First published in the United States of America 1983 by
Holmes & Meier Publishers, Inc.
30 Irving Place
New York, N.Y. 10003

Great Britain:
Holmes & Meier Publishers, Ltd.
131 Trafalgar Road
Greenwich, London SE10 9TX

Design by Stephanie Barton

Library of Congress Cataloging in Publication Data

Viteritti, Joseph P., 1946–
  Across the river.

  Bibliography: p.
  Includes index.
  1. Politics and education—New York (N.Y.)
2. Education and state—New York (N.Y.) 3. New York
(N.Y.). Board of Education. 4. Community and school—
New York (N.Y.) I. Title.
LC90.N7V57 1983   379.747'1   83-12714
ISBN 0-8419-0883-4
ISBN 0-8419-0884-2 (pbk.)

Manufactured in the United States of America

for Rosemary

CONTENTS

NOTABLE QUOTES

Livingston Street is the world of the "can't be done." If you want to do something a bit differently from the usual, they will tell you why you can't. If you try to, they will stop you.

—A New York City school teacher, April 1978

Executive Directors of the various divisions at Livingston Street did not like reporting to me. They saw their jurisdictions as franchises. They would accuse me of interfering in instructional issues. They would run to the Board every time I raised an embarrassing question. There they would get protection.

—A former deputy chancellor, May 1981

Budget controls? We have to be careful with that. If we had a tight financial management system those people across the river would know how we spent every penny. We don't need City Hall on our backs like that.

—A school system budget official, August 1978

I think that under the mayor's control we would have lost even more during retrenchment. The mayor is not elected by the 70 percent minority populace that is in the school system. We really don't have a powerful constituency. I believe in the tradition of a lay board.

—A community school superintendent, May 1981

The Board of Education is obstructionist and prohibitive. It has too much power and is not responsible to anyone. It diffuses responsibility. The members need a lot of attention and hand holding. Any one member can make your life miserable, but yet no one member is responsible for what happens. They interfere but they aren't substantive.

—A former senior assistant to the chancellor, June 1981

The idea that's been established over the last ten years that almost every service that someone might need in life ought to be provided, financed by the government as a matter of basic right, is wrong. We challenge that. We reject that notion.

—David Stockman, March 1981

PREFACE

In the fall of 1939 a neighborhood newspaper in Brooklyn first reported that the Board of Education, "New York's largest administrative department," would relocate its headquarters of thirty-seven years from Park Avenue and Fifty-ninth Street in midtown Manhattan, to the old Elks Club building on Livingston Street in Brooklyn.[1] According to the article, the decision to move was motivated by the need for more office space and the hope that centralizing all of the Board's administrative offices in one place would lead to greater efficiency in its operations.

The opening of the new school headquarters was a first in the history of New York City. Never before had a local agency established its executive offices outside the borough of Manhattan. But the move was hardly surprising. As a matter of custom the Board of Education had always carefully guarded its semiautonomous status within the local governmental structure. Politics and education were to be kept separate and apart. That was the American way. For thirty-seven years the Board of Education had been the only local agency that did not maintain its headquarters in the vicinity of City Hall, near the southern tip of Manhattan.

In terms of actual distance, the move to Livingston Street, across the Brooklyn Bridge from City Hall, brought the school board closer to the seat of municipal government than it had previously been. But it also resulted in a new psychological distance that cannot be measured in miles. When school officials at Livingston Street use the term "across the river" to refer to their counterparts within the municipal government, they are not reflecting on the three-minute car ride over the bridge. The term symbolizes a spirit of political and institutional separatism that continues to have a significant impact on educational policy making in New York City.

Today 110 Livingston Street is the home of the largest local public bureaucracy in the nation. Its administrative offices have overflowed the bounds of the original twelve-story structure; headquarters staff can now be found in several buildings in downtown Brooklyn or in another complex that has sprung up in Long Island City, Queens. The total budget of the school system exceeds $3 billion. Its full- and part-time employees combined number over a hundred thousand people. While the primary mission of the system is the education of the more than 900,000 children who attend New York's public schools, the managerial task before it is more complex than that of most large and middle-sized cities in the United States. Since the system contains over one thousand schools, its Division of School Buildings is responsible for one of the largest building maintenance operations in the nation. The Office of Food Services serves more than 500,000 lunches and 100,000 breakfasts per day, in more locations than those operated by the Howard Johnson restaurant chain. The Bureau of Pupil Transportation is responsible for the safe delivery of more than 140,000 children per day and administers a contract bus service larger than the public bus systems of either Chicago or Los Angeles.

By reputation, the central headquarters complex at 110 Livingston Street is a classic case of administrative incorrigibility. In his well-known study of that institution, David Rogers described it as "a model of bureaucratic pathology," characterized by overcentralization in its chain of command, horizontal and vertical fragmentation, compulsive rule-following, and insulation from its clients.[2] That assessment was made in 1968, just prior to the implementation of decentralization. However, even after more than a decade of experience with New York's moderate form of community control and decentralized governance, 110 Livingston Street is still widely perceived as a monument to bureaucratic inertia and ineptitude. Indeed, the image of the school headquarters is so poor that, upon his appointment in 1978, the new chancellor, Frank Macchiarola, suggested in jest that the address on the face of the building be changed from 110 to 112 Livingston Street.

This is a book about the politics of change. Specifically it is an account of some major policy initiatives undertaken during the administration of Chancellor Frank Macchiarola, with particular emphasis on the events of the first three years. It is not put forth as a complete chronicle of what happened during this important transitional period. It can more appropriately be described as a representative history that defines the general approach taken by the Macchiarola administration to a set of problems found in nearly every urban school system. It concentrates especially on explaining the kinds of institutional and political obstacles that must be overcome in order to make an urban school system such as New York's more responsive to the changing needs of its client population.

I have writen this book from the perspective of the superintendent's office or, as it is referred to in New York City, the Office of the Chancellor. I state that here at the beginning in order to alert the reader to both my interest and my bias: I served for nearly three years as special assistant to the chancellor during the very period covered in the forthcoming pages. I must also declare at the outset that I remain in fundamental agreement with the philosophy and the goals of the Macchiarola administration. However, for the sake of my former colleagues, I should also state that the conclusions presented are not meant to represent the thinking of the school administration, the chancellor, or the Board of Education. The truth of these claims will become more obvious as we advance through the text.

It is not my purpose here to evaluate the achievements of the school system or its leadership. That task can be better accomplished by outsiders, probably after the passage of more time. In describing the outcomes of particular episodes or policies, I have tried to rely especially on the judgments and assessments of informed individuals or groups within the broad educational and professional community. One always approaches this kind of project with the hope that the objectivity sacrificed by familiarity can be offset by the insights allowed through proximity. I began this enterprise with the basic assumption that one who has spent considerable time viewing the policy process from the vantage point of the chancellor's office becomes adept at defining the variables that stand between intent and implementation.

My role at Livingston Street was essentially managerial. The chancellor had given me responsibility for designing strategies and systems for gaining operational control of the bureaucracy so that it could be made responsive to the objectives of the administration.[3] Needless to say, that was a fascinating assignment for a student of public administration. While I do not intend to discuss the details of that personal experience in these pages, I will say that it did provide me with the basic premise on which this book was written. During my stay at Livingston Street I became thoroughly persuaded that the bureaucracy, however large and recalcitrant it may be, is manageable, controllable, and adaptable—as long as its leadership is committed to having it that way.

I left Livingston Street with a very deep-seated conviction that the major obstacles to change in a large urban school system like New York's are not found within the internal administrative structure but exist in the very complex and turbulent external environment that envelops the system. That idea drove the research for this book. That basic theme explains why this is more a book about politics than it is about management; for despite many well-meaning hopes to the contrary, the external environment of an inner-city school system is a highly political one.

I would be among the last to deny the validity of the image that has emerged in the literature about the bureaucracy at Livingston

Street. It is a well-deserved reputation. I will never forget a divisional meeting I attended on behalf of the chancellor in the summer of 1978, when a bureau director rose to his feet and announced to his colleagues that anyone volunteering information to a member of the chancellor's staff would be seen as a traitor. The walls around the Livingston Street fortress had always been impenetrable. Thus, during the first year of activity, the new chancellor's team of outsiders functioned more like a very small occupying army than as part of the institution it was trying to run.

I had come to Livingston Street with experience in more than a half-dozen of New York's municipal agencies, and in none of them had resistance to change been so blatant or hostile. I have a theory about that. Livingston Street had never really been effectively infiltrated from the outside, as most public bureaucracies are periodically. It simply did not know how to react. Seasoned bureaucrats have an astute ability to subvert change quietly and peacefully. The folks at Livingston Street had never needed to develop those skills very extensively, so they were clumsy in their resistance. What appeared as arrogance was really a well-insulated form of political naiveté.

Things are somewhat different now. As I have explained in some detail elsewhere, there is greater communication and cooperation within the bureaucracy.[4] There is a better integration of new ideas with old structures. While there is still much distance to be traveled, I think it is reasonable to claim that the state of the managerial art has genuinely improved at Livingston Street. It is important to make such pronouncements when they are legitimate, because it has become dangerously fashionable among people in public life to condemn the bureaucracy in an offhanded and irresponsible way. Bureaucracies are convenient targets for political candidates. Since few people want to identify personally with these institutions, it is possible to attack them without incurring much opposition. Even those who work in bureaucracies do not usually consider themselves bureaucrats.

The assault on the bureaucracy by individuals who are in office or want to be there is very often a technique for evading responsibility. If policies do not quite work out as the public would prefer, it is always possible to blame the faceless bureaucrats. If, for political reasons, a politician wants to reduce social benefits to the poor, it can easily be passed off as a war on administrative waste. If elected officials do not have the courage to demand meaningful controls in social programs, why not place the burden of failure on the bureaucrats, who are accountable to nobody?

There is good reason for focusing a book about the New York City public schools on the external environment. Not only might such an examination shed light on the policy-making process in education, but it can also provide an informed basis for recommendations on institutional reform. My immediate concerns are for a new institutional arrangement that will focus political responsibility for service delivery, and for a policy structure that is more inclined to be responsive to the needs of the present student clientele. I do not expect that all the relevant parties to these issues will agree with either my diagnosis or prescription. However, both can serve as starting points for rekindling a very important discussion on the future of New York.

There are more general implications to be drawn from a book of this sort. Granted, because of New York's extraordinary size, the managerial issues that have historically plagued Livingston Street might seem irrelevant to other school systems. However, all urban school systems must cope with the turbulence of a similarly complex political setting. All urban school superintendents must deal with a similar array of intergovernmental institutions, are accountable to a wide variety of constituents, and must respond to the problems of an inner-city community. The point to be made here is that we need not get lost in the details. This is as much a book about urban education as it is about New York City politics.

The discouraging predicament of the New York City school chancellor is that he must function in a political environment that is basically hostile to the interests of the students he serves. As will be explained at greater length later, I do not believe that the circumstances in other cities are very different. If we can concede at this point that New York has at least begun to address the crisis in the classroom that typically troubles many urban school systems, then perhaps there are some lessons to be drawn from the programmatic and policy initiatives that are about to be described.

NOTES

1. *The Brooklyn Heights Press,* October 27, 1939.

2. David Rogers, *110 Livingston Street* (New York: Random House, 1968), pp. 267–268. See also Marilyn Gittell, *Participants and Participation* (New York: Praeger, 1967).

3. See Joseph P. Viteritti and Daniel G. Carponcy, "Information, Organization and Control: A Study of System Application," *Public Administration Review* 41 (March–April 1981); Joseph P. Viteritti, "Policy Analysis in the Bureaucracy: An *Ad Hoc* Approach," *Public Administration Review* 42 (September–October 1982).

4. Viteritti and Carponcy, "Information, Organization and Control."

ACKNOWLEDGMENTS

The research for this book was supported by Grant No. NIE-G-81-0032 from the National Institute of Education, Program on Organizational Processes in Education.

One of the first individuals to take an active interest in the project was the late Professor Stephen K. Bailey of the Harvard Graduate School of Education. Steve provided me with some early important insights, encouraged me to take the project to Harvard, and offered me an opportunity to teach a course on organizational politics that was helpful in developing some of the central ideas.

Ron Edmonds provided the intellectual framework for much of the educational agenda carried out in New York between 1978 and 1983, and was instrumental in my own understanding of the issues. His work will have a lasting impact on future dialogues in urban education.

Among my other university colleagues who read drafts of the manuscript are Chris Argyris, Jeanne Chall, Joseph Cronin, Harold Howe II, Paul Lawrence, Norton Long, David Rogers, Rosemary Salomone, and Michael Timpane. Among my former colleagues in New York who reviewed the manuscript are Robert Bailey, Dall Forsythe, James Gifford, and Joseph Skerrett.

Brian Fitzgerald, my research assistant in Cambridge, did yeoman work in the stacks of the various Harvard libraries. Deborah Lefkowitz, my secretary, did an extraordinary job of typing, proof reading, and keeping things in general good order. Audrey Smith and Barbara Johnson picked up some last minute typing assignments in New York.

I regret that I cannot personally thank the numerous individuals within the New York City school system who provided me with information and documentation, and the many teachers, principals and school administrators who shared their opinions and insights in informal conversation. Their help is invaluable.

Finally, I owe special thanks to Frank J. Macchiarola, who not only offered me an opportunity to participate in a significant series of events in New York, but also maintained continued access and an open mind as I took up the task of writing about these events.

xvii

INTRODUCTION

We have come a long way in our thinking on school system governance. For more than the first half of the present century, the dominant principles of educational administration were hierarchy, centralization, and expertise.[1] This model of excellence was a legacy of the municipal reform movement, which was devoted to saving our cities from the evils of political corruption and to ridding public administration of the incompetence bred by patronage. According to the once popular managerial ethos, decisions about how to educate our young people were to be left to professionals, and the process should be protected from the influence of political forces at all costs.

There are still some of us who would prefer the past ideals to the present conditions.[2] But today we are more realistic; our perceptions and hopes have grown more cynical. We have come to realize that even the highest motives articulated at the turn of the century veiled a treacherous class warfare waged against the immigrant. Indeed the literature of the 1960s and 1970s told us in no uncertain terms that educational policy making is a political process responsive to the dictates of interest and power.[3]

Given our new understanding of schools as political institutions, it is no wonder that client and interest groups began to make demands on them that were customarily made only on governmental bodies. "Access," "Representation," and "Equity" all became rallying calls for the educational politics of the 1960s. At the outset of this turbulent decade, remnants of the traditional model were still so embedded in the structure of governance that decision making remained controlled by professional administrators. These educators, who were predominantly white, were rapidly losing touch with the changing population attending inner-city schools. Thus was born the movement for decentralization and community control; here began the campaign to wrest authority and power from local school-system bureaucracies.[4]

However, as the community revolution was being fought at the school-district level, other forces at work in education were moving discretion and authority out of the local realm. First of all, there was increased federal involvement, through grants in aid accompanied by

3

new regulations, and through legislation that would guarantee new rights under law.[5] Americans were also becoming a more litigious society. Coupled with newly defined legal protections, this proclivity to sue insured a greater role for the courts in educational policy making.[6] Much of the increased federal aid and regulation was channeled through the states, which in many cases were held accountable for the implementation of laws and the supervision of programs. Thus the expanded federal activism of the 1960s and early 1970s also brought increased state intervention in local education.[7] Finally, the 1960s were also a period of growing militancy on the part of organized labor, and the enlarged power of the unions was exercised at the state capitol as well as with the local school board.[8]

As commendable as it may have been in terms of our most fundamental democratic ideals, the community revolution, in a curious way, was extremely ill-timed. Client groups who sought to steal control of the policy process from local educators received stiff competition from institutions at other levels of government. By the time decentralization was implemented in many American cities, the stakes of educational politics were being carried off to other arenas. Hence it is with good reason that Frederick Wirt and Michael Kirst observe in the new introduction to their revised text: "The 1970s will be remembered as an era when the previous hallmark of American education—local control—became fully a myth. The political web surrounding the school district tightened and included many more participants."[9]

Historically, parallel lines of thought have determined our understanding of school-system politics and the role in which we have cast urban superintendents. There had been a natural symmetry between the reformist ideals of centrism and professionalism and the enhanced power and prestige of the superintendent. Equipped with pedagogical experience and the discretion of a chief executive, the superintendent emerged as the major figure in educational policy making at the local level. Throughout the 1960s and early 1970s, some of the most penetrating research on school politics documented the declining power of local school boards and the ascendancy of the superintendent. According to the observations of such scholars as Kerr, and later Ziegler and Jennings, the school board was seen as merely a legitimizing agent for the policy initiatives of the powerful superintendent.[10]

Notwithstanding the enhanced position of the superintendent vis-à-vis the school board, superintendents would soon come to know some unpleasant consequences of their enlarged roles. It is a basic fact of political life that those who seem to enjoy inordinate discretion in the policy realm become a target of the various advocate or interest groups in the larger social environment. Thus the superintendent quickly emerged as the focal point for school politics at the local level, becoming a victim of numerous cross-pressures. Taking its cue from the comparative study completed by Larry Cuban, the literature on urban superintendents now commonly describes them as a battered species.[11] Given the high turnover rate that has been evident over the last decade, one might also classify them as endangered. Between 1970 and 1973, twenty new superintendents were hired in the nation's twenty-five largest cities.[12] From 1975 until 1978, sixteen new superintendents were appointed in the twenty-eight largest American cities.[13]

Explaining the hazards of the job has become a common preoccupation of those who have studied the office. Because of some of the intergovernmental developments that have already been explained, the tendency to make increased demands on the superintendent coincided with the arrival of many new political actors on the educational scene. Thus, scholars such as William Boyd have recently described the power of the superintendent as less definite and more circumstantial. As the superintendent has become the object of higher expectations, his role in the policy process has become more circumscribed by other influential participants in a complex local and intergovernmental decision structure. Consequently, serving as chief educator of a school district is only part of the function of an urban superintendent; success and survival in office will be determined by his or her skill as a master politician.

Many of the problems put before school superintendents in the political forum during the 1960s and 1970s did have their origin in matters of a pedagogical nature. Throughout these decades there was mounting evidence on a national scale that public education had been failing. Between 1963 and 1981 the American people witnessed a steady decline in scores on the Scholastic Aptitude Test (SAT), from an average of 980 to an average of 890. There were many reasons given for the troublesome descent in recorded achievement: the proliferation of elective subjects, the deterioration of educational standards, the lack of student discipline, and the drain of talent from the teaching profession—not to mention the children themselves.

There were also some very predictable outcomes of the downward trend in the test scores. First, there was a significant loss of public confidence in the schools. In a national Gallup Poll on parental confidence taken in 1974, the mean rating on a possible scale of 5 was 2.80.[15] By 1979, the mean score on the annual survey was recorded at 2.38.[16] In 1980, a slight improvement was registered at 2.42.[17] This lower sense of confidence in public education was reflected in decreased enrollments. Between 1970 and 1978 public school enrollment dropped from 45.9 million students to 42.6 million students.[18] By 1981

Table 1-1
REPRESENTATION OF RACIAL MINORITIES IN LARGE URBAN
SCHOOL SYSTEMS, 1955–1975

City	Percent minority, 1955	Percent minority, 1975	Change
Baltimore	42%	73%	+31%
Chicago	30% (Est.)	77%	+47%
Dallas	16%	59%	+43%
Detroit	29% (Est.)	78%	+49%
Houston*	23%	63%	+40%
Los Angeles	24%	60%	+36%
Milwaukee	3% (Est.)	40%	+37%
New York City	28%	68%	+40%
Philadelphia	39%	67%	+28%
Washington, D.C.	64%	97%	+33%

Source: *Educational Redlining,* prepared by Irving Anker, chancellor of the New York
    City Public Schools, for the Council of Great City Schools, spring 1976.
*Ethnic categories were redefined in 1970.

these enrollment figures were down to 39.8 million.[19] No doubt part of this reduction is due to demographic factors, since there are now fewer school-age children in the general population. However, also contributing to the public school enrollment decline is the resort to private education, where, despite demographic changes in the population, enrollments have remained steady at about the 5 million mark and are now moderately on the rise.[20]

There were political implications of the enrollment declines. Since a smaller part of the American populace would have a direct stake in public education, the schools would lose important political support. Circumstances within the inner city were even more precarious. The children remaining in urban public schools increasingly came from racial minorities and the socially disadvantaged (see Table 1-1). These groups did not form a very strong political base. However, sparked by the refusal of local educational officials to change with the times, that base was sufficiently potent to launch an effort on behalf of community control.

NEW YORK UNDER DECENTRALIZATION

According to Diane Ravitch's seminal history, completed in 1974, the last of "the Great School Wars" in New York City was fought in the mid-1960s over decentralization and community control.[21] We are told in that chronicle, which begins with 1805, that school wars generally coincided with huge waves of migration, when the public schools became the battleground "where the aspirations of newcomers and the fears of the native population met and clashed."[22] In each of these episodes, Ravitch explains, "the role and purpose of the public school were bitterly disputed by intense and hostile factions."[23]

Between 1955 and 1975 minority enrollment in the New York City public schools grew from 28 percent to 68 percent. Black students have been the largest group since 1972; Hispanics the second largest since 1978. The white portion of the school population fell about 1 percent per year throughout the 1970s. The last school war was fought because minority parents wanted a voice in the school system that was educating their children. They wanted to be heard because they had lost faith in the white professionals, who for years had acted as if they were accountable to nobody.

Among the major proponents of school decentralization in New York were Mayor John Lindsay, the Ford Foundation, the Congress of Racial Equality, and several liberal Democratic organizations from Manhattan. The most vociferous opponent was Albert Shanker of the United Federation of Teachers. He was joined by the Council of Supervisors and Administrators, the leadership of the central school administration at Livingston Street, and an assortment of white middle-class neighborhood groups who equated community control with minority control.

The final outcome of the political debates over decentralization was a compromise reached in the New York State legislature in 1969. Under the new law, thirty-one community school districts would be established in the City—replacing the thirty districts that the central Board of Education had set up in 1965 through its own plan of administrative decentralization. An additional district would be carved out at a later date. According to the new plan for political decentralization, local school boards would be selected by direct election under a system of proportional representation. These school boards would choose their own district superintendents and would appoint principals found eligible according to criteria set by the central Board of Education.

Decentralization would involve only elementary and middle schools. The more than one hundred high schools of New York would remain under control of the central Board of Education, as would special education, bilingual education, and career education. The central Board would also maintain jurisdiction over the all-important budget, personnel, business, and support functions of the school system. All central functions would be administered by the Chancellor of Schools, who is appointed by and reports to the Board of Education (see Figure 1-1). The chancellor would also maintain responsibility for

Figure 1-1
CENTRAL ADMINISTRATION—NEW YORK CITY PUBLIC SCHOOLS, 1979

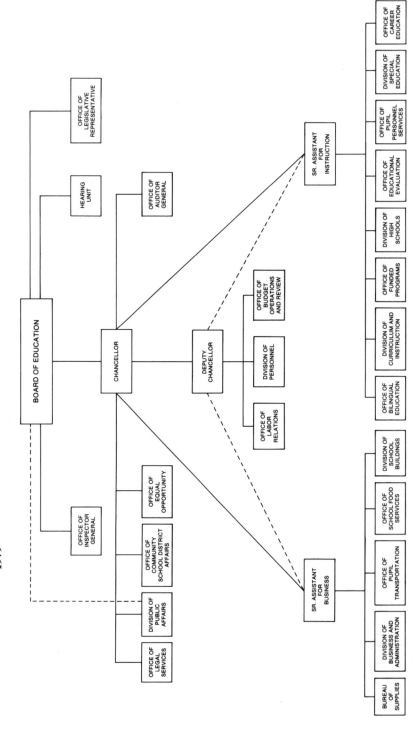

setting minimum educational standards for all schools in the city. As the chief executive officer of the school system, the chancellor is empowered to suspend, supersede, or remove a community school board or its members for failing to comply with the law or the bylaws, rules, regulations, or directions of the Board of Education.

The Decentralization Law passed in New York in 1969 was severely criticized by some of the most ardent proponents of community control. As a compromise, it is considerably more limited than had been hoped for in the level of discretion it granted to local school boards. Moreover, the process by which school board members are elected does not fulfill the participatory ideals of the neighborhood movement. Not only is the proportional representation scheme confusing to potential voters, but the timing of the balloting, which is separate from the general elections, also discourages voter turnout. Voter participation during the first school board election, held in 1970, was a meager 15 percent. In 1973 it dropped to below 11 percent. By 1980 voter turnout had fallen off to 10 percent.

In terms of representation, the outcome of school decentralization in New York City has been somewhat more encouraging. In a recent assessment Marilyn Gittell reports that between 1969 and 1979 the proportion of black and Hispanic principals at the elementary and middle school level has increased from 6 percent to 25 percent.[24] She observes that while in 1970 there were no black or Hispanic superintendents at the district level, by 1980 there were eight.[25] When local school board members were last appointed by central authorities at Livingston Street, there were 47 blacks, 30 Hispanics and 201 whites; in 1977, under decentralization, there were 72 black school board members, 34 Hispanics, and 180 whites.[26]

Gittell has also developed an index showing how well the school boards represent their respective district populations. She found that in 1977 the index of district population to board membership was 1:1 for blacks (equal), 0.9:1 for Hispanics (slightly overrepresented), and 1.2:1 for whites (slightly underrepresented).[27] These are rather favorable results, indicating that local school boards in New York City do reflect the populations of the districts they serve, and, in fact, are somewhat balanced in favor of minorities. However, these data are somewhat misleading.

When Gittell applies her index to the population that actually attends schools governed by the various community districts, the results are quite different. In 1977 the index of student population to school board membership was 1.5:1 for blacks (underrepresented), 2.1:1 for Hispanics (underrepresented), and 0.5:1 for whites (overrepresented).[28] While this situation is considerably better than that which existed in 1971 (2.8:1 for blacks, 2.5:1 for Hispanics, 0.6:1 for whites), it still serves to highlight a shortcoming in the governing structure of local school districts. Community school boards in New York City are more representative of the broad political constituency of their districts than they are of the clientele that attends their schools. This is a significant weakness if we consider that the intent was to achieve minority participation and client control. As we will see in some of the forthcoming chapters, it is a flaw in the local governing structure that is particularly highlighted when school boards are deliberating over racial issues.

School decentralization appears to have been a mixed blessing for New York City. It has become a subject of ridicule from many—both within the school system and without, at the central level of school operations and within the districts themselves. According to a *New York Times* poll taken in 1980 of the 650 elementary and middle school principals (366 of whom responded), 52 percent stated that they would recentralize the school system to the way it was prior to 1969, and 7 percent said they would opt for recentralizing to a five-borough system of governance.[29] Only 11 percent of those responding preferred to keep the system the way it is, and 10 percent claimed that they wanted to decentralize even further. Overall, the principals did not give high marks to the ten-year experience they had had with locally elected school boards, and they offered a variety of reasons for their dissatisfaction. As the *Times* reported:

> Many of the principals said the daily political pressures of decentralization had jeopardized what they should be doing first and foremost: spending time in the classroom. Citing what they said were millions of dollars in unnecessary operating costs, inefficient management techniques, political intrigue and administrative incompetence, they said that, as bad as they believed the centralized school system was years ago, the decentralized system that replaced it was worse.[30]

Few informed observers would deny that decentralization has further politicized educational decision making at the community level. That, in fact, was one of the goals. However, neighborhood politics has also brought favoritism, patronage, and occasional incidences of corruption. During the first decade under decentralization, six out of the thirty-two school boards were investigated because of charges of corruption. In District 5, located in Harlem, three school board members were convicted of conspiracy to misuse public funds in school board election campaigns. In District 23, located in Ocean Hill–Brownsville, a school board president and former state assemblyman was convicted for soliciting bribes from a producer of educational materials. On several occasions the chancellor has found it necessary to suspend or supersede local school boards because of findings of misconduct or the mismanagement of public funds.

In recent years public officials at both the state and local level have challenged the efficacy of the entire school board election process, which costs approximately $3.4 million every three years and now produces less than a 10-percent voter turnout, as compared to the average 40-percent turnout for regular elections in New York City. There has been much debate and disappointment, but at this time it does not appear that there is any earnest movement toward amending New York's current form of school decentralization.

SCHOOL GOVERNANCE AND LOCAL POLITICS

Prior to decentralization, all members of the central Board of Education in New York City were appointed by the mayor. Between 1961 and 1968 a screening panel had been established to allow the city's civic groups a role in nominating a list of eligible people from whom the mayor would choose. In 1969 the state legislature established a temporary five-person Board of Education, the membership of which was to be selected by the city's five borough presidents. Borough presidents in New York are elected on a countywide basis and are usually the product of the local party organizations, which are structured along the lines of the county boundaries. The 1969 law for the first time granted county-level officials authority in the area of education. In 1971 the temporary five-person Board of Education was replaced by a seven-member body. Under this plan, which is still in existence, the borough presidents kept their authority to appoint one person each. The remaining two members are chosen by the mayor. Unlike the previous board, which was unsalaried, members of this newly constituted body are compensated on a per diem basis.

The Decentralization Law of 1969 appeared to represent a significant loss of mayoral discretion in the area of education. The Board of Education is the official policy-making body of the school system. It chooses the chancellor, who functions as the chief executive officer of the operation at Livingston Street. However, one must be careful not to overstate the case. In reality, New York City mayors exercised little control over the school system. Many have preferred it that way, particularly when the school system began to slip, which started to occur in the early 1960s. Even though the Board of Education selected the superintendent or chancellor of schools, in all but a relatively few instances the person chosen was a product of the professional bureaucracy. Insofar as the power of the Board of Education was concerned, Livingston Street was a classic case of a situation in which the implementation phase of the policy process carried out through administration far outweighed the impact of original policy formulations. In effect, the superintendent or chancellor had not only been the candidate of the bureaucracy, but historically also functioned as both its instrument and guardian.

Mayor Lindsay endorsed the Decentralization Law of 1969 because he was an advocate of neighborhood government. However, his successors in office were far less enthusiastic about the community revolution and dismayed over the diminishing of their appointment power regarding the central Board. Since the city school district of New York is financially dependent, it is the responsibility of the municipal government to generate the dollars needed to support education. Livingston Street had been difficult enough to hold accountable when the mayor could determine the entire composition of the Board of Education. Now it would be nearly impossible.

In 1977 Mayor Abraham Beame proposed to legislative leaders a plan that would dissolve the central Board of Education. In its place Beame called for a commissioner of education, appointed by the mayor, and the creation of a nonsalaried advisory panel. The plan was vehemently objected to by the borough presidents, the United Federation of Teachers, and the administrative establishment at Livingston Street. It never made its way through the legislature. Beame's term in office came to a sudden end as the result of a bitter and surprising primary defeat in the summer of 1977.

In April of 1978 the newly elected Mayor Edward Koch sent another legislative proposal to Albany concerning school governance. Koch would retain the seven-person Board of Education, but would have all its members appointed, as before, by the mayor. His bill suffered a fate similar to that of his predecessor. But Koch remained determined to see to it that change took placed in the public school system. That had been his campaign pledge. Education in New York City was a public disgrace. The middle class was abandoning the system and the City because it had lost confidence in the schools. Businesses were relocating to other sections of the country because, despite the high taxes imposed by New York, its schools could not provide them with a capable work force. There was a direct relationship between the decline of the school system and the loss of tax revenues to the City. Something had to be done. If the mayor could not determine who would sit on the Board of Education, then perhaps he could influence the selection of a new chancellor.

Edward Koch is one of the great enigmas of New York City

politics. His political roots are in the liberal Democratic reform movement of Manhattan; his style as the city's chief executive often resembles that of a moderate or conservative. He began his political career in 1956 as a volunteer in the presidential campaign of Adlai Stevenson. It was at that time that he affiliated with the Village Independent Democrats, an insurgent club in Greenwich Village devoted to the defeat of bosses who ran the Democratic party of New York County. In the 1960s Koch was an active participant in the civil rights movement. He was an early opponent of the Vietnam war. During his nine-year service in the House of Representatives, he earned a reputation as an outspoken and articulate champion of liberal causes, and he had a voting record to support it.

But there is another side to Ed Koch. In 1971 he opposed the introduction of low-income housing in Forest Hills, Queens, arguing that the project would destroy the character of the neighborhood. During the Vietnam protests, he refused to march with demonstrators who had burned the American flag, claiming that their behavior was a liability to the peace movement. During his 1977 campaign for the mayoralty, Koch disappointed his longtime liberal supporters by coming out in favor of the death penalty, and he won the favor of conservatives by taking a tough stand against "poverty pimps." Koch likes to call himself a "sane liberal." He refuses to be backed into positions with which he disagrees.

There were serious drawbacks to Koch's sometimes pugnacious manner. Minorities in particular often saw him as insensitive or hostile to their needs. His campaign style caused him to lose a great deal of credibility in the black and Hispanic communities, which by 1980 were to account for 45 percent of the New York City population. The onus was upon him, as a newly elected mayor, to build bridges to the minority community, and there were mixed reports regarding his success in that sphere.[31] Nevertheless, Koch enjoyed a wide base of support.

Koch made political history in 1977 by being the first Democratic candidate in recent times to run a successful mayoral campaign against the public-employee unions. Organized labor had always been a major force in the electoral politics of New York City. Serious candidates for citywide office usually built their campaigns around union needs. By 1977 the dynamics of city politics had changed. The public was becoming increasingly disenchanted with worker militancy. Many civil service workers had moved outside the city boundaries, thus disqualifying themselves from voting. Moreover, New York could no longer afford to support generous collective bargaining agreements. So Koch defied both history and the unions and was elected on an anti-labor platform.

Koch had little choice but to approach his mayoralty as a fiscal conservative. The times demanded it. The New York City financial crisis had come into full bloom only two years prior to his election.[32] By law, Koch was required to live within the bounds of a four-year financial plan imposed by the New York State Emergency Financial Control Board.[33] Fiscal solvency and a balanced budget had to be the major priorities of his administration. Thus it was natural for Koch to declare war on waste and mismanagement within the municipal government. It is no wonder that the new mayor took aim at the overfed and undernourished bureaucracy at Livingston Street, which was costing more than $3 billion a year to run but showing unimpressive results in the classroom. Koch also understood that the revitalization of the public school system was a key ingredient to the economic redevelopment of New York.

Koch's first choice for schools chancellor was Shirley Chisholm, the black congresswoman from Bedford-Stuyvesant. The mayor's support of her candidacy represented an important gesture of goodwill to the minority community, whose children made up a disproportionate part of the student body. But the nomination was practically stillborn. The professional establishment in the school system did not take kindly to the appointment of outsiders to the highest post in their administrative structure, particularly when the outsider was not a career educator. The nomination received an immediate public rejection from teachers' union President Albert Shanker, which meant that it would be virtually impossible to obtain the needed majority vote on the Board of Education. The mayor appoints only two members of the central school board. He must rely on his own persuasive powers in order to line up the other votes. It was not easy to do so against the will and determination of Albert Shanker. However, Koch was also fully aware that the only chance to bring about significant reform within the school system rested with the appointment of an outsider as the new chancellor.

Koch's second choice for the job of chancellor was Frank J. Macchiarola. At the time Macchiarola was vice president of the City University of New York Graduate School and University Center, where he was also a member of the doctoral faculty in political science. Prior to that he had served as an assistant vice president of Columbia University, where he had earned both his Ph.D. and law degrees. As a scholar he had written several important papers on municipal finance in New York State, a field of expertise that would serve him well during the fiscal crisis.[34] For five years Macchiarola had been an active member of Community School Board 22 in Brooklyn, where his children attended public school. He had been elected president for the two years immediately prior to his appointment as chancellor.

Macchiarola's experience and expertise went beyond the field of education. In 1977 he took a leave of absence from the university in order to serve as deputy director of the state Emergency Financial Control Board (EFCB). During that time he played a key role in instituting the governmental and financial reforms required to put New York City back on the municipal bond market. In a career that constantly shuttled him between the university and public life, the thirty-seven-year-old candidate for chancellor had also served as a member of the Governor's Task Force on Higher Education, as special counsel to the Codes Committee of the state Senate, and as an adviser to the Temporary State Commission to Study the Governmental Operations of New York City.

Notwithstanding a rather full and impressive résumé of public service, Macchiarola was still considered an outsider by the professionals within the school system. Moreover, his previous involvement in the affairs of the city and state had sometimes placed him in an adversary position to individuals who would have a lot to say about the outcome of his nomination. If Albert Shanker responded to Shirley Chisholm with disapproval, his reaction to Macchiarola was one of outrage. While serving with the EFCB, Macchiarola was personally responsible for rejecting a contract that the union had negotiated with the city, claiming that the wage increase for teachers was too costly. Shanker never forgot that. He saw the Macchairola candidacy as a hostile act on the part of the mayor and promised to do all that he could to defeat it.

Koch's second nomination for the position of chancellor was not received with great favor by the minority community. There had been grave disappointment over the withdrawal of Chisholm's name. Understandably, many of the black and Hispanic leaders of the city believed that it was about time for one of their own to head up the public school system. While there was no concerted effort in the minority community to stop Macchiarola, many wondered if a school board member from the predominately white middle-class section of Midwood could be truly sensitive to their needs. Also, it was not easy for a segment of the population so reliant on local government services to become enthusiastic about a person who had developed a reputation as a fiscal conservative, particularly one brought in at the behest of Edward Koch.

Macchiarola enjoyed some substantial support. Through his various sojourns in public life, he had become acquainted with many of the most powerful figures in New York politics. As a candidate for the school board in his neighborhood, he became a known entity in Brooklyn's powerful Jefferson Democratic Club. Its leaders developed a fondness for him. To them, Macchiarola was an anomaly. Here was this university professor who would roll up his sleeves, declare himself a candidate for the local school board, and run a successful election campaign. Macchiarola enjoyed the camaraderie. He was almost "one of the boys," though never a very active member of their club. Over the years he developed a close friendship with Anthony Genovese, the political organizer who appeared to be the heir apparent of the powerful Brooklyn party leader Meade Esposito. Genovese's endorsement was to enhance Macchiarola's bid for the chancellorship.

When an announcement was made that a search would be conducted for someone to finish out Irving Anker's last year as chancellor of the nation's largest school system, more than seventy applications arrived at the Board of Education headquarters. In all, twelve individuals were actually interviewed. In the end, four finalists emerged. Two were recruited from inside the school system, two from without. Because of the public support he received from the mayor, Macchiarola was seen early on as the leading outside candidate. Koch, who had just been elected on a platform promising school reform, made it unambiguously clear to both the Board of Education members and the borough presidents who appoint them that he wanted his person chosen. The other leading nominee, a product of the professional establishment, was Theodore Wiesenthal. Wiesenthal was superintendent of Community School District 10, in the Riverdale section of the Bronx.

Koch lobbied heavily on behalf of his candidate. The Board decided that it would cast its votes on April 17; the position would become vacant on July 1, 1978. The Board would meet at an undisclosed location in Manhattan in order to avoid the attention of the press. A two-and-one-half hour heated debate ensued after the choice was narrowed down to Macchiarola and Wiesenthal. Finally, when the ballots were taken, Macchiarola was selected by a vote of 4–3. The Bronx, Staten Island, and City Hall (a Beame holdover) representatives opposed him until the end, as they were instructed to do by Albert Shanker. The Board gave Macchiarola a one-year contract, allowing him to complete the unfinished term of the retiring chancellor. Another contract would be voted on at a later date. Macchiarola was not in a strong position to launch a school administration bent on reform.

Irving Anker had served as chancellor for five years. He had been with the school system more than forty years—as teacher, principal, and deputy superintendent. On only a few previous occasions had an outsider been called upon to assume the leadership of the New York City public schools and the results had not been encouraging. John Theobald, a former deputy mayor under Robert Wagner, had been selected in 1958. In 1962 the Board of Education, under pressure from a coalition of outside groups, encouraged Theobald to resign because of his efforts on behalf of desegregation. Calvin Gross, the former superintendent of schools in Pittsburgh, was appointed in 1963. His tenure lasted for less than one year. Harvey Scribner, a commissioner of education from Vermont, took office in 1970. His administration lasted for two and one-half years. An intent reformer, he left New York frustrated. He was never able to form close alliances within the bureaucracy or on the Board, and the political support he received from outside the school system was weak at best. In 1978 there was hope that Macchiarola, a native New Yorker with strong political connections, would be able to proceed more effectively.

SETTING THE TONE

Macchiarola appointed an eight-person transition team to facilitate his entry. It began work in mid-May and continued to function until his formal appointment on July 1. All members of the transition team were people whom he had known for a number of years, from whom he could expect total loyalty. All would go on to join the administration as members of the chancellor's personal staff. Several of these individuals had served under Macchiarola at the Emergency Financial Control Board. Another contingent was brought in from the universities. To the surprise of some, there was no one from either City Hall or the Brooklyn clubhouse. To the surprise of none, nobody on the transition team was from the school system. However, a key function of the team was to identify people from the career civil service and the former chancellor's staff who might be asked to stay on with the new administration.

In early May, Macchiarola asked his City University colleague Alan Gartner to organize a conference on education as part of the transition process. Gartner was instructed to invite a cross section of relevant people, both locally and nationally, who could be expected to have something useful to say to a new chancellor on the instruction of New York City schoolchildren. A meeting was eventually held on May 18 and 19 at the Sterling Forest Conference Center in upstate New York. University participants included Benjamin Bloom of Chicago; Ronald Edmonds of Harvard; Frank Riessman of the City University; and David Rogers, the author of *110 Livingston Street*. Public-interest-group participants included David Seeley of the Public Education Association and Helen Heller of the United Parents Associations. While Albert Shanker chose not to attend, labor was represented by Ted Elsberg, president of the Council of Supervisors and Administrators, and several high-ranking members of the teachers' union. Also in attendance were representatives of several private foundations, a state senator, and a number of school principals and administrators.

Macchiarola and his staff listened to two days of presentations by their guests. However, they left the conference with more than just good advice. Bloom's and Edmonds' discussions of their research on the effective instruction of inner-city children would contribute to the formulation of a fundamental educational philosophy for the new administration. That philosophy would differ significantly from the "can't be done" attitude that was pervasive at Livingston Street. Macchiarola also returned from Sterling Forest with some additional recruits for his new team. Ron Edmonds was invited to join the chancellor's staff as Senior Assistant for Instruction—making him the top instructional officer of the school system under the chancellor, and the administration's highest-ranking black person. Nathan Quinones, the principal of South Bronx High School, was asked to become the executive director of the Division of High Schools. He was the first minority person ever to have held that important position in New York City.

Before its work was done, Macchiarola's transition team would define the basic components of a policy agenda that reflected his chief priorities as chancellor. There was to be a new emphasis on raising competency standards for students. There was to be an initial focus on early childhood programs. The administration would reach out to populations that had previously been unserved or underserved by the school system, including children with handicapping conditions, linguistic minorities, holdovers, and dropouts. The administrative hierarchy at Livingston Street would also be held to a new and higher standard of managerial accountability, as would all professionals within the school system.

The incoming chancellor was sworn in on June 29, 1978. In his first public statement as the head of the school system, Macchiarola condemned the "garrison mentality" and the "defensive attitude" that was so characteristic of Livingston Street.[35] In recognition of the financial condition that still continued to plague New York City, the chancellor warned that he would not tolerate any excuses that "we could have done better if we had more money." He pledged, "The money we have right now is the amount we are going to use, and that amount we are going to use well." These last words would come back to haunt him during some of the more difficult days of his administration. Macchiarola closed his remarks with a statement that was designed to set a new tone for public education in New York City:

> We cannot take the line that kids aren't what they used to be as an excuse for not doing the job, because the children we have in our

schools are the same children that we had thirty or forty years ago. They may have different faces, and they may have different needs, and they may come from different backgrounds, but they are our children and we have responsibility to them as we have them.[36]

What appeared to many at the moment as an expression of sentimental humanism was actually a serious philosophical statement. It was a commentary on past attitudes as well as a declaration of new expectations for children and professionals alike. It marked a delineation in time, leadership, and thinking.

As already noted, one of the important functions of the transition team was the identification of senior personnel at Livingston Street who would be invited to join the new administration. The rationale here was quite simple. It is common knowledge among students of public administration that the machinery of government is driven by career civil servants. While top-level appointees may establish the overall agenda for an agency, it is the individuals who understand the inner workings of the bureaucracy that convert policy into practice. Macchiarola wanted to recruit several career professionals to his personal staff. Certain members of his predecessor's staff were asked to stay on. An attempt would be made to integrate this experienced personnel with the new team of outsiders.

The first meeting of the chancellor's senior staff, held in early July, proved to be very telling. Macchiarola opened the session with a series of questions. How might we communicate our agenda to the public? How detailed should our public pronouncements be? Should we produce a "white paper" that officially represents our thinking? Is it advisable to articulate a set of specific goals so that the public knows exactly what we have set out to accomplish? An initial response to the chancellor's queries carried words of serious caution. One of the senior career people sitting at the opposite end of the long conference table warned that a new chancellor ought to be wary of promising more than could be delivered. That was a sure formula for failure. Another of his colleagues volunteered more of the conventional wisdom that evolves through long tenure. The chancellor was advised that the basic problems troubling schoolchildren in New York City are social, not academic. Neither a new chancellor nor anyone else could overcome these maladies in order to make the system, or the kids, look very good scholastically. "It is all very cut-and-dried," another added. "Only so much can be done. We had better learn to live with that reality from the beginning."

There was then disagreement. Edmonds recited his research findings on effective schools. He argued that, under certain replicable conditions, inner-city schools could be made instructionally effective, regardless of the social composition of the student body. A ninety-minute debate ensued. With a few notable exceptions, there was a clear dichotomy in the room between the career professionals and the more recent appointees. Perhaps at no other time in the history of the administration was the clash between the old regime and the new so dramatically illustrated. To the newcomers, the dialogue represented another manifestation of the "can't be done" mentality for which Livingston Street had become notorious. To the old-liners, the discussion was simply another confrontation with naive idealism.

Macchiarola finally closed off the meeting with his own observations. He commented that he would never have accepted the job as chancellor if he really believed that the situation in urban education was hopeless. The question of a white paper was shelved for another time, actually never to be taken up again. However, the new school chief was quite unambiguous in asserting that he wanted the message of his administration to be heard loud and clear. Based upon the social science research cited by Edmonds, that message and its underlying philosophy could be summarized in four words: ALL CHILDREN CAN LEARN. The administration would proceed on a belief in the fundamental educability of every child.

The final composition of the chancellor's staff was determined by mid-July. Except for the appointment of several school system insiders, it was not very different from that of the transition team. Richard Halverson, who had previously served as Macchiarola's chief aide at the Emergency Financial Control Board, was named Senior Assistant for Business. This position complemented the instructional role that had been assigned to Edmonds. Halverson also had responsibility for budget development and oversight—a role he later shared, after the selection of a permanent budget director.

Including Edmonds and Halverson, Macchiarola's personal staff consisted of a dozen people. It was the largest ever assembled by either a superintendent or chancellor of schools in New York City. At Macchiarola's request, the Board of Education had created a new title of Assistant to the Chancellor—a group of non-civil-service appointees who served strictly at the pleasure of the chancellor. Their existence provided Macchiarola with a cadre of individuals who supported his attempt to assume control of the sprawling bureaucracy that was Livingston Street.

The structure of Macchiarola's administration was conceived in a rather unorthodox fashion. Ordinarily the assistants to a chief executive perform a purely staff or advisory role. Most of Macchiarola's staff took on line responsibilities. Each top-level director within the bureaucracy reported directly to one of the senior assistants, depending upon the function of a given division or office. In addition to this formal reporting line, most assistants to the chancellor were assigned to one or more divisional or office directors, whose work they would oversee on a daily basis. Thus while each administrative office within the bureaucracy was run by a career civil servant, Macchiarola had at his disposal a shadow government that reported to him regularly. For at least the first two years of his tenure, Macchiarola's administration was, by design, a staff-dominated operation. In fact, what eventually became known as the chancellor's weekly cabinet meeting was restricted to the chancellor's assistants and his personal counsel, and excluded all line personnel. Policy was made at these meetings. Another weekly meeting was held for executive directors, but the purpose of this was more to inform than to consult.

Eventually the titles of Deputy Chancellor and Deputy Chancellor for Instruction were created in order to emphasize the line responsibilities of the two senior assistants. After the passage of two years, several members of the chancellor's staff returned to the university. Others, drawing from the benefit of experience, took on line positions within the bureaucracy. As time passed, so did the tendency to recruit assistants to the chancellor from outside the system. As the relationship between the chancellor's office and the bureaucracy grew more cooperative, the number of assistants diminished. Their functions became more staff-oriented and less concerned with supervision. The eventual reduction of tension between line and staff was achieved through the gradual aggregation of trust and the development of more formal, less personal management-control systems. But the peace that finally came was hard-earned.

Throughout the summer and fall of 1978 the local press in New York regularly reported on the enormous shakeup that was taking place at Livingston Street. It was the first time anything of this sort had ever occurred within the school system. Critics of the school bureaucracy applauded with amazement.[37] Others described the events as a managerial bloodbath. Before it was all over, the new chancellor had replaced every top-level director within the central headquarters. Over the next four years, more than 60 percent of the incumbent high-school principals were replaced.

Macchiarola also used his administrative authority under the law to initiate a more vigorous tenure-review process for principals and assistant principals. The Board of Education had been awarding tenure virtually automatically after someone had served in a position for a particular period of time. Within several months after his appointment, the new chancellor denied tenure to seventy-nine principals and assistant principals who he found had not produced sufficient evidence to prove that they deserved it. At the same time Macchiarola disqualified correspondence courses for teachers as a way to earn salary increments—a move that drew criticism from union President Albert Shanker.

Shanker and Macchiarola had already made some conciliatory moves toward each other, with the hope of forming a relationship that was at least workable, despite the union leader's public opposition to the chancellor's appointment. The attempt at a reconciliation began with the Sterling Forest conference, which several UFT officials received and accepted invitations to attend. Significant progress was evident when Macchiarola and Shanker reached an agreement on the terms of a new teachers' contract. During the early days of the administration, Shanker hosted a cocktail party at the union headquarters for the chancellor and his assistants so that the two staffs might become acquainted. Macchiarola and Shanker commemorated the affair with a cautious exchange of pledges for cooperation. The relationship seemed to be improving. Then came the Chancellor's Mid-Year Report.

Macchiarola had decided to prepare a report to the Board of Education containing the observations he had made of the public school system during his first six months in office. His remarks were highly personal—written, in fact, by himself rather than his staff. They were also devastatingly critical of the institution, its practices, and its personnel. The Chancellor's Mid-Year Report began with the assertion that while public education in New York City is better than some critics claim, it "is still in trouble" because "too many of our students are being failed by the system."[38] With regard to the attitudes of professionals at Livingston Street and in the schools, he alleged, "Too many of those who should be serving our children are only serving themselves." Once again underscoring the faults of automatic tenure, Macchiarola contended, "We cannot endeavor to evaluate our students and at the same time permit colleagues to escape similar evaluations." The chancellor also had some unkind words for teachers' "reliance on the union contract as a standard of professional responsibility," suggesting that "the job of teaching requires greater talents and abilities than many of our teachers presently possess." Finally, Macchiarola attacked the managerial structure at Livingston Street head-on, alleging, "We have not only tolerated mediocrity, we have developed, congratulated, and promoted it."

The Mid-Year Report was distributed widely throughout the city. It captured front-page headlines in almost every major newspaper. It was reprinted in several publications and was generally well received. However, the document infuriated Albert Shanker. The union president proclaimed publicly that he could not understand why the chancellor, who had spent six months trying to build a relationship with the teaching staff, would "attack them so unfairly."[39] In a personal letter to Macchiarola, Shanker expressed concern over the "disturbing tone" of the report, which, he said, "seemed to agree with the more demagogic critics of our schools."[40] In defense of his teachers, Shanker explained, "It is difficult to remain committed with increases in class size, disturbed children who have no guidance or clinical services to turn to, salary freezes, and threats of layoffs." As Shanker saw it, the last thing that his teachers needed during these difficult times was a verbal assault from the head of the school system.

Macchiarola had a significant message that he wanted to communicate on a grand scale. It was important for him as chancellor to dissociate himself from the traditional ways of the institution he had been so critical of before he took office. He wanted to point the finger of responsibility at the professionals who worked in the system, so that not only the kids or their backgrounds would be blamed for the poor performance of the public schools. Macchiarola wanted it to be known that, as chancellor, he would be more inclined to expose incompetence than to conceal or defend it. He wanted to project himself to the public as an agent of change.

Shortly after it received the Mid-Year Report, the Board of Education voted to grant Macchiarola a new two-year contract, so that his tenure in office would go beyond the one unfinished year of his predecessor, Irving Anker.

ABOUT THIS BOOK: PROPOSITIONS

There are generally two schools of thought concerning the superintendency of the New York City public school system. One is presented by David Rogers. In his assessment of the office, Rogers found that the authority and power of the superintendent are "far too limited for him to play a decisive role."[41] He commented that the superintendent "must spend too much time meeting with various interest groups, tending to particular crisis situations, and playing a purely public relations role."[42] Thus, he concluded, "If the superintendent uses what power he has, he gets stopped before he can carry out his plans."[43]

Another point of view appears in Sayre and Kaufman's classic study of power and politics in New York City. Sayre and Kaufman found that because claimants on each side of every controversy in school politics often include disparate groups, all policy decisions are the product of compromise. They saw the involvement of multiple interest groups as an opportunity for school executives to "play off one against the other" and follow their own preferences at least "part of the time."[44] Moreover, and even more significant, they perceived the "pluralistic" nature of decision making as testimony to the claim that the school system in New York, and the local government in general, was representative, open, and responsive to all groups within the city.

Both the above perspectives recognize the turbulence of the external environment and the multiplicity of parties who participate in educational policy making. Therefore both are consistent with the mainstream of the recent literature on the urban superintendent, which portrays that role as a highly political one susceptible to a battery of cross-pressures from a variety of actors. As a historical note, one might add that since the publication of these two major studies the New York City school system has undergone decentralization. This development has added thirty-two institutional participants to the external environment with which the superintendent (now called the chancellor) must deal. Their interests are represented by the thirty-two locally elected school boards and the community superintendents they appoint.

I begin this book with three major propositions concerning the impact of the external environment on the internal governance of the school system:

> PROPOSITION ONE: The constituents to whom the central administration must respond are so multiple and diverse that they function as a significant obstacle to the internal governance and control of the school system.
>
> PROPOSITION TWO: The conflicting demands which the multiple constituents impose on the system hinder the establishment of a unified policy direction.
>
> PROPOSITION THREE: On the whole, the external constituents to whom the central administration must respond are neither representative of nor responsive to the clientele which it serves.

I make no claims of originality regarding the first two propositions. Although less optimistic than the assertions of Sayre and Kaufman, they are generally consistent with the literature on the urban superintendent that has previously been cited. However, these two propositions provide an important basis for the third, which is the major point of departure for this book. The analytical distinction made here between *organizational constituents* and *organizational clients* is a serious and conscious one. The former refers to individuals, institutions, or groups to which an organization's leadership is accountable; the latter refers to individuals who receive services. While political scientists have recognized the distinction between these two analytical categories, there has been a tendency within the discipline to use the terms interchangeably. That tendency has led to analytical confusion, and it influences both the questions we ask and the observations we make as we go about our research on the public bureaucracy.

I will say more later about the significance of this analytical distinction within the broad context of organization theory. Now let it suffice to say that the dichotomy between constituents and clients in the external environment of an urban school system not only poses a major political dilemma for the superintendent, but also represents an important flaw in the institutional structure, which limits the capability of an urban school system to respond to the needs of the population it is supposed to serve. As will be explained later, this problem of governance applies to other human service systems that cater to a predominantly poor clientele.

I do not mean to suggest that any one school superintendent (or chancellor) has the accumulated wisdom to define with certainty policies that are in the best interest of the clients. Quite to the contrary, the policies of a school administration are often as much a result of the personal values of its leadership as they are a product of scientific investigation and discovery. Indeed, the absence of such certainty in the decision-making process is a fundamental aspect of the problem in educational governance and a cause of political conflict.

The important point is that once a superintendent charts a course he or she believes is consistent with the needs of the children who attend the public schools, the major impediments that stand between policy and practice are found in the external environment of the system. This is true even in situations where the goals of the school administration have the political support of the client population, because the leadership of the school system is not ultimately accountable to either that population or its representatives.

This book will show that the decision-making structure for education in New York City does not contribute to the ideals of representativeness or responsiveness. While the pluralistic nature of city politics may give school executives an opportunity to play one group off against the other in order to get their way, there is no incentive built into the system to guarantee the responsiveness of school executives to the clientele. In fact, the situation is quite to the contrary. While individual executives or a chancellor may be favorably disposed toward the clients, institutional factors in the policy structure can still prevent school officials from acting very effectively on behalf of the clients. While at one time the constituents to which the system had to respond may have represented the clientele it served, the composition of that constituency has not changed to keep up with the changes in clientele during the last two decades.

ORGANIZATION AND FORMAT

Each of the following five chapters (2 through 6) is developed around a specific case study dealing with an area of educational policy that concerned the school administration in New York between 1978 and 1983. Special attention is given to describing the role that an assortment of public and private actors at all levels of government played in the formulation, implementation, redirection, and obstruction of policy initiatives undertaken by the new chancellor. The topics include budgeting and school finance, competency standards, special education, desegregation, and staff accountability. The subjects were chosen according to three criteria:

- relevance to the concepts and propositions that have been posed;
- significance as educational and political issues in New York City during the time interval covered;
- general applicability to other urban school systems.

In order to expand the scope of the text beyond the details of the specific case studies, each chapter contains a historical analysis of the educational and political issues discussed, covering both the local and national scene. Each chapter also contains a discussion of the relevant research literature on the educational issues involved. Thus a conscious effort has been made to incorporate the details of specific cases within a general context. This wide treatment of the issues also allows for a fuller and more representative history of the Macchiarola administration. Given the nature of the events that took place in New York during this period, the episodes described also shed light on a variety of political and policy issues that go beyond the field of education. They include the subjects of fiscal retrenchment, intergovernmental relations, judicial policy making, legislative politics, and labor relations.

Chapter 7 serves as a conclusion. It begins with an update of the events portrayed in the previous chapters through the end of 1982. This update offers an opportunity to bring together the materials of the various case studies and to consider their relevance to the concepts and propositions presented earlier. The final analysis proceeds on several levels. It includes an evaluation of the educational policy-making structure in New York and a set of recommendations for institutional reform. These prescriptions are designed to assign definite political responsibility for the delivery of education services and to align more closely the interests of constituents and clients. The analysis in Chapter 7 also assesses the relevance of the institutional diagnosis for New York to other urban school systems and suggests some fundamental similarities that are found in their external political environments. Finally, based upon the substantive discourse that surrounded the several major policy debates that emerged in New York between 1978 and 1983, a set of policy options is outlined that can be applied to inner-city schools throughout the nation.

Attached to the basic text is an "Addendum for Social Scientists." This addition is an elaboration on some of the theoretical themes that have been developed. It examines the relevance of the present work to the existing body of literature on complex organizations, and the applicability of its concepts to public service agencies outside of education.

NOTES

1. See Raymond Callahan, *Education and the Cult of Efficiency* (Chicago: University of Chicago Press, 1962); David Tyack, *The One Best System* (Cambridge: Harvard University Press, 1974).

2. See Joseph P. Viteritti, *Bureaucracy and Social Justice* (Port Washington, N.Y.: Kennikat Press, 1979).

3. Ralph Kimbrough, *Political Power and Educational Decision-Making* (Chicago: Rand McNally, 1964); Lawrence Iannaccone, *Politics in Education* (New York: The Center for Applied Research in Education, 1967); Robert Salisbury, "Schools and Politics in the Big City," *Harvard Educational Review* 67 (Summer 1967); Lawrence Iannaccone and Frank Lutz, *Politics, Power and Policy* (Columbus, Ohio: Charles Merrill, 1970); Paul Peterson, *School Politics Chicago Style* (Chicago: University of Chicago Press, 1976); Ronald I. Campbell, *et al., The Organization and Control of American Schools* (Columbus, Ohio: Charles Merrill, 1978).

4. See Mario Fantini, Marilyn Gittell, Richard Magat, *Community Control and the Urban School* (New York: Praeger, 1970); Mario Fantini and Marilyn Gittell, *Decentralization: Achieving Reform* (New York: Praeger, 1973); Joseph Cronin, *The Control of Urban Schools* (New York: Praeger, 1973); George La Noue and Bruce Smith, *The Politics of School Decentralization* (Lexington, Mass.: D. C. Heath, 1973).

5. See Michael Timpane, ed., *The Federal Interest in Financing Education* (Cambridge, Mass.: Ballinger, 1979); Mary F. Williams, ed., *Government in the Classroom* (New York: The Academy of Political Science, 1978).

6. See Glenden Schubert, *Constitutional Politics* (New York: Holt, Rinehart and Winston, 1960); Gary Orfield, *The Reconstruction of Southern Education* (New York: John Wiley, 1969); John Hogan, *The Schools, the*

Courts and the Public Interest (Lexington, Mass.: Lexington Books, 1974); Raoul Berger, *Government By Judiciary* (Cambridge, Mass.: Harvard University Press, 1977); Donald Horowitz, *The Courts and Social Policy* (Washington: The Brookings Institution, 1977); David Kirp, *Just Schools* (Berkeley: University of California Press, 1982); Michael Rebell and Allen Block, *Education Policy Making and the Court* (Chicago: University of Chicago Press, 1982).

7. On the state role in education, see Stephen K. Bailey, *et al., Schoolmen and Politics* (Syracuse, N.Y.: Syracuse University Press, 1962); Nicholas Masters, *et al., State Politics and the Public Schools* (New York: Knopf, 1964); Jerome Murphy, *State Education Agencies and Discretionary Funds* (Lexington, Mass.: Lexington Books, 1974); Ronald Campbell and Tim Mazzoni, eds., *State Policy Making for the Public Schools* (Berkeley, Calif.: McCutchan, 1976).

8. See Harry H. Wellington and Ralph K. Winter, Jr., *The Unions and the Cities* (Washington: The Brookings Institution, 1971); William J. Grimshaw, *Union Rule in the Schools* (Lexington, Mass.: Lexington Books, 1979); Anthony Cresswell and Michael Murphey, *Teachers Unions and Collective Bargaining* (Berkeley, Calif.: McCutchan, 1980).

9. Frederick M. Wirt and Michael W. Kirst, *Schools in Conflict: The Politics of Education* (Berkeley, Calif.: McCutchan, 1982), p.v.

10. Norman D. Kerr, "The School Board as an Agency of Legitimization," *Sociology of Education* 38 (Autumn 1964); L. Harmon Ziegler and M. Kent Jennings, *Governing American Schools* (North Scituate, Mass.: Duxbury Press, 1974).

11. Larry Cuban, *Urban School Chiefs under Fire* (Chicago: University of Chicago Press, 1976). See also Jesse McCorry, *Marcus Foster and the Oakland Public Schools* (Berkeley: University of California Press, 1978); John Merrow, Richard Foster, Nolan Estes, *The Urban School Superintendent of the Future* (Durant, Okla.: Southeastern Foundation, 1974); Nancy L. Arnez, *The Besieged School Superintendent* (Washington: University Press of America, 1981).

12. Cuban, *Urban School Chiefs.*

13. *Wall Street Journal,* July 2, 1981, as cited in Julius D'Agostino, "The Urban School Superintendent's First Year: Implications of Two Literatures for School Management Practice," unpublished qualifying paper for the Ed.D. Harvard Graduate School of Education, May 25, 1982.

14. William Boyd, "The Public, the Professionals and Educational Policy Making: Who Governs?" *Teachers College Record* 77 (May 1976). See also Donald McCarty and Charles E. Ramsey, *The School Managers* (Westport, Conn.: Greenwood Publishing, 1971).

15. "A Decade of Gallup Polls of Attitudes towards Education," *Phi Delta Kappan* (September 1978).

16. "Annual Gallup Poll of the Public's Attitudes toward the Public Schools," *Phi Delta Kappan* (September 1979).

17. "Annual Gallup Poll of the Public's Attitudes toward the Public Schools," *Phi Delta Kappan* (September 1980).

18. United States Department of Health, Education and Welfare, National Center for Education Statistics, *Projections of Education Statistics* (Washington: U.S. Government Printing Office, 1980).

19. Ibid.

20. Ibid.

21. Diane Ravitch, *The Great School Wars* (New York: Basic Books, 1974). See also Marilyn Gittell, "Education: The Decentralization–Community Control Controversy," in Jewel Bellush and Stephen M. David, eds., *Race and Politics in New York City* (New York: Praeger, 1971).

22. Ravitch, *The Great School Wars,* p. xiii.

23. Ibid.

24. Marilyn Gittell, "School Governance," in Charles Brecher and Raymond D. Horton, eds., *Setting Municipal Priorities* (Montclair, N.J.: Allanheld, Osmun, 1980), p. 203.

25. Ibid., p. 202.

26. Ibid., p. 191.

27. Ibid.

28. Ibid.

29. *The New York Times,* June 25, 1980.

30. Ibid.

31. See, for example, Richard Wade, "Making a Case against Ed Koch," *New York* magazine, May 11, 1981; Jack Newfield, "Mayor Koch: Giving Bad Intentions a Good Name," *Village Voice,* December 17–23, 1980. For a more balanced view, see Ken Auletta, "Profiles: The Mayor," *The New Yorker,* September 10 and 17, 1979.

32. The authoritative text on the causes of the New York City fiscal crisis is *The City in Transition, The Final Report of the Temporary Commission on City Finances* (New York: Arno, 1978). See also Ken Auletta, *The Streets Were Paved with Gold* (New York: Random House, 1979); Charles R. Morris, *The Cost of Good Intentions* (New York: W. W. Norton, 1980). For another perspective, see Jack Newfield and Paul Dubrul, *The Abuse of Power* (New York: Viking, 1977); Roger Alcaly and David Mermelstein, eds., *The Fiscal Crisis of American Cities* (New York: Vintage, 1977); William K. Tabb, *The Long Default* (New York: Monthly Review Press, 1982).

33. The most comprehensive analysis of New York's political and institutional response to the fiscal crisis is found in Robert Bailey, *The Crisis Regime* (Albany: State University of New York Press, forthcoming).

34. See, for example, Frank J. Macchiarola, "The Theory and Practice of State and Local Government Relations in New York State," *Albany Law Review* 33 (Spring 1969); "Constitutional, Statutory and Judicial Restraints on Local Finance in New York State," *New York Law Forum* XV (Winter 1969); "Local Government Finance Under the New York State Constitution with an Emphasis on New York City," *Fordham Law Review* (December 1977).

35. Frank J. Macchiarola, "Remarks," June 29, 1978.

36. Ibid.

37. See, for example, David S. Seeley, "Winds of Change in New York

City's Public Schools: Can Chancellor Macchiarola Set a New Course?" *City Almanac* 13 (February 1979).

38. Frank J. Macchiarola, "Mid-Year Report of the Chancellor of Schools to the New York City Board of Education," January 1979.

39. *New York Post,* June 19, 1979.

40. Albert Shanker, correspondence to Frank J. Macchariola, January 18, 1979.

41. David Rogers, *110 Livingston Street* (New York: Random House, 1968), p. 255.

42. Ibid.

43. Ibid.

44. Wallace Sayre and Herbert Kaufman, *Governing New York City* (New York: W. W. Norton, 1960), p. 263.

THE BATTLES OF THE BUDGET 2

In no other sphere is the political liability of a poor clientele as apparent as it is in the budget process. The ability of an urban school system to procure the financial support needed to provide adequate service is directly linked to the composition of its clientele and the political power of that clientele—or, at least, its perceived power among policy makers. The budget is a key in determining the quantity, quality, and kinds of service that will be provided within a school system. Thus the budget is more than a financial document. It is a symbol of public priorities. It is a barometer of political support. It is a manifestation of individual and interest-group power.

Prior to the 1970s, the budget process in public organizations was understood to be incremental: The previous year's allotment determined the funding level for an agency, service, or program.[1] In most cases this incremental approach reaped at least slightly larger appropriations each year than it had the year before. The 1970s, which arrived on the heels of a national recession and an increasingly critical public attitude toward government spending, altered the entire dynamic of the budget process. The managerial techniques of the sixties, which were designed to make public sector activity more efficient and effective, were replaced by techniques aimed toward retrenchment.[2] Thus the typical managerial concern with "how to do better" gave way to a more painful preoccupation with "what can be done without?" The proverbial political question of "who gets what?" was replaced by a more troubling and controversial "who gets less?"

Some public officials initially saw the new politics of retrenchment as an opportunity to impose long-needed economies and eliminate waste. However, as we moved further into the 1970s, it became ever more apparent that retrenchment would really mean a substantive reduction in service.[3] As one high-ranking budget official in New York City explained it, "Up until about 1977 our major concerns had to do with reducing excess and making administrative cuts. We wanted to keep expenses down. After that we really became involved in service reductions."[4] Thus, by the middle of the decade, the realities of cutback management changed the stakes of the budget process. Client

31

groups that were once preoccupied with increasing the level of funding available to them were now fighting to hold on to what they had. To make matters worse, given the rapid growth of inflation during the 1970s, even maintaining a constant dollar appropriation would not be sufficient to maintain a comparable level of service.

Local school districts were among the major victims of the fiscal crisis that struck American cities during the 1970s and 1980s. According to a report published by the Council of Great City Schools in early 1981, all of its twenty-eight member school districts were expected to face some degree of financial difficulty during the coming year.[5] Chicago was confronted with a $15 million deficit and Cleveland with a deficit of over $46 million. In the same year, it took a court order to keep the Boston schools in operation, because they had run out of money by April. The Boston schools opened in September of 1981 with the layoff of over 1,500 teachers—a reduction of more than 20 percent in the teaching staff. That September, the Philadelphia schools did not open at all because of a teachers' strike protesting the layoff of 3,500 teachers and the recision of a 10 percent pay increase that had been provided in the contract.

Urban school systems were enduring this shrinkage in their operating budgets at the same time that they were experiencing a transformation of the populations they served. The middle class was taking its children out of inner-city public schools and placing them in private schools or moving out to the suburbs. As the middle class began to disassociate itself from urban schools, an unprecedented dichotomy over the issue of public education developed. It separated the middle-class taxpayer from the inner-city poor. While the middle class began to see its connection with public education as primarily one of footing the bill, the urban poor remained service recipients of the system. While the middle class often applauded the cutback in public spending for education, the poor looked with regret at the declining services being made available to their children.

The disinvestment in public education that began to take place during the 1970s was symptomatic of a changing national mood. The proponents of that change described it philosophically as a reevaluation of the function of government, which both inappropriately and unsuccessfully had cast itself as the agent of social change. The critics of this new conservative thinking associate it with a declining social consciousness. These philosophical differences had significant social implications in a country that had historically recognized public education as a means of social mobility for the poor. Because the consequences of the debate were so crucial, its battles were fought and its outcome decided in the arena of politics.

THE BATTLES OF THE BUDGET   33

The 1960s had been a period of rapid growth in educational spending. As the nation began to respond to the dictates of a technological society, as the sons and daughters and grandchildren of a generation of immigrants began to recognize the value of education, and as public officials began to address the needs of racial and linguistic minorities, education became a key national priority. The growth in spending for education took place on all levels of government. Between 1962 and 1972, the Office of Education's total budget grew from $477 million to $5.5 billion. However, the federal share of overall expenditures for elementary and secondary education grew only from 4.4 percent in 1962 to a little more than 7 percent in 1976. From 1960 to 1970, federal expenditures for elementary and secondary education increased by $1.9 billion, state expenditures by $9.86 billion, and local expenditures by $11.74 billion.[6]

The general trend notwithstanding, it was federal intervention in the sphere of education that was most responsive to the interests of minorities and the poor. As a result of the landmark *Brown* decision in the mid-1950s, the federal government first assumed its role as a protector of educational equality by challenging the historical violations suffered by blacks at the hands of the states. The federal agenda on behalf of educational equity did not take on a financial dimension until 1965, through the enactment of the Elementary and Secondary Education Act (ESEA).[7] Under Title I of this act, which was a cornerstone of Lyndon Johnson's Great Society program, federal education funds were appropriated on the basis of poverty. Between 1965 and 1966, federal grants for elementary and secondary education jumped from $1 billion to $2 billion. By the end of the decade, spending under Title I had reached nearly $3 billion.[8] It was the greatest infusion of federal funds for the education of the poor in the history of the nation.

The enactment of Title I specifically and ESEA in general was a major testimony to the political leadership of Lyndon Johnson. However, such leadership and legislation were made possible through the formation of a strong Congressional coalition of Southern Democrats and Northeastern liberals from states with large urban centers and numerous electoral votes. It was that Democratic coalition which made liberal presidential politics feasible since the days of Franklin Delano Roosevelt.[9] By 1968, this coalition had begun to crumble. Nixon strategists called upon Southern conservative Democrats to stand behind their Republican candidate, and began to tap a white urban and suburban electorate in the Northeast that was becoming disenchanted with the liberal politics of the 1960s.[10]

Richard Nixon interpreted his own election as a mandate to undo the federally funded social programs that had grown out of the Great

Society. His first budget request for elementary and secondary education was $400 million less than that of his predecessor, the lowest since
1965.[11] While the Democratic majority in Congress was able to prevent
a dismantling of Lyndon Johnson's legislative legacy, it was quite clear
that the generous growth in spending for education that had typified the
previous decade would now level off. Thus the former director of the
National Institute of Education, Michael Timpane, was both percep-
tive and prophetic when he wrote, "By 1972, every one of the financial
and demographic pressures for an additional federal finance commitment to education had abated; many promised actually to recede."[12]

The proponents of a strong federal role in education enjoyed a
short, though rocky respite with the Carter administration, whose tenure coincided with the rising power of a conservative voice in Congress. In 1980 the nation elected Ronald Reagan, and with him a
sympathetic Congress, which was prepared to carry out the mandate
that had just begun to be heard under Richard Nixon. The Reagan
administration promised a smaller federal role in education, less federal spending, and a transfer of discretion to the states. It had been the
denial of equal rights protection by some of the states that had
motivated federal intervention in the first place. Now Ronald Reagan
was pledging a retreat from that original federal commitment. His proposal for block grants would give the states a larger voice in deciding
how federal education dollars could be spent.

Speculation about the future distribution of federal dollars
through the states may be informed by several decades of scholarship
on state governments, none of which is encouraging for the prospects
of urban education or its clients. The history of state government in the
United States is a tale of rural domination, which has generally worked
against the interest of cities.[13] Through its judicial activism, the Warren
Court attempted to rectify the consequences of this anti-urban bias
when it outlawed the malapportionment of legislative seats in the various statehouses.[14] However, the net result of the "reapportionment
revolution" that took place was a redistribution of legislative seats to
the suburbs, where population growth was occurring, and whose representatives proved to be no more sympathetic to the interests and needs
of an urban population than were their rural colleagues.

By 1968, there began to appear a significant line of research that
showed a direct correlation between educational spending within the
various states and the property wealth of local school districts.[15] Despite the legal responsibility of the states to provide individuals with a
free and equal education, and the existence of state school finance
formulas that supposedly protected such rights, the research indicated
that children in property-rich districts were enjoying larger allocations
of educational funds than children in poor districts. The issue of state

school finance was by no means a solely urban issue, for many of the property-poor districts were either suburban or rural. However, given the differing needs of the urban school population, the higher costs of service, and the peculiar fiscal burdens of the cities,[16] inner-city schools were particularly hard hit by the maldistribution of educational funds imposed by many of the states.

The most significant challenges to the existing state finance formulas have come through the courts. The first such case was brought in California in 1971. The supreme court of that state found in *Serrano* v. *Priest*[17] that the state system of educational finance was discriminatory against the poor and therefore in violation of the Fourteenth Amendment of the federal Constitution and state constitutional law. Soon after the *Serrano* decision, the state courts of Minnesota, Texas, New Jersey, and Michigan handed down similar decisions. Then, in 1973, the Supreme Court handed down a decision in *San Antonio School District* v. *Rodriguez*[18] that appeared to be a setback in the litigation on school finance reform. In that case, the Supreme Court held that disparities in per capita expenditures for schoolchildren were not a violation of the equal protection clause of the federal Constitution, since education is not a guaranteed federal right. However, the Supreme Court did leave the way open for challenges based upon state constitutional law. Two weeks after the *Rodriguez* decision, the supreme court of the state of New Jersey unanimously upheld a challenge to the school finance formula on the basis of state legislative and constitutional enactments. The New Jersey court, in *Robinson* v. *Cahill*,[19] issued an opinion based on the entitlement of each child to a "thorough and efficient" education under state law. Thereafter, a spate of school finance cases proceeded, which challenged existing state formulas on the basis of state law. At the time of this writing, more than half the states in the nation have instituted some type of school finance reform. However, the result of the litigation and reforms remains an open question.[20] The outcome of school finance reform remains very much in the hands of the state legislatures. These bodies, being the political institutions that they are, remain reluctant to enact reforms that will redistribute funds away from the wealthier, more politically powerful districts in their jurisdictions in favor of the poorer districts, which are less capable of exercising a strong influence.

SCHOOL FINANCE REFORM IN NEW YORK STATE

New York State fits well into the national pattern that shows a correlation between school spending and local property wealth. In fact, in New York State the problem is particularly severe. A study of thirty-five states, performed by the Education Commission of the States in 1979, has shown that, according to two different disparity measures, New York ranked first and third in comparison to the other states.[21] In 1978, the per pupil property wealth for the richest school district in New York State was $612,733, while that for the poorest was $12,026, a ratio of 51 to 1.[22] Lawmakers in Albany have recognized the fact that education is constitutionally and legally a state function, and have designed a school finance formula that would supposedly alleviate the disparities in education spending that grow out of local differences in wealth. However, the state finance formula now in existence has gone only so far in overcoming these disparities. In 1978, the highest-spending school district in the state spent $5,753 per pupil, while the lowest spent $989 per pupil, a ratio of 5.8 to 1.[23]

A brief overview of the school finance formula for New York State shows why it has not succeeded in closing the funding gap among its more than seven hundred school districts.[24] Since the presumed goal of the formula is to bring greater equity in spending among the local districts, two basic criteria are used to determine a particular district's share of the state aid funds: full value of taxable property, and number of students in average daily attendance. The higher the property value of a district, the lower its share of state funds; the higher the average number of students in daily attendance, the higher the entitlement. Given the fact that the cost of educating some children is more than that of others, children are "weighted" according to different classifications of need. For example, secondary school students are weighted more heavily than elementary students; students with reading scores significantly below grade level are weighted more heavily than those with scores at grade level; handicapped children are weighted more heavily than nonhandicapped. Thus the overall scheme of the state finance plan seems to have all the ingredients for an equitable distribution of education funds among the districts. However, there exist exceptions, limits, and modifications of the general rules that undermine the overall purpose of the school finance formula.

First of all, the state has a set ceiling of $1,700 per student that it can allocate to any particular district. All expenditures above the $1,700 level are met entirely by local taxes. Given the fact that the average per pupil expenditure in New York State is well over $2,500, this ceiling significantly limits the ability of the state aid formula to readjust spending levels. Second, the state formula also assures that each district is guaranteed $360 per pupil, regardless of wealth. Therefore, a large portion of the state education money is allocated without respect to need. Third, a "save harmless" guarantee written into the law assures that no district will receive a total amount of aid that is smaller than its allocation in the previous year. Therefore, there is no downward adjustment for decreasing enrollment or increasing wealth. Fourth, a cap assures that no district will receive an increase of more than 13 percent above what it received the previous year, regardless of enrollment or attendance. Finally, the funding formula does not consider the differing costs of doing business among the various districts around the state. Despite hopes to the contrary, the New York State education finance law is a state-imposed mechanism that perpetuates inequities in spending. Thus, in 1978, the average spending level per pupil in those districts in the highest decile grouped according to wealth was $2,648, while the average spending per pupil for the districts in the lowest decile was $1,455. The wealthy districts in the state were spending 81 percent more per child than the poor districts.[25] It was this kind of inequity that brought New York State into court on the issue of school finance reform.

In 1976, twenty-seven local school districts from New York State initiated litigation challenging the school financial formula.[26] They alleged that the formula discriminated against property-poor districts in the support of primary and secondary education. The plaintiffs based their arguments on three major points: the denial of equal protection guaranteed by the New York State Constitution; a violation of the education article of the New York State Constitution, which requires a statewide system of common schools; and a violation of the Fourteenth Amendment of the United States Constitution.

Several months after the filing of the original complaint, the school boards of New York State's four largest urban districts—New York, Buffalo, Rochester, and Syracuse—entered the case as plaintiff intervenors. While these larger districts were in fact "property-rich" in comparison to many of the smaller districts in the state, they presented a rather novel and innovative argument regarding the impact of state school finance plans on inner-city schools. This line of argument, which has become known in the literature and the law under the general term "municipal overburden," added an urban dimension to the ongoing campaign for school finance reform.[27] The plaintiff intervenors put forward a four-point case:

- They argued that because cities must provide a number of municipal services within their jurisdictions which other districts do not require, and which drain off tax dollars that might ordinarily be allocated to education, the present formula is irrational and discriminatory.
- They argued that because of the higher cost of educational services in cities, the "equalizing" formula of the state does not

allow city districts the same purchasing power as other districts.

• They argued that because cities have a higher rate of student absenteeism than other districts, a funding formula based on average daily attendance rather than actual enrollment is irrational and discriminatory.

• They argued that because cities have a greater concentration of disadvantaged, handicapped, and other students with special needs, the present formula is irrational and discriminatory.

After 122 days of trial, 128 witnesses, and over 400 exhibits, the trial of *Levittown* v. *Nyquist* was concluded on January 12, 1977.[28] State Supreme Court Justice J. Kingsley Smith finally rendered an opinion on June 23, 1978, and issued a judgment on December 22, 1978.[29] He ruled in favor of both the plaintiffs and the plaintiff intervenors. He found factually that the level of educational expenditures in school districts is directly related to their property wealth. He also found that the disparity in expenditures affected the level of educational services provided to students. In accordance with the line of reasoning that came out of the *San Antonio* v. *Rodriguez* decision, Justice Smith found that although the inequities in the school finance plan do not violate the "equal protection" clause of the federal Constitution, they do violate equal protection rights and children's educational entitlements that are guaranteed in the state constitution.

In September 1978, three months after Justice Smith's opinion and three months before his decision, Governor Hugh Carey and Chancellor of the State Board of Regents Theodore M. Black announced the creation of a Special Task Force on Equity and Excellence in Education. The charge of the task force, to be headed by former state regent Max Rubin, was to evaluate and identify alternatives to the finance formula that were fiscally sound and constitutionally acceptable. Its thirty-five-person membership included educators from both private and public schools, government officials, and representatives of the business and labor communities. The task force published a report in September 1980 which confirmed the general findings of the State Supreme Court decision. Moreover, the research report found that spending differences in New York State had not diminished between the 1974–1975 school year (from which the data in the suit were derived) and the 1977–1978 school year (from which the data in the task force report were derived), but that in the most extreme cases spending differences had increased. During this period, the disparity between the per pupil spending rate in the richest district and the rate in the poorest district had changed from a ratio of 5.1 to 1 to ratio of 5.8 to 1.[30]

In the meantime, on April 7, 1980, the state argued its appeal of the original decision handed down by Justice Smith. The answer on that appeal finally came down on October 26, 1981, with a ruling from a four-judge panel of the Appellate Division of the State Supreme Court. The court upheld the original decision and found that the existing financing system impinges upon "the important right of education guaranteed to all children of this state."[31] It also upheld the "municipal overburden" argument of New York City and the other three large urban districts of the state. Shortly after the handing down of the forty-two-page Appellate Court opinion by Judge Leon Lazer, State Attorney General Robert Abrams announced his intention to take the appeal to the state's highest court. Given the unanimity of the Appellate Division ruling, speculation at the time suggested that a final Court of Appeals ruling would be both speedy and affirming. However, regardless of the temporary optimism that grew out of the favorable legal decision, the fact remained that the final resolution on the issue would be legislative and political.

The New York State legislature could be expected to exhibit the same kind of reluctance with regard to school finance reform that has been observed elsewhere. To begin with, few lawmakers were optimistic about the prospects of a plan that would radically redistribute education funds in a way that would penalize many politically favored districts. What the legislature had been doing instead, since the original *Levittown* decision, was to support incremental measures to supplement the allocations to "property-poor" districts. These adjustments were limited and were summarily dismissed by Judge Lazer as "insignificant." However a resolution to the school finance reform issue is worked out in New York, all factors suggest that any effective remedy will undoubtedly prove expensive. An estimate by the special task force appointed by the governor put the cost at $1 billion per year. Legislators in Albany had been circulating a figure of $2 billion per year. One cannot be optimistic about the prospects in a time of financial constraints. The funding problem is further exacerbated by New York State's already high level of education spending. According to a Citizens' Public Expenditure Survey based upon the federal Department of Education's National Center for Education Statistics, New York State ranks second in the nation on per pupil spending in education, surpassed only by the state of Alaska.[32]

While to a large degree the obstacles to school finance reform in New York are located in the Albany legislature, state-level politics only partially explains why an urban school system like that of New York City does not get its fair share of state operating funds. The other major aspect of the issue concerns politics at the local level. The New York City school system, like those in the other large cities of the state, is a dependent school district. This not only means that the city's municipal officials determine the size of its locally supported budget, but it also means that state operating funds for education must be channeled through the municipal government. This system of intergovernmental finance puts the city school system in a rather vulnerable position, particularly at a time when local governments are going through a period of financial austerity and retrenchment. With regard to local funds, fiscal dependence means that the school system must compete for support with other municipal services such as police, fire, and sanitation, all of which have a direct reporting relationship to the mayor, and many of which have more widespread and significant political support than the public schools. With regard to state funds, fiscal dependency has given rise to a practice called "supplantation." Supplantation is a tendency on the part of local governments to reduce funding when there is an increase in intergovernmental aid. The practice of supplantation is a reminder that the question of whether a school district like New York gets its fair share of state operating funds is not determined at any one particular level of government, but is the outcome of a very intricate process of intergovernmental finance, carried on between the city and the state.

THE NEW YORK CITY SCHOOL BUDGET: RETRENCHMENT AND SUPPLANTATION

In the 1980 fiscal year, which began on July 1, 1979, the total funding for the New York City public schools was $3.26 billion. Of this amount, $1.7 billion (50.6 percent) was derived from local tax levy sources, for operating expenses, and $137 million (4.2 percent) was derived from the City capital fund. Of the remaining dollars in the budget, approximately $1 billion (30.7 percent) came from state revenues, $396 million (12.1 percent) from federal revenues, and $31 million (2.4 percent) from other outside sources.[33] (Figure 2-1.) Thus, while the large part of the school budget comes from local sources, the contribution made from external sources—especially the state—is a significant one.

In the 1980 fiscal year, the total expense budget of the school system (which excludes capital items) was $3,111,543,000. As indicated in Table 2-1, 63 percent of the total amount of this funding was devoted to direct instructional programs (i.e., classroom instruction, school and field supervision), 4 percent was given to indirect instructional programs (i.e., counselors, attendance teachers, psychologists, etc.), and 10 percent to ancillary pupil support programs (i.e., security,

Figure 2-1
PUBLIC SCHOOL FUNDING SOURCES, 1980 ($3.26 BILLION BUDGET)

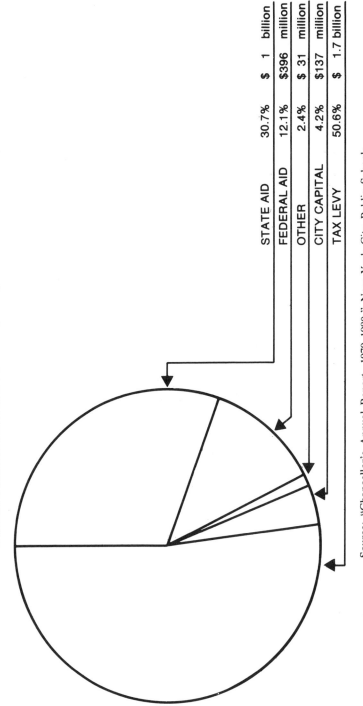

STATE AID	30.7%	$ 1	billion
FEDERAL AID	12.1%	$396	million
OTHER	2.4%	$ 31	million
CITY CAPITAL	4.2%	$137	million
TAX LEVY	50.6%	$ 1.7	billion

Source: "Chancellor's Annual Report, 1979–1980," New York City Public Schools, 1981, p. 27.

Table 2-1
**NEW YORK CITY BOARD OF EDUCATION 1979–1980 BUDGET
HIGHLIGHTS**

Selected Statistical Information—Public School Pupils

Functional Area	Budget (M = 1,000,000)	Average Cost per Pupil	Percent of Total Budget
Direct instructional programs (classroom instruction, school and field supervision)	$1,956 M	$2,037	63 %
Indirect instructional programs (counselors, attendance, psychologists, etc.)	$ 127 M	$ 133	4 %
Ancillary pupil support programs (security, transportation, lunch, etc.)	$ 321 M	$ 334	10 %
School buildings (custodial, maintenance, fuel, etc.)	$ 248 M	$ 258	8 %
City and districtwide administration (chancellor, personnel, business administration, district superintendents, etc.)	$ 108 M	$ 113	3½%
Miscellaneous expenses (unemployment insurance, collective bargaining reserve, etc.)	$ 41 M	$ 42	1½%
Debt service	$ 201 M	$ 209	6½%

Instructional/ Organizational Level	Budget		Average per Pupil Cost	Percent of Total Register
	Amount (M = 1,000,000)	Percent of Total		
Elementary	$1,181 M	39%	$2,774	44%
Junior high	$ 622 M	21%	$3,236	20%
High school	$ 790 M	26%	$2,716	30%
Special education	$ 409 M	14%	$7,958	6%

Source: "A Functional Analysis of the 1979–1980 New York City Board of Education Budget," Office of Budget Operations and Review, Board of Education of the City of New York, June 1980, p. II.

transportation, lunch). Of the remainder of the funds, 8 percent was spent on the upkeep of the system's more than one thousand school buildings (custodial, maintenance, and fuel), and 3½ percent was given to citywide and district-level administration (i.e., personnel and business matters). The remaining 8 percent was divided between miscellaneous expenses (1.5 percent) and the costs of debt service (6.5 percent). The latter was becoming a more important part of the total city budget as interest rates for borrowing rose.[34]

As was the case with other urban school districts throughout the nation, the New York City public school system began to experience an enrollment decline toward the second half of the 1970s. Between 1978 and 1982 alone, public school enrollment in New York declined from 1,100,000 students to approximately 924,000. Critics of the spending practices of the school system have often argued that such enrollment declines should have permitted a decrease in the overall expenses of the school system. However, such expectations do not take into consideration the rising costs of doing business, due to inflation. Nor do they take into consideration the change in the mix of services that has occurred within the school system over recent years, which has increased the per pupil operating expenses. The most significant of these changes in service is in the area of special education, where in an effort to comply with federal laws for the education of the handicapped, enrollment increased between 1978 and 1982 from 52,000 students to nearly 100,000. Since the cost of educating a child in special education is considerably more than the cost of educating a child in regular education, the increased special education enrollment has contributed significantly to the financial problems of the school system. Costs rose not only for instructional programs for children with handicapping conditions, but also for noninstructional services such as student transportation and support services. Thus in 1980, while only 6 percent of the total pupil population was receiving special education services, 14 percent of the total school budget was given over to special education. While the average per pupil costs in regular education were $2,716 (elementary), $3,236 (middle), and $2,716 (high school) at the respective grade levels, the average cost for a child in special education was $7,958.[35]

In order to appreciate fully where the public schools stood financially by the 1980 fiscal year, it is necessary to understand the impact of five years of retrenchment upon the city and its school system. The public schools were among the major victims of the fiscal crisis that struck New York in 1975. According to a report completed in 1976 by the office of the deputy chancellor, the schools took a budget reduction of $262 million during the first year of the crisis. This resulted in the layoff of more than ten thousand teachers and an overall staff reduction of twelve thousand personnel. The report further pointed out that while spending for education accounted for 21.6 percent of the total city budget during the three years prior to the fiscal crisis, the schools were being required to absorb 25.4 percent of the cutbacks that the city was making in its general operating expenses in 1975.[36]

The significant cutbacks in the Board of Education budget and the resultant layoffs in staff motivated the United Federation of Teachers and other education lobby groups to initiate legislative action in Albany, designed to protect the school system from a disproportionate share of further cutbacks. After a difficult legislative battle and a veto by the governor, the Stavisky–Goodman bill, named after its legislative sponsors, was written into law in 1976. The law requires that the city allocate to the Board of Education a share of the city budget at least equal to the average share it received over the three years prior to the fiscal crisis. A year after the law's passage, the city challenged its constitutionality in the courts, and the law was upheld.

City officials continue to criticize the law because it doesn't take into consideration decreasing student enrollments, which, they claim, should reduce the cost of education. School officials have also criticized the law for not insuring the protections it was meant to provide. They claim that the law does not have adequate safeguards against changes in the structure of the city budget. For example, in 1978 state and federal Medicaid reimbursements were taken out of the city budget, and payments were made directly to the hospitals. The city ceased accounting for these funds in its revenue and expense budget. This change reduced the city budget by $307 million in 1979 and $319 million in 1980.[37] It therefore reduced the base on which compliance with the Stavisky–Goodman law is measured. In 1980 debt service and pension costs were removed from the education budget and made part of the city's overall operating budget. This pullout, which came to $626 million,[38] is still included by the state comptroller in the education budget when monitoring for compliance with Stavisky–Goodman.

Despite the shortcomings of the protections for the Board of Education that were built into the state legislation, the school system was able to rehire some of the ten thousand personnel laid off after the initial shock of the fiscal crisis in 1975. However, whether the school system was able to keep its fair share of the local city budget is a more complex question.

One of the most comprehensive comparative analyses of budget retrenchment and service cutbacks among local agencies in New York was performed by Raymond Horton and Mary McCormick in the 1981 edition of the annual publication *Setting Municipal Priorities*.[39] Their analysis is primarily concerned with five major city services: education, transportation, police, fire, and sanitation. It covers two distinct historical periods: 1970 to 1975, and 1976 to 1980. Beginning with an overview of city finances, Horton and McCormick show that while the actual budget of the city increased by 86 percent during the first period, it increased by only 10 percent during the second. While city operating expenditures increased 10 percent to 18 percent annually between 1970 and 1975, the largest single-year increase between 1976 and 1980 was 4 percent. In 1980, the spending level actually fell. When the authors adjust their figures for the rate of inflation—using a 40 percent modifier, based on the local consumer price index—the data show a different pattern. When adjusted for inflation, the rate of expenditure between 1970 and 1975 increased only 33 percent. During the second half of the decade, the real expenditures of the city actually declined by 23 percent. These adjusted budget data are reflected somewhat in the patterns on employment. During the first half of the decade the citywide full-time workforce grew by 5 percent, while during the second half it was reduced by 21 percent. Thus, when taken together, the patterns on real expenditures and employment indicate, as might be expected, a general increase in city services during the early period of economic growth, and a decrease during the latter period of retrenchment.[40]

When Horton and McCormick go on to their comparative analysis of five major city services, their data suggest that education enjoyed the most rapid increase in expenditures between 1970 and 1975, and the second smallest decrease in the budget between 1976 and 1980. (See Table 2-2). The comparative data on employment, however, suggest that education held more of a middle ground. Education was one of three services to show a decrease in its personnel during the first period; it ranked third among the five in personnel cuts during the second period.[41] When one reviews the data presented by Horton and McCormick, it is difficult to argue that education suffered from a disproportionate amount of budget and staff reductions or that education was treated as a disfavored service by the city. However, there are several limitations in the data presented by these authors, and those limitations must be considered if one is to get a complete picture of how New York City dealt with retrenchment and what it meant to the school system.

To begin with, Horton and McCormick's comparative analysis of expenditures is based entirely on data from the expense budget. Under ordinary circumstances that would be an adequate way of studying changes in the operating capacities of various local agencies. But New

Table 2-2
**CONSTANT DOLLAR EXPENDITURES AND EMPLOYMENT FOR THE
CITY OF NEW YORK AND SELECTED FUNCTIONS, FISCAL YEARS
1970, 1975, 1980 (in millions of 1967 dollars)**

Function	Fiscal Year 1970	Fiscal Year 1975	Fiscal Year 1980	Percent Change 1970– 1975	Percent Change 1975– 1980	Percent Change 1970– 1980
Total city expenditures*	5,927.5	7,854.0	6,174.8	32.5	(21.4)	4.2
Police	518.1	614.1	391.9	18.5	(36.2)	(24.4)
Fire	235.9	263.7	172.9	11.8	(34.4)	(26.7)
Sanitation	148.5	169.2	118.3	13.9	(30.1)	(20.3)
Education	1,055.8	1,359.5	1,012.6	28.8	(25.5)	(4.1)
Transit	442.5	557.3	456.3	25.9	(18.1)	3.1
Total city employment†	241,827	253,677	194,308	4.9	(23.4)	(19.6)
Police	36,749	35,447	27,805	(3.5)	(21.6)	(24.3)
Fire	14,853	13,885	12,405	(6.5)	(10.7)	(16.5)
Sanitation	14,180	14,256	11,451	.5	(19.7)	(19.2)
Education	82,810	81,970	70,854	(1.0)	(13.6)	(14.4)
Transit	34,879	37,897	34,493	8.7	(9.0)	(1.1)

Source: Expenditure data for police, fire, sanitation, and education from City of New York, *Expense Budget*, as modified, for fiscal years 1971 and 1976, *Expense Budget*, as adopted, fiscal year 1980; employment data for police, fire, sanitation, and education provided by City of New York, Office of Management and Budget; transit data from *Transit Fact Book*, 1970–1971 and 1975–1976 editions; 1980 transit data provided by Office and Financial Planning, Metropolitan Transportation Authority. From Charles Brecher and Raymond Horton, eds., *Setting Municipal Priorities, 1981* (Montclair, N.J.: Allanheld, Osmun, 1980), p. 90.
*Total city expenditures include only city payments to the Transit Authority.
†Total city employment excludes Transit Authority employment.

York City does not provide us with an ordinary situation in financial practices. Until very recently, the City often provided for daily operating expenses out of the capital budget. However unsound this method may have been from an accounting perspective, it makes it imperative to look at changes in the capital budget when one is trying to assess fluctuations in operating expenses.

A second limitation of the Horton–McCormick analysis is that it looks at the overall expense budget of the City without distinguishing between locally generated revenues and funds from external sources. While that method of analysis was appropriate for the purposes of their study, it does not allow one examining the issue of retrenchment in terms of education to assess the important connection between state funding and local funding. To explain the point in another way, the data we have examined thus far do not allow us to recognize or understand the practice previously referred to as supplantation.

In July 1980 the chancellor's office completed its own analysis of the relationship between state funding and city funding over a six-year period between 1975 and 1980.[42] The staff report examined both the expense budget and the capital budget. It controlled for inflation in order to calculate constant dollar trends over the period. Table 2-3 indicates the report showed a 3.8 percent actual dollar increase in the education expense budget and a 16 percent per pupil expenditure increase. However, when these figures were adjusted for inflation, using a 37 percent modifier, they showed a constant dollar decrease in the expense budget of 25 percent, and a constant dollar decrease in per pupil spending of 16 percent.

When one analyzes the sources of the school budget over the six-year period between 1975 and 1980, a distinct pattern is evident. As state aid to education increased, local support declined. (See Table 2-4.) While the overall dollar increase in the budget was $109.75 million, the dollar increase in state aid was $142.4 million. Thus the state portion of the entire budget grew from 29.9 percent to 33.6 percent. While the city tax levy contribution to the school budget increased by $94.57 million, the city capital contribution decreased by $77.46 million and its intracity fund contribution decreased by $38.64 million. Thus the net decrease in city funding over the six-year period was $21.43 million. The overall city contribution to the budget decreased from 57.7 percent to 54.8 percent.

One cannot fully understand the extent of local disinvestment in education unless local support of the schools is seen in light of the

Table 2-3
TRENDS IN THE SIZE OF THE SCHOOL'S BUDGET 1975–1980*

	(Millions)	(Dollars)	(Millions)	(Dollars)
Fiscal year	Expense budget	Expense budget per pupil	Expense budget in constant† (1975) dollars	Expense budget in constant (1975) dollars per pupil
1975	$2,866.28	$2,605	$2,866.28	$2,605
1976	2,766.28	2,517	2,595.05	2,361
1977	2,805.18	2,604	2,573.56	2,389
1978	2,984.57	2,880	2,566.27	2,476
1979	2,892.75	2,896	2,274.17	2,277
1980**	2,976.03	3,028	2,139.49	2,177
	+3.8%	+16%	−25%	−16%

Source: "Report to the Chancellor on the Effect of State Funding on City Funding of the Board of Education," Chancellor's Office of Policy Analysis, Research and Planning, New York City Public Schools, July 1980.

*All amounts are end-of-year budgeted amounts, with the exception of 1980, where the amount is the budget as modified through February 15.

†Adjusted by the application of a Fiscal Year CPI.

**Includes pensions and debt service.

Table 2-4
SOURCE OF FUNDS, BOARD OF EDUCATION BUDGET 1975–1980*

Fiscal Year	Federal aid	(pct)	State aid	(pct)	Tax levy	(pct)	Capital	(pct)	Other intracity	(pct)	Total
Final 1975	356.25†	(12.4)	858.00†	(29.9)	1,366.97†	(47.7)	214.80†	(7.5)	70.26†	(2.5)	2,866.28†
Final 1976	291.56	(10.5)	812.05	(29.3)	1,387.53	(50.2)	198.21	(7.2)	76.97	(2.8)	2,766.32
Final 1977	286.17	(10.2)	828.98	(29.5)	1,467.53	(52.3)	183.87	(6.6)	38.63	(1.4)	2,805.18
Final 1978	351.84	(11.9)	853.92	(28.8)	1,550.26	(52.3)	185.99	(6.3)	22.58	(0.7)	2,984.57
Final 1979	300.16	(10.4)	939.99	(32.5)	1,418.85	(49.0)	183.20	(6.3)	50.55	(1.8)	2,892.75
Mod 1980	345.13	(11.6)	1,000.40	(33.6)	1,461.54	(49.1)	137.34	(4.6)	31.62	(1.1)	2,976.03
CHANGE	−11.12M		+142.4		+94.57		−77.46		−38.64		+109.75
1975–80	(+3.1%)		(+16.6%)		(+6.9%)		(−36%)		(−54%)		(+3.8%)

Source: "Report to the Chancellor on the Effect of State Funding on City Funding of the Board of Education," Chancellor's Office of Policy Analysis, Research and Planning, New York City Public Schools, July 1980.

*All amounts are from end-of-year condition except fiscal year 1980, which includes modifications through February 15.

†Figures are in millions of dollars.

Table 2-5
BOARD OF EDUCATION SHARE OF LOCAL REVENUES
(in millions)

Year	NYC tax levy revenues	NYC capitalized expenditures	Total	NYC funding (tax levy, capital & intracity) of BOE	Percent
1975	6,674.2	797	7,471.2	1,652.03	22.1
1976	7,372.5	861	8.233.5	1,662.71	20.2
1977	8,017.4	?	NA	1,690.03	NA
1978	8,432	577	9,009	1,758.83	19.5
1979	8,553	445	8,998	1,652.6	18.4
1980	8,976	282	9,258	1,630.5	17.6
Change 1975–1980	+2301.8 (34%)	−515 (−65%)	+1786.8 (+24%)	−22.5 (−1.3%)	

Source: "Report to the Chancellor on the Effect of State Funding on City Funding of the Board of Education," Chancellor's Office of Policy Analysis, Research and Planning, New York City Public Schools, July 1980.

city's own self-generated revenue base—that part of the city budget funded entirely by local sources, as opposed to intergovernmental aid from the state or federal levels. As the data in Table 2-5 indicate, the local contribution to the school budget was decreasing during a time when the local revenue base of the city was growing at a rather significant level (34 percent). The net result of these trends was a substantial reduction of locally generated revenues given to the schools. Between 1975 and 1980 the Board of Education's share of locally generated revenues decreased from 22.1 percent to 17.6 percent.

The data describing local disinvestment in education in the face of increased state aid provide us with rather straightforward documentation of the practice of supplanting local funds with state educational funds. However, one does not need to analyze the data in order to discover what is going on as a result of this rather intricate and convoluted scheme of intergovernmental finance. By midpoint in the 1970s, when the city was going through the painful motions required to cope with its own fiscal insolvency, the practice of supplanting education funds became widespread, blatant, and matter-of-fact. As Deputy Mayor for Policy Robert F. Wagner, Jr., explained:

> I might as well tell you, Fink and Anderson [state legislative leaders] tell us that aid to education is really part of an aid program to the city. In their eyes, it is not just education money. They tell us

that it is easier to get money that is earmarked for education than general aid to the city. They may tell Frank [Macchiarola] something else, but this is what they tell us.[43]

The practice of supplantation is indicative of a number of institutional inequities in state and local finances, all of which are felt by the local school system. To begin with, because the legislature in Albany has historically manifested a rather strong antiurban bias, particularly with regard to New York City, local city officials have attempted to put their own fiscal house in order by latching on to funds that have been made available through the state education aid package. The legislature has been known to be sympathetic and generous when it comes to general education aid. However, as the data and the litigation described in the previous section tell us, that sympathy and generosity have not shown themselves in an equitable fashion. Urban school districts such as New York and other property-poor districts have been discriminated against in the distribution of state education funds. The legislature has appropriated some marginal additional aid in response to charges of inequity and the early decisions of the courts. However, the few minor and temporary victories won on behalf of school finance reform are often lost at City Hall through the practice of supplantation.

In the end, the way the municipal government has chosen to deal with the biases of the legislature and its own fiscal problems has had a punitive impact upon the schools. The system of intergovernmental finance in New York City and the political dynamics that it creates make the municipal budget process crucial in determining the level of support the schools will enjoy in any given year. Individuals who participate in the budget process enjoy a great deal of authority and influence in determining what goes on in education. They are important actors because they not only determine the share of locally generated revenue that will be devoted to education, but also have a say in deciding what share of the state education budget will find its way to the schools.

THE PROCESS AND THE PLAYERS

Budget development within the New York City public schools is a full-year process. It begins in the late summer of each year, when the executive directors of the various central divisions of the school system submit their budget requests to the chancellor. By mid-December the chancellor has prepared a budget message for the Board of Education. The Board of Education puts the chancellor's budget under the scrutiny of its own budget review committee, holds public hearings on the merits of the proposal, and then sends it to the mayor. As has historically been the case in many large school districts around the country,[44] the Board of Education does not usually make many changes in the budget that is prepared by the chancellor.

Prior to the fiscal crisis that emerged in 1975, the usual practice within the city was for the mayor to review agency requests, including that of the Board of Education, from January through April. Then, in mid-April, he would submit his budget to the Board of Estimate and City Council. Between April 21 and May 16, the Board of Estimate and the City Council held public hearings on the mayor's preliminary budget. On May 1 the mayor submitted his final Executive Budget to the same bodies for consideration and approval. These steps have remained in the budget development process, but another crucial step has been added since the fiscal crisis. On September 9, 1975, the New York State legislature created an Emergency Financial Control Board, which was charged with the responsibility to oversee, approve, and modify a financial plan prepared by the city that was designed to achieve a truly balanced budget. As part of the monitoring process subsequently established, the mayor submits to the Control Board an annual financial plan outlining his budget goals for the forthcoming fiscal year and the progress made in achieving the long-term financial goals of the city.

This financial plan, now called the preliminary budget, must be prepared before January 15, not long after the schools chancellor has made public what will be his own budget request from the city. The difference between the articulated budget needs of the schools chancellor and the planned expenditure level of the mayor often sets the stage for a two-phase budget battle, which takes place in various arenas at City Hall. One phase involves a set of negotiations between school officials and municipal officials (usually from the Office of Management and Budget), prior to the formal announcement of the mayor's Executive Budget in the spring. A second and more heated phase occurs when school officials and members of various education interest groups lobby the local legislative bodies (Board of Estimate and City Council) to make their viewpoints on the budget known before it receives final approval.

The mayor does have authority to veto a budget agreed upon by the Board of Estimate and the City Council. However, this veto may be overturned by a two-thirds majority vote of either body. While the mayor is a member of the Board of Estimate, he does not vote on the budget. Since the governor and the state legislature are required by law to decide upon a state budget by April 15, local officials in New York usually have the advantage of knowing the amount of state aid that will be made available to them, prior to the approval of the city budget. According to the city charter, the city budget must be agreed upon by June 5 for the fiscal year that begins on July 1.

As the description of the process suggests, the major governmental actors in the development of the school budget are the mayor and the members of the Board of Estimate and of the City Council, each of which assumes a rather distinct role. Subsumed within the mayor's role are a whole host of actors who participate in the process on his behalf. Key among those individuals in the Koch administration is Deputy Mayor for Policy Robert F. Wagner, Jr., who acts as the mayor's chief representative to the school system. Wagner assumed that role in 1979, when Mayor Edward Koch asked him to serve as liaison between the Office of Management and Budget (OMB) and budget officials for the Board of Education, whose relationship had hit such a low point at that time that it was hardly workable. After his arrival on the scene, Wagner became a key player in both budgetary and policy roles regarding education. As he explains it, "My role is to act as a liaison, an ambassador if you wish, between the Board of Education and OMB. I have also gotten involved as a monitor of the Board of Education in terms of fiscal controls. My short-term concern was with overspending. I have more recently gotten involved in policy issues."[45]

The other major actors on behalf of the mayor are the staff in the Office of Management and Budget. OMB represents a group of financial technicians whose job it is to translate the mayor's priorities into a budget document. Because it is close to the mayor, OMB enjoys a great deal of authority. Because it controls the budget, it can influence policy, monitor performance, and hold agency people accountable for what they do. Because it possesses more information than anyone else on both the fiscal health of the city as a whole and the financial needs of individual agencies, it makes an enormous contribution to the annual dialogue that results in the formulation of a budget. As the former assistant director of the office admits, "OMB has an inordinate amount of authority. We know the mayor's priorities. It's our job to put them into policy."[46]

While the mayor and OMB look at the budget with an eye to economy, members of the Board of Estimate and City Council are more inclined to spend money. This is particularly true of those members who have less than a citywide constituency (i.e., the borough presidents and council members). Unlike the comptroller and the council president, who are elected citywide, the borough presidents and the council members are susceptible to neighborhood or community pressure for expanded services and increased spending. As one high-level OMB official explained it, "The Council and the Board of Estimate are more inclined to spend. They are concerned with providing services to their constituency. The mayor, on the other hand, must give priority to balancing the budget."[47]

The major figure from the school system in the budget process is the chancellor. He is the chief executive officer of the school system; he is the chief liaison with the mayor, and he is held accountable for what is spent. On occasion, the chancellor shares this role with the president of the Board of Education, to whom he formally reports. That was particularly the case with Board of Education President Stephen Aiello, whose candidacy for a position with the Carter White House during the first year of the Macchiarola administration made him a major figure on the local political scene. Aiello eventually left the Board of Education to go to Washington, upon his appointment as special assistant to the President.

There are several key administrative officials at the central school headquarters who act on behalf of the chancellor in the budget process. Ever since the reorganization of the central administration in March 1973, the most important person in that role has been the deputy chancellor,[48] and through the first year of the Macchiarola administration he continued to be. Then, with the appointment of Dall Forsythe as budget director for the school system in August 1979, the role became increasingly a shared one. Forsythe played a major part in healing relations between the Board of Education and the Office of Management and Budget after a year of conflict and controversy. Having previously served as chief budget analyst for the president of the City Council and having once worked with Macchiarola as a consultant to the State Emergency Financial Control Board, Forsythe knew both the issues and the people relevant to the budget process. His healing effect cast him as the major representative of the chancellor in dealing with budget officials at City Hall.

Numerous other individuals within the school system get involved in the budget negotiations with the municipal government. They include members of the Board of Education, members of community school boards, local community superintendents, principals, and the leaders of professional education groups. However, the activities of these players are usually carried out toward the end of the process, when the Board of Estimate and City Council are going through their final considerations of the mayor's executive budget. At that point, once the chancellor has set the tone of a negotiating strategy, and when the lobbying of local council members and the borough presidents can promise some results, these individuals enter the process. As one community superintendent explained it:

> The chancellor matters the most in determining the budget. He builds the ball park that I have to play in. . . . My only involvement in the budget comes after the mayor's budget comes out. After that there is always room for negotiation. I then go to the council members and the borough president. They are easier to get at. Their constituency is smaller. They are a bit more responsive.[49]

There was a time in New York City when the array of interest groups that stepped forward on behalf of education was both numerous and powerful. Now they are not so numerous and, some would argue, those that remain are not so powerful as they once were. As Deputy Mayor Robert F. Wagner, son of the former New York City mayor, explained:

> The constituency is strong, but not so strong as it once was when my father was mayor. The older interest groups such as UPA [United Parents Associations], and PEA [Public Education Association], are not so powerful as they used to be. Much of this is the result of changing demographics. There are few middle-class people left. The UFT [United Federation of Teachers] is now the principal source of strength. The EPP [Educational Priorities Panel] is fairly strong. It more represents a resurrection of the kind of movement that existed in the past. They have given what they say credibility, but they don't really have the power that used to be.[50]

The Educational Priorities Panel was founded in 1976.[51] Its evolution began in the heat of the city's fiscal crisis, when representatives from four groups—the United Parents Associations, the Public Education Association, the Community Service Society, and the Citizens Committee for Children—sought to establish a dialogue with school officials over the future of the education budget. The group, alarmed by the severe budget cuts imposed upon the schools, sought information about and participation in the Board of Education's deliberations on how its budget cuts would be absorbed. When its efforts proved futile, the group decided to form a broader alliance of interests and to seek foundation assistance to develop its own analytical capacity. Today the Educational Priorities Panel is an alliance of twenty-five interest groups. Its membership includes five major types of organizations: parent groups, child advocate groups, voluntary social agencies, civic groups, and ethnic-racial organizations.[52] While the association has been a major advocate for education in the city, it has also been a major critic of the way the Board of Education spends its money. In this way, EPP has carved a unique role for itself in the budget process. As Executive Director Stanley Litow explains it, "The role of EPP is to serve as an independent source of data on management and budget issues to the organizations, the media, the public. We consider ourselves an advocate for education and the parents. We also monitor the Board of Education."[53] Since its inception, the EPP has performed management and budget audits on a wide range of subjects at the school headquarters, including school building utilization, custodial services, the lunch program, school closings, special education, and pupil transportation. It prepares formal testimony on the budget for the City Council and Board of Estimate every year. It frequently confers with staff in the Office of Management and Budget on both management and policy issues. Because it has been critical of the Board of Education and school spending practices, the Educational Priorities Panel enjoys considerable credibility and influence with municipal officials.

The other organization that has carved out a major role in the budget process is the United Federation of Teachers. The manner and style of the union, led by Albert Shanker, are quite different from those of the EPP. While EPP's power in the budget process is a function of its ability to persuade, the union's ability to persuade is a function of its power. Shanker has been a major figure on the New York political scene for more than a decade. His teachers' jobs have been on the line, and many have been lost, each time the city goes about the business of cutting back on spending. Thus the union and its membership have a direct stake in the budget process and its outcome. The successful passage of the Stavisky–Goodman bill in 1976 was a clear manifestation of the union's interest and its power with regard to the budget. That exercise of strength in Albany also demonstrated that, because of its close association with the state teachers' union (New York State United Teachers), the UFT approaches the budget from both a local and state perspective.

The power of the union and other influential interest groups notwithstanding, most observers of the school scene in New York City would agree that the constituency for public education has certainly dwindled. Its clientele has become smaller in size, poorer in class, and less politically viable. The election of Edward Koch as mayor in 1977 led many to believe that the schools were headed for further setbacks. Koch had been elected with only meager support from the black and Puerto Rican communities, and it was their children who were attending the public schools. Koch's election campaign had been antagonistic to organized labor, and the teachers' union represented the most significant interest group on behalf of education in the city. Yet Koch was promising to upgrade the school system.

The selection of Frank Macchiarola as Chancellor of Schools in 1978 added to the curiosity. He had been chosen with the strong and outspoken support of the mayor. In fact, many individuals from both outside the school system and within referred to him as "Koch's chancellor." As a former deputy director of the State Emergency Financial Control Board, Macchiarola came to the schools with a reputation as a fiscal conservative. Moreover, his initial relationship with Albert Shanker was probably worse than that which the union president shared with the mayor.

The selection of "Koch's chancellor" gave rise to two streams of speculation. One scenario saw the chancellor as part of a scheme by the mayor to further dismantle the school system financially, so local resources could be invested in other services. Another scenario generated hope that the mayor would readily pour additional funds into the school budget to facilitate the recovery he and the chancellor had been promising. As things turned out, neither proved to be true.

ENTER "KOCH'S CHANCELLOR": THE BUDGET FOR FISCAL YEAR 1979

The new chancellor's participation in the budget process did not await his official inauguration. Frank Macchiarola had set up a transition team at the Livingston Street headquarters of the school system more than two months prior to his official swearing in on July 1. During that time, the transition team began to define the philosophical and programmatic priorities that would shape his administration. It also began to reveal an approach to budgeting that was indicative of a distinct personal style.

As the City Council was working on the final details of the fiscal year 1979 budget request submitted by outgoing Chancellor Irving Anker, Macchiarola made an eleventh-hour appearance before the Council's finance committee in order to request a change. The chancellor-designate proposed a plan that called for the removal of $15 million from the Board of Education's administrative budget and the reallocation of these funds into the budget for instruction. Within the next month the chancellor's staff found additional money in its own budget to be added to the transfer. The funds would be utilized to initiate three new programs at the school level:

1. The sum of $9 million would be used to hire 657 teachers in order to reduce class sizes in the first grade from an average of 32 pupils to an average of 25. This program was in line with the emphasis on early childhood development that was a key priority of the administration.

2. Another $5.4 million would be committed to a transitional class program for children who had been held over in the first three grades. In addition to fitting in with the administration's emphasis on early childhood development, this program was a forerunner to the remedial part of the Promotional Policy that would be the hallmark of the administration's instructional agenda. Under the transitional class program, children who had been held over would be placed in specially designed, nongraded, reduced-size classes for a period of six months to a year, depending upon need. During the 1978–1979 school year there would be 489 such classes, serving approximately 8,000 students in 358 schools.

3. Finally, $4 million would be devoted to after-school programs for children. This made 350 elementary and intermediate school buildings available for community-based activities. The proposal had a particular appeal to the Council members, whose neighborhood constituents stood to enjoy a direct and tangible benefit.

The chancellor's proposal to the Council, which was heartily approved, was one of those oft-sought-after legislative packages that had in it "something for everyone." Critics of the Board of Education's spending practices and its large bureaucracy were pleased to see the transfer of funds from the administrative to the instructional budget. Among the most vociferous of those critics had been the mayor himself. The members of the Council were pleased because the after-school programs gave them something to take home to their constituents. Albert Shanker greeted the proposal with praise because it would mean more jobs for teachers. This marked the beginning of an on-again, off-again relationship between the chancellor and the UFT president, which allowed them to cooperate when it seemed to be in their mutual interest. Finally, after some initial skepticism and suspicion, the new budget package received the support of the local community school boards and their superintendents, whose district schools were the direct beneficiaries of the programs.

In addition to signaling what the overall instructional strategy of the new administration would be, the eleventh-hour proposal made to the Council was significant on several other levels. To begin with, it represented an approach to budgeting that was program-oriented. The new administration was not just asking for more money; it was saying what it was going to do with the money, why it was important, and who would benefit. Given the ingredients of the legislative package that he put together, the new chancellor was also beginning to build the foundation for an important political alliance between a local district constituency and the teachers' union, which could and would be called upon at budget time, when the Board of Education was attempting to get its "fair share" of the resources allocated by the municipal government. In so doing, Macchiarola was also working to defuse two potential sources of opposition to the administration's initiatives, which were not particularly receptive to a new chancellor who was seen as an outsider to the school system. Finally, and perhaps most important, the chancellor's first turn at the budget trough demonstrated a willingness on his part to go directly to the Council to satisfy his budgetary needs, rather than through the mayor, who had been largely responsible for his appointment. That aggressiveness on the part of the new school chief was a revealing sign of things to come.

THE BATTLES BEGIN: THE BUDGET FOR FISCAL YEAR 1980

Almost immediately after the chancellor reaped the rewards of the minor budget victory he enjoyed during the summer of 1978, the directors of the various central divisions of the Livingston Street school headquarters began to prepare their initial budget packages for the 1980 fiscal year, which would begin in July 1979. Their requests were submitted to Deputy Chancellor Richard Halverson, who at that time had major responsibility for the school system budget. The new administration had originally retained the incumbent budget director, who had been appointed by Irving Anker, to operate and maintain the technical aspects of the budget office. However, it was Halverson who supervised the internal budget process on a policy level, and it was Halverson who served as the Board of Education's chief liaison with the Office of Management and Budget.

After several months of internal negotiation and revision, the chancellor finally had his first budget message to submit to the Board of Education. On December 15, 1978, Macchiarola made public a $3.03 billion proposal. The sum was slightly lower than the one requested by Irving Anker a year before. The total amount was based on the expectation of $130 million in state and federal aid and $41.6 million in savings through attrition and the reduction in the pupil register.[54] Of the money he asked for, the chancellor was proposing to spend $84.2 million for new programs or the expansion of existing programs, and $127.9 million for increased costs over which the school system exercised no control. Among the latter fixed costs were Social Security payments, pensions, and other personnel items. Among the new expenditures being proposed was $33.8 million to extend the transitional class program, $27.5 million for the hiring of 110 attendance officers to curtail truancy, $32.9 million for the expansion of special education services, and $32.9 million for the maintenance and repair of school buildings.[55]

Two days after the New Year, and less than three weeks after the chancellor submitted his budget message to the Board of Education, Mayor Edward Koch began to reveal preliminary figures on his own financial plan, which would soon be submitted to the New York State Financial Control Board. The mayor's preliminary citywide spending proposal called for a general saving of $147.7 million and the elimination of 7,073 full-time and 334 part-time city jobs. Of this total, $85.4 million of the spending reductions and 4,981 of the job cuts were to come from the Board of Education. The mayor's proposal, which had been prepared by the Office of Management and Budget, recommended in very specific terms the closing of fifteen schools, the elimination of reduced class sizes in the first grade, and the halting of the new transitional class program.[56] Board of Education President Stephen Aiello, enraged as much by the programmatic nature of the proposed cuts as by their amounts, issued a public condemnation, claiming that the Board of Education has "an obligation and responsibility to set its own budget priorities."[57]

On the next day the mayor announced that he was rejecting a contract that had just been negotiated between the chancellor and UFT President Albert Shanker. He ordered the chancellor to renegotiate the agreement because it was "too expensive" in its present form. He publicly stated, "To approve the contract would violate the standards I have established for settling economic issues with the municipal unions."[58] The contract that had been negotiated would have given a 4 percent wage increase to teachers. It would have also put ten thousand paraprofessionals who were hourly workers on an annual salary scale, thus making them eligible for fringe benefits and pensions. It was the latter part of the agreement that had most troubled the mayor.

Thus began a rather tense relationship between the new school administration and City Hall. Added to the issue of money, on which the two sets of players obviously stood far apart, was the institutional issue of control. Legally, the Board of Education is an independent state-chartered agency, which, within the guidelines set by the state commissioner, has sole responsibility for establishing educational policy. However, the city school district is also fiscally dependent, and that arrangement sometimes forces school officials to compromise their autonomy when they solicit funds from the municipal government. School officials have come to realize that it is easier to extract money from the local budget when they can be specific about what they want to do with it, why it is important, and who will benefit. However, jealous of their own autonomy, they do not like to be told these things. More than that, they do not like to be told where to take cuts. The issue of control had become a particularly sensitive one between the mayor and the members of the Board of Education since Koch had publicly advocated mayoral control of the school system during his election campaign. After all, at that time it did appear as though Koch had already managed to install his own chancellor.

On January 15, Mayor Edward Koch formally submitted the full proposal for his "Program to Eliminate the Gap" (PEG) to the Financial Control Board. It called for $250 million in spending cuts, which would be implemented on two levels. Level I cuts, implemented over the next fiscal year, would result in the loss of 6,033 job cuts citywide. Level II cuts, implemented as part of a continency plan if the City was unable to realize anticipated revenues, called for the elimination of 2,842 additional positions. The Board of Education was scheduled to absorb 3,597 of the Level I reductions and 829 of the Level II. While the total of these cuts was less than those announced by the mayor earlier in the month, the impact on the schools would still be severe.

On February 15 the chancellor appeared before the Board of Estimate to make a prepared statement on the mayor's proposed Program to Eliminate the Gap. His tone was moderate but direct. He said that he was not pleased with the proposed reductions, but praised the mayor for releasing the PEG document early enough so there could be reasonable discussion. He then stated the facts. The Board of Education was being asked to absorb 59% of the Level I cuts ($83.3 million out of $140.7 million). This was a reduction of 6 percent of the school system's tax levy budget. Other agencies were being asked to reduce theirs by 2 percent or 3 percent. The Board of Education was also being asked to absorb 30 percent of the Level II cuts ($16 million out of $52 million). On top of these cutbacks, the Board of Education was being asked to absorb $29.6 million in increased special education services that had been mandated by federal law. After reporting on education's share of the retrenchment measures, the chancellor outlined the programmatic impact they would have within the school system. He mentioned, among other things, the elimination of reduced class sizes in the first grade and the termination of transitional classes. He closed his remarks with a request that $70 million in increased state education aid promised by the governor not be used to balance the city budget.[60]

Within the next few weeks, the chancellor took his appeal to the New York City Council. There, in the course of regular departmental hearings, Macchiarola defended his original December 15 budget proposal. He once again explained how the mayor's PEG cuts imposed an unfair burden on education. He detailed the kinds of management improvements that his administration had made at Livingston Street. Then the chancellor noted that the three exemplary programs that same Council had endorsed at the beginning of his tenure were in danger of expiring.[61]

In the meantime, the leadership of the City Council began to speak out against the mayor's proposals. Soon a group of twenty-five Council members formed a coalition that promised to restore $33 million of the $83 million cuts the mayor had sought to implement.

As the battle lines were being drawn at City Hall on the adoption of the 1980 budget, a similar course of events was developing in Albany. Justice J. Kingsley Smith had issued his *Levittown* judgment on December 22. In January, Governor Hugh Carey had proposed a state budget including a school finance plan that would move toward greater equity in the distribution of resources around the state. His plan would increase operating aid to the poorer districts by $203 million, and at the same time would reduce the funds available to districts in the wealthiest quarter. New York City stood to gain $11 million from the plan. On February 7, Schools Chancellor Macchiarola appeared before a joint meeting of the New York State Senate Finance and Assembly Ways and Means Committees to support the governor's package. He appealed for a speedy solution to the *Levittown* issue and noted particular concern with the aspects of the decision regarding "municipal overburden." He then warned that $60 million of the $70 million in increased education aid proposed for New York City would be used to help balance the city budget and urged, "A way must be found to insure that schools receive these increases. We must insist that education aid goes to education."[62] When asked by a reporter after his testimony if the governor's proposal amounted to a plan to take away from rich districts to pay for the poor, Macchiarola responded, "If it's a choice between being on the side of Robin Hood, or on the side of the Sheriff of Nottingham, I'm on the side of Robin Hood."[63]

Unfortunately for the chancellor and the city school district of New York, not everyone saw the issue the same way. The Carey proposal drew immediate criticism from Senate Majority Leader Warren M. Anderson, a Republican from Binghamton. On March 21 legislative leaders in Albany decided to scrap the governor's new aid formula. They agreed that no district would get less aid in the next year than it was getting at present. As Democratic Assemblyman Arthur Kramer, chairman of the Ways and Means Committee explained, "The Robin Hood concept is dead this year. . . . There is a commitment on the part of the Assembly to see that there are no dollar losses for any school district in the state of New York. There will be no major changes in the formula."[64] On March 27 Carey and the legislative leaders tentatively agreed to a school aid plan that would increase statewide support by $185 million, with the "save harmless" guarantee that no district would receive less money than it had in the previous year. Later in the session, Assembly Speaker Stanley Fink, a Democrat from Brooklyn, proposed that an additional $35 million be given to the state's poorer districts.

The tentative agreement reached in Albany gave city budget negotiators definite boundaries within which to work and a good idea of just how much state aid to expect. However, they were far from agreement on how much local money could be committed to the expense budget under consideration. On April 28 the mayor unveiled his $12.8 million Executive Budget.[65] The reductions slated for the Board of Education were not as large as those originally cited in the mayor's January PEG proposal. In fact, according to the mayor's April figures, the education budget was in for an increase of $67 million over the budget of the previous year. Not included in the mayor's calculations, however, was $200 million in increased expenditures that would have to come out of the base budget, for collective bargaining agreements and federally mandated programs. In order to meet these new costs, the school system would still be required to take $73 million in program cuts (with the rest of the money coming from increased state aid). This could be translated into a loss of 1,800 teaching jobs and 400 administrative positions.

As the City Council Finance Committee started to hold its hearings on the Executive Budget, various proposals began to emerge from both the Council and members of the Board of Estimate. As the deliberations proceeded, the local legislature heard testimony for increased aid to education from the League of Women Voters, the Women's City Club, and, of course, again from the chancellor himself. At the end, Finance Committee Chairman Edward Sadowsky pledged that more money would be found for education, fire protection, and libraries. City Council President Carol Bellamy, a member of the Board of Estimate, publicly urged the mayor to add $12.8 million to the education budget.

On the evening of June 3 a meeting was held at the mayor's residence, Gracie Mansion. It was attended by Comptroller Harrison Goldin, City Council President Carol Bellamy, the five borough presidents, and the leadership of the City Council. The purpose of the meeting was to work out a final compromise on the budget, and education was one of the major points of contention. Several proposals were put on the table. The Council leadership proposed that $35 million should be added to the total City budget, with $26 million going to education. The members of the Board of Estimate, led by Comptroller Harrison Goldin, proposed a total increase of $28.4 million, with $15 million going to education. The mayor, who, as might be expected, took the most conservative stance in the negotiations, said that he would not agree to more than a $26 million addition to the entire budget. Finally, after twelve hours of bargaining, the impasse was broken. An agreement was made to add $27.5 million to the budget. Of this amount, $20 million would go to education. By that time the Board of Education was also expecting between $7 million and $12 million in supplemental aid from the state.

On July 27 Deputy Chancellor Richard Halverson made an announcement to the superintendents of the thirty-two school districts in the city. He told them that while they were about to start the school year in September with $1 to $2 million more each than they had had in the previous year, the additional money and more would be needed to pay for salary increases for teachers. He told them that, despite the increases, their districts would fall 2 percent below the level of funding needed to maintain the service levels of the past year.

On August 31 Halverson sent a five-page memo to the chancellor, recommending the closing of sixteen school buildings over the next year. The report was based on a reported enrollment decline of 150,000 students (19 percent) since the fall of 1975. Between 1975 and 1977, sixty school buildings had already been closed. The projected savings from the new closings were set at $1.2 million. The closings would result in the relocation of three thousand students.[66]

A TRIP TO THE WOODSHED: FISCAL YEAR 1980, PART II

Under ordinary circumstances, the battles over the 1980 budget would have ended in the spring of 1979. The school system would have received its cuts, it would have found some way to live with them, and it would have limped along until the next round of budget negotiations with the city began. But 1979 was not a typical year. It was problem-ridden, unpredictable, and loaded with explosive conflict. By the time the budget was adopted by the City Council and Board of Estimate in June, the relationship between budget officials at the Board of Education and those at the Office of Management and Budget had degenerated to animosity. School officials tried to protect their own prerogatives with regard to educational policy from what they perceived to be encroachments by the city. Individuals within the Office of Management and Budget were disturbed by what they saw as an unreasonable reluctance on the part of school officials to provide them with the information and cooperation they needed to make intelligent judgments on the budgetary needs of the Board of Education. As one high-level official in OMB explained, "Our conversations with them would always begin with the argument that the Board of Education is a state-chartered agency that is independent. Their attitude was that they didn't have to respond to our information requests. They made zero attempt to be cooperative."[67]

As things were quietly heating up with OMB, education officials were also getting involved in a more visible public conflict that had a direct impact on the city's schoolchildren. The second semester of the school year opened in February 1979 with a three-month strike by school bus drivers, which created an ordeal for 132,000 students who were not within walking distance of their schools or public transportation, and which proved particularly troublesome for 32,000 handicapped children who depended on the service. The striking drivers were not city employees. They were employees of the Varsity Bus Company, a private firm, which provided 65 percent of the school bus transportation for children in the city. They were striking because of a decision by the chancellor to create a system of competitive bidding for transportation contracts. The chancellor was disturbed by a nearly monopolized system of contracting, which did not give smaller bus companies an opportunity to compete on the open market. Furthermore, an analysis by the office of the deputy chancellor predicted a saving of $44 million over the next three years if a competitive system of bidding were adopted. The drivers from the Varsity Bus Company saw the new proposal as a threat to their job security. The strike launched by Local 1181 not only closed down service for the Varsity buses, but also succeeded in halting the operation of the forty-four smaller companies that had been serving the schools. While the strike, which began on February 15, finally ended on May 11, that settlement on the labor front marked only the beginning of the problems resulting from the new bus contracts.

On August 24, Dall Forsythe, the newly appointed budget director at the Board of Education, sent a memorandum to Deputy Chancellor Richard Halverson advising him that a collective bargaining agreement recently negotiated with the United Federation of Teachers would cost the school system $13.7 million in funds that had not been provided for in the 1980 budget. In addition to this, Forsythe estimated a future expenditure of $40 million for special-education and transportation services that had not been anticipated. The special-education costs were the result of increased enrollment brought about in response to a court-ordered federal mandate. The transportation costs resulted in part from the growth in special education and in part from the miscalculation of savings that would be realized as a result of the new bus contracts. These unanticipated expenditures would not only cause a serious deficit in the Board of Education's budget, but would also threaten to throw out of balance the financial plan that the mayor had submitted to the State Financial Control Board. To make matters worse, the financial management systems within the school system were in such poor condition that nobody really knew what the size of the deficit would be. In the meantime, special-education enrollments continued to grow, and so did expenditures.

During the month of September a series of meetings was held between Board of Education and OMB representatives to discuss both the size of the deficit and the manner in which it might be handled. On October 3 a meeting finally took place between the mayor and the chancellor. At that point the size of the problem was estimated at $80 million, and Koch informed Macchiarola that it would have to be resolved by a combination of spending reductions and whatever state and federal aid the chancellor could garner. The mayor insisted that he would not make any city money available to resolve the deficit. He then ordered the chancellor to prepare by October 15 a plan suitable for submission to the Financial Control Board. This plan was to include the following:

- a schedule of increased revenue expectations for fiscal year 1980;
- an expenditure-reduction plan;
- a timetable for the implementation of expenditure reductions;
- a contingency list of reductions in case anticipated revenue increases were not realized.

Within a week after the Koch meeting, Reuven Savitz, the senior assistant to the chancellor for business, who had been appointed in June, sent a report to Macchiarola projecting that the bus contracts would cost $105.05 million more than had been predicted in the previous estimate. This put the net deficit in transportation at $40 million. Upon learning this, the mayor made a public pronouncement that he would not bail out the Board of Education. He insisted that school officials would "eat their deficits." He pledged, "We will not lay off cops and firemen to make up for their deficits."[68]

On October 12 the chancellor sent a memorandum to the Office of Management and Budget projecting a total budget gap of $84 million and outlining a cost-reduction and revenue plan designed to eliminate that gap. The mayor's Office of Management and Budget agreed with Macchiarola's $84 million figure. But OMB disagreed with the chancellor's revenue projections and found his cost-reduction plan too vague. In the meantime, Comer Coppie, executive director of the State Financial Control Board, sent a letter to the mayor reminding him that the FCB was expecting a revised financial plan for the city within the next week. That plan was to include cutbacks in the overall spending of the city so that its finances could be put in balance by 1982, as had been required by law. It was also to describe a method for dealing with the expenditure problem at the Board of Education.

On October 30 Mayor Edward Koch summoned Board of Education officials to his office at City Hall. There, once again, he warned the chancellor and Board President Stephen Aiello that they could not expect any help from him in overcoming their deficit. The mayor also used the occasion to inform them that he was assigning Deputy Mayor Robert Wagner, Jr., to serve as his personal liaison with the Board of Education. At that same meeting, the chancellor proposed a plan to the mayor that would result in $45 million worth of cuts. Included in the proposal were the elimination of free transportation for students living less than 1½ miles from school, and the layoff of up to 2,300 teachers.

The chancellor's recommendations set off a series of reactions around the city. From that point onward, much of the criticism of the budget was heaped on the chancellor himself. Five members of his own Board of Education objected to the chancellor's plan and called upon him to cut back his personal staff. Members of the Board of Estimate and City Council demanded that the chancellor scrap his "horror list" and come up with a plan that focused on administrative cuts. Comptroller Harrison Goldin threatened to make his own suggestions to eliminate entire bureaus at the Livingston Street headquarters. City Council President Carol Bellamy accused school officials of "living in a dream world" if they believed they could lay off 2,300 teachers without touching the central bureaucracy. In a radio interview on a local station, City Councilwoman Mary Pinkett charged that everyone at the Board of Education headquarters was more expendable than teachers. She went on to say, "Before the City allows larger classes, layoffs of teachers and paraprofessionals, or cuts in lunch programs and transportation for low-income children, Chancellor Macchiarola would have to go first."[69]

By mid-November the budget gap at the Board of Education was put at $92.1 million. At that point, the chorus of criticism led by elected officials was joined by the editorial boards of the local press. On November 14 both *The New York Times* and the *New York Post* ran editorials calling on the Board of Education to take control of its spending and to implement the kind of financial management systems that had obviously been lacking. They also noted that the Board of Education had proposed to resolve its deficit by cutting instructional services. In the meantime, the Board of Estimate and the City Council set a November 20 deadline, by which time school officials were expected to work out an acceptable plan to resolve their $92 million problem.

As budget analysts at Livingston Street went back to the drawing boards to devise a new prescription for cuts to meet the November 20 deadline, a number of efforts were made to locate additional sources of revenue so as to reduce the required cuts. Besieged by representatives from the school system, and with the help of the city Office of Management and Budget, State Comptroller Edward Reagan was able to come up with $11.3 million in state funds to which the Board of Education was entitled. Assisted by Deputy Mayor Robert Wagner, school officials launched a strong lobbying effort among members of the Board of Estimate and City Council on the afternoon of November 19. Then, on that same evening, Board President Stephen Aiello, who was about to leave his position in New York to join the Carter administration in Washington, made a call to White House aide Jody Powell that resulted in the expedition of $14 million in Impact Aid money earmarked for New York City.

On Tuesday, November 20, Chancellor Frank Macchiarola appeared before the Education and Finance Committees of the City Council to outline his plan for closing the $92.1 million budget gap. The proposal provided for an actual spending reduction of $23.6 million, and $68.5 in revenue offsets. Of the $23.6 million in cuts, $5.7 million would be realized through administrative cutbacks—requiring the layoff of 150 administrative personnel and the freezing of 490 administrative vacancies. In addition to the additional state and federal aid that the Board of Education was able to expedite, it identified $35.6 million in firm revenues that did not appear in its original budget. It was also allocated $7.6 million in tax levy reserve funds from the city. The balancing plan did not involve the layoff of any teachers, nor did it include the reduction of free and reduced transportation services to children.[70] In exchange for the availability of city reserve funds, school officials verbally agreed to the establishment of a set of financial monitoring procedures by the city.

While the resolution of the deficit meant that the worst part of the budget crisis was over, the school administration was not yet out of the woods with regard to the credibility it had lost or the restitution that would still be demanded of it. On the evening of November 20, the *New York Post,* armed with a report prepared by the Educational Priorities Panel, printed an editorial criticizing the Board of Education for taking only $23.6 million in cost reductions. On November 24, the *Daily News* issued an editorial entitled, "Good News, Bad News," which criticized the temporary solution to the fiscal headaches within the school system. It further chastised the chancellor for "miraculously" discovering that there was fat in the administrative budget, after having first denied it.[71]

Before the ink was dry on the November 20 agreement to close the deficit, another conflict began to emerge, concerning the structure of the education budget. On the next day, Harrison Goldin, in his capacities as City Comptroller and member of the State Financial Control Board, sent a letter to the chancellor and Board President Aiello, demanding the implementation of tighter financial controls. He urged the development of "a control mechanism that will provide a basis internally for the Board to monitor and control its expenditures and that will assure compliance by the Board of Education with appropriation limits imposed by the city." Goldin's letter included a list of recommendations of the kinds of information and mechanisms he desired. It closed by requesting, "To the extent that your recent agreement with the Office of Management and Budget meets these standards, I request copies of the resulting reports." When first asked about having agreed to any outside financial controls, the chancellor responded, "It serves everybody to have as much information as possible available, as long as the autonomy of the Board is maintained and their prerogatives protected."[72]

Within a few days, the Educational Priorities Panel issued a report that was highly critical of the budget process at the Board of Education and the manner in which the Board had decided to take its cuts. It recommended a process that would be public, providing for informed discussion; and based on accurate data and presentation of all the facts." The report went on to state, "Lack of full public discussion tends to obscure the shaky foundations upon which budgets are being built, not only from the public, but possibly even from the budget builders themselves." The report then outlined nine specific pieces of information that the EPP wanted to have made public on a regular basis.[73]

The debate over the school budget finally reached the state level at a December 5 meeting of the Financial Control Board. It was there that Governor Hugh Carey and Mayor Edward Koch agreed that they would ask the Board of Education to give formal approval to the monitoring mechanisms it had informally accepted during the previous month. That public statement inspired a *New York Times* editorial urging the Board of Education to "get its payroll data in better order" but warning the city not to intrude in matters of education judgment.[74]

On December 11, Mayor Koch and Comptroller Harrison Goldin sent a joint letter to Board President Stephen Aiello, asking for the establishment of ten specific financial-management procedures, "to monitor the progress of the Board's 1980 expenditure-reduction program and prevent the development of any future deficit conditions." The requirements of the two city officials, however, involved more than just an information exchange. What they wanted was authority to veto the hiring of any new nonpedagogical or nonteaching employees. This marked the major point of difference between education officials and the city concerning monitoring. While school officials understood monitoring as the disclosure of information, those in the municipal government saw it in terms of actual control.

On December 20 Board President Aiello responded to the Koch–Goldin request in writing on behalf of his colleagues at the Board of Education. He began by noting, "We wish to assure you of our cooperation and our determination to control our expenditures so that we do not exceed our financial resources." Aiello assured the mayor and the comptroller that the Board would direct the chancellor to supply the reports required throughout 1980. However, on the issue of control the Board president took a rather firm stand, which, while not atypical of the one the Board of Education had taken historically, was particularly strong under the circumstances. He stated:

> The Board of Education cannot agree to interference by the Office of Management and Budget in the hiring of either pedagogical or nonpedagogical personnel. . . . Over the long run we believe that the Board of Education should have more fiscal autonomy, not less, and we want to be certain that no technical agreement on financial management and monitoring compromises that autonomy. When the Board's budget is once again balanced, we will reduce or eliminate external reporting requirements, although we will, of course, maintain controls for internal monitoring.[75]

GATHERING THE TROOPS: THE BUDGET FOR FISCAL YEAR 1981

The budget process for the 1981 fiscal year did not start on a very positive note. Board President Stephen Aiello's provocative letter to the mayor and the comptroller arrived on their desks three days after the chancellor had made public his budget message to the Board of Education. Moreover, the school administration had not yet recovered from the political fallout of the 1980 crisis. As budget director Dall Forsythe put it, "We didn't start '81 in very good shape. We had just gotten our asses kicked because of $92 million in overspending. Now it was time to come back for money."[76]

The appointment of Forsythe by the chancellor did help immensely to mend relationships between the Board of Education and the Office of Management and Budget. He was competent, trusted, and well liked by all parties involved. As one OMB official explained, "Dall Forsythe's arrival on the scene improved relations between OMB and the Board. Dall, having worked for [City Council President] Bellamy, understood OMB's role. Dall contributed to the budget process. He gave us information. By hiring Dall, Frank [Macchiarola] bought a channel of information and goodwill."[77] Stanley Litow, executive director of the Educational Priorities Panel, concurred. "Dall gave the Board of Education credibility. He gave us someone we could deal with. He is a realiable source of information."[78] Macchiarola's recruitment of Forsythe proved to be a key appointment. However, despite the goodwill that seemed to be developing, the mayor's office and the chancellor's office were still worlds apart on the issue of the budget. Neither went to any great length to hide that difference.

On December 17, 1979, Schools Chancellor Frank Macchiarola submitted to the Board of Education the largest budget package on record as of that date. The $2.68 billion expense budget* included $248 million to maintain current levels of service, $29 million to restore educational programs affected by previous cuts, and $52 million for new programs. Among the programmatic items appearing in the request were $79.7 million for register increases in special education, $15 million to expand transitional classes for all eligible students and to maintain reduced class size in the first grade, and $14.3 million for remedial programs to help high school students achieve new state-mandated performance standards.[79]

As might be expected, the reaction of public officials to the chancellor's new budget was cool. Harrison Goldin remarked, "Since the city already has a budget gap of $400 million in 1981, the City would be hard pressed to come up with programs of this kind." City Council President Carol Bellamy commented, "It's not clear the Board of Education knows how it's spending its money. There are serious questions whether they have the capacity to judge what they need to spend, and it would appear that they do not." Queens Borough President Donald Manes, usually a strong supporter of education, quipped, "We'll give very careful evaluation and consideration to the chancellor's proposal.

---

*It would actually come to more than $3.3 billion when pension and debt service costs were added.

We always check and double check figures that come out of Livingston Street."[80]

The mayor's response to Macchiarola's budget message was uncommonly reserved. However, as commentary about the chancellor's request was making its way around the city, OMB was in the process of preparing the next installment of the mayor's citywide financial plan for submission to the State Financial Control Board. On January 16, that plan was revealed, and it proved to be an ambitious one. The plan was designed to balance the city's finances in 1981 instead of 1982, one year prior to the legally required mandate set by the state. Doing so would be a significant political feat for a mayor who was up for reelection in 1981. However, carrying out the city's fiscal rehabilitation a year early would require the gravest retrenchment that the city had experienced since 1975. Koch proposed $299 million in reductions citywide for 1981. This was more than twice the amount that had been imposed during the previous year. He also called for an additional $461 million in cuts in 1982. To achieve these cuts, he would remove 13,000 jobs from the city payroll in two years. According to Koch's plan, 7,186 of these jobs would come from the school system, which would have to lay off 4,000 teachers; the remainder of the positions would be eliminated through attrition. In real dollars, Koch's proposal mandated for the Board of Education $111 million in cuts during 1981 and $182 million in 1982.[81]

The 1981 Program to Eliminate the Gap (PEG) sent a shock wave through the city. It also became an impetus for the formation of the most formidable and far-reaching coalition on behalf of public education in New York City since the institution of community control. Even before the Koch plan was made public, as word was leaked about what OMB had recommended to the mayor, *The New York Times* ran a strong editorial entitled "Cutting Schools to the Bone," which explained how the reductions meted out to education were "proportionately larger than the reductions meted out to police and fire." It personally criticized the mayor, who "justifies exacting so much from the school system on the ground that it is doing an unsatisfactory job with what it has." It noted that the mayor "has remained lamentably silent about where education fits among his priorities." It demanded, "The public needs a better explanation."[82]

On the same day the PEG proposal was announced, the Board of Education issued a formal public statement expressing deep disappointment with Mayor Koch for taking the advice offered by his Office of Management and Budget, which had "shown a consistent lack of understanding of the schools and the needs of our children. . . ."[83] The most severe and threatening reaction to the new budget came from

Albert Shanker of the United Federation of Teachers, who accused the mayor of assuming that "only minority kids and children of parents who don't vote attend city schools." He promised Koch "the toughest fight of his administration."[84] At a public meeting of the Board of Education on January 24, Bill Scott, a high-ranking assistant to Shanker, pledged, "We are going to fight him [Koch] by registering every teacher, every parent, every eligible student in the New York City public schools and turning them out to vote in the next mayoral primary. We are going to try our damnedest to have a new mayor on election day 1981. . . ."[85]

Thus began a bitter series of exchanges between the mayor and the union president, which took place in the news media, on television talk shows, and at public meetings. Koch would not be intimidated. Never at a loss for words when on either the defense or the offense, the mayor assured the Senate Banking Committee in Washington, during a hearing on the New York City federal loan guarantees, "Albert Shanker is not Moses, and he does not make up that budget." And for those who had wondered about his own priorities, the mayor offered, "We're not going to lay off cops to keep teachers on the payroll."[86] On January 24, the City Office of Management and Budget informed the schools chancellor that it would be eliminating one thousand CETA (Comprehensive Employment and Training Act) jobs from the school system because of federal cutbacks.

The campaign to restore the school budget began to gather momentum on several fronts. Almost immediately after the announcement of the mayor's financial plan, an Ad Hoc Coalition of education groups, consisting of parent associations and neighborhood associations, was formed to discuss a strategy for opposing the cuts. The union was at the center of a movement called Save Our Schools (SOS), which coordinated two marches around City Hall and began a rather intense lobbying campaign within the City Council and the Board of Estimate. On March 14 Albert Shanker and State Senator Vander Beatty, chairman of the Black and Puerto Rican Legislative Caucus, held a joint news conference announcing that they were burying long-standing differences to join in a "life-and-death" struggle against cuts in the education budget. The teachers union had often stood on the opposite side of the fence from the black community since the divisive battles over school decentralization in the sixties. Now these two groups were pledging to stand together in a common fight against a mayor who, they alleged, felt safe in making reductions in an education system largely populated by minority children. They accused the mayor of "counting votes." Beatty announced, "I'd like to thank Ed Koch for bringing us together."[87]

In the meantime, the administration at school headquarters was launching its own campaign. The chancellor made his usual appearance at the joint hearings of the City Council and Board of Estimate regarding the mayor's Program to Eliminate the Gap. As might be expected, Chancellor Macchiarola protested the unfair burden the schools would be required to absorb. But Macchiarola's efforts went beyond the elected officials of the city. He and his budget people also began meeting with the editorial boards of the major newspapers of the city to discuss the severity of the proposed cuts, their inequity, and the impact they would have on educational services. In addition to this, the school administration began to urge its principals, district superintendents, and professional education groups to lobby local council members.

A third and rather distinct campaign was being organized under the auspices of the Educational Priorities Panel. EPP had been a long-time critic of the Board of Education and the way it spent its money. However, even that group was concerned about the size of the reductions reflected in the mayor's plan. As the executive director, Stanley Litow, explained it, "Koch came up with more than $100 million in cuts. We were forced at that point to attack PEG."[88] Nevertheless, the EPP strategy was quite different from that of the union and the Board of Education. The latter two groups opposed all the cuts, in accordance with their hard-driving political approach to the budget debate. EPP was more conciliatory, accepting some cuts, opposing others, and hoping to come up with a compromise that would lead to smaller reductions in the school budget. Thus EPP was not in total agreement with either school officials or the union. As Litow pointed out, "We again here hit loggerheads with the chancellor's office. They wanted to oppose all cuts. We felt that this didn't leave anyone options." Litow was particularly critical of the union strategy. "SOS also said no cuts. It was a complication for us. We never felt they played a significant or useful role. . . . They may have exercised some muscle. But many people said that SOS should have been called 'SOJ,' for Save Our Jobs."[89]

On March 10 EPP presented a report on the PEG proposals at the joint hearings of the Board of Estimate and City Council. The major point of the report was to argue, "The proposed PEG reductions would devastate the education system."[90] It noted that the schools were being asked to absorb 64 percent of the personnel cuts planned by the mayor. The report also offered a counterproposal that focused on administrative savings and other gap-filling measures. On March 31 *The New York Times* ran an editorial entitled "Better Homework on New York's Schools," praising the Educational Priorities Panel for its analysis of the Koch budget and for finding $60 million in administrative savings that could be implemented. The work done by the EPP was beginning to substantiate the argument that the school administration's and the union's reactions to the Koch budget were not just a cry of "wolf." However, there was still a long process of negotiating ahead before a final budget was formulated. Whether the budget process would prove to be the political contest that the union and school officials perceived it to be, or whether it was responsive to the voice of informed reason, as EPP hoped, remained to be seen.

As the machinations of the budget process moved into full gear within the city, negotiations regarding the state budget were under way in Albany. These would determine the amount of state aid to be expected for local school districts. When Governor Carey announced his new budget on January 21, he made it clear that he was temporarily shelving any plans for significant changes in the education formula. The total $13.8 billion state budget called for a $188 million increase in education aid, $103 million of which was destined for New York City. The education proposal received a moderately cool reception from Republican leaders, one of whom labeled it "a political document," while Assembly Speaker Stanley Fink said he would recommend an increase in education aid.[92]

By the end of March, Republican and Democratric leaders in the legislature had agreed to a budget that raised aid to education by $319 million statewide. That agreement was based on the "save harmless" presumption that there would be no spending reductions for property-rich districts in the state. Of the total aid package, $124 million was set aside for New York City. The New York City figure was not arrived at, however, until an agreement had been worked out between Assembly Speaker Stanley Fink and Mayor Edward Koch. At the end of a Sunday afternoon meeting held on March 23, Fink and Koch announced a pledge on the part of the mayor that, of the $124 million in anticipated state aid to education coming to New York City, no less than $60 million would go to the schools.[93]

The final composition of the state education budget and the manner in which it was designed were indicative of two significant school finance issues that were nowhere near a resolution. First of all, the new state budget made it clear that while incremental supplements would be forthcoming to property-poor or municipal districts in the name of equity, no radical redesign of the school finance formula was in the offing. Second, it was clear that the budget process by no means guaranteed that whatever supplemental aid was squeezed out of the legislature would in fact find its way to the schools. On the contrary, the process demonstrated that the practice of supplantation had become so open and matter-of-course that it was nearly an institutionalized aspect of the finance system between the state and the local governments.

Meanwhile, as the budget development process in the city began to approach its final stages, there emerged some signs of a moderate reconciliation between the Board of Education and the Office of Management and Budget. On February 20 a letter of agreement was sent to Comer Coppie, executive director of the State Financial Control board, which outlined a set of procedures designed to allow city budget officials to monitor the financial activities of the school system, but at the same time did not compromise the decision-making prerogatives of the Board of Education. The letter was signed jointly by the chancellor, newly elected Board President Joseph Barkan, the director of the Office of Management and Budget, and the first deputy comptroller. The procedures were based on those originally proposed by the mayor and the comptroller in their December 11 letter to Board President Aiello.

The mayor delivered his executive budget to the City Council and Board of Estimate on May 9. In his own words, this $13.6 billion package was "the first truly balanced budget for the City of New York in more than a decade."[94] This budget-balancing act, carried out one year earlier than required by the city's four-year financial plan, brought the mayor widespread editorial praise in the local media. The only major change in the budget from the original January proposal was a $91 million increase for the Board of Education. That increase, when taken at face value, could be seen as both significant and misleading. Approximately $69 million of the total was included to cover mandated increases in services and the loss of $15 million in federal aid. Approximately $13 million had been restored to the education budget to maintain basic instructional services. The net result of the mayor's Executive Budget was that the Board of Education would still be left with an $89 milion PEG cut.

Within three weeks of the time the mayor's budget was made public, the Educational Priorities Panel published its own analysis. As it had done in its previous report, the EPP criticized some of the education cuts proposed by the mayor, endorsed others, and made several of its own recommendations on how the Board of Education might reduce its spending. However, the bottom-line message of the report, which was presented in testimony before the City Council, suggested that $34 million must be restored to the education budget for the next year in order to maintain the current level of service within the school system.[95]

In the meantime, the chancellor stepped up his own campaign on behalf of the education budget. On May 30 Macchiarola called a meeting in the auditorium of Park West High School in Manhattan. He invited the directors of all the major offices within the central headquarters of the school system, and the superintendents of the thirty-two community school districts. However, the major purpose of the meeting was to bring together the nearly one thousand elementary, middle, and high school principals of the city school system. The meeting was the first of its kind. Since the institution of decentralization in 1969, the Chancellor of Schools had never taken it upon himself to meet en masse with the community school district principals, who both legally and practically reported to their own community superintendents. Macchiarola decided to break with precedent. His meeting was attended by more than twelve hundred educators from around the city. Many, perhaps, came more out of curiosity about what this chancellor had to say than out of any sense of responsibility or deference.

The ground rules were firmly set. No press would attend. The chancellor and his staff would make a series of presentations. Then representatives of the various principals' associations would be allowed to ask questions of the chancellor.

The chancellor began with a general status report on the schools. He discussed the problems of the system and the major programmatic changes of the past year. He noted the accomplishments, giving particular attention to a preliminary report that showed a rise in citywide reading scores, but also noting improvements in attendance and some significant managerial innovations. He congratulated those present for their good performance. He then went on to the major topic of discussion, the budget. Budget Director Dall Forsythe gave the large audience a detailed report on the mayor's proposed budget and what it meant to the schools. The chancellor explained that while 19 percent of the city expense budget for the previous year had gone to education, 30 percent of the PEG cuts that the mayor was proposing would come from the schools.

As the chancellor got into the heart of his presentation about the budget, it became quite apparent to those who were in attendance that the purpose of this meeting was not merely to inform. To the surprise of many educators who had once perceived Macchiarola to be "Koch's chancellor," the meeting turned out to be a call to political action on behalf of the school budget. Macchiarola was unambiguous in the opinion he offered about city budget officials, saying, "The Executive Budget was developed by city budget officials, who are distant from you and our children, not by those who understand schools and children's needs." He was straightforward in pointing out to the principals that the budget problems of the school system were their problems: ". . . however difficult the cuts of the past have been, the proposed cuts are even worse because they are targeted at the schools and at the districts."

The chancellor was unrestrained in his call for action, urging:

> I hope your voices will be raised with mine in proclaiming that our schools are a vital service and that our children are essential resources. Let me be more specific. I am not asking you simply to content yourself with moral indignation or an occasional letter to the editor, I am asking all of you to speak out forcefully for schools.

Macchiarola was also quite direct in telling the group before him just what he expected of them and how they could do it:

> Next week the City Council and the Board of Estimate will be holding hearings on the Executive Budget. I urge you to write and to telephone the Mayor, the President of the City Council, the Comptroller, the Borough Presidents, and the members of the City Council. Do not stop there. Write, telephone members of the state legislature and ask them to speak out for schools. Ask your relatives, friends, and neighbors to do the same.[96]

In addition to copies of the budget and management reports of the chancellor, a packet of material was distributed that included a League of Women Voters publication listing the names, addresses, and phone number of every elected official in New York City. Thus began the last stage of a concerted lobbying campaign on behalf of the school budget. Principals and district superintendents began meeting in groups with City Council members, state legislators, members of the Board of Estimate, and representatives of the mayor's office. As one top-level person from OMB described it, "This year [fiscal year 1981] had the most political advocacy of all. They [school people] felt that they had to do that to maintain their status. The size of the cut caused them to act very strongly."[97]

As the chancellor went about the city in an effort to raise support for the school budget, the mayor went on his own tour, criticizing the Board of Education and the way it spent its money. During one public meeting, held at PS 98 in Queens, Koch described the school budget as being out of control and complained, "I don't have control over the Board of Education budget. I'm not allowed to tell them how to spend their money."[98] Once again the mayor was underscoring a point he had been making all along—that his attitude toward the school budget was in part motivated by the fact that, unlike the mayoral agencies that report to him directly, the school system was not directly accountable to him, once the budget was appropriated.

On June 4 Chancellor Macchiarola made his final appeal on behalf of the 1981 budget before the joint hearings of the Board of Estimate and City Council. Propelled by the momentum evident at the principals' meeting only a few days before, the chancellor began his testimony in a strong and direct fashion, touching on a sensitive nerve of the two legislative bodies: "It is unfortunate that I must talk of the needs of our children in the context of an Executive Budget that does not offer a sense of hope. It is more unfortunate that some very significant needs that were recognized by the leadership of New York City government two short years ago, when I first became chancellor, now need to be pleaded anew." In response to the Educational Priorities Panel report, which advocated a $34 million increase in the mayor's budget, the chancellor pointed out that the EPP recommendation was only a "hold-the-line proposal." He also emphasized that any resotration below that amount would result in increased class size, closed after-school programs, and reduced support services. He asked for a full restoration of the $89 million in PEG cuts exacted by the mayor, promising in return an expanded transitional class program, reduced class sizes in the first grade, school-based support teams for special education, new programs for the gifted and talented, and more after-school programs. The chancellor closed his testimony with an appeal to the political sensibilities of the legislature, offering an interesting commentary on the social structure of the city and its relationship to school system politics:

> . . . in the city agency with the greatest number of middle class employees, we will be the only agency to lay off employees, presenting a novel twist to saving the city for the middle class. . . . The child denied teachers today will need counselors and psychologists tomorrow, and prison guards and wardens the day after. Our budget is truly the capital budget of human resources.[99]

Macchiarola left City Hall with a pledge from Finance Committee Chairman Edward Sadowsky to add more money to the education budget. It soon became apparent, however, that what Sadowsky had in mind was the $34 million sum advocated by the Educational Priorities Panel. On June 11, as the council went into its last round of negotiations on the 1981 budget, *The New York Times* published an editorial entitled, "School Children Should Come First." The editorial cited both the chancellor's testimony and the EPP report on the potential damage inflicted by the Koch cuts, and recommended that "classroom services ought to be at the top of the list of restorations as the Board of Estimate reviews the mayor's proposals."[100] The Educational Priorities

Panel had obviously made a persuasive case on behalf of education. The question was whether Koch was convinced.

The Council leadership originally went into negotiations with the hope of adding $60 million to the Koch budget, $34 million of which would go for education. When it appeared that the Board of Estimate was supporting that Council plan, Koch came up with a counter-proposal that would increase the total city budget by $35 million and shift $6.3 million in city funds to education. The mayor also said that he would make available to the Board of Education $15 million in cost savings that OMB had identified in the current school budget. What Koch was doing in effect was giving their own money back to the schools. The Council leaders immediately turned down this offer by the mayor, and on the next day (June 12), came up with a new package that would increase the total city budget by $49 million, with $29.5 million going to education. On that same day a compromise was finally worked out with the mayor. A total of $39 million was added to the proposed Executive Budget. Of that, $21 million would be allocated to the Board of Education—considerably less than the $89 million the chancellor had asked for, and even less than the $34 million hold-the-line supplement recommended by the Educational Priorities Panel. The agency to receive the next highest supplement in the final budget was the Police Department, which had $17.2 million restored.

As the long series of battles over the 1981 budget seemed to be coming to an end, budget director Dall Forsythe was asked to comment on the $21 million increase that the mayor and the legislature had finally provided, in comparison to the previous proposals. Forsythe replied, "I obviously think its better. It's gone from a catastrophe, to a disaster, to simply a set of serious problems for the next year."[101]

"FROM CATASTROPHE TO DISASTER": FISCAL YEAR 1981

As matters turned out, Forsythe's words proved to be as much prophetic as they were descriptive. On June 25, the Municipal Assistance Corporation issued a report on the city's proposed spending plan for 1981. It concluded that the plan "aspired to, but did not guarantee a truly balanced city budget for the coming year."[102] As the mayor began to meet with Governor Carey and state legislative leaders, he discovered that the city would not get $142 million in state aid that had originally been anticipated. At that point Koch began to issue warnings concerning possible layoffs to balance the city budget.

In mid-July, Koch sent a letter to Board President Joseph Barkan, stating that he would have to cut $29.5 million from the Board of

Education's 1981 budget, to cope with a fiscal deficit resulting from recently negotiated labor contracts. As stated, the mayor's request would require $26.5 million in the form of personnel cutbacks, and $3 million from the supplies budget. On Monday, July 21, the chancellor and Board President Barkan met with Deputy Mayor Wagner to appeal the cuts, but, in Barkan's words, "All he gave me was sympathy."[103] Two days later Koch and Comptroller Harrison Goldin sent a joint letter to Barkan, stating that insufficient progress had been made by the Board of Education in establishing the monitoring techniques it had agreed to set up. The letter was particularly critical of the continuing problems concerning the integration of the Board of Education's financial management system with the city's.

On August 11, the mayor made public his new financial plan. He announced it on the opening day of the national Democratic convention in New York City. He used the unveiling as an occasion for requesting more federal aid to the city. He accused President Carter of broken promises, and threatened, "If you don't carry the cities of the country, Mr. President, you ain't going to be the next President."[104] These were strong words from a Democratic mayor hosting a national convention for an incumbent president. But they were no harsher than the details of the plan that was about to be revealed. The mayor's proposal called for $87 million in midyear cuts in the 1981 budget citywide. Of this total, $12 million would come from the school system.[105] While this amount was considerably less than the $29.5 million the mayor had just threatened to ask for, it brought the total cuts imposed upon the Board of Education for the 1981 fiscal year up to over $100 million.[106] This was only $11 million less than the amount Koch had originally requested in his January PEG announcement. On August 21, Koch met with Comer Coppie of the State Control Board, State Comptroller Edward Reagan, and Special Deputy State Controller Sidney Schwartz, all of whom were critical of his plan because, in their estimation, many of the balancing devices incorporated in it were not on firm ground. The mayor asked Chancellor Macchiarola and Police Commissioner Robert McGuire also to attend the meeting at City Hall, to explain to the members of the Control Board why further reductions in their budgets would be difficult. The Control Board officials accepted their arguments by the end of the ninety-minute meeting. On September 17, Koch, Macchiarola, Barkan, and City Comptroller Goldin sent to Comer Coppie a final agreement outlining the implementation of an improved financial management system at the Board of Education. The letter described the measures that had already been taken, the steps that remained, and the matters "the Board contends that it cannot agree to." While there was a basic consensus concerning the exchange of information, school officials continued to refuse to accept the city's right to approve its budget modifications.

The 1980–1981 school year began that September with the layoff of 2,200 teachers. Although most were regular substitutes, it was the largest single layoff action implemented by the Board of Education since the height of the fiscal crisis in 1975.

ELECTION YEAR FORTUNES: THE BUDGET FOR FISCAL YEAR 1982

Despite the teacher layoffs mandated by the mayor's financial plan, the 1980–1981 school year did begin on some positive notes. The first sign came from within the school system itself when the chancellor announced the results of the annual citywide reading test. The scores from the California Achievement Test taken in the spring indicated a marked improvement in all grades from two through nine. The percentage of students reading at or above the national average had risen from 40.3 percent to 46.7 percent over a one-year period. The results of the test were greeted with guarded praise from both municipal officials and the local press. To be sure, good news was not usually expected from Livingston Street, so the announcement was a welcome one. But many observers adopted a wait-and-see attitude. Were the test scores the beginning of a real turnaround in the public schools, or were they merely a temporary aberration? There were also some unconvinced cynics who questioned the very validity of the scores themselves.

On September 29, Mayor Edward Koch and City Council Finance Committee Chairman Edward Sadowsky met to work out a final amendment to the 1981 budget. In exchange for Council approval of an increase in the property tax, Koch agreed to restore $9 million to the expense budget. Most of this would be used to hire five hundred more patrolmen in the Police Department, but some would find its way to the schools. While there was no reversal of the decision on teacher layoffs, approximately 1,060 school crossing guards that had been scheduled for dismissal would be kept on the payroll. An additional $1 million would be given to the schools for building maintenance.

On November 23 Special Deputy State Comptroller Sidney Schwartz issued a report predicting that the city would end the 1981 fiscal year with a budget surplus. According to his estimate, this surplus could amount to as much as $156 million. If this were true, the surplus would be the first in the city budget in over twenty years. Schwartz, whose approach to financial matters was characteristically cautious, was not inclined toward such optimism with regard to the

New York City budget. However, the truth is that the city had received higher revenues than anticipated during the first four months of the fiscal year, and this trend was expected to continue. The city Office of Management and Budget responded to the Schwartz announcement with its own projection of a slightly lower surplus. In an official financial plan statement prepared for the United States Treasury Department, city OMB Director James Brigham calculated an end-of-year surplus amounting to $109 million.[107] The spring and summer of 1981 were punctuated by a series of predictions from the state comptroller, the city comptroller, and OMB, all of which tried to get a fix on just how much surplus cash the city would have on hand by June of 1981. All contributed to an emerging climate of hope that surrounded the preparation of Mayor Koch's election-year budget.

Schools Chancellor Frank Macchiarola took full advantage of the tenor of the times as he prepared his budget message for the 1982 fiscal year. His agency had just endured the largest reductions of any in the city. In the face of these serious cuts, the schools were showing signs of progress—a feat that at least partially disarmed the perpetual critics. For the first time since the outbreak of the fiscal crisis, it also appeared that the city was finally getting its own financial house in order—a factor that itself had to make that year's budget process somewhat smoother. Moreover, it was now clear to all concerned that Edward Koch was about to run for reelection on a service budget—that is, a budget that promised more rather than less service to the people of the troubled city.

Macchiarola delivered his budget message to the Board of Education on December 15, declaring:

> The New York City school system has withstood six years of austerity. But because of our children's resilience, and the efforts of our staff, we can point with pride to some modest improvements, even while absorbing some hundreds of millions of dollars of service cuts.[108]

The chancellor's budget proposal amounted to $3.1 billion. The local tax levy and general state aid portion of the total was $2.7 billion. This represented a $392 million increase over what the schools had received from the city in the previous year. The chancellor was quick to point out, however, that his budget request included $18 million in state funds that City Hall had illegally laid claim to through the practice of supplantation. He also noted that $276.6 million of the increase was needed to "just keep abreast" of rising costs.

The fastest-growing part of the chancellor's budget was devoted to special education. Because of increased compliance with federal mandates, special education costs were projected to climb from $296 million to $370 million over a one-year period. The budget also included a substantial sum of money for improved building maintenance and repair ($25.2 million). However, the underlying message in the chancellor's budget request was clear. It demanded that the city "invest in basics."[109] Included were proposals to expand full-day kindergartens, upgrade vocational education programs, and increase course offerings in the high schools. Most important of all, the chancellor was requesting funds to support the program that was the centerpiece of his administration's instructional agenda—Promotional Policy. Promotional policy would cost, according to his estimate, $63 million. Approximately $34 million of that amount was requested from the city. The remainder would be paid out of federal and state reimbursable funds.

The chancellor's large, ambitious request aroused criticism in the press. The *New York Post,* in customary fashion, chastised the Board of Education for its "bloated bureaucracy,"[110] and the *Daily News* ran an editorial on the chancellor's "Mind Boggling Budget."[111] To the surprise of many, however, reaction from the mayor's Office of Management and Budget was moderate and supportive. Assistant OMB Director Edward Burke was quoted as saying, "A year ago the Board [of Education] was overspending its budget by $100 million. This year, they are running a small surplus, and the city already has some of the increases set aside."[112]

Interspersed with these new words of encouragement emerging from City Hall were signs of a more lasting reality. On December 10, Mayor Edward Koch announced that he was about to launch a new legislative campaign in Albany. The purpose behind it was nothing less than an amendment to the state education law that would give the mayor virtual control over the Board of Education. Koch wanted to expand the membership of the seven-person Board so that he could appoint a majority of its members, rather than just the two he appointed under the current law. By bringing such a proposal to Albany, Koch was escalating the control issue from a technical discussion of the budget to a basic question of institutional reform. As might be expected, the five borough presidents, who choose the majority of the Board members, reacted in strong opposition to the plan, while their appointees protested Koch's attempt to "politicize" the school system. Another strand of strong though quiet resistance came from the chancellor, who dispatched his own legislative lobbyist to Albany to help organize the struggle against the Koch takeover. Later that month, the Board of Education voted to sue the mayor for the state education funds that were "supplanted" to balance the city budget. Macchiarola delivered the message of the impending suit to City Hall personally, and, armed with this threat, left the mayor's office one afternoon in early January with $19 million in supplanted state education funds.

In the meantime, Albany was about to go through its annual ritual of preparing of the state education budget. This year events began a bit early. On September 20, the Governor's Special Task Force on Equity and Excellence in Education released an interim report demonstrating that between 1974 and 1978 spending differences among local school districts had become worse. On January 19 Governor Hugh Carey presented his new budget to the legislature. His proposal called for only a 2.17 percent increase in education spending statewide, but, in an attempt to effect a *Levittown*–related remedy, would decrease aid to wealthier school districts and redistribute it to the poorer ones. Unfortunately, the impetus that might have been provided by the September report never reached the legislature. True to form, Republican legislative leaders criticized the governor's budget. Responding to the Robin Hood analogy that had come to surround attempts at school finance reform, Senator Joseph Pisani, a Republican from Westchester County, remarked about the governor, ". . . even a superficial glance at our suburban districts will show that he is functioning more like a random mugger, who can't tell the rich from the working class."[113] That year's budget negotiations between the governor and state legislative leaders went well beyond the April 1 deadline set by law. An accord on state education aid was not reached until May 8. While it would increase the state education budget by $287 million, it provided that no school district would receive less aid than it had in the previous fiscal year.[114]

Mayor Koch announced his financial plan for 1982 amidst great ceremony on January 16. It was celebrated as the "second genuinely balanced budget in the city's recent history" and, in the mayor's own words, was said to "mark the end of New York's search for fiscal recovery."[115] For the first time since 1975, the city budget would include "significant service enhancements," but it would also be constructed according to standard and acceptable principles of accounting. This was a remarkable achievement, for which the mayor received considerable praise. Koch's election-year budget, however, proved to be a telling commentary not only on his own personal priorities, but on his view of the voting public. The greatest infusion of funds would take place in crime-related services—adding 1,500 patrolmen to the Police Department, 200 patrolmen to the Transit Authority, and 336 officers to the Department of Corrections. The Board of Education was slated to receive 440 new positions.[116] This was not a very substantial increase, given the relative size of the school system, the severity of the cuts it had recently been required to absorb, and the significant rise in mandated services. Moreover, Koch's proposal left the greatest amount of uncertainty with regard to the chancellor's key program, Promotional Policy—promising only to leave its future to a more personalized level of negotiation: "Though funds are not now available for the Board of Education's proposed student Promotion Policy, the city will work closely with the Board to develop an affordable program and identify state, federal, and city sources to support it."[117]

On the day after he presented his new financial plan, the mayor appeared before a meeting of the United Parents Associations, where he praised the education system of the city, claiming, "Things are changing and looking better." Encouraged by the reading scores announced in September, candidate Koch was now becoming more inclined to take note of the positive achievements apparent in the public schools. Nevertheless, the mood within the school system itself was far from jovial. The chancellor had recently made public an implementation plan for the closing of fifteen schools around the city, which would necessitate the relocation of 4,500 elementary and middle school children. At that point Macchiarola became the target of a strong lobbying campaign conducted by local politicians and parent groups, all of whom were determined to protect their community schools from becoming the victims of local retrenchment. In its usual, political form, the campaign was carried out through meetings demanded of the chancellor by an array of community representatives, including parent group leaders, City Council members, state legislators, and even congressmen. In its more militant form, the effort resulted in formal appeals to override the chancellor's decisions, which found their way to the Board of Education, the State Commissioner of Education, and the courts. In one extreme case the chancellor found it necessary to supersede a community school board that refused to close a school as planned.

On January 20 Ronald Reagan was sworn in as President of the United States, promising cutbacks in federal aid to urban areas in general, and education in particular. Therefore, as local municipal officials began to anticipate the temporary benefits of an election-year budget, speculation also began to emerge about the permanent consequences of federal retrenchment. On March 12 Mayor Koch held a press conference at City Hall, where he offered an initial estimate, putting the cost of federal cutbacks for New York at $353 million in 1982.[119] Soon thereafter, State Commissioner of Education Gordon

Ambach addressed a meeting of elementary and secondary school teachers, where he predicted a loss of $220 million in federal education funds statewide.[120]

On March 10 Chancellor Frank Macchiarola appeared before a joint meeting of the Board of Estimate and City Council to testify on the mayor's 1982 financial plan. He began by pointing out that because of the proposed Reagan cutbacks, the city schools stood to lose between $106 and $125 million in federal aid. He then noted that while the city was planning to fund the conversion of 2,026 lost federal CETA positions by creating jobs on the municipal payroll, only 7 of those conversions were going to education. He further explained that while the school system had been required to absorb 58 percent of the dollar retrenchments and 67 percent of the job losses during the 1981 fiscal year, it was scheduled to receive only $20 million for new programs in 1982. He added that this $20 million represented disputed state funds, which the mayor agreed to "at least in part to avoid a suit."[121]

Macchiarola closed his testimony by restating the budget request he had made to the Board of Education in December. He placed particular emphasis on the need for $34 million in local tax levy funds to implement his Promotional Policy. In the past the chancellor had done moderately well in his monetary appeals to the local legislature. However, in this election year the dynamic of the budget process was different. And the new dynamic did not necessarily benefit the schools. In the past the chancellor's appeals to the legislature had focused on the reduction of impending cutbacks. Now he was asking for the enhancement of projected increases. In the previous year, the crisis atmosphere surrounding the school budget had helped mobilize the constituency for public education in the city. This year's optimism produced a dead calm. The most visible pawn in the budget negotiations was the chancellor's Promotional Policy, which enjoyed only mixed support in the educational community. Some disagreed with it philosophically; others believed it was too expensive. Indeed, if the chancellor could not persuade his philosophical adversaries, it was crucial for him to show the others that the new policy could be paid for. Thus the battle of the 1982 budget became a highly personal one.

On the day before Mayor Koch was scheduled to deliver his Executive Budget message for 1982, OMB Director James Brigham announced that the city would end the 1981 fiscal year with a surplus of $243 million. This was more than twice the sum he had originally predicted. He said that the money would be used to help offset the impact of the federal budget cutbacks promised by President Reagan. The $14.7 billion Executive Budget released by Edward Koch on May 12 did not include any great surprises. In a manner consistent with his original January financial plan, the budget allowed for the hiring of 1,500 patrolmen in the Police Department, 300 new police officers in the transit and housing authorities, and 627 corrections officers. The mayor was direct and unambiguous in explaining where his priorities were: "No issue is more important than personal security and public safety. That is why my first priority in the restoration of essential services has been to increase the city's police protection."[122]

The $2.95 billion allocated to the Board of Education in the mayor's Executive Budget represented a 7.7 percent increase over what it had received in 1981. A major portion of the funds ($18.9 million) was put aside to cover registration increases and program enhancements in special education. Money was also provided to pay for federal CETA conversions ($11.3 million), the expansion of the school security force ($5.4 million), and the replacement of obsolete equipment in vocational education ($5 million). In total, 568 personnel were to be added to the Board of Education payroll. Since the announcement of the mayor's January financial plan, negotiations had been taking place between the chancellor's office and OMB regarding Promotional Policy, which led school officials to lower the sum of money requested of the city from the original $34 million to a revised figure of $20 to $25 million. Nevertheless, the mayor's Executive Budget included only $7.1 million for Promotional Policy.[123] It was clear that the chancellor had a lot of work to do before the City Council and the Board of Estimate took their final actions on the mayor's budget in June. That task would be a lonely one for the chancellor, but, as things turned out, he did not proceed from a position of weakness.

In mid-April, Macchiarola had made public a report prepared by the office of the city comptroller on the subject of financial controls within the school system. The major finding of the report, which was completed a month before its official release, stated: "In the aggregate, the Board of Education has made significant progress toward improving its financial controls since last year. This is evidenced in the contrast in financial condition existing in December 1979 with December 1980."[124] This was a flattering assessment from an unexpected source. City Comptroller Harrison Goldin had been a major critic of the financial practices at Livingston Street and was one of the first to call for the establishment of new monitoring mechanisms by the city. His office was an important recipient of the monthly status reports required of school officials. Thus such a favorable finding could be seen as a sign that the Board of Education had begun to get its own financial house in order.

A second positive sign came from another unexpected source. On May 22, less than two weeks before the chancellor was scheduled to outline his budgetary needs to the Board of Estimate and City Council, the Educational Priorities Panel published a report entitled "Belt Tightening at 110 Livingston Street." The purpose of the study was to describe how and where school officials had implemented budget cuts in response to the fiscal crisis. The major finding of the report stated:

> EPP's analysis of payroll and budget data reveals that by and large, since 1976, the Board has executed a policy of supporting instructional rather than administrative service. When cuts were necessary, administrative or ancillary units were more often the target than were instructional services. . . . The Board reduced its total staff by 4 percent net between 1976 and 1980. Administrative and ancillary staff decreased by 16 percent.[125]

The report revealed that a similar policy had been followed in 1980, when the Board of Education was attempting to eliminate its $91 million deficit. At that time, staff in the central administration had been cut by 12 percent, while personnel in the Division of Special Education, the original source of the deficit, had grown by 35 percent. Thus, the general conclusion of the long-awaited study was strongly complimentary:

> Despite increasing financial pressures, it [the Board of Education] has adhered to a policy of maintaining instructional services instead of administrative and ancillary services. The EPP applauds this policy and supports the Board's efforts to maintain the level of instructional services in New York City.[126]

Coming from the group that had historically been one of the most severe critics of Livingston Street's "bloated bureaucracy," the new round of praise was much appreciated by school officials. Coupled with the favorable comment from the comptroller's office, it did much to bolster the rising credibility of the chancellor's administration.

But the best news was yet to come. And the source of that news was the schools themselves. On May 28 Chancellor Frank Macchiarola held a news conference at the Livingston Street headquarters to announce the results of the most recent citywide reading tests, administered in April. For the second consecutive year the scores revealed a general improvement in reading for all grades between two and nine. The scores showed that 50.7 percent of the children in these grades were reading at or above grade level—a 4 percent increase above the 1980 scores and a 10.3 percent improvement over 1979. Most important of all, in the twelve years that this citywide examination had been given, these scores marked the first time that New York City public school students placed above the national average.[127]

When the chancellor was about midway through his news conference, in walked Mayor Edward Koch. Koch had not made it a practice to appear at the Board of Education headquarters, but he wanted to demonstrate his satisfaction. Before a group of cameras and reporters, the mayor described the improved reading scores as a "Herculean increase."[128] He offered particular praise to the chancellor, while at the same time he underplayed the role of the seven-member Board of Education, of which he was trying to take control. He stated, "The Board of Education deserves credit, but the person who deserves the most credit is the one who implements policy—that's the chancellor."[129]

Koch's appearance sparked off a series of questions from the reporters in attendance, several of whom focused on the budget that was under consideration. When asked if the chancellor's performance would be rewarded by a more generous appropriation, Koch responded, "You're not leaving me anything to discuss with the Board of Estimate."[130]

Since the first positive report on the reading scores appeared in September of 1980, the mayor had begun to change his public posture on the school system from a highly critical one to a moderately hopeful one. The 1981 results of the citywide tests made school improvement an integral part of Koch's reelection campaign. He pointed proudly to the significant advancements in public education made under the leadership of his chancellor; these achievements were noted in public appearances, campaign literature, and even television commercials. A *New York Times* editorial appearing on the first day of the 1981 school year was indicative of both the improved image of the city's public schools and the political capital this image would represent during the ongoing election campaign:

> When campaigning politicians identify with the public schools, educators must be doing something right. So Mayor Koch's television advertisements touting improvements in New York City's schools, which open today, are a welcome indication of their returning health.[131]

Only six days after the announcement of the reading scores, it was Macchiarola's turn to appear at the budget hearings before the Board of Estimate and City Council. By that time he was no longer just the Chancellor of Schools, he was becoming a local hero. Nevertheless, the chancellor's approach was moderate and low-keyed. He noted the accomplishments of his administration and thanked those present for their past support. He did not attack the mayor's "miracle budget" but termed it adequate. He expressed confidence in the school system's ability to manage the basics but advised, "It is time to raise our sights."[132] The chancellor then offered a number of educational options that could be taken if more money were provided in the budget. Included in the list were more subject classes in high schools, intensive intervention in the kindergarten and first grade, restoration of arts programs, and improved education for the gifted and talented.[133] Not included in his budget request was an appeal for additional funds to support Promotional Policy, an item he chose to keep as part of his personal negotiations with the mayor.

Immediately prior to the chancellor's testimony before the Board of Estimate and the City Council, the Educational Priorities Panel had prepared its own analysis of the mayor's Executive Budget and submitted it to the legislative bodies. The EPP report provided a telling commentary on how the school system was faring in comparison to the municipal agencies in the city.[134] It began by noting that the $128.5 million reduction in the Board of Education's base budget over the previous two years had constituted 27.5 percent of the total citywide reductions. In return for this, the school system had been allocated 20.6 percent of the total city expenditures. Then, turning its attention to the 1982 fiscal plan, the report pointed out that the Board of Education's portion of the local tax levy budget would decline from 19.6 percent to 19.3 percent, a difference that could be translated into $30 million. The mayor's Executive Budget had included a provision that would pay for the conversion of a portion of the CETA positions lost under federal cutbacks. However, while the school system held 18.9 percent of these positions citywide, it was scheduled to receive only 15.7 percent of the reimbursements. This disparity could be translated into 164 positions. Finally, the EPP report showed that of the $211 million increase for education in the 1982 Executive Budget, only $18 million or 8.55 percent of this increase was for new services. This was a not-so-generous portion of an election-year budget, particularly at a time when the public schools were beginning to show positive signs of improvement.

On June 16, the leadership of the City Council and the members of the Board of Estimate reached an agreement to propose adding $62.3 million to the mayor's Executive Budget. Koch responded with a counterproposal of $24 million. On the next day a compromise was worked out between the mayor and the legislative leaders to add $49.1 million to the 1982 budget. The largest part of this supplemental appropriation would go toward hiring a thousand more policemen than the mayor had originally requested. Thus, as the election-year budget was finally determined, it was clear that police were everyone's priority. Approximately $7 million was added to the Board of Education budget for Promotional Policy, thereby bringing the total amount of local support for the chancellor's program to $14 million. This was considerably less than the $34 million that had originally been requested.

SUMMARY COMMENTS

The budget process of the New York City school system is a case study in institutional dependency. Support for public education in this large city school district is determined by politics at three levels of government—state, local, and federal. Recent history has shown that, despite efforts by education officials and their allies, the schools of New York City have not done particularly well in this complex, power-driven process.

In accord with the traditional anti-urban bias that has historically existed in state legislatures throughout the country, the school finance formula in New York has been found inequitable. Claims of inequity were substantiated in the courts, where the battle for reform was begun in the *Levittown* case. However, temporary gains on behalf of reform made in the courthouse were soon lost in the state house and further compromised at City Hall. State legislators will not support a total redistribution of education funds on behalf of poor or financially burdened local districts. Moreover, a significant part of the marginal benefits wrung from the legislature in the spirit of fairness has been supplanted by the municipal government and applied to local deficits.

The problems inherent in this intergovernmental system of school finance have been further compounded by a recent federal commitment to reduce education spending. For nearly two decades Washington has served as an important source of support for inner-city school systems. Now, in response to an increasingly conservative climate that is evident on a national scale, financial assistance from the federal government has dwindled. Moreover, according to a plan instituted under the Reagan administration's New Federalism, financial authority is devolving from the federal to the state level. Given what we already know about the predispositions of state legislatures, such developments do not offer encouragement for the future of urban public education.

Retrenchment has become the governing principle for public budgeting at all levels of government. The data reviewed in the preceding pages demonstrate that schools have carried a large share of the burden resulting from the cutbacks.

An important reason why urban school systems have done so poorly in the politics of the budget is the nature of their clientele. The population attending an inner-city school district like that of New York is increasingly drawn from racial minorities, linguistic minorities, and the poor—all of whom lack the kind of political leverage that is a prerequisite for success in budgetary politics. The events of the three-year period described in this chapter illustrate quite clearly just how politically impotent that clientele is. The strongest base of support for public education in New York City is composed of those who work in the school system, not those who are served by it. In this case, that base consisted of two major groups: the administrative leadership of the school system, led by the chancellor; and organized labor, spearheaded by the United Federation of Teachers. The Educational Priorities Panel—a coalition of twenty-five separate organizations—constitutes another significant force in the budgetary politics of the school system. But EPP is an anomaly in New York City politics. Its source of strength is moderation, not power. It represents a rather peculiar version of interest-group politics that is not typical of the coalitions one usually reads about in the literature of politics. Among the local functions in New York City, only in education does a client group derive its influence from its willingness to criticize how its service agency spends money. In reality, the EPP plays an ever-changing role in education, shifting back and forth between that of an advocate and that of consumers' union.

A large part of the dynamic behind the budget process observed here was the product of a relationship between two personalities, Mayor Edward Koch and Chancellor Frank Macchiarola. Koch's frustration with the institutional arrangement of school governance was real. He was required to pay a large part of the bills incurred by the school system, but he couldn't really control it. He could criticize, harass, tease, and bargain, but he could not rule. He could not really insure the kind of financial accountability that he thought was necessary. That factor must be a consideration when the mayor decides where to put his money. At least part of the budgetary problem the school system has with the mayor must be interpreted as an institutional one.

A chancellor whom the mayor personally disliked would have been a significant liability to the school system. Despite all the tugging and fighting, that was not the case here. Koch liked Macchiarola, he put him on the job, and he wanted him to succeed. Macchiarola proved to be a strong advocate of the public schools. He was outspoken and politically astute. He mobilized professionals within the system in a way unusual for a chancellor or superintendent. He appealed to the local media. He managed to change the image of the public schools from that of a dying system to one where significant and positive change was occurring.

Nevertheless, the personal attributes of the chancellor highlight the political weaknesses of the school system itself. Macchiarola helped put together the strongest coalition on behalf of public education that was possible in New York. The reward for these efforts was the most catastrophic retrenchment that any agency in New York experienced. In an election year, when the city was enjoying a surplus, when the credibility of the schools was on the rise, and when the mayor was using that credibility as part of his campaign for reelection, education lost ground in the percentage it received of the local budget. Given the extraordinary set of circumstances, which strengthened the hand of education advocates during the years 1980 and 1981, the best that can be said about the chancellor's efforts is that perhaps they prevented matters from becoming as bad as they could have been. In the end, the cutbacks suffered during the 1980 through 1982 fiscal years was not nearly so severe or inequitable as the pattern that was evident between 1975 and 1980.

NOTES

1. Aaron Wildavsky, *The Politics of the Budgetary Process* (Boston: Little Brown, 1964).

2. Peter A. Pyrr, "Zero-Base Budgeting," *Harvard Business Review* 48 (December 1970); *Zero-Base Budgeting* (New York: John Wiley, 1973); "The Zero-Base Approach to Government Budgeting," *Public Administration Review* 37, (January–February 1977); Aaron Wildavsky, *Budgeting: A Comparative Theory of the Budgetary Process* (Boston: Little Brown, 1975); "A Budget for All Seasons: Why the Traditional Budget Lasts," *Public Administration Review* 38 (November–December 1978).

3. See Charles Levine, *Managing Fiscal Stress* (Chatham, N. J.: Chatham House, 1980); Charles Levine et al., *The Politics of Retrenchment* (Beverly Hills, Calif.: Sage Publications, 1981); Charles Levine and Irene Rubin, eds., *Fiscal Stress and Public Policy* (Beverly Hills, Calif.: Sage Publications, 1980).

4. Edward Burke, private interview, May 4, 1981.

5. *Boston Globe,* February 15, 1981.

6. Michael W. Kirst, "The Changing Politics of Education," in Edith Mosher and Jennings Wagner, Jr., eds., *The Changing Politics of Education,* (Berkeley, Calif.: McCutchen, 1978), p. 148.

7. See Stephen Bailey and Edith Mosher, *ESEA: The Office of Education Administers a Law* (Syracuse, N.Y.: Syracuse University Press, 1968).

8. P. Michael Timpane, "Federal Aid to Schools: Its Limited Future," *Law and Contemporary Problems* 38 (Winter 1974), p. 495.

9. Nelson W. Polsby and Aaron Wildavsky, *Presidential Elections* (New York: Scribners, 1971).

10. Kevin Phillips, *The Emerging Republican Majority* (New Rochelle, N.Y.: Arlington House, 1969); Richard W. Scammon and Ben J. Wattenberg, *The Real Majority* (New York: Coward–McCann, 1970).

11. Timpane, "Federal Aid to Schools," p. 499.

12. Ibid., p. 505.

13. See Malcolm E. Jewel, *The State Legislature* (New York: Random House, 1962).

14. Gordon E. Baker, *The Reapportionment Revolution* (New York: Random House, 1967); Andrew Hacker, *Congressional Redistricting* (Washington: The Brookings Institution, 1964); Malcolm E. Jewel, ed., *The Politics of Reapportionment* (New York: Atherton Press, 1962).

15. John Coons, William Clune, and Stephen Sugerman, *Private Wealth and Public Education,* (Cambridge: Harvard University Press, 1970); Arthur Wise, *Rich Schools, Poor Schools* (Chicago: University of Chicago Press, 1968).

16. See Betsy Levin, Thomas Muller, and Caragon Sandoval, *The High Cost of Education in Cities* (Washington: The Urban Institute, 1973).

17. *Serrano v. Priest,* 5 Cal. 3d 584 (1971).

18. *San Antonio Independent School District v. Rodrieguez,* 411 U.S. 1 (1973).

19. *Robinson v. Cahill,* 62 N.J. 473 (1973). For an analysis of the events leading to this case and how it was resolved, see Richard Lehne, *The Quest for Justice* (New York: Longman, 1978).

20. See Michael W. Kirst, "What Happens at the Local Level after School Finance Reform," *Policy Analysis* 3 (Summer 1973); Stephen J. Carrol and Rolla Edward Park, *The Search for Equity in School Finance* (Cambridge, Mass.: Ballinger, 1981); Richard F. Elmore and Milbrey McLaughlin, *Reform and Retrenchment* (Cambridge, Mass.: Ballinger, 1982).

21. Education Finance Center, Education Commission of the States, *Equity in School Finance* (Denver, Colo.: Education Commission of the States, October 1979).

22. New York Special Task Force on Equity and Excellence in Education, "Research Findings and Policy Alternatives: A Second Interim Report," September 1980, p. 25.

23. Ibid., p. 24.

24. See Educational Priorities Panel, "A Citizen's Guide to the New York State School Aid Formula," New York, 1980–1981.

25. New York State Special Task Force on Equity and Excellence in Education, "Research Findings," p. 26.

26. For an overview of the case, see James P. Gifford and Frank J. Macchiarola, "Legal, Technical, Financial and Political Implications of School Finance Reform in New York State," *Tulane Law Review* 55 (1981).

27. For an opposing view, see Jay M. Stein, "Municipal Overburden as State Educational Aid: Is It Equitable?" *Urban Education* XII, 4 (January 1978).

28. Gifford and Macchiarola, "Legal . . . Implications."

29. *Levittown* v. *Nyquist,* Supreme Court of the State of New York, County of Nassau, index No. 8208/74, June 27, 1978.

30. New York State Special Task Force in Equity and Excellence in Education, "Research Findings," pp. 24–25.

31. *Levittown* v. *Nyquist,* Appellate Division of the State Supreme Court, October 26, 1981.

32. *The New York Times,* October 18, 1981.

33. "The Chancellor's Annual Report, 1979–1980," New York City Public Schools, 1981, p. 27.

34. "A Functional Analysis of the 1979–1980 New York City Board of Education Budget," Office of Budget Operations and Review, Board of Education of the City of New York, June 1980, p. II.

35. Ibid.

36. Bernard Gifford, "Public Education in New York City: Reflections on the Immediate Past and Some Thoughts About the Future . . . a Budgetary Perspective," Board of Education of the City of New York, Office of the Deputy Chancellor, September 1976, pp. 13–15.

37. "A Report to the Chancellor on the Effect of State Funding on City Funding of the Board of Education," Chancellor's Office of Policy Analysis, Research and Planning, New York City Public Schools, July 1980, p. 16.

38. Ibid.

39. Raymond D. Horton and Mary McCormick, "Services," in Charles Brecher and Raymond D. Horton, eds., *Setting Municipal Priorities, 1981* (Montclair:, N.J.: Allanheld, Osmun, 1980).

40. Ibid., p. 87.

41. Ibid., pp. 87–88.

42. "A Report to the Chancellor on the Effect of State Funding on City Funding of the Board of Education."

43. Robert F. Wagner, Jr., private interview, May 18, 1981.

44. H. Thomas James, James A. Kelly, Walter I. Garms, "Determinants of Educational Expenditures in Large Cities of the United States," (Stanford Calif.: Stanford University School of Education, 1966); L. Harmon Ziegler and M. Kent Jennings, *Governing American Schools* (North Scituate, Mass.: Duxbury Press, 1974); William L. Boyd, "School Board–Administrative Staff Relationships," in Peter Cistone, ed., *Understanding School Boards,* (Lexington, Mass.: Lexington Books, 1975).

45. Robert F. Wagner, Jr., private interview, May 18, 1981.

46. Edward Burke, private interview, May 4, 1981.

47. Richard Frankan, private interview, May 19, 1981.

48. See, David Rogers, *Can Business Management Save the Cities?* (New York: The Free Press, 1978), Chapter 4.

49. Jerome Harris, private interview, May 6, 1981.

50. Robert F. Wagner, Jr., private interview, May 18, 1981.

51. For a history of the Educational Priorities Panel, see Amy Plumer and Edward T. Rogowsky, "The Educational Priorities: An Evaluation," unpublished report, Educational Priorities Panel, November 1977.

52. Member groups in the Educational Priorities Panel include: Advocates for Children, Alliance for Children, American Jewish Committee–New York Chapter, ASPIRA of New York, Association for the Help of Retarded Children, Citizen's Committee for the Children of New York, The City Club of New York, City-Wide Confederation of High School Parents, Coalition of 100 Black Women, Community Council of Greater New York, Community Service Society, The Junior League of New York City, League of Women Voters of New York City, National Association for the Advancement of Colored People, New York Urban Coalition, New York Urban League, Parent's Action Committee for Education, Presbytery of New York, Public Education Association, Queensboro Federation of Parents Clubs, Rheedlen Foundation, United Neighborhood Houses, United Parents Associations, and Women's City Club of New York.

53. Stanley Litow, private interview, May 8, 1981.

54. "Chancellor's Budget Message for the 1980 Fiscal Year," submitted to the New York City Board of Education, December 15, 1979.

55. Ibid.

56. *The New York Times*, January 4, 1979.

57. Ibid.

58. *New York Daily News*, January 5, 1979.

59. Office of the Mayor, City of New York, "Financial Plan for 1980–1981," January 15, 1979.

60. "Statement of Frank J. Macchiarola, Chancellor of the New York City Schools, before the Budget Review Hearings before the Board of Estimate and the Legislative Office of Budget Review," February 15, 1979.

61. "Statement of Frank J. Macchiarola, Chancellor of the New York City Schools, before the Departmental Hearings of the New York City Council," March 5, 1979.

62. "Testimony by Frank J. Macchiarola, before the Joint Meeting of the New York State Senate Finance and the New York State Assembly Ways and Means Committees," February 7, 1979.

63. *New York Post*, February 8, 1979.

64. *Newsday*, March 21, 1979.

65. "Message of the Mayor, The City of New York Executive Budget, Fiscal Year 1980," April 26, 1979.

66. Richard Halverson, "Recommendations for School Consolidations and Closing," August 31, 1979.

67. Edward Burke, private interview, May 4, 1981.

68. *Newsday*, October 14, 1979.

69. *Newsday*, November 18, 1979.

70. "Testimony of Chancellor Frank J. Macchiarola before the Education and Finance Committees of the City Council," November 20, 1979.

71. *New York Daily News,* November 24, 1979.

72. *The New York Times,* November 22, 1979.

73. Educational Priorities Panel, "Service Cuts and Budget Deficits in New York City Schools, 1979," November 27, 1979.

74. *The New York Times,* December 8, 1979.

75. Stephen Aiello, correspondence to Edward Koch and Harrison Goldin, December 20, 1979.

76. Dall Forsythe, private interview, May 1, 1981.

77. Edward Burke, private interview, May 4, 1981.

78. Stanley Litow, private interview, May 8, 1981.

79. "Chancellor's Budget Message for the 1981 Fiscal Year," submitted to the New York City Board of Education, December 17, 1979.

80. *Newsday,* December 18, 1979.

81. Office of the Mayor, City of New York, "Financial Plan for 1981–1984," January 11, 1980.

82. *The New York Times,* January 14, 1980.

83. "Statement by the New York City Board of Education Regarding the Announcement of PEG Cuts," January 16, 1980.

84. *The New York Times,* January 17, 1981.

85. *Newsday,* January 25, 1980.

86. *New York Post,* January 30, 1981.

87. *Newsday,* March 15, 1980.

88. Stanley Litow, private interview, May 8, 1981.

89. Ibid.

90. Educational Priorities Panel, "A Proposal to Rescue the 1981 School Budget," March 10, 1980.

91. *The New York Times,* March 31, 1980.

92. *The New York Times,* January 23, 1980.

93. *New York Daily News,* March 26, 1980.

94. "Message of the Mayor, The City of New York Executive Budget, Fiscal Year 1981," May 9, 1980.

95. Educational Priorities Panel, "Education Budget Options: 1981," May 27, 1980.

96. "Statement of Frank J. Macchiarola, Chancellor of the New York City Public Schools, Before the City-Wide Principals' Conference," Park West High School, May 30, 1980.

97. Richard Frankan, private interview, May 19, 1981.

98. *Newsday,* May 22, 1980.

99. "Testimony of Frank J. Macchiarola, Chancellor of New York City Public Schools, before the New York City Council and the Board of Estimate, City Hall, New York," June 4, 1980.

100. *The New York Times,* June 11, 1980.

101. *Newsday,* June 13, 1980.

102. *The New York Times,* June 26, 1980.

103. *Newsweek,* July 24, 1980.

104. *The New York Times,* August 12, 1980.

105. Office of the Mayor, "City of New York Financial Plan, Fiscal Years 1981–1984," August 11, 1980.

106. Frank J. Macchiarola, memorandum to the Board of Education, "Adoption of the Budget for the 1980–1981 Fiscal Year," August 22, 1980.

107. *New York Daily News,* November 29, 1980.

108. "Chancellor's Budget Message for the 1982 Fiscal Year," submitted to the New York City Board of Education, December 15, 1980.

109. Ibid.

110. *New York Post,* December 18, 1980.

111. *New York Daily News,* December 22, 1980.

112. *Newsday,* December 16, 1980.

113. *The New York Times,* January 21, 1981.

114. *The New York Times,* May 9, 1981.

115. Office of the Mayor, City of New York, "Financial Plan for Fiscal Years 1981–1985," January 16, 1981.

116. Ibid.

117. Ibid.

118. *The New York Times,* January 18, 1981.

119. *The New York Times,* March 13, 1981.

120. *The New York Times,* April 7, 1981.

121. "Testimony of Frank J. Macchiarola, Chancellor of the New York City Public Schools, before a Board of Estimate/City Council Joint Hearing on the Mayor's Program to Eliminate the Gap," March 10, 1981.

122. "Message of the Mayor, The City of New York Executive Budget, Fiscal Year 1982," May 12, 1981.

123. Ibid.

124. "Status Report on the Board of Education's Budget and Financial Controls," Office of the Comptroller, March 1981.

125. Educational Priorities Panel, "Belt Tightening at 110 Livingston Street: How One Agency Has Responded to the Fiscal Crisis," May 1981.

126. Ibid.

127. Board of Education, City of New York, press release, May 28, 1981.

128. *Newsday,* May 29, 1981.

129. *The New York Times,* May 29, 1981.

130. *Newsday,* May 29, 1981.

131. *The New York Times,* September 10, 1981.

132. "Statement of Frank J. Macchiarola, Chancellor of the New York City Public Schools, before the Joint Budget Hearings of the City Council and Board of Estimate," June 3, 1981.

133. Ibid.

134. Educational Priorities Panel, "Education Budget Options, 1982," May 1981.

RAISING COMPETENCY STANDARDS

Promotional Policy represented many of the principles for which the new administration at Livingston Street stood. From a programmatic perspective, it was the foremost manifestation of the philosophy that stated, "All children can learn." It symbolized an expression of faith in the fundamental educability of all children and, at the same time, spelled out a set of expectations to which children would be held. It was also indicative of professional standard of accountability based on the premise that inner-city schools can and should be instructionally effective.

A study of the formation and implementation of Promotional Policy in New York City can teach us several important lessons about the public policy process. It shows the important role social science research can play in determining the outcome of policy decisions. It illustrates the multiplicity of parties, public and private, educator and noneducator, that participate in the policy process in a large urban school system. It demonstrates the kind of resistance that arises when one tries to change policy in a system that must respond to the demands of a varied constituency. Change, we will see, is particularly difficult when those to whom the system is accountable and those whom the system must serve are not one and the same.

Promotional Policy in New York City is not a unique phenomenon. It can be seen as part of a national movement for competency, developing in response to the declining literacy rate that has been afflicting American youth since 1963, and the consequent decline in public confidence in the schools, the education profession, and the instructional process itself. The competency movement represents a demand for higher standards in education. It has been supported by public officials calling for more accountability from the schools, and by parent and community groups clamoring for more effective teaching and learning. Competency standards have been embraced by civil rights advocates as a means to educational equity that will insure a quality education to all children, regardless of race or class. The business community, whose prospective talent pool is linked to the level of skill possessed by students emerging from the public schools, has also appealed for higher standards.

A key component of the competency movement is the administration of standardized tests. As of 1980, thirty-eight states required students to demonstrate competency in basic skills by their performance on some kind of standardized test. Some twenty states have established minimum course requirements for graduation. But only a few are experimenting with competency tests to determine eligibility for graduation or grade advancement. In 1977 both houses of Congress held exploratory hearings on the question of establishing national standards in reading, writing, and mathematics. That same year President Jimmy Carter reportedly considered the development of a national competency examination.[1]

Despite the momentum that the competency movement has gained, support for the use of standardized tests has been both limited and guarded. A report prepared by the National Academy of Education in 1978, at the request of HEW Secretary Joseph Califano, warned against the inappropriate application of competency tests and issued a particular note of caution regarding their use in determining eligibility for graduation. According to the late Stephen K. Bailey, a former New York State Regent, and chairperson of the study group:

> . . . the setting of statewide minimum competency standards for awarding the high school diploma . . . is basically unworkable, exceeds the present measurement arts of the teaching profession, and will create more social problems than it can conceivably solve.[2]

The report did recommend the use of standardized tests in the lower grades for diagnostic and prescriptive purposes. It concluded, in its characteristically cautious tone, that, if properly administered, "minimum competency testing can be a positive educational development."

Minimum competency testing remains one of the most controversial issues in education today. Its proponents believe that it will help restore training in cognitive development as the primary function of the school.[3] Advocates hope that the new focus on basic skills will motivate teachers to teach more purposefully and students to work harder. Many of those who oppose the testing, however, criticize it as a response to political pressure rather than educational judgment. They claim that there is an inadequate match between the tests and the skills that are supposedly being measured.[4]

It is not difficult to understand why the competency movement has aroused such controversy. The history of testing in the United

States has been rather mixed. True, many well-intentioned educators have seen competency tests as a tool for improving the instructional process. But there are also those who have used them as instruments for unfair discrimination, exclusion, and tracking. Tests have been used to segregate certain populations from the mainstream, and in this way have served the purposes of those who would deny some individuals or groups the opportunity of an adequate education. For these reasons, competency testing has not only been debated on instructional grounds, but has also been challenged as both an ethical and legal issue.[5]

One of the first significant legal challenges to the use of testing in education came in 1967, when a federal judge in the District of Columbia ordered a tracking system in the Washington public schools abolished. In *Hobson* v. *Hansen*,[6] Judge Skelly Wright found that a testing system that disproportionately places poor and black students in lower tracks is discriminatory and in violation of the due process clause of the Fifth Amendment to the federal Constitution. Judge Wright also "breathed in" an equal protection provision to the due process clause, stating that while not all tracking can be deemed discriminatory, any situation where there has been a history of racial segregation requires close scrutiny. The judge did not rule on the validity of the achievement tests themselves.

The District of Columbia case set an important legal precedent in the application of the due process and equal protection clauses of the Constitution for protection against unfair testing practices. It was particularly relevant to situations where school systems had been recently desegregated. Four years after *Hobson* v. *Hansen* was handed down, a federal district court in Louisiana held that testing could not be used as a basis for student assignments or tracking in a school system that had recently been desegregated.[7] That same year a federal appeals court in Georgia ruled that a previously segregated school system would be required to function as a unitary system for several years before testing could be used for placement.[8] The rationale behind the argument was that black children had received an inferior education in the segregated schools and therefore could not be expected to achieve at the same level as white children.

Litigation on the discriminatory effects of testing seemed to be moving at full steam until 1976, when the United States Supreme Court ruled on a test that ws being used as a criterion for the hiring of police officers in Washington, D.C. While the examination in question was not the type of competency test found in schools, the principle laid down by the Court was certainly applicable. In *Washington* v. *Davis*,[9] the Court ruled that while the disproportionate impact of testing was not irrelevant, this result, in itself did not constitute a violation of the equal protection clause of the Constitution. It ruled that such a violation would exist only if a plaintiff could prove discriminatory intent on the part of the defendant. In handing down this decision, the Court raised the plaintiff's burden of proof from mere discriminatory effect to discriminatory intent. While *Washington* v. *Davis* was seen by many as a setback to litigation on behalf of the disadvantaged, it did not put an end to legal challenges of testing. In 1979 a federal district court in California found that the use of IQ tests to place students in classes for the educable mentally retarded was a violation of federal law.[10] Laws cited were the Civil Rights Act of 1964, the Rehabilitation Act of 1973, and the Education for All Handicapped Children Act of 1975.

The first direct legal challenge to a statewide competency test took place in Florida in 1978.[11] Two years earlier, the Florida state legislature had passed a law requiring students to pass examinations in functional literacy and mathematics as a prerequisite for a high school diploma. When the tests were first administered in 1978, 36 percent of the students failed,[12] including a disproportionate number of minority students. The results led to widespread criticism from a variety of groups, including the National Association for the Advancement of Colored People and the statewide teachers' union. In *Debra P.* v. *Turlington*,[13] the plaintiffs challenged the legality of the statute and the tests, alleging that the tests discriminated against minorities, lacked validity and reliability, and measured skills that were different from those taught in schools. The federal district court, recognizing possession of a high school diploma as a property right, found that the testing program had failed to give adequate notice of the new standards to students and was therefore a violation of procedural due process rights. The court also considered the effects of past discrimination as a factor and enjoined Florida from implementing its diploma requirements for four years. On appeal, the Court of Appeals for the Fifth Circuit affirmed the lower court's ruling as to inadequate notice and remanded the case for further findings on the curricular validity of the test. In 1979 a state Supreme Court in New York issued a similar finding of inadequate notice when it enjoined the state deputy commissioner of education from rescinding the diplomas of two handicapped students.[14] The students had been granted diplomas from their local school board but had not passed the newly instituted competency examinations required by the state for graduation.

While the courts have not rejected the use of minimum competency examinations for determining student eligibility for graduation or promotion, they have subjected testing practices to rather close scrutiny and have found the use of such examinations to be fair and legal if certain conditions are satisfied. While no definitive guidelines have been laid down, a careful analysis of the case law does point to some key requirements. In a comprehensive review of the literature and the law, Merle McClung has identified five factors to be considered in establishing minimum competency standards.[15] These include:

- appropriateness of test content so that tests do not include items of coerced belief, invasion of privacy, or unteachable or unmeasurable content;
- adequacy of phase-in period, insuring that students are given adequate prior notice when new standards are to be imposed;
- instructional match so that test content reflects the objectives of the curriculum and course of study;
- protection against racial or linguistic discrimination so that tests are able to withstand scrutiny as to discriminatory motives behind their use and as to cultural or linguistic bias;
- protection of the handicapped by special consideration where appropriate, either through exemption, different standards, or different assessment procedures.

Looking at the issue from a less legal and more educational perspective, William Spady has emphasized the important role of the instructional program in the attainment of competency. He suggests that competency-based education does not consist of evaluation and certification systems alone, but depends on the teaching system to give all students the opportunity to meet certification standards.[16] Francis Archambault has expressed an additional concern about the issue of remediation.[17] He claims that too often states that have set new competency standards have left responsibility for remediation to the local districts, without providing either additional funds or adequate diagnostic instruments for helping students who have not achieved the desired standards. He notes with regret that politicians at the state level often act as though achievement can be legislated. Like Haney and Madaus,[18] he warns that remediation can be one of the most expensive hidden costs of a competency program that is carried out well.

Competency testing has thus proved to be a double-edged sword. In a positive sense, it may be seen as a technique for monitoring, if not guaranteeing, the delivery of quality education to all children. In a perverse form and application, it has been used as a tool for discrimination, segregation, and the denial of equal educational opportunity. Thus one of the first matters to consider about these tests is the intention of those who put them into effect. Once that issue is resolved, the next important question concerns the care with which such a program is implemented. That attention from educators will determine whether children are the beneficiaries or the victims of the movement toward higher standards. The fact of the matter is that education has been failing. More specifically, public education has been failing the children of the poor, the minorities, and the inner cities. A system that has no standards, no expectation of excellence, and no regard for failure can no longer be tolerated.

The proponents of Promotional Policy in New York City saw it as a vehicle for both effective instruction and educational equity. Their approach was steeped in a philosophy of education based on an extensive body of social science research. That philosophy, and the research supporting it, was no less controversial than the competency movement itself. However, an analysis of its origins and precepts is important to understanding how Promotional Policy developed.

PHILOSOPHICAL FOUNDATIONS: THE SEARCH FOR EQUALITY

The philosophy of the administration headed by Chancellor Frank Macchiarola was in large part a response to the sense of despair that had emerged within the educational profession. It was a reaction to the belief that factors outside the school environment had a more significant impact on the ability of children to master basic skills than factors within the school. It was a rejection of the idea that certain children, particularly those within the inner city, are uneducable. The philosophy of despair was a convenience. It relieved educators of responsibility and provided a rationale for failure. Yet the resignation it engendered was genuine, built on a significant body of social science research. It was not always the intention of the purveyors of this research to provide such a rationale, but their work was used to do so, and it was used effectively.

One of the first such studies was completed by James Coleman and his colleagues in 1966.[19] The report, entitled *Equality of Educational Opportunity,* was prepared at the request of U.S. Commissioner of Education Francis Keppel in fulfillment of a mandate appearing in the Civil Rights Act of 1964. The law required that the Office of Education undertake a survey concerning the relationship between equal educational opportunity in public schools throughout the United States and the race, color, religion, or national origin of children. The "Coleman Report," as it became known, was a landmark study. One of the largest social science projects in history, it involved the testing of more than 570,000 school children and 60,000 teachers, and the surveying of facilities in 4,000 public schools. Prior to the preparation of the Coleman Report, educational opportunity in the United States was usually measured through an analysis of inputs, i.e., staff, resources, facilities, etc. The Coleman Report analyzed these also, but then took the analysis a step further by examining educational outcomes as reflected in achievement tests. The major findings of the report were as follows:

- Most black and white children attend segregated schools.
- The measured characteristics of these schools, i.e., their facilities and resources, showed these inputs to be equal among black and white schools.
- The measured characteristics of these facilities, resources, and inputs had little impact on black or white performance on standardized tests.
- The presence of classmates from affluent backgrounds showed a positive relationship to student performance on standardized tests.

The major conclusion of the report was profound. It stated that the quantity and quality of school inputs have little or no bearing on student achievement; what counts more is the student's home environment and peers. Needless to say, this conclusion had significant implications in terms of social policy. While it advanced the cause of racial integration, it struck a harsh blow at instructional strategies based upon the principle of compensatory education. It gave rise to a plethora of studies that contributed to the notion that public funds put into educational programs in the name of equality were funds poorly invested.[20] And thus was born the idea that "schools don't matter."

In 1972 Christopher Jencks and a group of his colleagues from the Harvard Graduate School of Education completed a reanalysis of the data from the Coleman Report. Their study, entitled *Inequality*,[21] was as much a radical critique of the American class and social structure as it was a book about education. But while the findings in *Inequality* offered a provocative commentary on economic classes in the United States, they also supplied scientific ammunition to those who were advocating a disinvestment in public education. What began as a Marxist analysis of America became a tool of conservative politicians.

Jencks and his colleagues used achievement data to show how little school conditions affect pupil performance. They found that school administrators and educational experts do not know what to do in order to raise test scores, and suggested that compensatory education was a failure. They proposed that, no matter what was done at the school level, only a fundamental change in the economic structure of the nation would lead to the social advancement of poor black children. Thus, in terms of the discourse on equal opportunity, what was added to the notion that "schools don't matter" was the observation "and they wouldn't be enough anyway."

The most controversial and disturbing research on school effects was the work of Arthur Jensen, which appeared in the *Harvard Educational Review*[22] in 1969. Jensen tied achievement to native intelligence and found intelligence to be a product of genetic inheritance. He began his research with the premise that compensatory education has failed to produce significant effects in both the IQ and achievement levels of children. This being the case, he tells us, we must start to question the assumption on which compensatory education is based. That assumption implies that IQ is environmentally determined. Jensen's work, on the contrary, suggested that genetic factors are much more significant in determining IQ differences than are environmental ones. He noted, however, that the most crucial of the environmental factors is family. He discussed evidence that variations in intelligence among races and social classes do not result largely from differences in environment, but must be attributed partially to genetic differences. Jensen found the effect of educational programs on IQ scores to be small. He presented environment as a "threshold variable," arguing that while extreme deprivation can prevent a child from performing at his or her genetic potential, an enriched educational program cannot push a child above that potential.

While the aforementioned studies all varied significantly in purpose, scope, and content, they did share common ground, some intentional, some not. Most obviously, all gave credence to the idea that "schools don't matter" and provided a rationale for reducing the national commitment to public education. Educators who chose to do so could use this literature as an excuse for their own inadequacies—blaming the poor performance level of children on the children themselves rather than on the schools they attended. This use of social science research legitimized a cynical and desperate philosophy of education based on the premise that certain children, particularly poor minority children in inner-city schools, are uneducable. The literature, however, also gave rise to a new line of research arguing that, in certain places, under certain conditions, inner-city schools attended by the urban poor can be instructionally effective.

One of the first studies to appear in this new literature on effective schools was conducted by George Weber in 1971.[23] Weber studied four inner-city schools in New York, Kansas City, and Los Angeles, which were found to be successful in teaching reading to poor minority children. In contrast to the work that had been done before him, Weber drew some startling conclusions about the relationships among student characteristics, school performance, and achievement. Commenting on the schools he examined, he stated, "Their success shows that the failure in beginning reading typical of inner-city schools is the fault not of the children or their backgrounds, but of the schools."[24] In 1974, the New York State Office of Education Performance published a study confirming Weber's findings.[25] Comparing two New York City schools—one high-achieving, one low-achieving—the research showed that the differences in student performance were attributable to factors that were within the control of school personnel. In 1976 Maden, Lawson, and Sweet[26] completed a comparative analysis of forty-two elementary schools in California, half of which had proved effective on the basis of test scores, half of which had not. This study identified ten institutional characteristics associated with the high-achieving schools. In the following year Wilber Brookover and Lawrence Lezotte[27] of Michigan State University published the results of a study of eight urban schools—six improving, two declining—which offered a similar set of school characteristics found to have a positive impact on student success.

The research on effective schools was appearing at the same time that new evidence was emerging on the efficacy of compensatory education. Investigations of major federal programs such as Title I and Head Start were beginning to show that these efforts did produce positive cognitive and affective results for those children to whom they were made available.[28] The research on effective schools was not limited to the American scene. In 1979 a group of social scientists in London published a significant study on twelve urban secondary schools. Their book, entitled *Fifteen Thousand Hours*,[29] showed that the time a child spends in school not only can make a critical difference in academic performance, but can also influence such behavioral factors as delinquency and truancy. It concluded by offering a list of school characteristics similar to those variables of effective instruction identified by American scholars.

Since its original appearance in 1971, research on effective schools has become part of a popular literature in education. Contributed by journalists and other nonacademic writers, the new literature has directed attention to the increasing number of success stories among schools for the urban poor.[30] Taken as a whole, this scholarly and journalistic writing has been responsible for two major advances toward equal educational opportunity. First of all, it has begun to provide support for a new way of thinking in the education community—an awareness that schools do matter, and therefore what happens in them makes a difference in terms of student performance. Second, it had led to a new line of inquiry within urban education. That research has focused on the discovery and implementation of effective instructional strategies for those same urban schools that once were written off by many members of the educational and political community.[31]

One contributor to the new body of literature was Ronald Edmonds, who had joined the staff of Chancellor Frank Macchiarola as Senior Assistant for Instruction. Edmonds had previously served as assistant superintendent of education in Michigan and had collaborated on a preliminary study of effective schools with two colleagues from Michigan State. Their work, which began in 1974, involved ten thousand students from twenty elementary schools in the Detroit Model Cities Area. Using data from the Stanford Achievement Test and the Iowa Basic Skills Test, and controlling for family background and school environment, Edmonds and his colleagues found that family background neither causes nor prevents effective education in urban elementary schools.[32] That initial study served as an impetus for the Search for Effective Schools Project, which Edmonds directed while on the faculty of the Harvard Graduate School of Education.[33] Conducted with a Cambridge colleague, John Fredericksen, the Harvard-based project aimed to confirm what institutional behavior and circumstances contributed most to creating and maintaining a climate of pupil progress and instructional success. It went beyond the original Detroit data base to include five elementary schools in Lansing. Student performance was measured by standardized tests. A successful school was defined as one that eliminates the relationship between pupil performance and social class. Considering the results of his own work in the context of the larger body of literature on the subject, Edmonds identified the following tangible characteristics he believed to be indispensable to effective schools for poor children:

- strong administrative leadership;
- a climate of expectation in which no children are permitted to fall below minimum but efficacious levels of achievement;
- a school atmosphere that is orderly and conducive to instruction;
- a set of priorities placing pupil acquisition of basic school skills above all other school activities;
- the use of some formal means by which pupil progress is frequently and regularly monitored.[34]

The Edmonds research played a major role in defining an overall instructional strategy for the administration at Livingston Street. That strategy called for a focus on the development of basic skills, with a particular concentration on the early childhood and elementary grades. It included the selection and application of standardized tests for the periodic evaluation of student performance. It was based on a belief in the fundamental educability of all children, regardless of race or class. The statement "All children can learn" was meant to be both empirical and normative. It was more than a statement of fact growing out of a select body of social science research. Given the context of the literature from which it emerged, it represented a claim that the expectations with which educators approached their task affected the outcome. It did not mean that all students could be expected to function at the same level of achievement, nor was it designed to disregard the severe obstacles that children from disadvantaged backgrounds would need to overcome. The basic message was that, if properly taught, all children were capable of mastering a minimally acceptable level of basic skills. Thus, in a philosophical context, the corollary of the statement proposing "All children can learn" was the mandate requiring "All children must be taught."

FROM PHILOSOPHY TO PRACTICE: PROGRAMMATIC INNOVATIONS IN THE NEW ADMINISTRATION

The Search for Effective Schools Project, begun in Michigan and completed at Harvard, set the stage for an experimental program of school site intervention in New York City, administered through the office of the chancellor. The School Improvement Project as it was called, was an attempt to help participating schools increase their effectiveness by developing practices and conditions that research had found conducive to successful teaching and learning. Edmonds initiated the New York City project in the 1978–1979 school year. The purpose of the first phase was to validate the characteristics of effective schooling he had previously identified in Detroit and Lansing. In order to examine the relationship between these factors and educational outcomes, Edmonds developed case studies of nine New York City elementary schools. The result of the studies was a confirmation of the original findings about the characteristics that distinguish effective from ineffective schools.[35] As already mentioned, these included strong administrative leadership, a schoolwide climate conducive to learning, an emphasis on basic skills instruction, optimistic expectations by teachers, and ongoing assessment of pupil progress.

The implementation phase of the School Improvement Project began in the 1979–1980 school year, with generous support from the Ford Foundation, the Carnegie Corporation, and the New York Foundation.[36] It involved ten elementary schools, all of which were selected on a voluntary basis, according to the expressed interest of the principal, staff, and parents. Each school was assigned a liaison representative from the chancellor's office. This person was to conduct an assessment of the school's needs and help the principal form a planning committee to develop and implement strategies for meeting those needs. The school planning committee was to be composed of teachers, parents, supervisors, and paraprofessionals. The committee's school improvement plan, submitted to the chancellor's office, was to include objectives, activities, and evaluation procedures, focusing on the five factors for school effectiveness referred to in the research. Technical assistance, training, and other support services were provided through the chancellor's office. In the 1980–1981 school year seven of the original ten schools implemented their plans, and nine additional schools that had joined the project began developing theirs.

In January 1980 a similar project was developed by the New York Urban Coalition, with the support of Board of Education President Stephen Aiello and the chancellor. The Local School Development Project, as it was called, initially involved thirty-seven elementary and middle schools throughout the city.[37] The primary goal of the project was to improve academic achievement through the establishment and support of a planning team at the school. This team, composed of administrators, staff, parents, and, in the case of some middle schools, students, would develop a comprehensive school plan. A Council on Local School Development was set up by the Urban Coalition to serve as an advisory group to the project and conduct an ongoing review of the program. In the 1980–1981 school year three of the thirty-seven original schools left the program, and one new one was added.

Both the School Improvement Project (SIP) and the Local School Development Project (LSDP) emphasized a school-based approach to the improvement of basic instruction. While one was conducted under the auspices of the chancellor's office and the other by an outside group, both had the support of the central school administration. However, there were subtle differences between the two programs, which serve to highlight the major direction in which the new administration was moving. LSDP was built on a relationship forged with the local district superintendent; SIP was primarily concerned with designing a strategy around the principal as the key actor. This emphasis on the principal not only grew out of the priorities set down in the Edmonds' research but also reflected a growing body of literature that points to the principal as the key person determining school performance.[38] While both programs recognized the importance of acquiring basic skills, SIP had a more direct focus, and it was backed up by an emphasis on regular formal evaluations. Finally, while LSDP included both elementary and middle schools, SIP was devoted entirely to the former. This reflected the emphasis on early childhood development that was a key ingredient of the initial instructional strategy of the Macchiarola administration.

The administration had signaled the direction in which it was moving, early on, when the chancellor made his first appeal to the City Council in the summer of 1978, requesting that funds be made available for the reduction of class size in the first grade and the implementation of the Transitional Class Program. Both of these programs illustrated a fundamental policy approach. Both were based on a significant body of social science research. The literature on class size seemed to suggest rather persuasively that reductions are beneficial with regard to cognitive and affective outcomes in circumstances when certain conditions are met: when children are in their early years; and when reductions are substantial (i.e., from twenty to fifteen, or fifteen to ten), when the objective is geared to elementary school reading or mathematics.[39] Thus came the proposal for reduced class size in the first grade and an important part of the strategy adopted in the transitional classes.

The Transitional Class Program was particularly significant. It was a precursor of things to come, setting a foundation for the broader-based Promotional Policy and the administration's effort to raise competency standards. It was designed to address a grievous problem that was far too typical, both within New York City and around the country: children who do poorly in early grades fall further behind as they advance to later grades. Thus the initial policy statement which introduced the transitional class program read as follows:

> Urban school systems throughout the country, including New York City, have traditionally responded to the problem of early academic failure in one of two ways. Pupils are either held over at the same grade level and repeat a year of instruction or they are given a social promotion into the next grade along with some remedial instruction. Experience has demonstrated that many of these pupils do not profit from either of these approaches and in fact, continue to fall behind academically.[40]

The Transitional Class Program that began in the fall of 1978 was advanced on the premise that pupils who fail to learn basic skills in grades one, two, and three will profit most if placed in special non-graded, small classes. During the 1978–1979 school year, funds were made available to set up 489 classes for approximately 8,000 pupils in 358 schools. As a result of budget cuts imposed during the following year, the program was reduced in 1979–1980 to 391 classes for 7,425 pupils in 313 schools. The chancellor allocated funds among the districts, based on the number of pupils who had been held over in the first three grades the previous June. Citywide guidelines were established. Each class would be composed of between fifteen and twenty first-, second-, and third-grade pupils who had been held over as a result of falling a year or more below grade level in reading ability. However, up to three potential holdovers could be admitted to a class if there were not enough holdovers to fill it. In his articulation of the program principles, method of allocation, and guidelines for implementation, the chancellor was making his first policy statement on the issue of social promotion and providing an incentive to community superintendents and their school principals to end the practice.

The administration was committed to making the program a positive experience for children, upgrading both their academic skills and self-concept. Citywide criteria for teacher selection included the following qualifications: demonstrated success in working with slow learners, a minimum of three years' experience in teaching early childhood grades, demonstrated flexibility in classroom management, and a willingness to participate in staff development. Teachers were given the responsibility for holding an initial parent orientation meeting and bimonthly parent-teacher conferences. They were also required to attend special training sessions in diagnostic prescriptive assessment, classroom management systems, and the integration of the reading process in different curriculum areas.

In December 1980 the administration completed an evaluation of the program. The report revealed a high incidence of noncompliance with the citywide standards at the district level. A substantial number of teachers did not have the required years of teaching experience, some ineligible pupils had been placed in the program, instructional techniques had not always conformed to those established, and some staff had not been rigorous in testing students for the purposes of evaluation.[41] In the final assessment of the program prepared by the Office of Educational Evaluation, pre- and post-test data were available for only 54 percent of the second- and third-grade students. This data did show, however, a mean reading gain of one month per month of instruction among second-graders, and a mean gain of 1.12 month per month of instruction for third-graders. The program was eliminated at the end of the second year because of loss of city funding. While the test scores were moderately encouraging regarding the efficacy of the remediation, the degree of noncompliance exhibited at the school district level offered several important, though discouraging lessons. No doubt at least part of the noncompliance could be traced to problems of implementation at the central level. However, the message coming back to the administration was quite clear. It warned that new standards of competency and performance could not be set by administrative fiat from the chancellor's office. The road between a policy decision and its successful implementation is a long one, and it needed to be traveled carefully before a workable Promotional Policy could be put in place.

ROUND ONE: COMPETENCY STANDARDS AS A STATE ISSUE

The campaign to raise competency standards in New York was not launched at the local level. It began as a state issue, and, ironically, the administration at Livingston Street was on the opposing side. In 1975 the New York State Board of Regents had adopted a policy requiring students graduating from high school in 1979 and thereafter to pass state-developed Basic Competency Tests (BCTs) in reading and math before they could qualify for a diploma. A competency test in writing was to be added to these requirements in 1980. These Basic Competency Tests were similar to those that had been developed in many other states and were designed to evaluate a student's coping skills—skills needed to function as a responsible adult in contemporary society. In academic terms, this meant the measurement of basic literacy skills, or the ability to read, write, and calculate at the eighth-grade level.

When the BCTs were first administered in June of 1978, they were severely criticized by some of the Regents, who claimed that the tests were too easy. In July the Regents instructed the Commissioner of Education to establish tentative standards for new and more difficult tests in reading comprehension, writing, and math. These standards were set tentatively, to allow for a public statewide review in the form of Regents/Commissioner Regional Conferences. The Regents were scheduled to take a formal vote of approval on March 1. Under the new standards, the BCTs would continue to apply only to the graduating classes of 1979 and 1980, and new examinations would go into effect in 1981. The Regents Competency Tests (RCTs) were designed to change the basic philosophy and purpose of the state competency program. Unlike the BCT, which was concerned with measuring basic life skills and functional literacy, the RCT was meant to assess content and academic skills at the high school level. This high-school-level standard is the most distinguishing feature of the RCT, and at the time it was the only test of its kind in the nation used for determining eligibility for high school graduation.

Before 1978, New York State was responsible for a comprehensive program of competency testing, but the applications of the exams used varied extensively from those of the BCT and the RCT. Most tests were used for broad evaluative purposes. The Pupil Evaluation

Program (PEP) in reading and math is administered statewide each year to third- and sixth-grade pupils in both public and private schools. Children who score below the established "state reference point" on the PEP test become eligible for remedial help. A Preliminary Competency Test (PCT) in reading and writing is used to identify students who might have trouble passing the minimum competency tests in high school. Regents Examinations are offered in twenty-two subject areas each year for students in grades nine through twelve. These examinations are used as a standard of excellence. Students who pass them and complete appropriate course work are granted the distinction of receiving a Regents high school diploma. The state also administers a high school equivalency examination for individuals who do not finish four years of high school, but who wish to demonstrate proficiency on five general education development tests in order to obtain an equivalency diploma.

It is not difficult to understand the Regents' motivation for implementing a new test that would determine eligibility for a regular high school diploma. Except for Alaska, where the costs of nonacademic support services are unusually high, New York spends more money per child on education than any other state in the nation. The results of this level of expenditure had not been commensurate with the cost. There had been widespread public dissatisfaction with the level of competency exhibited by high school graduates, and this dissatisfaction was voiced by political, business, and community leaders in all corners of the state. A major force behind the new competency examination was Dr. Kenneth Clark, the psychologist and educator, who was the only black member of the Board of Regents. Clark was a major figure in the civil rights movement in the United States. He had served as a key expert witness on behalf of the plaintiff in the famous *Brown* v. *Board of Education* Supreme Court case, where he testified about the psychological damage inflicted on black children as a result of segregated schooling. He was a strong believer in state competency standards as a mechanism for assuring quality education for poor and minority youngsters. Clark brought a lot of credibility to the competency debate, on behalf of the test.

However, the test had its problems and its opponents. New York was proposing to establish the most rigorous standards for high school graduation in the nation. But no such standards existed in the lower grades. There was great concern about the potential outcome of the test. Almost immediately after the first battery of BCTs was administered in 1978, the Puerto Rican Legal Defense Fund in New York City filed a complaint with the United States Office for Civil Rights, alleging that the test had a disparate impact on Hispanic students. Other major opponents who spoke out against the test were the New York State United Teachers and the New York State School Boards Association.

On January 11, the state Commissioner of Education and the Regents held a public hearing in New York City to discuss the merits of the newly proposed standards. Among the participants at the hearings was City Schools Chancellor Frank Macchiarola, who used the occasion to join the ranks of those who had come out in opposition to the new standards. He argued: "I believe that a hasty and ill-considered implementation of what is, potentially, an extremely useful educational strategy may undermine the very educational process that it seeks to support.[42] The chancellor had made it clear that he was not opposed to the new competency requirements in principle. What he objected to was what he saw as a sudden imposition of new standards that were not consistent with either the present curriculum or any existing state curriculum. He was also concerned that while the state was establishing new standards for graduation, it was not providing any means of remediation for those students who did not pass the proposed examinations. Macchiarola recommended that both the BCT and the RCT testing programs be phased in "to assure that all students have been provided a reasonable opportunity to meet the standards."[43] He urged the Regents to consider a comprehensive approach that would integrate competency testing, diploma requirements, and a promotional policy for the elementary grades. He also suggested that local school boards be allowed to grant their own diplomas to students who met the requirements of a state-endorsed curriculum or program but did not pass the new examinations.

At the close of these hearings, the Regents voted to provide one additional offering of the BCT examinations in August 1979 for students who had not passed in either January or June. They also decided, however, not to request state funds from the legislature for remedial programs. In the meantime, they proceeded with their plans to approve the more difficult RCTs on March 1. Soon thereafter, the chancellor made arrangements to go ahead with his own remediation program to help students pass the state examinations. In the absence of any funds, the effort was organized on a volunteer basis in cooperation with David Seeley of the Public Education Association and members of the Board of Education's School Volunteers Corps. In all, approximately 4,000 volunteers contributed to the "Campaign for Competency." The chancellor's office was still predicting, however, that more than 7,000 students would not graduate because of their failure to meet the test requirements.

By February the chancellor had convinced State Education Commissioner Gordon Ambach to add an amendment to the proposed competency standards that would allow the granting of "certificates of achievement" to students who did not pass the examinations but had completed their course work for high school. Under this plan, students would be entitled to a free education in pursuit of a high school diploma until they reached the age of twenty-one. Macchiarola offered public praise to the commissioner for his conciliatory action, saying, "The commissioner appears to be responding to the need to treat children fairly."[44] But not all were in agreement. Regent Kenneth Clark condemned the certificate-of-competency plan, calling it a "Jim Crow diploma."[45] Several of Clark's colleagues on the state board saw the certificates as a way of undermining what they were trying to accomplish with the new standards. On February 9 a seven-member Regents Committee on Elementary and Secondary Education directed Commissioner Ambach to revise his proposal and remove the certificate plan.

On February 28, the day before the Regents were expected to take their final vote, Macchiarola sent a letter to Ambach, threatening to ignore the Regents' decision. He said that he would use his own "broad powers" as chancellor to issue local certificates of achievement rather than deny them to more than 7,200 students. Macchiarola argued that any regulation forbidding local districts to award certificates was inapplicable in New York City, since state law gives the chancellor authority to determine all educational policies for the city school district, including the establishment of minimum educational standards. As might be expected, the letter to Ambach did not sway the opinions of the Regents. In fact, it only added to their determination. State Regent Louis Yavner reacted in a punitive way and scolded the chancellor publicly, declaring, "New York City must be shamed. . . . It must wear a scarlet letter."[46]

On March 1 the Regents voted unanimously to approve a new set of regulations, deeming that "New York now has the highest diploma standards for foundation skills in the nation."[47] Under these regulations, students scheduled to graduate in 1981 would be expected to pass the RCTs in reading, writing, and math unless they had passed the BCTs before 1979. Students would also be given an option to use scores from the College Entrance Examination or American College Testing Program in order to demonstrate competency. The regulations authorized the use of alternative testing procedures for handicapped and bilingual students. That same day, the Regents voted 9–6 to approve the awarding of certificates to special-education students with retarded mental development who had passed their Individualized Education Programs (IEPs). Then, after a two-and-one-half-hour debate, the Regents voted 10–5 against the issuing of certificates of achievement.

During the spring of 1979, the city Board of Education, in cooperation with the Public Education Association, continued its volunteer-based "Campaign for Competency" to help students get through the state examinations. In addition to this effort, the chancellor put aside $200,000 to set up a tutoring program during the spring recess. When the results of the BCT examination were announced that July, the outcome was not nearly as gloomy as had originally been expected. Of the 42,908 seniors registered in the city's 112 high schools, only 956 were denied graduation because of their poor performance on the BCTs. That summer, 973 students, including juniors and seniors, registered for remedial classes.[48]

The test scores released in July 1979 allowed for only a brief sigh of relief. As the city school district moved to bring its students to the required competency level, the Regents were taking further measures to enforce their higher standards. On July 27 the state board, in a 13–1 vote, proposed a new regulation that would place on probation any high school that had a student pass rate of less than 85 percent in the statewide competency examinations. Such probationary status would jeopardize the authority of a school to grant diplomas and its eligibility for state and federal funding. To make matters worse, while students entering their senior year in 1980 could still qualify for graduation by passing the BCTs, those eligible for graduation thereafter would be required to take the more difficult RCTs. These new exams began to be administered to students during the 1979–1980 school year.

In the summer of 1979, the chancellor assembled a Regents Competency Test Task Force, which was given the assignment of revising the basic high school curriculum so that it was consistent with the standards set in the new state examination. This task force of central school personnel would also be responsible for the development of training programs for staff and remedial programs for students. These programs were in place by September. In the meantime, however, the administration continued its campaign against the new standards. In an extensive interview with *The New York Times* that fall, Nathan Quinones, executive director of the Division of High Schools, complained:

> We think it terribly unfair to immediately implement a more difficult test when that test has not been validated and when we don't have a clear curriculum to base the test on. These examinations should be phased in over a period of time.[49]

In January, as the new tests were to be administered for the first time, the chancellor issued his own public statement. He again made the point that a uniform curriculum should have preceded the establishment of a standard exam—this time comparing the Regents program to his own Promotional Policy, which was then in its developmental stage. He explained, ". . . my model has been reversed. . . . We have been asked to administer tests in the absence of validated standards and a curriculum."[50]

On March 29, 1980, the administration, upon the advice of Nathan Quinones, submitted a set of recommendations to the Board of Education regarding new local requirements for the high school diploma.[51] There was nothing in the proposal that contradicted or undermined the state standards. However, it was also meant to be consistent with the new Promotional Policy for grades kindergarten through 9 that the chancellor had introduced in November. Moreover, there was an important message in the local diploma requirements that were finally adopted in June. It emphasized that while the administration was supportive of the effort to upgrade basic skills, it would not do so at the expense of a wider variety of programs. Among other things, the regulations included a new foreign language requirement, the establishment of a new global history curriculum, and more "hands on" experience in such areas as shop classes, home economics, and business. The number of credits required for graduation was increased from 38 to 40.

In the summer of 1980 the High Schools Division began experimenting with a Mastery Learning Program, a technique developed by Professor Benjamin Bloom of the University of Chicago. Bloom had been a participant in the original conference held at Sterling Forest by the Macchiarola transition team in May 1978. His approach asserts that, with appropriate instruction, all students can "master" basic subject matter.[52] It includes several major components:

- the formulation of a set of behavioral objectives that all students should achieve;
- frequent formative/diagnostic evaluation;
- corrective or rememdial instruction for students who have not achieved their objectives;
- an overall evaluation on the basis of what has been taught.

These basic tenets of Mastery Learning, which were adopted by the High School Division on an experimental basis, were consistent with the overall philosophy of the administration, the characteristics of success identified in the literature on effective schools, and the effort to raise competency standards.

Throughout the 1980–1981 school year, the High Schools Division continued, and in fact stepped up, its remedial efforts with regard to the RCTs. By then, the chancellor had restructured his central budget so that local tax levy funds and federal aid dollars could be channeled into the program. Nevertheless, as the June 1981 test date came closer, the anxiety level of both students and staff rose higher. On June 18, Chancellor Macchiarola sent a twenty-two-page letter to Willard A. Genrich, chancellor of the New York State Board of Regents, once again registering his disagreement with the impending examinations. However, this document was more than a letter of protest. Prepared by his Office of Legal Services, it read like a scholarly research brief, outlining the legal issues, the constitutional issues, and the precedent case law. It touched upon all relevant points: inadequate notice, test validity and reliability, the absence of a standard core curriculum, the denial of remedial services, and differences in impact. What the letter amounted to was a veiled threat of a lawsuit against the state.

The results of the Regents Competency Examination were announced during the last week of July. Of the 42,363 seniors who were to have graduated in 1981, only 716, or 1.7 percent, were denied diplomas because of unsatisfactory performance on the statewide examination. Given the severity of the examination and the dire consequences that had been anticipated, these results were both a surprise and a tribute to all concerned. Perhaps they were also a testimony to the efficacy of the remediation campaign that had been launched. The outcome of the test results was to make the debate over state competency standards moot in New York.

PROMOTIONAL POLICY: THE INITIAL DESIGN

If there was one thing that the debate over state competency standards accomplished, it was to give the administration at Livingston Street a clear sense of how it wanted to design its own Promotional Policy for the elementary and middle grades. The draft policy document made public in November 1979 was based on the intial recommendations of the Task Force on Graduation Requirements, Promotion Policies, and Minimum Competencies, which had worked under the direction of Ron Edmonds for one year. The proposed Promotional Policy was composed of five major parts:

1. a citywide standard curriculum;
2. a testing program;
3. clearly defined promotional standards;
4. promotional gates;
5. a remediation program.[53]

A proposed *citywide standard curriculum,* which was introduced the same week as the draft policy document, was an integral part of Promotional Policy. These "Minimum Teaching Essentials," as they were called, were designed to "ensure that all students receive sequentially planned instruction enabling them to acquire mastery of basic skills for each grade."[54] If the policy were successful, children at specific grade levels throughout the city would be given a basic body of instruction within a similar time frame and would show a minimum level of proficiency in reading, writing, and mathematics. Districts, however, were encouraged to "enrich" these minimum essentials with their own materials, "provided that assurances are given that the basic curriculum requirements are met." The purpose behind this curriculum was to establish minimum teaching standards for staff, as a first step towards minimum competency standards for students. Thus the citywide curriculum was scheduled for implementation one year before the promotional standards. This curriculum for kindergarten through grade nine was designed to be consistent with the high school curriculum being planned to prepare students for the Regents Competency Tests.

The draft Promotional Policy called for the use of *criterion-referenced tests* in reading, writing, and mathematics, to be administered as an aid to determining grade placement beginning in 1982. These tests were to measure student achievement in relation to the citywide standard curriculum—that is, students were to be evaluated on the basis of the materials they were taught. Up until this time, the annual citywide examination given to comply with the State Decentralization Law had been "norm-referenced." Norm-referenced exams evaluate students in the context of a broader group, i.e., a national "norm" or grade level. The criterion-referenced test called for under the Promotional Policy would evaluate students according to a specified absolute score. In the spring of 1980 the Board of Education began experimenting in community school districts 8, 16, and 24 with a state-developed instrument called the Degree of Reading Power test (DRP). The DRP was a criterion-referenced test that could also be used for diagnostic purposes and instructional planning.[55] The chancellor hoped to adopt this examination on a citywide basis after one or two years of experimentation. In the meantime, the administration's plan was to use the norm-referenced test on a temporary basis. This examination was believed to be consistent with the citywide curriculum, and it made possible year-to-year comparisons on a citywide basis.

The heart of the chancellor's proposed policy was the promulgation of *promotional standards.* Here both the policy and the purpose were quite clear:

Student promotion will be determined by the degree to which the student has mastered the basic skills required in each grade. Automatic advancement from grade to grade without evidence of achieving required performance standards in basic skills places an unfair burden on students in succeeding grades. The early mastery of basic skills will help ensure that today's elementary school student is not tomorrow's high school dropout.[56]

Once again, the administration was making a connection between competency standards in the earlier grades and those imposed at the high school level—portraying the former as a logical foundation for the latter. However, except for the grades governed by the promotional gates (4 and 8), the administration left some discretion at the district level for interpretation and enforcement of the broad policy. Instead of mandating, it recommended specific guidelines for promotion, consistent with the criteria set at the promotional gates. These included:

- satisfactory completion of academic areas of study;
- achievement of a standardized reading score of not more than one (in grades 2, 3, 4, 5, 6) or one and one-half (in grades 7 and 8) years below grade level; after 1982, norm-referenced tests were to be replaced by criterion-referenced tests in all basic skills;
- achievement of required performance standards on basic skills criterion-referenced tests;
- satisfactory attendance, behavior, and punctuality.

The proposed *promotional gates* to be established in grades four and eight were designed to serve as checkpoints, and the criteria for promotion set here were rigid. Achievement of a standardized reading score of one year below grade level in the fourth grade or one and one-half years below grade level in the eighth grade would mean denial of promotion. A math score of two years below grade level at either of the gates meant the same. These norm-referenced standards would be replaced by criterion-referenced standards in 1982. Grade 4 was selected as a gate because relevant literature seemed to suggest that the sequence from reading readiness to reading comprehension should be completed at that point. Grade 8 was selected because it is, for many students, the last year before high school. The administration went to great lengths to demonstrate that it was not treating retention lightly. The proposed policy statement read as follows:

The retention of a student is a most serious step which, if improperly handled, can have a severe negative effect on the student. Emphasis on student retention should be in the elementary grades. . . . The purpose of retention is to ensure that students so retained are provided opportunities for success through programs designed for their needs and capacities.[57]

All students not meeting the standards in the gate grades would receive *remedial instruction* similar to that given in the transitional classes. A special summer program would be set up for eighth-graders to give them the opportunity to advance to high school before September. Fourth-grade holdovers would receive remediation in the following school year. The administration was careful not to set up gates or mandate retention in any grades where it could not provide remediation. In fact, the original policy statement specified quite clearly that the establishment of the gates was contingent on the availability of funds for remedial programs.

The draft Promotional Policy allowed for certain exceptions in the case of special-education and bilingual students. In select cases, alternative testing methods would be made available to handicapped children, and in a limited number of cases, depending on the child's individualized program, special-education students would be exempt from participation. Students enrolled in bilingual education programs for less than four years and found to be of limited proficiency in English would be tested in both English and their native languages, the proportion being determined by the number of years a student had been in a bilingual program. Students in bilingual programs for more than four years, or proficient in English, would take the exam in English.

A hidden issue behind the Promotional Policy concept was that of staff accountability. Ron Edmonds, the policy's chief architect, had seen a long-term potential in the policy for use in staff evaluation. This was not a part of the original design because it was not the major purpose of the policy. The administration did not want to make Promotional Policy a union issue. It wanted to put the policy in place with teacher support. But the potential use was there, and it was obvious. As Edmonds explained:

> The other side of it all is that the program will allow us to evaluate teachers and principals. We will find teachers and principals that are not performing. You know what I mean—if teachers and principals working within the same socioeconomic environments are having more trouble getting their kids through the gates, it tells us more about the professionals than about the kids. That is the genius of the program. The policy is now being offered with an emphasis on the child, but I see it as a basis of professional accountability. I have avoided the latter issue in our past discourse because I don't want to complicate matters. I don't want to fight

that battle now, but that is the obvious question that must come about.[58]

The administration extended itself to cover all bases in the design of Promotional Policy, to make the program workable. It planned to implement a standard curriculum before imposing competency standards. It would try to assure that instructional materials were consistent with test content. It was committed to providing remediation for children held over in the gate grades. The policy would be phased in gradually, and handicapped or bilingual children who could not be expected to perform at the desired level of proficiency would be given special consideration. The design of the Promotional Policy was one of the most self-conscious and deliberate efforts of the administration.

The chancellor did not want to be susceptible to the same kind of criticism he himself had so forcefully directed at the state. However, in some measure, the issues were not the same. From a legal perspective, the courts had applied the due process clause to test the legality of competency standards for high school graduation because they had deemed possession of a diploma a property right. No diplomas were at stake in the Promotional Policy, and there had been no firm legal precedent on the issue of grade-to-grade advancement. Instructionally, the appropriate phase-in period for a policy governing fourth- or eighth-grade advancement could not be expected to be as long as one related to a twelfth-year diploma. Moreover, by the time Promotional Policy was proposed, competency testing was already in practice under state law. Thus one of the strongest arguments on behalf of a Promotional Policy for the lower grades was the existence of state competency standards for high school graduation. If implemented effectively Promotional Policy would help prepare children for high school.

Despite the care that went into the policy design, there were still critics outside the administration who would not accept it. Some rejected competency testing as a legitimate concept; others had problems with the way the administration would put the policy into practice. Thus Promotional Policy became a highly charged educational and political issue in New York City.

ROUND TWO: COMPETENCY STANDARDS AS A LOCAL ISSUE

The chancellor had made a commitment to a Promotional Policy from the beginning of his tenure. The forces behind the demand for higher competency standards in the city were as strong as those at the state level. Among the major advocates was Mayor Edward Koch, who had frequently expressed outrage at the poor performance levels of children in the public school system. The first set of citywide reading scores to be announced by the Macchiarola administration appeared in March 1979. The scores were based on the California Achievement Test, which had been taken by pupils in grades 2 through 9 in the previous March, four months before the new administration formally took office. The results showed that only 43 percent of the pupils who took the exam scored at or above grade level on a national scale. To make matters worse, there was a discernible pattern showing that the longer a child stayed in school, the further below grade level he or she fell. Ron Edmonds referred to this pattern as the "accumulated academic deficits of inferior instruction."[60] A *Daily News* editorial aptly described the overall test results as a "Sorry Showing" for New York.[61] The outcome contribued to a heightened criticism of the City's public schools and added to the outrage of the mayor.

The tests taken by city schoolchildren in March 1979 were scored within two months. Because local law requires competitive bidding on the purchase of such tests, a different one was administered this year from the one given previously. The scores for the Metropolitan Achievement Test (MAT) showed erratic results. There were very great gains in some grades and significant losses in others. On May 14, Macchiarola ordered that the test scores be withheld pending an investigation of their validity.[62] He directed that decisions on student promotions should be made primarily according to teacher judgment and classroom performance. He withheld payment from the Psychological Corporation, from which the examinations had been purchased. Within two weeks, the chancellor announced that the tests had been found invalid.[63] He ordered that a new test be administered on June 6 and decided to use the California Achievement Test. The decision caused some dissension among personnel in the community school districts, who were not pleased with the prospect of administering another exam and were not accustomed to such strong direction from the central office. One community school board in Manhattan (District 3) refused to administer the test and sought a court injunction against it. Macchiarola got the injunction overturned by a State Appellate Division Court, used his powers under the Decentralization Law to supersede the community school board, and sent in his own trustees to administer the new exam on June 6.

Apart from the validity issue, using the California Achievement Test again carried another distinct advantage, comparability. Longitudinal analysis of systemwide progress is not possible unless the same test is used consistently over time. However, the need to disqualify the previous examination struck a severe blow to the credibility of standardized tests in general. It raised significant questions regarding their use in making educational decisions about individual children, and added fuel to the ongoing campaign against competency testing. The results of the test, announced in June, showed that only 40.3 percent of the city schoolchildren in elementary and middle schools were reading at or above grade level. This was even less than the 43 percent rate recorded in the previous year.[64]

On October 30 the Public Education Association hosted a Convocation for Competence in Manhattan. Among the honored guests was Mayor Edward Koch, who called for a "crackdown" that would flunk students who can't read, and end social promotion. That same week Charlotte Frank, executive director of curriculum and instruction for the New York City public schools, announced a conference for community school district and high school superintendents. The conference, to be held on November 13, was to introduce the newly proposed citywide standard curriculum for kindergarten through grade nine. Each district was invited to send six representatives. It was urged that the individuals chosen should be "key people" who were instructional leaders in the district.[65] Present at the conference would be the chancellor, who would describe the intent of the new curriculum; Ron Edmonds, who would explain its relationship to Promotional Policy; and State Regent Louise Matteoni, who would discuss its implications regarding the state competency program. The afternoon would be devoted to workshops, run by the Division of Curriculum and Instruction, that would focus on the design and content of the new citywide curriculum.

On November 7 the chancellor made public the draft of his proposed Promotional Policy. This document for general review was to be the subject of public hearings by the Board of Education on December 6. It was expected that the Board would approve some form of this proposal by the end of the school year. The chancellor proposed his Promotional Policy, under the authority granted to him by the Decentralization Law, to establish minimum educational standards and curriculum requirements for all schools throughout the city school district. As the press release that accompanied the nine-page document stated, this was the first time that a New York City chancellor had exercised his responsibility in such a way.[66] Chancellor Irving Anker had prepared a draft promotional-standards document at the end of his tenure, but in anticipation of his departure the Board of Education decided to table it and await the selection of a new chancellor.

Promotional Policy would introduce a new element in the relationship between community school districts and central administration. However, it was part of a distinct pattern of governance emerging under Macchiarola's leadership. This chancellor would use his authority to the fullest to implement his policies. Macchiarola had made a philosophical commitment to focus on the elementary grades, and that meant a series of centrally administered initiatives in the school districts. From a managerial perspective, focusing on the high schools would have been easier, since the executive director of that division is appointed by, and reports to, the chancellor. However, the administration chose to move ahead with such projects as reduced class sizes in the first grade, Transitional Classes, the School Improvement Project, and now, Promotional Policy. The district reaction to Promotional Policy was mixed at first. Some community school board members and superintendents saw it as an infringement on their own prerogatives, others were supportive, but most greeted the new policy with sincere skepticism as to its feasibility. Livingston Street in their eyes was the "world of the can't be done." Why should things be different now? Was this a serious effort at educational reform? Or was it a political maneuver carried out at the behest of the mayor? Did the administration really know what it was doing? Was it committed to doing things right?

Alfred Melov, who was a community superintendent in Brooklyn and the president of the Citywide Association of Community Superintendents, explained the general district reaction as follows:

> When Promotional Policy was proposed, I didn't look upon it seriously. It looked like pie in the sky. I didn't expect them to get the funds for it. . . .
> The initial reaction of the Superintendents was pro. They agreed philosophically. Many believed, however, that money was the key. . . .
> A strong Chancellor would have moved in this direction years ago. We needed minimum standards. There had been an abdication of leadership by the Chancellor. The Superintendents were forced to build their own policies. It caused inequity and a lack of continuity in the city. . . .
> Once you give up that power, however, it's hard to get it back. Superintendents are suspicious of the central Board of Education and are extremely jealous of their own prerogatives.[67]

Philip Kaplan, president of a community school board in Brooklyn and also head of the New York City Community School Boards Association, offered another cynical view:

> I am not a supporter of Promotional Policy. . . . I could be convinced.
> I agree with the principle of Promotional Policy. You have to stop promoting kids who can't read. . . . But there are problems

with the program. It hasn't been packaged together yet. They don't have the money. What programs do we have to cut to do this?[68]

The district reaction to Promotional Policy was very telling. Superintendents and school board members did not respond to it purely as an issue of control. What they seemed to be telling the administration was, "If you're going to assume authority over educational policy, first show us what you can do with it." They had seen competency tests imposed at the high school level, without the resources available for support services. They were fearful that the same scenario would be played out in the districts with Promotional Policy. The major concern on everyone's mind was remediation. The administration had stated in its draft it would not require retention for any child if there were no funds for remediation. But most people in the districts were not convinced that the political forces behind Promotional Policy would allow the administration to abide by that pledge.

There was also opposition to Promotional Policy on philosophical grounds. Among the strongest of the opponents was Meryl Schwartz, president of the United Parents Associations (UPA). Schwartz had no confidence in competency tests as an instrument for evaluating pupil performance. She and her organization took the position that a policy requiring children to be held over was punitive and unfair. They demanded measures against unsatisfactory teachers instead of against pupils, whom they regarded as the victims of ineffective instruction. Schwartz was to remain one of the most outspoken critics of Promotional Policy in the city, and her group would be joined by others, such as Advocates for Children. These were formidable opponents, and their viewpoint had to be taken seriously. They were not enemies of public education; they were not among those who had given up on the school system. They represented a significant part of the educational establishment in New York.

These influential groups, however, did not represent the entire clientele of the city school system. There was considerable support for Promotional Policy within the minority community, whose children made up a large majority of students. This support was reflected among the community superintendents. As Alfred Melov explained, "Minority superintendents are supportive. It's the white middle-class liberals that are opponents."[69] Influential members of the black community had also supported competency standards at the state level. The previous spring (1979) the Reverend Carl E. Flemister, executive director of the American Baptist Churches of Metropolitan New York, had made a public appeal for greater emphasis on basic skills in public education.

His organization had endorsed the Regents program advocated by Dr. Kenneth Clark, although it urged that remediation must be a key component of the competency program. Like Clark, the ministers saw competency standards as a means toward achieving quality education for black children. Minority parents also seemed supportive of tougher standards generally and of Promotional Policy in particular. Anthony Alvarado, then community superintendent of District 4 in East Harlem, has pointed out that such support seems to be consistent with a more general outlook among the less advantaged:

> Most lower-middle- and lower-class parents are hard-nosed. They say that if a student doesn't do well, he should be left back. Therefore, minority parents support Promotional Policy.[70]

Meryl Schwartz of the UPA, however, offered a more cynical view of minority support for the new policy:

> Supposedly minority parents love it. They are the most vulnerable people. We [the schools] never did anything for them anyway. Minority parents have faith in test scores because they don't have confidence in teacher judgment.[71]

The Board of Education held its public hearings on adoption of the proposed Promotional Policy on December 6. The hearings got considerable attention in the local press. Several days before they were held, the *New York Daily News* announced that the Board of Education would be meeting to hear testimony on "one of the most revolutionary proposals it has offered in some time."[72] The turnout was so large that it was necessary for the Board to schedule an additional day of hearings. Representatives of more than a half-dozen local community school boards offered formal testimony. Most agreed with the policy in principle, although many asked for more discretion at the district level, and nearly all were concerned about the availability of funds for remedial programs. Alfred Melov, speaking on behalf of the Citywide Association of Community Superintendents, complimented the chancellor for "seeking to establish curriculum standards for achievement"[73] but raised a number of questions considering the implementation of the new policy:

- Should it be adopted when funding is problematic and unsure?
- Are the gates at the appropriate grades? Why not three and seven instead of four and eight?
- Will there be adequate planning at the school level for pupils who don't pass the gates?

- Will there be changes in the use of Title I and state aid to allow for more effective use to help marginal learners?
- Will there be effective overall planning and development regarding curriculum standards and the tests?

Melov closed his testimony with a statement that fairly well described the sentiments of the superintendents he was representing: "In summary, we look with favor upon the broad base draft, but we in the field take the position of the natives of Missouri, 'We have to be shown.' "[74]

Meryl Schwartz spoke on behalf of the United Parents Associations. She began her presentation with a discussion of her philosophical disagreements with the policy of retention and the burden it places on pupils rather than on school personnel. She criticized the administration for not consulting more with parents in the original design of the program. Then she read off her organization's own list of practical questions about the implementation of the program. Among these were:

- What support services will be provided for holdovers?
- Should the gates be established if dollar resources and supports are not in hand?
- What tests will be used until criterion-referenced tests are developed and validated? Is it valid to use norm-referenced tests to hold students over?
- Can youngsters be held over repeatedly? If so, is that acceptable?
- Are the fourth and eighth grades appropriate for the gates?
- Will all holdover classes be organized for fewer than twenty? Twenty-five?[75]

Carla Precht of Advocates for Children began her testimony by saying that her organization supported Promotional Policy in principle, but presented a litany of questions and concerns similar to those from Meryl Schwartz. The Coalition of Organizations and Advocates for Children with Handicaps, representing twenty-two separate organizations, expressed general disagreement with the policy and particular concern with the provisions governing special-education students. Several groups representing different sectors of the bilingual community in the city attended the hearings and, while offering general support of the principles behind the Promotional Policy, were fearful of the impact it would have on students whose dominant language was not English. Addressing the issue in a more critical tone, the Puerto Rican Educators Association castigated the plan, which, it claimed punished students but did not hold staff accountable.

Individuals and organizations who came to the hearings to offer support for the proposed Promotional Policy carried the weight of some rather influential sectors of the New York community. They included David Seeley of the Public Education Association and Lloyd Cooke of the Economic Development Council of New York City. But perhaps the most important supportive remarks were those made by Sandra Feldman of the United Federation of Teachers, who said, "We've come to praise you, not to bury you." The UFT agreed with the basic philosophy and purpose of Promotional Policy. It had been intimately involved in its actual design. If implemented according to its original plan, the proposal would also result in more jobs for teachers. While UFT support for the program would not guarantee its passage, strong opposition from the union would have severely weakened its chances.

The Council of Supervisors and Administrators (CSA), which represents supervisory personnel in the school system, was more guarded in its support than was the teachers' union. That organization's spokesperson at the hearings expressed a concern with the "logistics" of implementation. However, the fact of the matter was that there was a real split within the CSA. High school principals were generally in favor of promotional policy because it raised the hope that students received from the lower grades would be better prepared. Middle school principals were lukewarm at best, because an implication in the policy suggested that the administration might be moving toward a kindergarten-through-eighth-grade organization that would eliminate the middle schools. Elementary school principals were downright skeptical because it was they who would have to deal with the holdovers and whatever hardships resulted. Thus CSA President Ted Elsberg explained:

> We are for standards. We support it. We are concerned with the implementation. High School principals are 100 percent for Promotional Policy. Elementary and junior high school principals are against it. Elementary school principals are most concerned with implementation. They have doubts about the funds for remedial programs. Many of them think that this is being done just because it looks good.[76]

As the public hearings came to a close, the administration drew nearly unanimous praise from the local media concerning the proposal it had put forward and the goals it had set out to accomplish. A *Daily News* editorial entitled "Strong Medicine" cited Promotional Policy as an end to the "anything goes era of public education."[77] A *New York Times* editorial entitled "An End to Social Promotions" described the previous practice as a "mixture of kindness and defeatism." It noted that "Mr. Macchiarola can't yet answer all the doubts," but pointed out, in the terms of the administration's philosophy:

> There is some evidence, in any case, that the most effective schools in poor neighborhoods are those that set high academic standards and keep evaluating their pupils' progress. The chancellor's new Promotional Policy is an encouraging step in that direction.[78]

Despite the good press, there was still a great deal of work to be done. Many professionals within the system who accepted the policy in principle had little faith in the administration's ability to carry through on what it had said it would do. There were questions about the details. There was widespread skepticism that the mayor and the city would not provide the necessary funds for remedial programs, and even its most ardent advocates believed that Promotional Policy could not be effective without funds.

Six months were to pass before the Board of Education reached a final resolution on the chancellor's proposal. Board approval was expected. In the meantime, however, the administration "took to the streets." Macchiarola and Edmonds began meetings with PTAs, good-government groups, community school boards, and all others concerned, in order to build confidence in the administration's program and make revisions that would render it workable. Edmonds put together an advisory group of seven community superintendents and concentrated on hammering out some of the details on implementation.

The Board of Education took its final vote on Promotional Policy at the same June meeting in which it approved the new local requirements for the high school diploma. As expected, it approved an amended version of the draft proposal submitted by the chancellor in November 1979. Most of the revisions in the policy document had been recommended by the administration after consultations with a large variety of groups over the previous six months.[79] Among these was a change in the later gate grade from 8 to 7. This was done in order to allow for remediation before a child entered a terminal grade. However, in changing this gate grade, the administration also stiffened the promotional standard. It required that any student one year below grade level in reading (instead of the original one and one-half years) be held over.

The administration also changed the policy with regard to bilingual students. It required any student in a bilingual program for less than four years to take standard examinations in reading and math in "English as a second language." The previous proposal would have allowed such students to take the examination in both English and their native languages, the proportion being determined by the amount of time spent in the bilingual program. In making this change, the administration was emphasizing the "transitional" rather than the "maintenance" goals of the bilingual program. In making his recommendations to the board for revisions, the chancellor also built in a new appeals procedure for parents who might feel that the holdover of their child was not justifiable or in line with the new regulation. This procedure would go from the school level, to the community superintendent, to the community school board, and finally to the chancellor.

The Board of Education approved all the revisions the administration recommended in the final Promotional Policy document. However, it also made one change that the administration had not recommended. That change was the removal of the all-important funding contingency. This reversal not only took the chancellor's office by surprise but went against everything the administration had promised in its campaign to win support for the policy. As Ron Edmonds explained:

> I had said that Promotional Policy would not go ahead without the funding for the remedial program. That was my public position. That was Frank's [Macchiarola's] position. The Board of Education decided to delete the funding piece on the day that they adopted the policy. I was damned surprised. They said that they thought the policy was wise and sound. They believed that it was so important that they would go ahead no matter what. It made Frank and me look like liars. We had said publicly that we would not go ahead without money.[80]

In removing the funding contingency, the board members informed the chancellor that they were not going to tie educational standards to money. In the words of Board member Amelia Ashe, they instructed him to "make every effort, absolutely every effort, to make sure it gets funded and implemented."[81] However, by removing the funding contingency, the Board actually weakened the chances that the policy would get funded. It weakened the incentive for the mayor. It got the politicians off the hook. The Board gave them a policy at no cost. In so doing, it weakened support for the policy in the field— among the superintendents, among the principals, and among the teachers. Promotional Policy was adopted as everyone had feared it would be, without the proper supports. But everyone also knew that, no matter what the Board or the chancellor adopted at the policy level, what happened in the field would determine the real viability of the program. If lack of funds didn't kill the program, lack of cooperation at the district and school levels could.

ROUND THREE: FROM ADOPTION TO IMPLEMENTATION

As the administration approached the beginning of the 1980–1981 school year, the tasks before it were quite clear. First, it had to prove to the people in the field that, despite the removal of the funding contingency, it had every intention to implement Promotional Policy according to the original design. Thus the summer of 1980 was devoted to planning how to translate the initial policy concept into a set of workable programs. Second, the administration had to convince people in the field that although the Board of Education was prepared to move ahead without funding, money for Promotional Policy would be forthcoming. This would not be accomplished easily, since the administration had suffered a loss of credibility as a result of the Board's last-minute decision. Finally, and most important, the chancellor had actually to produce from the mayor and the local legislature the funds that were needed. However, since those municipal officials had already gotten what they wanted from the Board of Education, the chancellor was in a rather weak bargaining position.

All the signs coming from Livingston Street seemed to indicate that Promotional Policy was moving ahead without any ambivalence. The Board of Education had given final approval to the citywide standard curriculum in June. In September the Division of Curriculum and Instruction began to work with the districts to develop instructional programs to be used as models for the remedial effort required by Promotional Policy. While the administration was preparing its own remediation effort for the gate grades, it wanted to encourage the districts to cooperate in developing their own programs for the other grades. The announcement of a 6.4 percent improvement in the citywide reading scores that September was certainly expected to put the chancellor in a stronger position to negotiate for the money needed. Moreover, these scores, which showed that 53.3 percent of the children in grades two through nine were still reading below grade level, served to emphasize once more that serious action had to be taken to raise the competency levels in the city schools.

When the chancellor submitted his budget message to the Board of Education on December 15, the $63 million figure he attached to Promotional Policy was based on an estimate that 43,000 students would be held over—17,000 from the fourth grade, and 26,000 from the seventh grade.[82] Approximately $39 million of the total would be used to hire 1,539 teachers for remedial classes, and $2.1 million would be for teacher training. A central staff of thirty-eight people was expected to cost $1.5 million, and contractual fringe benefits were projected to cost $17.5 million. The remaining money would be allocated for test development and the purchasing of materials. The administration was planning to divert $29 million of its federal and state reimbursable funds into its remediation. This left $34 million that it was requesting from the city.

On December 22 Ron Edmonds distributed a preliminary draft of the chancellor's rules, regulations, and programs for the implementation of Promotional Policy. The draft was sent to all community school board presidents and superintendents "to give you some sense of our work thus far, but primarily so that you may know the instructional programs we are recommending for your consideration."[83] The superintendents were asked to react to the programs and provide alternatives to those with which they disagreed. However, the preamble of the document stated the basic policy directive in no uncertain terms: "The administration remains committed to the basic educability of all the children we serve."[84] In accordance with this, the document explained, the administration had adopted a uniform curriculum, committed itself to a citywide testing program based on the curriculum, and instituted a variety of school improvement projects. It explained further that Promotional Policy "obtains to each grade in the basic skills areas" and is not confined to grades 4 and 7. It noted that the significance of grades 4 and 7 "derives only from the central administration's monitoring of promotion practices of those grades and centrally supportive services for students who fail those grades."[85] In closing, the draft regulations declared, "We fully anticipate that all districts will enforce this policy at each grade and will appropriately respond to students making inadequate progress at any grade."[86]

The administration was doing all it could to convince the district people that Promotional Policy was a reality with which they would have to deal. However, its campaign to develop credibility in its new programs was still an uphill battle. The financial plan announced by the mayor in January carried an endorsement of the chancellor's Promotional Policy, but stated clearly that funds were not yet available for remediation. This announcement only added to the skepticism of those who were undecided and fueled the efforts of those who were opposed. The latter launched a last-ditch effort, aided by the uncertainty of the mayor and the vulnerability of the chancellor to persuade the Board of Education and the administration to postpone the implementation of Promotional Policy to a later date.

In February 1981 the chancellor appointed Thomas Minter Deputy Chancellor for Instruction to succeed Ron Edmonds, who was returning to the university. Changing the title of the top instructional position in the administration from Senior Assistant, which Edmonds held, to Deputy Chancellor, which was given to Minter, symbolized the differing needs and expectations the two men fulfilled. Edmonds, who had been recruited from the university, served as a senior policy adviser. He was a planner and a thinker, whose job was to design the overall instructional agenda of the administration. Minter was recruited from the federal bureaucracy, having served as assistant secretary of education in charge of elementary and secondary programs. He would function more as a line administrator who was responsible for the implementation and administration of instructional programs. In that same month the chancellor appointed Alfred Melov to serve as assistant superintendent in charge of Promotional Policy. Melov would report to Minter and assume responsibility for the final development and operation of the Promotional Policy. His appointment was a key one, for the superintendents had a great number of concerns with regard to the chancellor's programs, and their support was crucial to its success. Melov, who had been elected president of the Citywide Association of Superintendents, and had previously been their spokesperson on Promotional Policy, could help gain their support by seeing that their concerns were built into the final implementation plan.

On February 18 the chancellor distributed to the superintendents another draft of guidelines for the implementation of Promotional Policy. This revised draft reconfirmed the policy goals of the document Ron Edmonds had circulated in December, and outlined the responsibilities of the superintendents. These included the identification of students likely to fall below required performance standards, the selection of viable remediation programs, the selection of qualified teachers for remediation, the development of communications with parents, and the selection of appropriate testing and evaluation instruments to measure student progress regularly throughout the school year.[87] From February to October 1981, the Division of Curriculum and Instruction conducted curriculum workshops where teachers could share effective programs for the application of *Minimum Teaching Essentials,* the basic document of the citywide standard curriculum. On March 12 the chancellor held a citywide conference for superintendents at Glen Cove, New York. While Promotional Policy was not the only topic on the agenda, it certainly was the most significant and time-consuming one. During the course of the three-day conference, the chancellor and his top-level staff, including Minter and Melov, explained the rationale behind Promotional Policy and answered questions concerning its practical operation and long-term implications.

On March 24 Budget Director Dall Forsythe received a note from Richard Frankan, Deputy Assistant Director of the City Office of Management and Budget. The note stated that OMB was in the process of formulating its final recommendations to the mayor on the Board of Education's 1982 budget request. It explained further, ". . . before

OMB completes its evaluation of the chancellor's new Promotional Policy, several outstanding questions need to be resolved." The cover note was followed by six pages of questions, which, it was later learned, had been prepared with the assistance of the United Parents Associations, the leading opponent of Promotional Policy in the city. The questions covered the following broad topics:

- What average salary figure for teachers was used in the cost projection?
- What functions will central support staff perform? At what rates will they be compensated?
- How were cost figures arrived at for the teacher training program?
- What relationship is there between grade-equivalent test scores and the ability to master the curriculum at a given level?
- How will one measure the relative benefits/injury to youngsters from inclusion in holdover classes?
- How will errors of measurement be accounted for?
- Will all districts apply discretion to the standards in a uniform way?
- Can the new promotional standards be postponed until a more adequate measuring device for identifying holdovers is developed?
- How will student progress be evaluated?
- How long will students be retained in holdover classes if they fail to meet required standards?
- In what ways will the promotional policy curriculum differ from prior or existing programs?
- Will this policy force teachers to "teach to the test"?
- How will the standards be applied to bilingual and special-education students? What recourse will parents have?
- From what reimbursable programs will funds be drawn?
- How will funds be allocated to the districts?
- What qualifications will there be for participating teachers?
- If the funds requested are not allocated, are there alternative plans for a program of smaller size and scope?

The nature of the questions in the OMB communication indicated the serious doubts many had regarding the preparedness of the administration to implement its policy. In addition to the philosophical differences many opponents had, fears began to grow about that Promotional Policy might bring about. People talked in a half-joking way about those "bearded fourth-graders" who could not get past the gates. Others wondered if the policy would give rise to a new population of dropouts who, discouraged by failure at a young age, would never get to high school. The OMB correspondence made it clear to school officials that support for Promotional Policy was far from assured. It also carried the message that negotiations with municipal officials would go beyond the subject of dollars and would concern the details of pedagogical issues, policies, and practice.

On March 31 Macchiarola announced that he would be holding five boroughwide meetings for community superintendents and principals in order to discuss Promotional Policy. These meetings were to be held between April 28 and June 5 and would be attended by all the chancellor's top-level staff. The meetings were reminiscent of the citywide meeting of principals held the year before in order to mobilize support for the shool budget. This year the chancellor was reaching out to the principals on a boroughwide basis in a more intimate setting, in order to respond to their concerns about Promotional Policy and to assure them that he would get financial backing for it. It appeared that the more doubtful city financing of the remedial programs became, the more determined grew the chancellor. There were some members of the administration who started to wonder if it might be better to put the whole matter off for another year. But Macchiarola knew that this was an election year. If funding could not be gotten now, it would not be gotten at all. As Melov explained the chancellor's position, "Frank said, 'NO BACKING OFF!' "[88]

The citywide reading test was administered to students in grades 2 through 9 on April 6. As in the previous year, the instrument used was the California Achievement Test, a norm-referenced exam. On April 10, nearly three weeks after the initial inquiry, Dall Forsythe issued a "preliminary response" to the questions he had received from the mayor's office about Promotional Policy. The response was thirteen pages long, and it addressed all the issues that had appeared in the initial OMB inquiry. On April 14 the chancellor issued to the community districts the final set of guidelines for the implementation of Promotional Policy. This document was a revised form of the two previous drafts, incorporating the concerns raised by various district personnel and, at the same time, clarifying the responsibilities of the superintendents.

On the day after he distributed the final policy guidelines, Macchiarola received a three-page letter from Deputy Mayor Robert F. Wagner, Jr., advising him that there had been "considerable internal discussion at City Hall" regarding the proposed Promotional Policy and its accompanying budget request. Wagner was suggesting a face-to-face meeting to discuss "the issues that have surfaced as being the most problematic." He assured the chancellor, "I am in sympathy with the basic concept of Promotional Policy and the purpose of the meeting, in my view, will be for me to get a more precise understanding of recent developments." The developments Wagner wanted to discuss concerned cost projections, the availability of other-than-City funds, and implementation strategies. Wagner also listed a number of specific issues he wanted Macchiarola to address, and these were not very different from the ones included in the original OMB inquiry to Forsythe. Wagner closed his letter in a conciliatory and supportive tone, writing: "Once again let me emphasize that I ask these questions in a constructive spirit and with the hope that a Promotional Policy is effectively implemented in the city.[89]

It would take several weeks before the meeting between Macchiarola and Wagner took place, and the outcome of that meeting would determine the future of Promotional Policy. In the meantime, Forsythe began to meet with the OMB staff in order to take a second look at the original cost projections submitted by the Board of Education. The first round of negotiations resulted in a new and lower projection for the cost of remediation programs, taking it from the initial $63 million total down to a $42 million total. Three elements contributed to this projection:

- A revised teacher salary estimate from a $20,000 per year average to a $17,000 per year average.
- A revised child count. The initial projection assumed that all children who were absent from the exam and all children with limited English proficiency would fail. The new projection assumed that half the absentees would fail, and that children of limited English proficiency, taking the exam in English as a second language, would have the same pass rate as other children. The new child count also factored in enrollment declines that were not considered in the first estimate.
- Both of the above factors reflect a change in mathematical assumptions, and perhaps also the usual kind of dollar "padding" found during the initial phases of a budget process. However, the third factor contributing to the downward decline of the cost projection was an amendment to the actual policy standards set by the chancellor and the Board of Education. It called for a revised standard of promotion that changed the seventh grade holdover criterion from one year below grade level in reading to one and one-half years below grade level. This new standard would undoubtedly reduce the number of seventh-grade holdovers and the cost of their remediation. It represented a rather significant amount of influence on instructional policy wielded by budget officials in the mayor's office.

These revisions notwithstanding, it was still not determined how much, if any, of the total cost package would be paid for by the city. Macchiarola continued his borough meetings with the principals. On April 27 he held a general conference for the members of the thirty-two community school boards around the city. The conference, which was held at the City University Graduate Center, was arranged by Philip Kaplan, president of the Community School Boards Association. Kaplan had not been a supporter of Promotional Policy but was willing to give it a hearing. By then it was apparent that the community school board members had more reservations about Promotional Policy than their superintendents. The superintendents had seen themselves as implementers of policy. If packaged well, the chancellor's plan could clarify policy among the districts and make their jobs easier. However, the board members had for ten years played a rather singular role in making instructional policy in their districts, and the chancellor's initiatives would compromise that role. Macchiarola understood the concerns of the local school board members and enjoyed a good rapport, for he had been one of them once, having served as a member and president of a school board in Brooklyn. He and his team were joined in their presentations by Board of Education President Joseph Barkan. The presentations focused on three general topics: the policy directive, the implementation plan, and the budget. Macchiarola used the occasion to present the revised $42 million budget and to explain how it had been calculated.

Three days after the school boards conference, the executive board of the New York City Elementary School Principals Association voted to reject Promotional Policy as it was then written. On May 1 it issued a press release that alleged: "It is our considered opinion that this [policy] document reflects political concerns and not the educational needs of the children of New York City."[90] The press release was handed to Macchiarola personally on the same day, as he entered Forest Hills High School to begin one of his boroughwide meetings with the district principals. The outlook was clear. The negotiation of the budget for remedial programs made Promotional Policy seem more political than ever. The principals, who once were skeptical, were now angry. First they had been told Promotional Policy would not go ahead without funding. Then the Board had changed that. Afterwards, they were told that the money for remediation would be sought. Then, as the budget process was about to reach a climax, they were told that they would not need as much as was originally expected. Macchiarola was trying to maintain the credibility of his new Promotional Policy, but he wasn't getting much help from either the Board of Education or City Hall, both of whom wanted him to put the program in place.

The mayor was scheduled to submit his Executive Budget on May 12. Macchiarola and Wagner scheduled their meeting for the first week of the month. It was meant to be cordial. The two men liked each other personally; they worked well together. Wagner was a strong advocate of public education, a believer in the chancellor, and a supporter of Promotional Policy. But the money was still in doubt. The two decided to meet at Macchiarola's home in Brooklyn. The tone would be relaxed and friendly. However, Macchiarola had already made an important personal and professional decision before the meeting had begun. He had been the key force behind the design and adoption of Promotional Policy. He did not want to see it implemented without the necessary financing for remedial programs. He did not want to be responsible for raising competency standards in a manner which he had found inadequate at the state level. So, after a number of serious discussions with his family, close friends, and staff, Macchiarola had decided that he would resign his position as chancellor if the city did not allocate the funding for the program. That decision was never made public, but it set the stage for the meeting between him and Wagner.

Macchiarola's resignation would not have come at an opportune time. The mayor was in the midst of a reelection campaign, and the chancellor's record played a key part in that campaign. When the mayor's budget was announced on May 12, the figure for Promotional Policy was still under consideration. However, in the final delilberations, the total cost for Promotional Policy was put at $36 million; $11.4 million would come from the city.

EDUCATIONAL OUTCOMES: MOST CHILDREN DID LEARN

The citywide reading scores were announced on May 28. Of course, the big news of the year was the fact that New York City schoolchildren in grades 2 through 9 had moved above the national average for the first time in a decade, with 50.7 percent reading at or above grade level. It was a 4 percent increase over the 1980 scores, and a 10.4 percent improvement over 1979.[91] (See Figure 3-1.) The results of the math scores, announced that same day, were not so positive, but were better than had been expected. The scores on the Stanford Diagnostic Math Test showed that 49.6 percent of the students in grades 2 through 9 were either at or above grade level. More than 50 percent of the students in grades 2 through 6 were at or above grade level, while less than 40 percent of those in grades 7 through 9 were at grade level. (See Table 3-1.) The administration of this test was the first step toward the development of a standardized citywide instrument consistent with

Figure 3.1

READING ACHIEVEMENT OF STUDENTS IN NEW YORK CITY PUBLIC SCHOOLS, GRADES 2–9* 1978–1981 (1981 Preliminary)

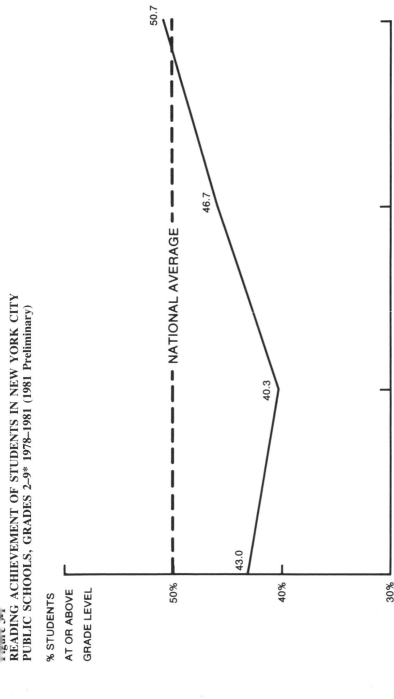

Source: Board of Education, City of New York, Division of Public Affairs, May 28, 1981.

*Students with limited English proficiency who did not take the test are included in these results as reading below grade level.

Table 3-1
DISTRICT PERCENT OF STUDENTS AT AND ABOVE GRADE LEVEL
IN MATHEMATICS,* 1981

				Grades					
District	2	3	4	5	6	7	8	9	Total
1	40.4	54.2	35.9	43.2	42.9	23.4	26.7	16.4	35.1
2	64.6	72.6	69.8	70.3	67.6	58.9	54.3	39.9	63.4
3	44.2	52.9	40.6	43.9	44.0	29.5	29.5	15.5	39.0
4	45.5	49.6	39.7	36.0	40.3	24.9	23.7	9.4	33.8
5	42.2	49.2	38.7	48.1	42.9	27.8	24.2	15.3	37.0
6	35.6	47.5	36.0	45.0	36.2	23.6	22.5	13.8	34.3
7	37.6	47.5	39.2	39.5	33.5	24.6	20.8	34.7	34.2
8	42.5	56.0	50.7	43.8	42.2	25.8	26.5	15.9	38.6
9	39.0	47.2	34.1	30.6	26.8	20.5	21.8	13.1	31.3
10	47.9	52.7	41.4	44.0	43.3	27.8	26.6	16.8	39.1
11	57.4	65.9	58.1	59.0	58.7	41.0	39.9	21.2	51.5
12	43.1	54.9	37.1	45.8	34.6	16.2	17.2	8.0	36.9
13	50.9	61.9	47.8	45.7	52.3	27.9	26.4	6.7	43.5
14	50.2	62.8	59.5	57.7	52.3	28.2	37.7	21.4	48.9
15	50.3	62.6	54.1	53.7	49.0	26.2	32.2	17.1	48.1
16	46.0	59.0	48.3	45.2	51.5	19.3	17.7	4.1	40.4
17	42.8	50.2	48.4	45.6	37.4	22.3	20.8	60.9	38.7
18	66.3	69.5	63.6	62.3	61.5	40.7	37.3	26.8	52.7
19	43.7	52.5	42.8	42.3	43.9	31.1	31.0	28.4	40.9
20	60.7	71.2	64.2	65.0	62.0	45.5	48.6	33.6	56.4
21	59.8	68.5	60.2	62.6	61.4	49.8	49.8	34.7	56.8
22	64.9	72.4	67.2	69.7	65.8	59.4	57.0	38.6	63.7
23	34.8	44.3	45.6	39.9	35.4	17.2	16.4	45.2	33.4
24	56.9	69.3	60.3	61.9	56.9	49.0	52.0	38.3	56.3
25	77.1	85.5	30.3	79.9	81.0	71.8	67.9	50.7	74.2
26	81.8	90.9	84.9	88.2	84.7	76.3	68.8	57.9	79.2
27	57.4	64.4	58.2	60.9	56.8	44.0	44.5	32.7	54.3
28	52.7	67.8	57.5	59.0	62.3	49.6	45.3	32.5	54.1
29	67.0	67.0	59.0	65.6	57.1	39.1	40.9	37.3	55.9
30	64.6	73.1	64.2	64.8	59.4	44.9	49.0	37.4	58.5
31	74.0	84.1	78.0	77.5	70.2	63.5	65.1	31.9	72.2
32	44.3	49.5	41.9	38.6	40.5	30.0	27.7	16.5	38.3
33†				70.0	55.3	64.0			60.2
City	53.4	62.5	54.6	55.5	52.6	38.9	38.8	29.5	49.6

Source: Board of Education, City of New York, Division of Public Affairs, May 28, 1981.

*Includes students excused from testing because of limited English proficiency.

†Experimental intermediate school.

the math curriculum taught in the schools. Since the Promotional Policy guidelines did not prescribe a math standard until 1982, this test would not be used to determine advancement at the gates until then. Given the newness of the test, no year-to-year comparisons were possible in math.

The reading improvement over the previous year was reflected in all of the city's thirty-two school districts. However, as might be expected, there was a wide difference in the achievement levels between middle-class school districts and those with predominantly poor populations. Thus, in the highest-scoring district (District 26), Bayside–Douglaston–Little Neck, Queens, a rather affluent neighborhood on the New York City–Nassau County border, 83.6 percent of the students read at or above grade level. The lowest-scoring district (District 9), located in the impoverished South Bronx, reported 30.6 percent of its students reading at or above grade level. However, another distinct pattern showed that the most significant year-to-year improvements took place in the low-achieving districts located in predominantly poor areas. Thus the largest district-wide improvement in the reading scores (8.8 percent) for 1981 was in District 4 in East Harlem. This pattern becomes even more prounounced when one reviews reading score improvements over the two-year period between 1979 and 1981. (See Table 3-2). There is an 18.7 percent improvement in East Harlem (District 4), 12.8 percent in Central Harlem (District 5), 13 percent in Williamsburg–Greenpoint (District 14), 15.8 percent in Ocean Hill–Brownsville (District 23), 13.9 percent in Queens Village–Hollis–Springfield Gardens (District 29), and 12.5 percent in Bushwick (District 32).

The overall results of the 1981 reading scores were a harsh reminder of the kinds of obstacles children from disadvantaged backgrounds must overcome in order to reach acceptable levels of proficiency in basic skills. However, the test scores also demonstrated that, with the right motivation, expectations, and instruction, it is possible to upgrade the achievement levels of all children, regardless of social condition. District 4 in East Harlem is a significant case in point. Led by Anthony Alvarado, a strong superintendent, who instituted a Promotional Policy at the district level a year before the chancellor's centrally administered effort, it enjoyed the highest increase in reading scores of any district in the city.

There was also other encouraging evidence suggesting that intervention at the school site, if properly planned and administered, could be effective in upgrading the basic skills of city public schoolchildren. This was borne out by data from both the School Improvement Project and the Local School Development Project.

Table 3-2
DISTRICT PERCENT OF STUDENTS READING AT AND ABOVE
GRADE LEVEL,* 1981, AND COMPARISON OF DISTRICT TOTALS
1979–1980–1981 (Preliminary)

District	2	3	4	5	6	7	8	9	1981 Total	1980 Total	1979 Total
1	34.1	43.1	34.1	45.8	43.1	33.2	36.6	34.4	37.9	32.8	25.8
2	51.4	50.4	55.9	63.2	61.1	64.5	60.5	52.1	56.2	54.8	50.5
3	33.9	38.8	35.8	46.6	46.6	43.8	40.0	33.3	40.6	37.1	—
4	48.2	45.7	41.6	47.5	52.1	42.8	37.4	40.8	44.4	35.6	25.7
5	36.1	37.2	34.3	47.3	45.7	46.9	41.9	39.1	41.8	35.3	29.0
6	28.6	30.5	29.4	40.1	35.0	30.3	32.4	30.3	32.3	29.2	24.7
7	30.3	30.6	32.5	38.7	30.9	31.6	29.3	61.6	32.7	28.9	22.0
8	43.4	43.3	41.3	45.6	41.4	42.6	42.0	39.3	42.6	37.8	32.1
9	30.9	30.5	28.1	32.1	29.9	30.4	33.8	26.9	30.6	27.8	22.3
10	36.7	37.7	34.4	40.0	40.1	39.1	39.8	39.5	38.5	34.9	30.4
11	54.3	55.5	55.2	64.9	62.6	60.9	55.7	47.2	57.6	54.1	47.3
12	35.4	39.7	32.2	45.0	36.8	31.6	28.4	33.7	36.2	30.9	25.2
13	48.6	51.2	41.8	48.1	51.4	46.0	42.4	23.0	46.0	41.0	29.8
14	43.1	44.8	46.7	45.2	39.6	34.3	39.0	35.5	41.5	36.3	28.5
15	47.1	47.9	43.9	50.5	46.5	39.9	39.0	32.3	45.1	40.5	35.5
16	39.5	42.9	43.9	45.5	51.8	32.1	30.8	22.8	40.5	39.1	29.6
17	46.0	49.3	47.5	50.2	43.3	36.7	38.2	94.2**	45.2	41.3	34.0
18	69.0	63.9	65.3	67.1	64.7	55.7	57.8	56.3	62.2	59.1	51.0
19	36.5	39.5	34.7	42.0	40.3	38.8	37.8	47.1	38.7	34.0	27.9
20	59.2	62.8	57.9	62.9	59.6	55.6	57.7	57.7	59.0	55.5	48.9
21	51.0	57.4	53.6	60.9	62.5	58.2	61.7	62.8	58.7	55.0	48.3
22	62.6	64.5	64.1	68.3	66.6	71.0	69.8	64.8	66.5	62.8	56.6
23	29.7	31.3	35.1	41.4	37.9	35.7	40.3	90.3**	36.2	29.5	20.4
24	47.6	52.3	53.1	57.3	54.9	56.5	57.7	54.1	54.3	51.5	47.4
25	66.2	73.7	70.8	73.7	74.2	75.8	72.7	70.0	72.3	69.4	64.3
26	77.8	82.7	82.5	87.8	84.3	87.4	82.0	82.3	83.6	77.8	71.9
27	52.8	52.7	52.5	60.6	57.8	54.3	53.9	53.1	55.0	52.4	43.6
28	50.6	56.0	51.5	61.2	62.3	60.4	55.2	51.6	56.4	51.9	47.4
29	67.4	62.6	60.3	66.4	59.2	54.3	55.9	65.4	60.9	55.6	47.0
30	63.5	61.4	53.7	63.0	55.4	55.5	58.8	60.5	58.9	54.7	47.9
31	71.7	75.5	77.2	78.0	70.5	77.2	75.6	62.7	74.9	70.3	64.2
32	38.4	35.0	33.4	36.1	40.1	36.7	38.3	34.6	36.9	30.0	24.4
33†				80.0	68.1	80.4			74.0	65.4	
City	48.5	50.4	48.6	54.7	52.1	50.3	50.0	50.5	50.7	46.7	40.3

Source: Board of Education, City of New York, Division of Public Affairs, May 28,
1981; September 2, 1980.

*Includes students excused from testing because of limited English proficiency.

†Experimental intermediate school.

**Based on 31 students in that grade in District 23 and 242 students in that grade in
District 17.

All but one of the schools participating in the School Improvement Project (SIP) showed gains in the percentage of students reading at or above grade level between 1980 and 1981. The gains ranged from 0.8 percent to 11.8 percent. The seven schools in SIP for two years showed an average gain of 7.2 percent between 1980 and 1981. The nine new schools had an average gain of 4.6 percent. The average gain for all sixteen schools was 5.8 percent. The average citywide gain was 4 percent. Gains for the two-year schools in SIP between 1979 and 1980 averaged 8.4 percent, compared to the citywide average of 6.4 percent. The two-year gain was 15.4 percent compared to the citywide gain of 10.4 percent.[92]

The data for the Local School Development Project (LSDP) schools were almost as encouraging. Of the thirty-two schools participating in LSDP, twenty-six showed gains in the percentage of students reading at or above grade level between 1980 and 1981. Four schools showed declines, and two alternative schools did not administer the exams. The average gain for all LSDP schools was 5.2 percent. The gains for the improving schools ranged from 0.7 percent to 20.6 percent. Between 1979 and 1980, LSDP showed an average gain of 9.1 percent of students reading at or above grade level, as compared to a 6.4 percent gain citywide. The two-year gain for LSDP schools between 1979 and 1981 was 14.0 percent, as compared to 10.4 percent citywide.[93]

When the final analysis of the citywide reading scores was completed, it was found that 23,509 students would be held over at the gates. This total included 10,023 fourth-graders and 13,486 seventh-graders.[94] The number was considerably less than the 40,000 that had originally been predicted. Once the individual norm-referenced scores from the California Achievement Test were computed, an effort was made to perform a criterion-referenced analysis of the exam in order to make it useful in the remedial effort that was planned. The practice drew criticism from some outsiders, who felt that the citywide test was being inappropriately used for too many purposes.[95] However, the launching of the administration's summer remedial program received a large amount of coverage and praise from the local media, which heralded the end to social promotion in the public schools. This acclaim included an editorial in *The Amsterdam News*, the City's largest black newspaper, which endorsed the chancellor's Promotional Policy but issued a caveat that there should also be more evaluations of teachers.[96]

In June approximately four hundred veteran teachers were hired and trained for participation in the six-week remedial program for holdovers. While the original Promotional Policy plan required that such a summer program be offered only to seventh-grade holdovers, the 1981 summer program was made available to all students (in grades 4 and 7) who had failed to make it through the gates. In addition to the centrally administered remedial effort, ten community school districts initiated supplementary programs of their own.[97] A total of 9,495 students participated in the administration's summer program, which ran from July 6 to August 14. On the last day, all students who had not passed through the gates in June, including those who had not participated in the remediation, were given an opportunity to retake the test. A total of 15,917 students sat for the exam. Of this number, 5,999 achieved satisfactory scores and passed through the gates. This represented a 37.7 percent passing rate. A remaining 17,510 would be held over in the fall.[98] On September 2, the central Division of Curriculum and Instruction began a two-week training program for approximately fifteen hundred teachers and two hundred supervisors, who would participate in the promotional gate remedial program during the forthcoming school year.

In October the Board of Education's Office of Educational Evaluation completed an assessment of the summer remedial program.[99] The evaluation showed that there was a direct relationship between the number of days a student attended the summer program and the rate of promotion. It found that 41.4 percent of the fourth-graders and 44.5 percent of the seventh-graders who regularly attended (twenty-four out of thirty days) the chancellor's six-week program met the criteria for promotion in August. It also found that 40.3 percent of the fourth-graders and 41.7 percent of the seventh-graders who regularly attended district summer school programs were promoted. These data can be compared to a passing rate of 30 percent of fourth-graders and 42.5 percent of seventh-graders who received private tutoring during the summer. Only 9.6 percent of the fourth-graders and 13.8 percent of the seventh-graders who received no instruction over the summer passed the August examination.[100]

The outcome of the six-week summer program gave a great deal of credibility to the idea of remediation. As the chancellor observed:

> This gives us a good indication of what can be accomplished in the regular school year program. If students attend school regularly and if instruction is conducted with the same degree of purposefulness and enthusiasm as it was in the summer, we will be able to significantly raise the level of achievement of our lowest-achieving students.[101]

The August results also pointed to the potential and serious problems that would need to be faced in the forthcoming school year. The fact of the matter is that only 67.7 percent of all the June holdovers even bothered to take the August exam, and of that amount, only 37.7 percent managed to pass. (See Table 3-3.) This points to a population which can be expected to have more difficulty in getting through the gates. It may mean that the children with the most serious learning problems did not benefit from remediation. The administration acknowledged those potential difficulties but refused to despair. As the 1981–1982 school year began, it continued to search for effective methods of dealing with children who had the most serious learning problems. Charlotte Frank, executive director of the Division of Curriculum and Instruction, explained:

> With regard to the pupils being held over more than once, we are thinking about alternative designs. We must work with the kids who have not advanced. To the extent that we narrow the pool, we will continue to refine our approaches. It's our job to find a way to make these kids learn.[102]

At about the same time that the administration was reviewing data from its summer program for the elementary and middle grades, another report emerged from the office of the deputy chancellor for instruction, concerning the high schools. It showed that the mean scores on the Scholastic Aptitude Test (SAT), which had been consistently decreasing in New York since 1968, had increased in 1981 by 12 points in math and 7 points in verbal performance.[103] These improvements compared favorably with those recorded in the rest of New York State, where mean gains for both public and private schools were 6 points in math and 3 points on the verbal test. No improvements occurred on either the math or verbal scores nationally in 1981. However, despite the gains, the mean SAT scores in New York City high schools continued to lag significantly behind both the state and national averages. In 1981 the mean math score in New York City was 431, as compared to 479 in the state and 466 nationally. The mean verbal score was 384 in the city, compared to 435 in the state and 424 in the nation.

The SAT results demonstrate that while progress was made in New York City high schools between 1978 and 1981, the achievements were not so significant as those in the elementary and middle schools. There is no easy explanation for the varying rate of improvement. Most educators would agree that it is more difficult to overcome the accumulated deficits of inadequate instruction at the secondary level than it is in the lower grades. That is simple logic. However, at least some of the difference must be attributed to the emphasis that the administration placed on early childhood and elementary instruction. This overall strategy was dictated as much by financial constraints as by pedogog-

Table 3-3
AUGUST 1981 CALIFORNIA ACHIEVEMENT TEST RESULTS FOR
HOLDOVERS IN GRADES FOUR AND SEVEN, BY SCHOOL DISTRICT

District	Number of holdovers,* June 1981	Number and percent of holdovers tested, August 1981		Number and percent of holdovers promoted,† August 1981		Percent of retested holdovers who were promoted** August 1981
		N	%	N	%	%
1	580	411	70.9	126	21.7	30.7
2	359	213	59.3	106	29.5	49.8
3	494	381	77.1	154	31.2	40.4
4	648	255	39.4	119	18.4	46.7
5	606	367	60.6	126	20.8	34.3
6	669	604	90.3	223	33.3	36.9
7	938	603	64.3	194	20.7	32.2
8	1079	768	71.2	327	30.3	42.6
9	1598	905	56.6	314	19.7	34.7
10	1699	1066	62.7	352	20.7	33.0
11	591	451	76.3	213	36.0	47.2
12	751	483	64.3	151	20.1	31.3
13	830	480	57.8	195	23.5	40.6
14	853	560	65.7	159	18.6	28.4
15	878	653	74.4	220	25.1	33.7
16	582	357	61.3	107	18.4	30.0
17	1284	833	64.9	267	20.8	32.1
18	445	309	69.4	124	27.9	40.1
19	1217	998	82.0	291	23.9	29.2
20	612	371	60.6	139	22.7	37.5
21	545	418	76.7	168	30.8	40.2
22	461	342	74.2	158	34.3	46.2
23	751	465	61.9	176	23.4	37.9
24	569	476	83.7	221	38.8	46.4
25	209	148	70.8	80	38.3	54.1
26	73	57	78.1	36	49.3	63.2
27	1050	775	73.8	342	32.6	44.1
28	514	401	78.0	151	29.4	37.7
29	673	495	73.6	241	35.8	48.7
30	564	344	61.0	152	27.0	44.2
31	548	414	75.6	213	38.9	51.5
32	839	514	61.3	154	18.4	30.0
Citywide	23,509	15,917	67.7%	5,999	25.5%	37.7%

Source: Office of Educational Evaluation, New York City Public Schools, "The Promotional Gates Program: An Analysis of Summer School Participation and August, 1981 Test Scores," October 5, 1981.

*Students were designated "holdovers" if they scored below 6.2 (grade equivalent) in seventh grade or below 3.7 (grade equivalent) in fourth grade on the April 1981 CAT. The figures in column one were supplied by the Office of Promotional Policy; all other figures were derived from August 1981 test documents.

†These numbers and percentages pertain to students promoted from among all holdover students, even those who did not retake the CAT in August 1981. Therefore, 25.5 percent of students who did not meet the promotional standard in April were able to meet it in August.

**These numbers and percentages pertain to students promoted from among those holdover students who retook the CAT in August. Therefore, 37.7 percent of students who retook the CAT met the promotional standard in August.

ical considerations. Nevertheless, the outcome shows that what educators do with regard to policy and school practice does have an impact in the classroom.

SUMMARY COMMENTS

This chapter is a case study in educational policy making. More specifically, it is an analysis of the attempt by the schools chancellor to change the policy on competency standards that had been in place for more than a decade, and replace it with a policy consistent with his own educational philosophy. That philosophy was an innovation because it ran contrary to the thinking within a large part of the city school system, not to mention a large part of the general educational profession. The philosophy was provocative because it raised the standard of performance for both students and staff. It constituted a rejection of the negativism that contributed to the idea that certain children are uneducable.

The new philosophy articulated at Livingston Street was designed to alter significantly the way things operated within the school system. This change was particularly evident as the administration began to address the needs of children with the most severe learning problems, who had fallen below the standards of proficiency. These were the hard-core failures. These were the students who could not be promoted. These were the ones whom some would have counted among the "uneducable." The administration responded to these children on several levels. First, it sought to demonstrate that they were the exception rather than the rule. However, it also recognized that it must identify them in order to deal with their needs effectively. Once this identification took place, educational professionals would have to discover how to proceed with instruction and programs, but expectations were to remain high. Whether the administration and the school system could respond to this ambitious calling would be determined over a longer period of time.

The debate over competency standards in New York demonstrates that there are many steps between policy design and implementation. The former is essentially a planning process; the latter is more concerned with securing cooperation and compliance. Both processes represent important aspects of policy making, but successful implementation usually demands the involvement of more parties. Therefore, it is in the implementation of policy that it is most possible for things to go wrong.

The participants in the competency standard debate in New York were both numerous and diverse. It involved, first of all, the Board of Regents, which established its own state standards. These Regents standards had a direct impact on high school students in the city and set the context for a Promotional Policy in the earlier grades. The debate involved the chancellor, who opposed the Regents standard and sought to establish his own policy. It involved personnel within the school system—including community superintendents and school board members, who were ambivalent about the chancellor's proposal, and building principals, some of whom were downright opposed to it. It involved the mayor and the Board of Education, who were troubled by the poor competency levels of the city's public school students, adamant about raising the standards, but only moderately supportive on the funding issue. Ironically, from the chancellor's perspective, the public postures of the mayor and the Board of Education became an obstacle to his winning support and credibility for Promotional Policy among district personnel.

There were also considerable differences about the merits of the chancellor's Promotional Policy among the client groups of the school system. Blacks and other minorities appeared to support it. Many of the more established middle-class educational interest groups were opposed. Both factions argued their cases on very solid grounds. The debate among these groups once again highlights the significance of the distinction between constituents and clients in a school system composed of predominantly minority students. This is not to say that the more established educational interest groups in the city are separate and apart from the clientele of the system, but this chapter certainly raises the question of whether these influential groups, however well-meaning, always represent the preponderant school clientele.

There is as much respectable social science research that speaks against the use of competency exams for determining promotion as there is literature that supports it. This division, at least in part, explains the controversy the issue provokes and the number of perspectives on it. One might say that in developing his Promotional Policy the chancellor had a wealth of evidence, opinion, and allies from which to choose. In the end, however, the determination of competency standards for schoolchildren in New York City was the product of conflict and the compromise worked out among the many participants in the policy debate. And notwithstanding all the discussion among professional educators and their clients concerning policy design, it was the OMB budget analysts who eventually had the final word on the standards.

There remains no consensus within the education profession concerning either the efficacy or fairness of competency testing. Many of those who oppose it are still sensitive to a malevolent strain in the history of American schooling, wherein tests were used to deny opportunity to certain groups. Some of the most enthusiastic supporters of competency testing see it as a means of linking educational quality to human equality. The fact remains, however, that there is no established relationship between competency testing and student achievement.

The history of the competency movement has taught us that once a decision has been made to use testing as a basis for graduation or promotion, certain guidelines must be followed to increase the probability of a desirable outcome. For example, competency tests should be based on a standard curriculum that is taught to all students. Newly developed standards should be implemented on a gradual basis, and the tests used should be free of cultural biases. It is equally important to assure that any competency-based policy is supported by an effective remedial program for children who cannot achieve the standard. This case illustrates an inherent danger in the competency movement—that some of the most outspoken political supporters of higher standards may not be sensitive to the need for support services.

There is also a singularly important positive lesson to be drawn from New York City's experience with the competency movement. It suggests that there is a relationship between adult expectations and student achievement. This was borne out by student responses in New York to both the graduation standards set by the Regents and the promotional standards set by the chancellor. Such policies produce the most successful results when they are reflected in the attitudes of classroom teachers. While these policies do not guarantee positive attitudes, they are a first and important step toward the development of effective teaching.

NOTES

1. Joseph A. Califano, Jr., *Governing America* (New York: Simon and Shuster, 1981), pp. 293–299.

2. National Academy of Education, "Improving Educational Achievement: Report of the National Academy of Education Commission on Testing and Basic Skills," 1978, p. iv.

3. See Robert Ebel, "The Case for Minimum Competency Testing," *Phi Delta Kappan*, 59 (April 1978).

4. See Walt Haney and George Madaus, "Making Sense of Competency Testing," *Harvard Educational Review* 48 (November 1978); Gene V. Glass, "Standards and Criteria," *Journal of Educational Measurement* 15 (1978); Chris Pipho, "Minimum Competency Testing," *Phi Delta Kappan* 60 (December 1979).

5. For an overview of the legal issues, see Merle S. McClung, "Competency Testing Programs: Legal and Educational Issues," *Fordham Law Review* 47 (1979); Donald M. Lewis, "Certifying Functional Literacy: Competency Testing and Implications for Due Process and Equal Educational Opportunity," *Journal of Law and Education* 8 (April 1979); Paul Tractenberg and Elaine Jacoby, "Pupil Testing: A Legal View," *Phi Delta Kappan* 59 (December 1977); Donald Carter, "The Emerging Legal Issue in Competency Testing," *Education and Urban Society* 12 (November 1979).

6. *Hobson* v. *Hansen*, 269 F. Supp. 401 (D.D.C. 1967).

7. *Moses* v. *Washington Parish School Board*, 33 F. Supp. 1340 (Ed. La. 1971).

8. *Lemon* v. *Bassier Parish School Board*, 444 F. 2d 1400 (5th Cir., 1971).

9. *Washington* v. *Davis*, 426 U.S. 299 (1976).

10. *Larry P.* v. *Riles*, 495 F. Supp. 926 (N.D. Cal. 1979).

11. For opposing views on the Florida case, see Thomas A. Fisher, "Florida's Approach to Competency Testing," and Gene V. Glass, "Minimum Competence and Incompetence in Florida," *Phi Delta Kappan* 59 (May 1978).

12. Fisher, ibid., p. 601.

13. *Debra P.* v. *Turlington*, Docket No. 78-13 62R 1978.

14. *Board of Education of Northport–East Northport Union Free School District* v. *Ambach*, Sup. Ct. Albany Country, Special Term, August 24, 1979.

15. Merle S. McClung, "Competency Testing Programs." See also Merle S. McClung, "Are Competency Testing Programs Fair? Legal?" *Phi Delta Kappan* 59 (February 1978).

16. William G. Spady, "Competency Based Education: A Bandwagon in Search of a Definition," *Educational Researcher* 6 (January 1977), p. 11.

17. Francis X. Archambault, Jr., "Remediation in Minimum Competency," *Education and Urban Society* 12 (November 1979).

18. Haney and Madaus, "Making Sense of Competency Testing."

19. James S. Coleman *et al.*, *Equality of Educational Opportunity* (Washington, D.C.: Office of Education, National Center for Educational Statistics, 1966). See also Frederick Mosteller and Daniel P. Moynihan, eds., *On Equality of Educational Opportunity* (New York: Vintage, 1972).

20. See, for example, Victor Cicirelli *et al.*, *The Impact of Head Start, A Study by the Westinghouse Learning Corporation and Ohio University* (Washington, D.C.: Office of Economic Opportunity, 1969); Harvey Averich *et al.*, *How Effective Is Schooling?* (Santa Monica, Calif.: Rand Corporation, 1972); Joel Berke and Michael Kirst, *Federal Aid to Education: Who Benefits? Who Governs?* (Lexington, Mass.: D. C. Heath, 1972). Ruby Martin and Phyliss McClure, *Title I of ESEA: Is It Helping Poor Children* (Washington, D.C.: A Report Research Project of the Southern Center for Education Studies in Public Policy and the NAACP Legal Defense of Education Fund, Inc., 1969); Michael Wargo *et al*, *ESEA Title I, A Reanalysis and Synthesis of the Evidence* (Palo Alto, Calif.: American Institute for Research, 1972); Gene Glass *et al.*, *Education of the Disadvantaged: An Evaluation Report on Title I, Elementary*

and Secondary Act of Fiscal Year 1969 (Boulder: University of Colorado, 1970).

21. Christopher Jencks *et al., Inequality: A Reassessment of the Effect of Family and Schooling in America* (New York: Basic Books, 1972).

22. Arthur Jensen, "How Much Can We Boost IQ and Scholastic Achievement," *Harvard Educational Review* 39 (Winter 1969).

23. George Weber, *Inner City Children Can Be Taught To Read: Four Successful Schools* (Washington: Council for Basic Education, 1971).

24. Ibid.

25. New York State, Office of Education Performance Review, "School Factors Influencing Reading Achievement: A Case Study of Two Inner-City Schools," Albany, New York, March 1974.

26. J. V. Madden *et al., School Effectiveness Study: State of California,* State of California Department of Education, 1976.

27. Wilber B. Brookover and Lawrence W. Lezotte, *Changes in School Characteristics Coincident with Changes in School Achievement* (East Lansing, Michigan State University College of Urban Development, 1977).

28. See, for example, National Institute of Education, *The Compensatory Education Study, Final Report to Congress from the National Institute of Education,* September 1978; Edward Ziegler and Jeannette Valentine, eds., *Project Head Start: A Legacy of the War on Poverty* (New York: The Free Press, 1979); Thomas C. Thomas and Sol H. Pelavin, *Patterns of ESEA Title I Reading Achievement* (Menlo Park, Cal.: Stanford Research Institute, 1976); Robert J. Rossi *et al., Summaries of Major Title I Evaluations* (Palo Alto, Calif.: American Institute for Research, 1977).

29. Michael Rutter *et al., Fifteen Thousand Hours* (Cambridge: Harvard University Press, 1979).

30. See, for example, Phi Delta Kappan, *Why Do Some Schools Succeed? The Phi Delta Kappan Study on Exceptional Urban Elementary Schools* (Bloomington, Ind.: Phi Delta Kappa, 1980); Diane Brundage, ed., *The Journalism Research Fellows Report: What Makes an Effective School?* (Washington, D.C.: Institute for Educational Leadership, April 1980); Robert Benjamin, *Making Schools Work* (New York: Continuum, 1981); Gene Maeroff, *Don't Blame the Kids* (New York: McGraw–Hill, 1981).

31. See, for example, the symposium on effective schools in *Educational Leadership* 40 (December 1982).

32. Lawrence Lezotte, Ronald Edmonds, and George Ratner, *A Final Report: Remedy for School Failure to Equitably Deliver Basic School Skills* (East Lansing: Michigan State University, Department of Urban and Metropolitan Studies, 1974).

33. Ronald R. Edmonds and John Fredericksen, *Search for Effective Schools: The Identification and Analysis of City Schools That are Instructionally Effective for Poor Children* (Cambridge: Harvard Unversity, Center for Urban Studies, 1975).

34. Ronald Edmonds, "Effective Schools for the Urban Poor," *Educational Leadership* 137 (Ocbober 1979).

35. "School Improvement Project, Program Description," Office of the Senior Assistant to the Chancellor for Instruction, New York City Public Schools, November 1978.

36. "SIP Report, The School Improvement Project," Office of the Deputy Chancellor for Instruction, New York City Public Schools, 1981.

37. "Local School Development Project: A Summary of the First Annual Assessment Report," Office of the Deputy Chancellor for Instruction, New York City Public Schools, 1981.

38. See, for example, Joan Shoemaker and Hugh W. Fraser, "What Principals Can Do: Some Implications from Studies of Effective Schooling," *Phi Delta Kappan* 63 (November 1981).

39. See Mary Lee Smith and Gene V. Glass, *Relationship of Class-Size to Classroom Processes, Teacher Satisfaction and Pupil Affect: A Meta-Analysis* (Boulder: Laboratory of Educational Research, University of Colorado, July 1979); *Meta-Analysis of Research on the Relationship of Class-Size and Achievement* (Boulder: Laboratory of Educational Research, University of Colorado, September 1978); Leonard S. Cahen and Nikola N. Filby, "The Class-Size/Achievement Issue: New Evidence and a Research Plan," *Phi Delta Kappan* 61 (March 1979); Gene V. Glass *et al.*, *School Class Size: Research and Policy* (Beverly Hills, Calif.: Sage Publications, 1982).

40. "Evaluation Report for the Transitional Class Program, 1979–1980," Office of Educational Evaluation, New York City Public Schools, December 1980.

41. Ibid.

42. "Statement of Chancellor Frank J. Macchiarola on the New York State Regents Competency Testing Programs," January 11, 1979.

43. Ibid.

44. *The New York Times*, February 7, 1979.

45. Ibid.

46. *Newsday*, March 2, 1979.

47. "The Regents Competency Testing Program: Regulations and Procedures," New York State Education Department, Albany, New York, March 1979.

48. Board of Education, City of New York, press release, July 11, 1979.

49. *The New York Times*, November 11, 1979.

50. *Newsday*, January 10, 1980.

51. Frank J. Macchiarola, "Memorandum to the Board of Education Regarding High School Diploma Requirements," March 26, 1980.

52. See Benjamin Bloom, *Human Characteristics and Learning* (New York: McGraw–Hill, 1976); Benjamin Bloom, "An Introduction to Mastery Learning Theory," in James H. Block, ed., *Schools, Society and Mastery Learning* (New York: Holt, Rinehart and Winston, 1974); Thomas R. Gusky, "Individualizing within the Group-Centered Classroom: The Mastery Learning Model" (Lexington: Office of Educational Research, University of Kentucky, 1980); Thomas R. Gusky, "Mastery Learning: Applying the Theory," *Theory Into Practice* (February 1980).

53. "Draft Regulation of the Chancellor, Required City-wide Educational Standards and Curriculum Requirements for Students in Grades Kindergarten through Grade 9, City School District of the City of New York," November 2, 1979.

54. Ibid.

55. See Michael W. Kibby, "Test Review: The Degrees of Reading Power," *Journal of Reading* (February 1981).

56. "Draft Regulation of the Chancellor, Required City-wide Educational Standards and Curriculum Requirements.

57. Ibid.

58. Ronald Edmonds, private interview, May 14, 1981.

59. Board of Education, City of New York, press release, March 6, 1979.

60. Ronald Edmonds, private interview, May 14, 1981.

61. *New York Daily News,* March 8, 1979.

62. Board of Education, City of New York, press release, May 14, 1979.

63. Board of Education, City of New York, press release, May 31, 1979.

64. Board of Education, City of New York, press release, September 5, 1979.

65. Charlotte Frank, "Memorandum to All Community Superintendents and High School Superintendents, Regarding Conference to Introduce Curriculum Bulletin, *Minimum Teaching Essentials: Grades K-9*" October 25, 1979.

66. Board of Education, City of New York, press release, November 7, 1979.

67. Alfred Melov, private interview, April 30, 1981.

68. Philip Kaplan, private interview, May 6, 1981.

69. Alfred Melov, private interview, April 30, 1981.

70. Anthony Alvarado, private interview, May 18, 1981.

71. Meryl Schwartz, private interview, May 1, 1981.

72. *New York Daily News,* December 2, 1979.

73. Alfred Melov, "Presentation Regarding Promotional Policies Draft," December 6, 1979.

74. Ibid.

75. United Parents Associations' Testimony Prepared for the Public Hearings on Draft Promotional Policies at the Hall of the Board on Thursday, December 6, 1979.

76. Ted Elsberg, private interview, May 6, 1981.

77. *New York Daily News,* January 2, 1980.

78. *The New York Times,* December 31, 1979.

79. "Chancellor's Regulations, Promotional Policy for Students in Grades Kindergarten through Grade 9," June 30, 1980.

80. Ronald Edmonds, private interview, May 14, 1981.

81. *Newsday,* June 19, 1980.

82. "Chancellor's Budget Message for the 1982 Fiscal Year," submitted to the New York City Board of Education, December 15, 1980.

83. Ronald Edmonds, "Draft, Required City-wide Policy on Educational Programs for the Promotional Gates," December 22, 1980.

84. Ibid.

85. Ibid.

86. Ibid.

87. Frank J. Macchiarola, "Draft Guidelines for Implementation of City Promotional Policy for the Promotional Gates," February 18, 1981.

88. Alfred Melov, private interview, April 30, 1981.

89. Correspondence between Robert F. Wagner, Jr., and Frank J. Macchiarola, dated March 15, 1981.

90. New York City Elementary Schools Principals Association, news release, May 1, 1981.

91. Board of Education, City of New York, press release, May 28, 1981.

92. Frank J. Macchiarola, "Memorandum to the Board of Education on Student Reading Achievement in the School Improvement Project (SIP) and the Local School Development Project (LSDP) 1980–1981," October 27, 1981.

93. Ibid.

94. Office of Educational Evaluation, New York City Public Schools, "The Promotional Gates Program: An Analysis of Summer School Participation and August, 1981 Test Scores," October 5, 1981.

95. See, for example, Eugene Radwin et al., *A Case Study of New York City's City-wide Reading Testing Program* (Cambridge, Mass.: The Huron Institute, May 1981).

96. *The Amsterdam News,* July 11, 1981.

97. These included Districts 1, 4, 9, 13, 14, 17, 21, 25, 28, 31. Board of Education, City of New York, press release, June 23, 1981.

98. Office of Educational Evaluation, New York City Public Schools, "The Promotional Gates Program."

99. Ibid.

100. Ibid.

101. Board of Education, City of New York, press release, October 19, 1981.

102. Charlotte Frank, private interview, December 8, 1981.

103. Thomas Minter, "Memorandum to Frank J. Macchiarola Regarding Gains in SAT Scores," October 26, 1981.

4
EDUCATING THE HANDICAPPED

While significant strides were made during the 1960s in educational equality for racial minorities, it was not until the next decade that such progress was realized on behalf of children with handicapping conditions. These parallel movements in the advancement of human rights faced many similar obstacles—judicial and legislative battles, a lack of consensus on goals and techniques, a concern for the costs and affordability of compensatory programs. No group was more severely victimized by unfair testing and tracking practices than were the handicapped. For these children, the label "uneducable" represented more than a prevailing public attitude; in many instances it was an explicit public policy. There was a substantial amount of overlap between the two disadvantaged populations. A large proportion of children who suffered from discrimination, segregation, and denial of educational opportunities because of handicapping conditions or designations came from the ranks of racial minorities and the poor.

This chapter concerns an attempt by the administration in the New York City public schools to comply with a federal court order enforcing the Education for All Handicapped Children Act of 1975. It allows us to analyze the local impact of both a legislative mandate and judicial intervention. The case serves to illustrate once more the variety of cross-pressures to which an urban superintendent is subjected. It documents the way such conflicting demands inhibit the ability of a local school system to respond adequately to the needs of its clientele. Moreover, given the nature and scope of the mandate imposed, the issue demonstrates, more than any other faced by the administration, the organizational and managerial consequences that can follow changes in instructional policy.

The passage of the Education for All Handicapped Children Act (Public Law 94-142) in 1975 came after a long and trying period of legislative and judicial debate.[1] First, there was an incremental campaign to sensitize federal programs enacted on behalf of the poor to the newly recognized needs of the handicapped. Between 1965 and 1969, the Elementary and Secondary Education Act was amended five times in order to guarantee funds at the state and local levels for programs to benefit handicapped children. In 1968 Congress mandated that at least 10 percent of each state allotment of funds under the Vocational Education Act be earmarked for programs specifically designed for handicapped persons. That same year the Handicapped Children's Early Education Assistance Act established experimental preschool and early-education programs for the handicapped to serve as models for the state and local levels. While the channeling of resources through several federal mechanisms in the 1960s helped in overcoming the adverse conditions of the handicapped, it was apparent that much more needed to be done. Many handicapped children were still being denied the right to an education, and many of those receiving education were being placed in programs that were either not responsive or counterproductive to their needs.

By 1968 research in the field of special education had begun to focus more on quality issues. A significant article written by Lloyd M. Dunn attracted much attention to the fact that schools too often assigned labels to students and altered their educational status without conducting appropriate evaluations.[2] The fact that a disproportionate number of children separated from the mainstream were from racial minorities gave rise to suspicions of what many social scientists would call second-generation segregation.[3] Additional research and writing argued that labeling children according to handicapping condition produces adverse psychological and behavioral effects.[4] Thus three major and often conflicting problems seemed to be emerging. First, there was a need to provide educational opportunities to handicapped children who had been unfairly denied access to the schools. Second, there was the problem of children who had been placed in special-education programs but didn't belong there. Third, and most complex, was the development or identification of programs appropriate to the individual needs of that large and diverse population of children who required special-education services.

Many students of the subject agree that the most significant early advances on behalf of the handicapped occurred in the area of litigation rather than legislation.[5] The *Hobson* v. *Hansen*[6] decision against tracking in 1967 laid the legal groundwork for subsequent cases that would deal more specifically with the handicapped. Three years later, in *Diana* v. *State Board of Education,*[7] the parents of nine Mexican-American schoolchildren in California brought a successful class-action suit into federal court alleging that their children had been inappropriately placed in classes for the educable mentally retarded (EMR) because of the use of culturally biased IQ tests. They produced evidence that while 13 percent of the children in the entire school population had Spanish surnames, 26 percent of the children segregated into EMR classes were Hispanic. The court ordered that all children whose primary home language was not English be retested in their own language. When retested, seven of the nine children scored above the cutoff point. In 1972 the United States District Court in *Larry P.* v. *Riles*[8] supported a similar class action brought on behalf of six black elementary schoolchildren in San Francisco. There again the evidence was persuasive, with blacks constituting 66 percent of the population in EMR classes and only 28 percent of the district enrollment. The court ruled that these disproportionate numbers constituted a "suspect classification." It found that incorrect placement of children in EMR classes constituted irreparable injury because the curriculum was less demanding, teacher expectations were low, and students were subjected to ridicule and feelings of inferiority. The court issued a preliminary injunction requiring that no black student be placed in an EMR class on the basis of criteria that rely primarily on the IQ tests currently being administered. In 1974 the court affirmed the order in an appeal, giving further injunctive relief to the plaintiffs.

While judicial remedies were being ordered in California to protect minority students from inappropriate placement in special education, legal battles were being fought on other fronts to assure that children were not being unfairly excluded from educational service. In 1971 the Pennsylvania Association for Retarded Children (PARC) brought a class-action suit on behalf of fourteen mentally retarded children, challenging a state statute under which retarded children could be excluded from public education.[9] The suit was brought to secure a child's rights to notice and full due process procedures before any change in status. It also sought the etablishment of free public education programs appropriate to the child's needs, and compensatory education for children who had been excluded from school. The plaintiffs argued that denial of an education was an unconstitutional violation of equal protection. They argued that placement without notice or the opportunity for a hearing was a denial of due process. In this landmark case, *PARC* v. *Pennsylvania,* the United States District Court found that all mentally retarded children can benefit from an educational program and that "the earlier such training and education begins, the more thoroughly and more efficiently a mentally retarded person will benefit from it."[10] The court also held, "It is the Commonwealth's obligation to place each mentally retarded child in a free public program of education and training appropriate to the child's capacity." However, the court explained that "appropriate" implies the presumption that among alternative programs, "placement in a regular school class is preferable to placement in a special public school class."[12] The case resulted in a consent agreement between the plaintiffs and the defendants and the court's appointment of two masters to oversee its implementation. In its resolution, the *PARC* decision attempted to remedy the three major legal and educational issues surrounding special eduation—unfair exclusion, inappropriate placement, and quality of instruction.

In 1972 a similar class-action suit was brought on behalf of seven "school-excluded" children in the District of Columbia. There the defendants argued that the plaintiffs were attempting to force them to divert funds from other educational programs in order to benefit exceptional children, and that such action would violate the rights of other children. Here again the federal court based its reasoning on the equal protection and due process clauses of the Constitution. In *Mills* v. *Board of Education*[13] it decided that the claim of insufficient funds was an inadequate defense. If sufficient funds were not available to provide all desirable educational programs, the money should be spent so that no child is entirely excluded from public education. In 1975 a motion of contempt was filed by the plaintiffs, and the court appointed a master to oversee the special-education program of the District of Columbia.

The *PARC* and *Mill* decisions set the stage for the passage of Public Law 94-142, which, at the end of a long lobbying campaign and considerable legislative debate, was signed by President Gerald Ford on November 29, 1975.[14] In 1973 Congress had overridden a presidential veto to extend Section 504 of the Vocational Rehabilitation Act, directing state agencies to give priority to clients with severe handicaps and to allow such clients a role in determining their rehabilitation programs. Section 504 also specifically prohibited discrimination against handicapped individuals in any program receiving federal assistance. The revisions in Section 504 were significant because they marked a point at which federal legislation began to regulate programs for handicapped people rather than merely provide compensation. However, Public Law 94-142 went much further. It was designed to assure that all children receive "a free appropriate education and related services designed to meet their unique needs."[15] The text of the legislation included the finding that more than one-half of the estimated eight million handicapped children in the United States were not receiving appropriate educational and related services. It included the claim that one million of these children were entirely excluded from school.

It was not the intention behind 94-142 to establish new rights for the handicapped. The purpose was to implement, reinforce, and clarify the constitutional and legal rights already in existence. It would accomplish this by defining standards of appropriateness, providing steps for ensuring due process, and defining the respective obligations of state and local jurisdictions. In so doing, the new law reduced handicapped people's reliance on Section 504 for deriving educational benefits. More important, 94-142 made litigation on behalf of the handicapped easier. While prior to its passage, plaintiffs had to rely on complicated constitutional reasoning as the basis for a suit, now they had available specific statutory requirements on which they could build their legal arguments.[16]

The requirements of the mandate imposed under Public Law 94-142 are quite unambiguous. In terms of evaluation and placement, due process procedures are required to assure that no student is unduly excluded from service or inappropriately assigned. Racially and culturally biased tests are excluded, as is the reliance on any single criterion for evaluation. All tests must be given in a child's native language. Once an evaluation is completed, parents must be granted provisions for a grievance procedure that includes the right to counsel. According to the law, any child found in need of special educational services must be placed in the "least restrictive environment." This means that handicapped students must be "mainstreamed," or placed with nonhandicapped children, as much as is possible and appropriate. In addition to this, each handicapped child must be provided with an "individualized educational program" (IEP), which must be reviewed and revised annually so long as a child is in a special-education program.

In order to offset the costs of the law to state and local jurisdictions, Congress authorized funding for a part of the expenses. The *authorized* federal assistance was to be progressively phased in over a five-year period. It would begin at 5 percent of the total national cost in 1978, the year in which the law took effect, and increase to 40 percent by 1982.[17] Entitlements would be computed by multiplying the number of handicapped children in a state by a percentage of the nationwide average expenditure per pupil. While local educational agencies are expected to prepare annual applications for funds, in the form of program plans submitted to the state, the law explicitly places responsibility for monitoring, evaluation, and compliance at the state level. Moreover, the specific obligation to identify, locate, and evaluate all handicapped children is placed with the states. The text of the law includes an expectation (not requirement), based on an estimated national average, that 12 percent of the school population in any given state will need special-education services.

Notwithstanding remarkable efforts to be explicit, those drafting the legislation in 1975 could not have anticipated all the problems that would intervene between the original intent and actual implementation of the law. It is now part of conventional social science wisdom that something gets lost along the way from the point where policy is made to the point where it is put into practice. Sometimes the change is a result of bureaucratic resistance; other times, it is the result of poor management or planning. The literature on implementation is replete with case studies of well-intentioned programs gone awry at the action stage of the policy process.[18] Recently the experience with special-education reform has added to this literature.[19]

The local problems that have grown out of the federal law governing special education are multiple and complex. To begin with, Congress never appropriated the funds necessary for the federal government to absorb its share of the financial burden. Therefore a disproportionate share of the responsibility has fallen upon the states and local districts. This responsibility is particularly burdensome during a period of economic scarcity and fiscal retrenchment. To make matters worse, the costs for implementing compliance are much higher than anyone had anticipated.[20] In addition to the financial problems resulting from Public Law 94-142, there are managerial ones. The due process requirements for evaluation and the emphasis on mainstreaming often necessitate significant changes of an organizational type in social services.[21] Such changes are difficult and don't always get the support of school personnel. Many local districts simply do not have the data-collection capabilities necessary for the required evaluation and placement procedures.[22]

The overall strategy underlying Public Law 94-142 was certainly consistent with the philosophy that was beginning to dominate the special-education profession during the early 1970s. This philosophy of mainstreaming, which dictated that children be taught in the "least restrictive environment," intended to prevent the stigmas attached to labeling and the stereotypical behavioral and learning expectations imposed by teachers.[23] However, notwithstanding the credibility, conviction, and good intentions of the mainstreaming philosophy, it is important to note that the profession is not unanimous concerning its merits. Much of the disagreement with the emergent norm is well founded. A significant body of research, for example, suggests that regular teachers are not receptive to mainstreamed handicapped pupils, and many are not confident of their own ability to deal with such children.[24] It is common knowledge that one of the major reasons why certain students are referred for special-education services is that many regular teachers do not want to deal with them or their problems. As the research on effective schools referred to in Chapter 3 suggests, poor teachers' attitudes and low expectations are generally associated with unsatisfactory student performance.[25] To compound these problems, it has been shown that handicapped pupils in mainstreamed classes also have difficulty winning acceptance by their own peers—a factor that can further contribute to their psychological damage.[26] It is not the purpose here to resolve the debate over the merits of mainstreaming. It is important at this point only that the context of the disagreement be known. The fact of the matter is that the school administration in New York City believed in and supported the philosophy embodied in Public Law 94-142. Indeed, the emphasis on the educability of handicapped children was in basic accord with the administration's own philosophy. However, the difficulties local school districts have had in complying with the law also apply to New York. In this sense, the case study that follows illustrates a set of problems many urban school districts have faced since 1978.

NEW YORK CITY: THE BUREAUCRACY VS. THE LAW

The New York City public schools began providing services to handicapped children in 1906. By 1934 the array of available programs included ungraded classes for the mentally retarded, special schools and classes for the physically handicapped, homebound instruction, and "schools of opportunity for behavior problem boys who are unable to make suitable adjustment in the traditional school."[27] The Board of Education regarded its commitment to special education as a noteworthy and progressive innovation. In her annual report to the Superintendent of Schools, Associate Superintendent Margaret McCoovey in 1934 proudly explained that new programs had been established "to give every child an equal chance with his brother, and a chance to become a self-sustaining member of society."[28] She further explained that parents no longer regarded special education as a stigma, since the categorization of handicapped children focused attention on their educational needs and strengthened appeals for financial support.

Superintendent McCoovey could never have anticipated that the programs she had developed would give rise to a structure of bureaus within the central school administration that possessed unmitigated power. Each bureau was developed in response to the demands of a special needs group within the special-education community. Thus both bureau and client enjoyed a reciprocal relationship remote from outside interference or control. In return for the special services they derived from the central administration, these client groups served as political advocates who supported the growth of the bureaus and the budgets they commanded. Special education spawned the most entrenched bureaucracy in the central school administration, guarded by the professionalism of its own specialized service and defended by a select group of interests that were well organized, articulate, and aggressive.

One might argue that there was nothing inherently wrong with the arrangement. The respective client groups were probably able to maintain their own system of quality control and accountability, which would be the envy of the most adamant proponent of community control. The problem was, however, that the system was exclusive. Not all handicapped children were served. Not all had their own personalized bureaus with which to work. The bureaus did not have to deal with a larger public and wouldn't. As one attorney for Advocates for Children explained:

> Under the old system, the bureaus ran everything. They were untouchable. They each served their own special constituency, but the point is that many kids were not served at all. They were excluded. Only some of the kids were represented under the old system.[29]

Representation was only one problem with the bureau structure. By 1978 this organizational design, which emphasized categorization, labeling, and the segregation of children on the basis of handicapping condition, was in conflict with federal law. It appeared to many reformers in the special-education profession that the antiquated administrative structure was serving the needs of the bureaucrats better than it was the children. The major service-delivery mechanism of the division was its Office of Field Operations, which was primarily composed of six instructional bureaus. (See Figure 4-1.) Each bureau was set up to deal with children in self-contained classes formed on the basis of handicapping condition. Alongside the bureau programs were self-contained nonbureau programs for children with multiple handicaps.[30] Mainstreaming was not a common practice. In addition to the Office of Field Services, the division was composed of an Office of Finance and Administration and an Office of Pupil Certification. The former was concerned with business matters. The latter performed the important functions of evaluation and placement. Unfortunately, neither office performed its functions very well. The data systems in the business offices were primitive and unreliable. The evaluation and placement operations were so inefficient that they became a source of major litigation long before Public Law 94-142 was on the books.

Since the early 1960s, Section 4407 of the New York State Education Law had required local school districts to evaluate their own schools in order to determine whether they were capable of meeting the individual needs of handicapped children. In cases where the local

Figure 4-1
FORMER TABLE OF ORGANIZATION, DIVISION OF SPECIAL EDUCATION

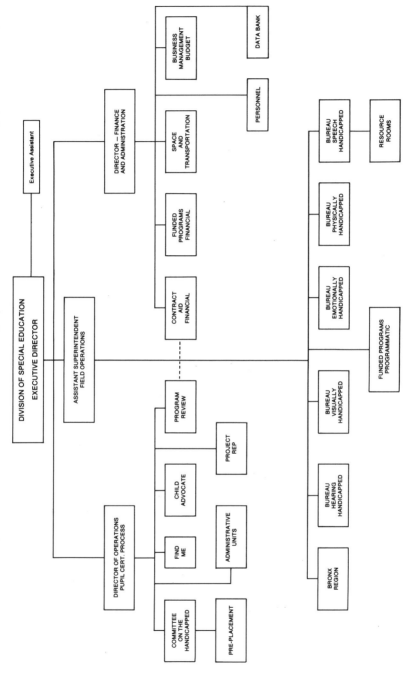

school was found not to have the necessary means, a recommendation would be made for a private placement. The state would then enter into a contract with a private school and would contribute funds of up to $2,500 per year. In 1974 the state law was amended. Under its new provisions, local school districts would be required to assume financial responsibility for all private placements, except for cases of out-of-state residential treatment. If enforced, this new law could place a severe financial burden on the local school district in New York City, for it had been a common practice to deem many handicapped children "uneducable" and exclude them from service in either a public or private setting. As one attorney from an advocate group, who later joined the school system's legal staff, explained, "Medical discharges were not unusual around here. We were discharging kids who were said to be unfit for education. This was common practice within the Board of Education at one time."[31]

By 1971 proceedings had been introduced in federal court on behalf of brain-injured and other handicapped children in New York City who had not been receiving appropriate educational services. The plaintiffs also brought to the attention of the court lengthy waiting lists for evaluation and placement. On June 22 the United States District Court denied the plaintiffs' motion for a preliminary injunction against the Board of Education, which they alleged was denying equal educational opportunities to brain-injured children.[32] However, on December 14 the United States Court of Appeals held that the district court should have retained jurisdiction in the case, pending the clarification of state law.[33] At that point the plaintiffs began administrative proceedings before the state commissioner of education.[34] On November 26, 1973, Commissioner Ewald Nyquist ruled in the momentous *Riley Reid*[35] decision that the Board of Education's failure to evaluate and place handicapped children was in violation of state law. He ordered the Board immediately to place all children diagnosed as handicapped in an appropriate public or private program. He also ordered the Board to devise a long-range plan to eliminate the waiting lists for evaluation and placement.

Between 1974 and 1975 the special-education enrollment in New York City increased by 19.2 percent, growing from 33,170 students to 39,553 students.[36] It was then the largest single-year increase in the history of the school system, which no doubt had begun to serve a population it had never reached before. However, before long outside advocates began to ask, "How?" When that happened, the Board once again found itself in federal court. On June 11, 1975, the parents of seven black and Puerto Rican children attending special day schools for the "socially maladjusted and emotionally disturbed" (SMED) brought a class-action suit in the United States District Court in *Lora v. Board of Education*.[37] The plaintiffs in the *Lora* case claimed that their constitutional rights regarding due process, equal protection, and involuntary servitude were violated when they were placed in racially segregated SMED schools. They challenged the evaluation and placement techniques and produced data showing that while 59.8 percent of the school population was black or Hispanic, 92 percent of the children in SMED schools were from those minority groups.

It was not long after the *Lora* case was brought into court that President Ford signed Public Law 94-142. Within the next year, the New York State legislature passed the Guiffreda bill, which sought to codify into state law all the rights and procedures guaranteed in Public Law 94-142. In the meantime, the administrative apparatus in the Division of Special Education had become overloaded with requests for evaluations and placement. Many parents took advantage of the remedies provided in the commissioner's *Riley Reid* decision and opted to put their children in private schools. Special-education officials in the city were not pleased with this practice because the costs of private schooling were paid from their budget.

On April 6, 1976, the commissioner reaffirmed his original decision. He stated that parents who had enrolled their children in private schools because the Board of Education had failed to provide a timely evaluation or placement were entitled to tuition reimbursements.[38] He added that the Board of Education could not transfer such children during the school year when public placements became available. On June 30, 1976, the commissioner established due process procedures whereby students could appeal placement decisions if they were not satisfied.[39] By September of 1977, the size of the waiting list for evaluations had grown to over 5,000 children. Added to these were 2,100 pupils who were awaiting placements. The situation brought more appeals to the commissioner, who then held that the Board of Education must diagnose and place a child within sixty days of referral.[40] He ordered that no child be transferred from a private placement unless that placement was found to be inappropriate. Finally, he instructed the Board of Education to submit a new plan to eliminate its waiting list on January 2, 1978.

In the meantime, the Division of Special Education was in the process of examining the merits of its bureau structure, which by then was in conflict with the educational principles embodied in the federal and state laws. In October 1977 a pilot project for regional management was set up in the Bronx. The Bronx Regional Office, which covered the entire borough, was designed to incorporate all special-education services under a single management structure. Its responsibilities would include evaluation, placement, program development, supervision, monitoring, and support services. The pilot operation abolished the old bureau structure and placed emphasis on the elimination of labels. It was also hoped that under the Bronx plan, special-education personnel would work more closely with regular school principals and teachers. Under the old structure, staff in the districts usually regarded special-education people as an arm of the central administration. The Bronx Regional Office hoped to achieve some level of integration.

The ideas behind the regional plan appeared to be sound, but the project was put into place rather late. Helen Feulner, the executive director of the division, had proposed a reorganization plan based on a regional structure as early as April 1976. There was no action on the proposal. Now in October 1977, eight months before a new administration was due to take office, a pilot program was begun. The incumbent administration would not even have adequate time to evaluate its own experiment.

In February 1978, a month after it was due, the Division of Special Education submitted its "Plan for Elimination of Waiting Lists for Evaluation and Placement" to the state commissioner. In a letter to the commissioner, the plaintiffs reacted to the plan by calling it vague, ambiguous, and unsatisfactory. By this time the United States Office for Civil Rights had found the Board in violation of Section 504 of the Rehabilitation Act of 1973. The reason for the violation was the "denial of appropriate education services to handicapped students due to excessive waiting lists." On June 23, eight days before the new administration was due to take office, the Division of Special Education submitted to the state commissioner a new plan for the elimination of waiting lists.

THE ADMINISTRATION'S INHERITANCE: BACKLOGS AND BAD WILL

As Frank Macchiarola took office on July 1, the Division of Special Education was under criticism from the state Commissioner of Education, the Office for Civil Rights, the federal courts, and an assortment of advocate groups. While the regional experiment was going on in the Bronx, the old bureau structure was still alive and well in the four other boroughs. One of the first executive actions of new chancellor was to place all senior officials in the central administration at Livingston Street on probation for a period of six months. By the end of this time, a decision would have been made regarding each individual's tenure. This was a common practice within the public sector and was an ordinary feature of municipal government in New York. But it had never been done at Livingston Street. Needless to say, Macchiarola's announcement was not well received by the bureaucracy. In particular, Helen Feulner, who had served as executive director of the Division of Special Education for eight years, took exception to the chancellor's action. She demanded a meeting, at which she told the new school chief that she would not wait six months for a decision. She wanted the issue to be resolved immediately. It was. Feulner was replaced by Charles Schonhaut, who would serve as acting executive director until a permanent one was chosen.

Charles Schonhaut had formerly served on the staff of Chancellor Irving Anker and had played a major role in that administration. He did not consider himself a special educator, but he knew the system well. On a temporary basis, he could keep things from falling apart in that troubled division. Afterwards, he would remain with administration as Superintendent of High Schools for the Borough of Brooklyn.

On July 5 the chancellor received a letter from the state commissioner, criticizing the Board of Education's June plan to eliminate the waiting lists.[41] More work had to be done. Schonhaut was directed to develop a new plan. In August, Macchiarola commissioned Alan Gartner of the City University of New York to conduct an evaluation of the Bronx Regional Office. Gartner, who had a reputation as a strong advocate for decentralization in New York City and a supporter of the mainstreaming concept, was expected to favor the thinking behind the regional plan.

On November 22 Schonhaut compiled a "Status Report on Evaluation and Placement."[42] The report showed that 8,259 children were awaiting evaluation. Of this group, 2,428 had been on the list for more than sixty days without an offer for an appointment. It also showed that 4,449 students were awaiting placement, of whom 2,765 had never been offered a site. In January 1979 the commissioner's office prepared its own "Report on New York City's Education of Handicapped Students."[43] The report noted the growing size of the waiting lists. It observed that the Board's efforts to evaluate and place handicapped children had been a "chronic problem." It found that the Board's June 1978 plan to reduce the waiting lists "failed completely." On January 16, 1979, the chancellor submitted to the commissioner a new "Plan to Evaluate Children in Compliance with the Commissioner's Regulations."

The Gartner study on the Bronx region was completed in December 1978. The two-hundred-page document ended with guarded praise and a good number of cautionary recommendations. From a comparative perspective, the evaluation found that the regional design was a "more workable and better strategy" than the centralized bureaucratic system in terms of operations, accountability, and the general delivery of services.[44] However, beyond the issues of organization and management, Gartner and his colleagues found much that was wanting in the Bronx region. They did not see any distinct inclination in the regional setting to emphasize placements in the "least restrictive environment." They did not find any close integration between district personnel and regional staff. They warned of a "real danger" that over a period of time "a set of regional systems will develop their own hierarchies and bureaus, create a series of autonomous units, and become even more inaccessible than the present system is."[45]

There was a clear message to be found in the Bronx report. While the regional plan was marginally preferable to the bureau structure, it did not go far enough. There was a basic flaw in any organizational design that assumed a central division or region could be responsible for the day-to-day operation of programs carried out in school buildings in the districts. There was little chance that handicapped children could be mixed into the mainstream if their teachers were not. Gartner wanted more decentralization. He saw a monitoring role for the division, but emphasized that all educational initiatives should be run from the school and district levels. He explained:

> Our proposals are based on the assumption that the local school districts are responsible for the education of all youth residing within that district. We see little chance of change . . . unless there is a major structural realignment of the DSEPPS [Division]– Districts relationship.[46]

Not long after the Gartner report was completed, Brooklyn Legal Services, a small public-interest law group located off Livingston Street, began litigation in the United States District Court concerning the unresolved waiting lists. The original affidavit filed in *José P. v. Ambach*[47] on February 15, 1979, initiated a class-action suit on behalf of all handicapped children deprived of a free, appropriate education because of the Board of Education's failure to perform timely evaluations and placements. The attorneys for the plaintiffs cited a long history of frustration they had experienced at both the city and state levels. Indeed, the new litigation indicated that the plaintiffs had even lost faith in the state commissioner's ability and will to bring the situation to a satisfactory resolution. As John "Chip" Gray, the original attorney from Brooklyn Legal Services, explained:

> The State Commissioner appeared to be abandoning the *Riley Reid* decision. He was becoming less aggressive. At that point, we chose to start litigation against the state and the city because the

law states that it is the state's responsibility to assure compliance with 94-142.[48]

Public Law 94-142 made litigation easier for special-education advocates. The *José P.* case was the first to be brought against New York on the basis of its statutory provisions. It would prove to be the most significant special-education case in the city, but it would not be the last. On March 2 United Cerebral Palsy of New York initiated another class-action suit againt the Board of Education on behalf of all handicapped individuals residing in New York City legally entitled to a free, appropriate education.[49] This case went beyond the evaluation and placement issues cited in *José P.* to questions of quality—i.e., timeliness of evaluations, kinds of programs available, mainstreaming opportunities, accessibility of facilities, and the preparation of individualized education plans (IEP's).[50] Taken as a whole, these questions moved the case beyond the policy formation phase and pushed it to the level of implementation. As Michael Rebell, attorney for UCP, explained, "In short, the UCP plaintiffs were advising both the defendants and the court that solutions to the long-standing special-education problems in New York City would require a structural reform of the entire system."[51]

One of the first major court proceedings of the *José P.* case took place on May 16, 1979. At that time Charles Schonhaut, representing the Board of Education, stood before Judge Eugene Nickerson and admitted that the Board had failed to evaluate and place children in a timely fashion. The judge issued a Memorandum and Order certifying the class action and finding that the Board had failed to comply with federal and state requirements. A final judgment would not be issued in the case until more facts were gathered concerning the problems of implementation and their prospective solutions. In order to facilitate the fact gathering, Nickerson appointed former federal Judge Marvin E. Frankel to serve as special master in the case. Frankel came to the case with a reputation as a judicial activist. As a judge, he had been intimately involved in prison reform in New York. In 1974 he presided over the *Aspira*[52] bilingual education case, which involved the city school system. Now he was to play a major role in *José P.* As Judge Nickerson's Memorandum and Order prescribed:

> . . . he [the master] will not be limited to receiving and reporting evidence. He will be permitted to consult informally with the parties and with outside experts and others and receive materials not in evidence.
> The master shall evaluate the plans promulgated by the Board and shall make such recommendations as he deems appro-

priate as to what decree the court should enter to provide the requisite public education to handicapped children in the City of New York.[53]

In August, Judge Nickerson recognized the overlap between the *José P.* and the *UCP* cases and issued an order in the latter, deferring it until the receipt of a final report by the special master in *José P.* On October 2 another case was brought before Judge Nickerson on the basis of the rights ensured under Public Law 94-142. *Dyrcia S.* v. *Ambach*[54] was argued by the Puerto Rican Legal Defense Fund on behalf of a group of handicapped students who were in need of bilingual and bicultural special educational services but had not yet been properly evaluated or placed. The *Dyrcia S.* case would eventually add a new dimension to the *José P.* proceedings.

As litigation was being brought against the school system under Public Law 94-142, the *Lora* case was still pending in federal court. Suing in 1975 before the enactment of Public Law 94-142, the plaintiffs had originally argued on constitutional grounds. The case was finally decided by United States District Court Judge Jack Weinstein on July 2, 1979. Weinstein ordered the following relief in this case concerning the segregation of minority students in special day schools for the "socially maladjusted and emotionally disturbed":

- the identification and evaluation of students illegally placed in special day schools;
- the development of nondiscriminatory standards, criteria, and procedures for evaluation and placement of emotionally handicapped students;
- the development of a full continuum of services for emotionally handicapped children, with placement in the least restrictive environment;
- the preparation of documents explaining parents' due process rights;
- the development of an in-service training program and a continuing training program for all current and future staff within the school system in order to sensitize individuals about the dangers of racial and cultural biases and the needs of special-education children;
- increased services and programs for the special day schools;
- the establishment of a comprehensive reporting and monitoring mechanism to ensure compliance with the court order.[55]

Judge Weinstein's decision was far-reaching and innovative. It had significance as a constitutional case. However, to a large extent it was dated. Some of the remedies ordered were already at the implementation stage. Some of its more important features would be included under the statutory issues covered in the *José P* case. In the end, *Lora* came to a rather curious conclusion. The administration agreed with the mandates in the judge's order but differed with it on an important matter of principle. Hence, within six months of the original decision, the Board of Education appealed the case. The problem, from the point of view of the administration, was the court's finding of intentional discrimination. As one attorney for the administration explained,

> We appealed *Lora* because we did not want it said that there was intentional discrimination. We were not so interested in its results because, in fact, there were none. We just wanted to be on the right side of the issue.[56]

When the United States Court of Appeals handed down its decision on *Lora* in March 1980, it came out in favor of the Board. Citing *Washington* v. *Davis,* Judge Milton Pollack found that ". . . inferences from evidence of discriminatory impact will not substitute sufficiently for a finding of actual motivation. . . ." He added, "The burden of proof remains with the plaintiffs."[57] The administration had won its point of principle. The fact of the matter is, however, that by 1980 it had already begun to move toward compliance, and there was no intention of changing direction. The Division of Special Education was in the process of reevaluating the children in special day schools. In December 1979 the "*Lora* Decree Staff Development Program" began, designed to acquaint school personnel with laws and regulations governing the handicapped, the special needs of handicapped pupils, and the problems inherent in racial, ethnic, and cultural stereotyping. Under the direction of Alan Gartner, the monumental training program reached 55,000 teachers and 15,000 administrators throughout the school system over the 1979–1980 school year.[58]

By March 1980, all the other major issues of the *Lora* case were either decided, or under negotiation within the broader framework of the *José P.* case. Recognizing the overlap of the two cases, Judge Pollack himself recommended in his appellate decision:

> In order to avoid potentially conflicting mandates, and in the interests of avoiding waste and duplication, the District Court should consider the feasibility of consolidating the present case with *José P.* v. *Ambach* . . . since so many of the same issues are common to both cases, it might be in the interests of judicial husbandry and all concerned.[59]

As things turned out, the two cases were never consolidated. *Lora,* at that point, became a moot issue. It, like most other special-education litigation in New York City, was simply overshadowed by *José P.*

THE JUDICIAL MANDATE: "SPECIAL EDUCATION IN TRANSITION"

On July 5, 1979, after the completion of a year-long national search, the chancellor appointed Dr. Jerry Gross as the new executive director of the Division of Special Education. The thirty-nine-year-old educator had been serving as director of the La Grange Area Department of Special Education in Illinois since 1974. Between 1969 and 1974, Gross had served as assistant director of the Special Education Division in the Minneapolis public schools. Prior to that, he had held positions as a special educator in Torrance, California; Tucson, Arizona; Carbondale, Illinois; and Boston, Massachusetts. At the time of his appointment in New York, Gross was vice president and president-elect of the Council of Administrators of Special Education, a national organization.

Gross had impeccable credentials as a special educator. He possessed a sterling reputation nationally as an articulate advocate of decategorization. Among the goals he stated at the time of his appointment were the expansion of mainstreaming opportunities for special-education children and the relocation of referral and placement services closer to the schools. Gross also promised a reorganization of the division. He came to New York with his own working model for special-education services. That model was an encapsulation of all the principles and mandates included in Public Law 94-142. It was consistent with the recommendations in the Gartner report on regionalization. Gross even brought with him a small corps of his own people, who would help him implement the plan.

Gross's appointment gave birth to a new optimism. The selection of a permanent executive director of special education had been long awaited. However, the problems he and his staff would face were enormous. There were a court order, pending lawsuits, and an emerging budget crisis. There were those long, ineradicable waiting lists that continued to grow. And there was that large, cumbersome, obstreperous bureaucracy that defied change. By 1981, the student population in the Division of Special Education would be larger than that of the entire school systems of Buffalo, Rochester, Syracuse, and Yonkers combined. if the division itself were an independent school district, it would be the sixteenth largest in the nation, approximately the size of the Cleveland school system.

The summer of 1979 was a busy one for the new executive director and his staff. By its end, they had designed a new plan for the division. In early September, the plan, entitled "Special Education in Transition," was voted on and approved by the Board of Education.[60] Under a newly proposed divisional structure, an Office of Student Support Services would assume responsibility for pupil evaluation and certification, and an Office for Instructional Programs and Services would replace the existing Office of Field Operations. (See Figure 4-2.) An Office of Finance and Administration would continue to administer personnel, budget, and other housekeeping operations. Two central themes governed "Special Education in Transition":

1. delivering special-education services close to the child and teacher, where those services can be most effective;
2. defining the services in order to minimize reliance on categories and labels.[61]

Under the old structure, children referred for special education were evaluated by a distict Committee on the Handicapped (COH), which was part of the central divisional structure. This district COH usually included a psychologist, an educator, and a parent. There was one of these units in each of the thirty-two school districts, but in most cases the professionals who sat on it were not from the child's home school. If this district unit found a child in need of special services, its decision required approval by the central COH, to which it reported. At that point the child would be placed by an administrative unit reporting to the central COH. The placement would usually be made in a "self-contained" program run by a central bureau that was part of the Office of Field Serives. By definition, self-contained programs did not allow handicapped children much opportunity to be mainstreamed with children in regular education. Parents did possess due process rights to appeal evaluation and placement decisions at each stage of the process and could make a final appeal to a hearing unit appointed by the Board of Education.

A basic concept distinguishing the Gross plan was the school-based approach. Under his model, each school would contain a School-Based Support Team (SBST), which came under the new Office of Student Support Services. The SBST would consist of a psychologist, a social worker, a special educator, the school principal (or designee), a guidance counselor, and the regular classroom teacher of the child. All children referred for special education would be reviewed first by the SBST within the environment of the home school. The SBST would make an initial evaluation of whether a child was in need of special services, and if so, what kind. At that point the SBST

Figure 4-2
TABLE OF ORGANIZATION, PROPOSED DIVISION OF SPECIAL EDUCATION

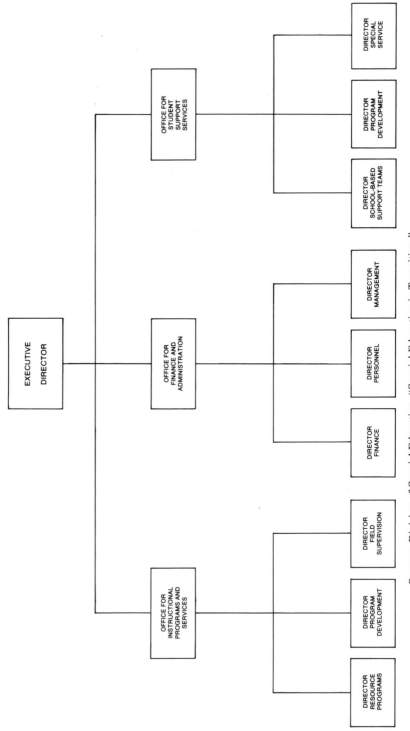

Source: Division of Special Education, "Special Education in Transition."

would attempt to prescribe a program of educational and support ser-vices to be provided to the child at the home school. This prescription would ordinarily include a resource-room program in the school, ad-ministered through the new Office for Instructional Programs and Ser-vices. Resource-room programs are designed for mildly handicapped students, who spend approximately 80 percent of their school time in a mainstreamed setting with regular-education students. The other 20 percent of their time, spent in the resource room, is meant to provide for each child's special needs. This SBST approach not only allows the maximum opportunity for mainstreaming, but also calls for a good deal of joint planning between regular and special-education teachers at the home school.

Under the Gross plan, only special students whose handicapping condition did not allow them to use a resource room would be referred by the SBST to the COH. "Low incidence" programs for these chil-dren, which might take place in a self-contained day school or alterna-tive school, would also be operated by the Office of Instructional Programs and Services. However, even in these settings, an attempt would be made to provide whatever mainstreaming opportunities are feasible within a particular "continuum of service." Under the new office, the bureau structure was eliminated. The office would also pro-vide support services to all schools that housed special-education pro-grams and classes.

The message behind Gross's school-based proposal was quite clear: Keep a child within the regular educational setting as much as is practicable. Also incorporated in "Special Education in Transition" were commitments to timely evaluations and placements, parental in-volvement in all stages of the educational process, procedural safe-guards, and staff development and training. The new organizational structure would include six regions, which would coordinate and inte-grate the work between the central division and the thirty-two commu-nity school districts.

Gross's plan was designed with an eye toward the law and the impending judgment from Judge Nickerson in the *José P.* case. In fact, Gross consulted with the plaintiffs in the case as he planned the future of his division. In the end, "Special Education in Transition" would become the basis of a prenegotiated court judgment. Gross did not see either the court or the plaintiffs as adversaries, for he was in basic agreement with the law and their determination to enforce it. That is the reason he was hired. And this attitude led to an initial exchange of confidence and goodwill with the plaintiffs. As one attorney for the latter observed,

Jerry Gross was a professional committed to reforming the system. He early on appeared to have decided to view the court mechanism as an opportunity to promote reforms in the system, rather than as an outside intervener to be resisted at every turn.[62]

Another major force behind the spirit of cooperation pervasive before the final judgment was handed down, was the role assumed by the court-appointed master, Marvin Frankel. Frankel had originally been appointed as a fact-finder, someone who would provide relevant information to the judge in order to help him reach a fair and workable solution. Frankel sought to perform this function by bringing the plaintiffs and the defendants together so that a judgment acceptable to both sides could be negotiated for the court. In short, Frankel drove the negotiations. As one party in the case explained,

Frankel expedited negotiations. He was very good at finding a middle ground, although he tended to get involved only when negotiations broke down. He played an active role, but it wasn't done in terms of making decisions. He managed to get the parties to reach their own resolutions.[63]

As the negotiations advanced toward an agreement, and as the special master came closer to making a recommendation to the judge, there was still disagreement among the members of the Board of Education on how to handle the judgment legally. Should the Board enter into a consent decree and become legally bound by its provisions? Should it merely accept a judgment and, in a more flexible form of cooperation, agree not to appeal it? Or should the Board merely accept a judgment, attempt to carry it out, but leave the future legal options open?

On November 27 Chancellor Macchiarola sent a memorandum to the Board of Education.[64] It stated that he fully supported "Special Education in Transition." However, he added that he could not recommend consenting to the proposed *José P.* judgment because it contained requirements that extended into the next two fiscal years. He reminded the Board members that the Board of Education does not control its fiscal future, so it could not commit itself to that extent. When the Board met the next day, it agreed to accept the chancellor's advice to accept a judgment and not enter into a consent decree. Two days later, an attorney for the city who had been present at the Board meeting, and was handling the case for the Board, sent a letter to the master. It stated that the Board had decided not to consent to the proposed judgment, but that it would not appeal it.[65] The letter provoked fury at the Board of Education. On December 12 Board member

Amelia Ashe sent a letter of concern to the chancellor and the other members of the Board, saying that the Board had never agreed not to appeal the judgment.[66] She advised them that the Board had agreed neither to enter into a consent decree nor to waive its right to reopen the case in the future. She requested that the attorney's letter to the special master be removed from the record.

On December 14, 1979, Judge Eugene Nickerson issued an order and judgment. As expected, it was a combined product of Public Law 94–142, "Special Education in Transition," and the negotiated recommendations of the special master. The relief ordered included the following requirements:

- an outreach office, with adequate bilingual services, for the identification of all children in need of special-education services;
- the establishment of SBSTs in all schools by April 1981;
- the provision of resources by the spring of 1980 for the timely evaluation of children, either by Board staff or by approved outside facilities;
- appropriate programs in the least restrictive environment, with the provision of a continuum of services including preventive services, resource rooms, and sufficient programs for handicapped students in both high incidence and low incidence programs, as close to the home as possible, with appropriate bilingual programs;
- commitment to hire personnel for all related services, such as physical and occupational therapy;
- facilities that are fully accessible to handicapped students, and close to their homes;
- commitment to issue a parents' rights booklet in English and Spanish.[67]

The final judgment also included several specific time limits for the implementation of the SBSTs and the elimination of the waiting lists. The order would be implemented under the continued supervision of the special master. It called for the creation of a management information system and periodic reporting to the master and the parties. Also required were two additional plans. A "January Plan" (1980) would set forth the detailed procedures for implementing the judgment. An "April Plan" (1980) would specify staff, space, and instructional materials needed to fulfill the judgment and the January Plan. Both plans were to be negotiated with the plaintiffs and approved by the court.[68]

It was clear at this point that both the master and the plaintiffs would have a legally defined long-term role in the Division of Special Education. This role would take them beyond the initial judgment, through the implementation, supervision, and monitoring of the agreed-upon plan. It would make management within the division a negotiated process. On February 27, 1980, the court issued a consolidated judgment incorporating all the provisions of the December 14 *José P.* order into the *United Cerebral Palsy* and *Dyrcia S.* cases. The Public Education Association and Advocates for Children, both of whom participated in negotiating the original judgment, were eventually granted *amicus* status on behalf of the plaintiffs.

THE COSTS OF COMPLIANCE: AN EMERGING CONTROVERSY

Judge Nickerson handed down the *José P.* judgment less than a month after the $92 million school budget deficit was made public in 1979. Special-education spending had indeed contributed to that deficit, since school officials had already made a commitment to eliminate the waiting lists and improve services for children with handicapping conditions. Now, as the administration went about the task of complying with the court order, the financial situation became further exacerbated. Here was a classic case of a superintendent (the chancellor in this case) caught in a set of cross-pressures from outside: on the one hand, ordered by the court and federal law to increase services for special-education children; on the other hand, urged by the mayor and municipal officials to reduce spending.

Within a week after the judgment, school and city officials began public speculation and debate on the anticipated costs of complying with the new mandate. In addition to the 68,000 students then receiving special-education services, new referrals were growing at a rate of 4,000 per month. Executive Director Jerry Gross projected that three hundred new classrooms would be needed by September, and he estimated that special-education costs would rise by $350 million over the next three years. City Budget Director James Brigham declared that Gross's estimate was ridiculously high.[69] By then, the battle over budget controls was in full bloom. Just a few days earlier Board President Stephen Aiello had sent his controversial letter to the mayor and city comptroller, advising them that school officials had no intention of compromising their autonomy on spending.

On January 27, 1980, Mayor Edward Koch appeared in Washington, where he delivered a major address before the United States Conference of Mayors. The subject was mandates. Koch complained that New York, like other cities, was required by the federal and state governments to provide services that would cost $17.5 billion. He pointed out that, of this amount, the federal government provided only $6.5 billion, and the state, $4.7 billion, leaving the financially beleaguered city to pay the remaining $6.25 billion. He added that the city that year was spending $427 million for educating the handicapped, of which $35 million was contributed by the federal government and $71 million by the state, while the remaining $221 million came from local sources. Koch ended his address by asking for a new policy that would not permit federal or state governments to mandate services from cities without providing funds to pay for them.[70]

Throughout the remainder of the school year, considerable local attention was given to the mandate issue in news stories, editorials, and speeches of protest by public officials. An editorial by WCBS-TV, aired in late June, is an example. While acknowledging the need for more and better services for the handicapped, the editorial attacked Congress, which "has not picked up the tab for the very expensive education it has required."[71] These protests about costs did nothing to help the literally thousands of handicapped children throughout the city who still were not receiving adequate educational services, to which they were both morally and legally entitled. Nor, despite their consternation, did the protesters weaken the intent of the federal courts.

On June 30 the United States Federal District Court, in *Riley* v. *Ambach,* handed down a decision concerning eighteen learning-disabled children in nine Long Island school districts.[72] While the case did not directly involve New York City, the implications were significant. At issue were the state's criteria for identifying children as "learning-disabled." A student was considered learning-disabled if there was a 50 percent discrepancy between expected and actual achievement at grade level. Plaintiffs argued that the 50 percent rule was too restrictive and inconsistent with federal standards. They testified that the use of the rule caused the number of children in the state receiving services as learning-disabled to drop from 28,172 to 12,167 over one year. Deciding in favor of the plaintiffs, Judge Charles P. Sifton found that "the use of the 50 percent standard interferes with the proper identification of learning-disabled children."[73]

The decision was likely to have a considerable impact on the city, increasing the number of children legally entitled to special-education services and contributing further to the large budget deficit. As might be expected, Mayor Koch denounced the decision as "simply another foolish mandate."[74] He warned that the city might join the state as an *amicus* in an appeal of the decision. Koch then let loose with his own analysis of the local situation, reminding his public and the judge that the additional burden on the budget would reduce other local services:

> There's just a limited pot of money for the city. . . . If I were the judge, I would ask myself, "Where will they have to take it from? From nonhandicapped children? From police? From firemen?" . . . This is ridiculous. It can't go on this way. This country, every city, every county, is fed up with mandates.[75]

In mid-July the chancellor's office completed an in-depth study on the projected costs of instruction and related services in special education expected to result from an attempt to comply with Public Law 94-142 and the *José P.* mandates over the next three years. Based on the existing referral rate (then 3,500 per month), the report projected a register increase that would amount to 91,732 in June of 1981; 105,176 in June of 1982; and 116,668 in June of 1983.[76] While these growth figures were dramatic from a local perspective, they were consistent with a nationwide trend that began with the passage of Public Law 94-142. In fact, on a national scale, the percentage of the total student population in New York in 1980 receiving special education services was rather low (7.5 percent). A survey conducted by the National School Boards Association the year before found that in 261 school districts of various sizes throughout the country, special-education enrollment averaged 8.6 percent.[77] In districts of 25,000 pupils or more, the average enrollment was 9 percent. A preliminary study from the United States Office of Education revealed that 8.9 percent of the total American public school population was receiving special-education services in the 1979–1980 school year.[78]

To these national surveys, the chancellor's office added its own, which focused on twenty-two large urban school systems. Special-education enrollment in these cities ranged from 4.2 percent in Detroit to 18.4 percent in Boston. When compared with the entire group, New York's 7.5 percent enrollment rate in 1980 came out to be the fourth lowest. (See Table 4-1.) If the projected rate of growth in New York was valid, the portion of children receiving special education by 1983 would be 13.3 percent. Given the continued rise of special-education enrollments around the country, this percentage would still be consistent with the national norm. However, when the 1980 staff-to-pupil ratios were applied to the registration projections for 1981–1983, the resulting cost figures appeared overwhelming. Costs within the Division of Special Education would rise from $311,689,582 in 1981 to $361,583,297 in 1983. (See Table 4-2.) When fringe benefits and contract bus services were added to these figures, the real amount in

Table 4-1
SPECIAL-EDUCATION POPULATION IN MAJOR U.S. CITIES

City	Percent of public school enrollment
Boston	18.4
Buffalo	15.2
Baltimore	14.9
Pittsburgh	14.7*
Philadelphia	12.4
Milwaukee	12.0 (estimate)
Chicago	11.7
Minneapolis	11.4
Newark	11.0 (estimate)
St. Louis	10.4
Cincinnati	9.8*
Denver	9.7*
Columbus	9.6
Houston	9.6*
Indianapolis	8.4*
Los Angeles	8.3
Dallas	7.8*
Miami (Dade County)	7.7
New York City	7.5 (as of 4/30/80)
San Diego	7.3*
Portland	6.4
Detroit	4.2

Source: New York City Public Schools, Chancellor's Office of Policy Analysis, Research and Planning, "Costs of Compliance; A Report to the Chancellor on the Projected Costs of Providing Services to the Special Education Population in New York City in compliance with P.L. 94-142" July 1980.
*Figures marked with an asterisk are for school year 1978–1979; all others are for school year 1979–1980.

spending would grow between 1981 and 1983 from $510,963,769 to $584,139,393. (See Table 4-3.)

As the chancellor's office was in the process of completing its cost projections, other officials in the city and state, concerned with the rising expenditures in special education, began to conduct their own inquiries. On August 19 Macchiarola received a letter from Comer S. Coppie, executive director of the State Financial Control Board. The letter expressed "serious concerns" regarding "the impact of federal mandates and recent judicial determinations on the Board of Education Budget and the city's Financial Plan."[79] Enclosed was a seventy-seven-page draft report, which Coppie was planning to release after he received a reaction from the chancellor's office.

Table 4-2
PROJECTED COSTS FOR THE DIVISION OF SPECIAL EDUCATION

	FY 1981, adopted budget	FY 1982	FY 1983
Instuctional and related services	$209,571,827	$228,788,781	$244,081,818
Office of Instructional Programs and Services— Administration	5,712,607	5,712,607	5,712,607
Office of Student Support Services	42,501,866	49,123,228	50,009,412
Office of Finance and Management	3,246,225	3,246,225	3,246,225
Non-public school tuition	31,295,000	35,714,864	39,171,178
Other	19,362,057	19,362,057	19,362,057
Total (FY 1981 dollars)	$311,689,582	$341,947,762	$361,583,297

Source: Chancellor's Office of Policy Analysis, "Costs of Compliance."

The FCB report noted that the city was facing a $1 billion budget deficit for the 1982 fiscal year, the year in which it was legally bound to have a balanced budget. Focusing on the "acute impact" the special-education program had on the city's financial condition, the report explained that $98 million in projected cost savings within the school budget would be more than offset by the rising expenditures in special education.[80] The FCB document criticized the semi-autonomous reporting arrangement enjoyed by the school system and demanded more external controls. It called the cost ceiling projected in the city financial plan "unrealistically low." It expressed concern with the impact the recent *Riley* v. *Ambach* decision would have if it was not successfully appealed. Finally, the FCB report included a strong attack on the management of the Division of Special Education, which, it claimed, had a direct bearing on the current financial crisis.

Table 4-3
PROJECTED COSTS FOR SERVICES TO THE SPECIAL EDUCATION
POPULATION

CATEGORY	FY 1981	FY 1982	FY 1983
DSE	$311,689,582	$341,947,762	$361,583,297
Fringe benefits	95,176,957	104,838,427	110,867,923
Contract bus service	104,097,230	108,465,734	111,688,173
Total cost	$510,963,769	$555,251,923	$584,139,393

Source: Chancellor's Office of Policy Analysis, "Costs of Compliance."

Instructional programs for handicapped students have been organized and administered in such a way as to confound any rational decision-making process. . . .

In summary, the historical development of the special-education program has produced an archaic programmatic and management structure. As a result, the Division of Special Education has been unable to effectively manage the rapid growth of enrollment resulting from recent court decisions.[81]

As school was about to open in September, City Comptroller Harrison J. Goldin began another investigation of special education, holding hearings at the Board of Estimate chambers at City Hall. Among those to appear at the hearings were Mayor Edward Koch, Council President Carol Bellamy, Chancellor Frank Macchiarola, union leader Albert Shanker, and Board of Education President Joseph Barkan. A common theme to emerge from two days of well-publicized testimony was the unfair burden of nonsupported federal mandates. Koch described the legislative and judicial mandates as "classic examples of well-intentioned intervention which is insensitive to local needs and local fiscal conditions."[82] Carol Bellamy warned, "In our desire to redress the unequal treatment of handicapped students, we may end up dismantling what is left of our public education system."[83] She also urged the Division of Special Education to "put its house in order." Answering his own question as to whether the city could simultaneously assure a decent education for all children and balance its budget, Albert Shanker shouted, "I don't believe it can be done."[84]

Macchiarola used the hearings as an opportunity to describe the changes that were going on in special education in terms of mainstreaming opportunities, related services, and management reforms. He discussed "Special Education in Transition" and its relationship to the law. He presented data from his recent report on enrollment and cost projections and explained them in a nationwide context. The chancellor also registered his agreement with the emerging theme of the day, the need for more federal support. But beyond that theme, he gave quite a different message from those who had preceded him to the podium. He pledged:

We are committed to provide direct and support services to children with handicapping conditions, which are both required by law, and morally right in themselves; doing so in the knowledge that the costs must be borne by New York City taxpayers with insufficient help from Washington and New York State.[85]

Within a few days after his testimony at City Hall, Macchiarola sent off a response to Comer Coppie regarding the FCB report. The chancellor's reaction to the state document was highly critical. He held that data in the draft report were inaccurate, untimely, and unconfirmed. He stated that the analysis of management practices within the Division of Special Education "addresses an organization and system which no longer exists."[86] In October the Financial Control Board released a study that contained both the FCB report and the chancellor's response. In the meantime, the city Corporation Council joined the state Commissioner of Education as an *amicus curiae* in an appeal of Judge Sifton's decision in *Riley v. Ambach*.

In February 1981 the Educational Priorities Panel released a report on special-education funding that documented the inequities local officials had been pointing out all along. Subtitled "A Story of Broken Promises," the report concluded that "the federal government has not fulfilled its funding commitments."[87] At issue here was not whether the federal government would pay for all the costs incurred by local districts as a result of Public Law 94-142. Rather, the concern was the difference between the level of funding authorized by Congress in the law, and the amount of federal monies spent. Congress had appropriated funding on a rising scale that would increase from 5 percent of the national costs for special education in 1978 to 40 percent in 1982. By 1981, the national commitment had not gone beyond 12 percent. (See Table 4-4.) In New York City, this difference could be translated into a loss of $20 million in federal support. Under the existing arrangement, the city was paying for 59 percent of the special-education expenditures, while the federal contribution amounted to a mere 8 percent.[88] The remainder was paid by the state.

The EPP report did not reserve any kind words for the state's role in special-education funding. It included an analysis of the new state aid formula that went into effect in 1980–1981. It found that while the new state allocation had increased by $12 million (or 10 percent) over the previous year, it actually provided fewer dollars per pupil and $34 million less than the old formula would have provided. As a result, the city, which was a codefendant with the state, had to increase its spending by 47 percent to meet the costs of mandated services.[89]

COURT INTERVENTION: EDUCATIONAL REFORM AND ORGANIZATIONAL CHANGE

Compliance with the court order would require significant changes in the way that the Division of Special Education was managed and organized. In organizational terms, educating children in

Table 4-4
FEDERAL EXPENDITURES FOR SPECIAL EDUCATION (NATIONALLY)

| Federal fiscal year | Authorization for PL 94-142 | |
	Dollars authorized	% national average expenditures
1978	$387 million	5%
1979	$566 million	10%
1980	$1.2 billion	20%
1981	$2.12 billion	30%
1982	$3.16 billion	40%

| Federal fiscal year | Appropriations for PL 94-142 | |
	Dollars actually appropriated	% national average expenditures
1978	$387 million	5% (fully funded)
1979	$566 million	10% (fully funded)
1980	$804 million	12% (instead of 20%)
1981	$862 million	12% (instead of 30%)
1982	Unknown	Unknown

Source: Educational Priorities Panel, "Special Education Funding: A Story of Broken Promises."

the least restrictive environment meant designing an entirely new ser-vice-delivery structure. It meant redefining the role of regular-education teachers. It meant the certification of a new generic teacher's license for special-education personnel who had been trained to work with more restricted categories of children. All this would have to be supported by training and retraining. All this would have to be done while the division was going through a period of rapid growth. All this would have to be imposed on a bureaucracy deeply entrenched in the ways of the past.

Implementing the court order became an intricate process, to be carried out under the supervision of the special master and with the involvement of the plaintiffs. Special master Marvin Frankel sought to define his role during the implementation phase in very much the same way that he cast it during the negotiation of the original court order and judgment. He urged the plaintiffs and the defendants to work out their differences among themselves. When this was difficult, he brought them together and attempted to effect a compromise. He would, as one party in the case described it, "lubricate the negotiation process."[90] After a set of negotiations on a particular issue was completed, Frankel would send his recommendations to Judge Nickerson in the form of a

Special Master's Report. If a compromise could not be reached, he would make recommendations on the basis of his own analysis of the issues and the facts. After receiving a report from the Master, the judge would give the plaintiffs and defendants an opportunity to submit affidavits outlining their own positions on the case. He would then issue an order. In most cases, the judge's order was consistent with the recommendations of the Special Master.

The way the court defined its role in this case was a rather peculiar one. It sought to be as inactive as possible. It served as an intervenor of last resort. If anything, *José P.* was a case of plaintiff intervention carried out under the auspices of a court order and judgment. The relationship between the plaintiffs and the defendants under this arrangement was a delicate and changing one. Both parties wanted compliance with the law. Both wanted to be cooperative. But what constituted compliance? When one gets to the implementation stage of a court order, compliance is not clearly defined by the law. It is negotiated. It becomes a question of settling details. And in an organization of significant size, administrative details are numerous and intricate. These details would raise more philosophical questions on the process of intervention. At what point could it be said that the plaintiffs had overstepped their bounds? At what point would they be infringing on managerial prerogatives? Who really knew? One attorney for the defendants explained the issues in a rather inconclusive manner, which is indicative of the problems inherent in the arrangement worked out, and the mixed sympathies of the parties:

> To a large measure, our relationship with the plaintiffs has been cooperative. They have been willing to compromise. At times, however, they have attempted to intrude into areas that should have been left up to management discretion. On the other hand, they have been dealing with an institution that has a poor track record. They sometimes have excess caution. They don't trust that the Board of Education will be able to do what it should do. Because of their intervention, the outcome has been very much more favorable to kids.[91]

A major requirement of the *José P.* order and Jerry Gross's special-education plan was the establishment of School-Based Support Teams (SBSTs) for evaluation, placement, and service delivery at the school level. These teams were to be phased in initially in three experimental community school districts (Districts 12, 15, 31). The phase-in process was to be monitored by the Office of Children with Handicapping Conditions from the State Education Department. The first monitoring report was completed in April 1980. The findings of this early evaluation touched on some deep-seated problems that were to plague the administration throughout the implementation process. The report began with words of praise for the overall concepts and goals of the SBSTs as they were outlined in "Special Education in Transition." It identified several "major strengths" evident in places where the plan was well implemented. These included more meaningful evaluations and placements, an emphasis on instructional and behavioral goals rather than labeling or categorization, a higher level of parent participation, and more involvement of school principals in special education. Unfortunately, these positive features were the exception rather than the rule in the three pilot districts.

The general conclusion of the evaluation was that "problem areas appear to outweigh the strengths and may undermine the success of further efforts if not resolved."[92] Among the major problems uncovered were shortages of personnel, including evaluation personnel, resource-room teachers, bilingual staff, and related service personnel. The fact was that the system was not hiring staff at a fast enough pace either to deal with the growing evaluation backlog or to provide adequate services for children once they entered the system. The other major problem was organizational. Gross was attempting to impose a new structure on the division. This would be mediated by newly created regional offices which were to act as intermediaries between the central administration and the districts. Evaluation and placement responsibilities once belonging to the districts were to go to the newly created SBSTs. And it was all to be done quickly. That was the law. That was the mandate. That was what the seven-member Board of Education wanted. Needless to say, there was confusion—confusion about responsibility, authority, and lines of communication. As the evaluation report stated, "Accountability seems fuzzy."[93]

In June the Division of Special Education began to work with the City Board of Examiners to develop a new generic teacher's license. It was proposing not the elimination of all categorical licenses, but a two-tier, broad-banded approach to licensing that would provide the system with teachers who could work with a larger, more integrated variety of students. These licenses had to be consistent with state law and the structure of university teacher education programs, the underlying philosophies of which predated Public Law 94-142. At about the same time, the division began to administer recertification exams for regular-education teachers who had been laid off because of the fiscal crisis and could be rechanneled into special education. Added to these efforts was a large-scale recruitment campaign, which reached out through the universities, the media, and communities where English was not the dominant language.

In the fall of 1980 the January and April Plans, which were supposed to have been submitted to the court by the defendants in the
respective months, were still under negotiation. As the parties to the
negotiations became more involved in details, the details appeared to
become more significant and more controversial. The major remaining
issue delaying agreement on the January Plan, now nearly a year late,
concerned preventive services. These include any service or activity
that, to a greater or lesser degree, can be said to prevent a nonspecial-
education student from being classified as having a handicapping condition. All agreed that the judgment required such services. The
question was: who was entitled to them? The plaintiffs argued that all
children within the school system were entitled to such preventive
services. The defendants held that the judgment required such services
only for those children in the plaintiff class, i.e., those who had been
referred for evaluation. The plaintiffs pointed out that, by definition,
preventive services were designed for the benefit of nonhandicapped
children, and therefore all nonhandicapped students should be included. They also demonstrated that the defendants had originally
agreed to include all children in an earlier draft of the plan, which was
now in its sixth revision.

The defendants argued that no federal or state law requires such
preventive services for nonhandicapped students. They said that the
plaintiffs' interpretation of the judgment would extend the mandate to
every student in the school system. They proposed to deliver preventive services to "nonclass" members only after other mandates in the
judgment were met—i.e., timely evaluations, related services to handicapped children, preventive services to postreferral children. They did
not want to be legally obliged to offer such services before then, and
they wanted a paragraph defining this stipulation included in the approved plan.

After several hearings and much negotiation, the special master
submitted his report and recommendations to the court on November
8. He made it clear that at issue here was not the law but the requirements of the judgment. He reviewed the text of "Special Education in
Transition," which was incorporated in the judgment and had a strong
recommendation for broad-based preventive services. He noted that it
was "interesting, if not decisive," that previous versions of the January
Plan agreed to by the defendants prescribed preventive services for all
children. He explained that upon further deliberations, the defendants
concluded that "budgetary constraints required postponement of the
projected SBST services to 'nonhandicapped children.' "[94] Frankel
then recommended that the proposed January Plan be approved by the
court, without the qualifying paragraph requested by the defendants.

The January Plan was 75 pages long, and it included a 185-page appendix. An even larger April Plan was still under negotiation by the parties. While the judge was deliberating over the recommended January Plan, the local press evinced more general concern with the overall implementation of the court order. Within the past year, the number of children identified as needing special-education services had increased from 50,000 to 72,000 students. However, the number of children on waiting lists still amounted to over 7,000 and the division still needed 1,000 additional personnel.[95]

On January 8, 1981, a year after its original due date, Judge Eugene Nickerson approved the January Plan that had been submitted to the court. However, contrary to the recommendation of the special master, Nickerson ordered that the qualifying paragraph sought by the defendants regarding preventive services be incorporated in the final document. Finding that the defendants had made a "good faith effort to advance towards the objectives set forth in the judgment,"[96] the judge ruled that the city district would not be required to provide preventive services on a prereferral basis until the other major mandates of the judgment had been carried out.

Within a few days after the approval of the January Plan, debate began among the parties on the provisions of the long overdue April Plan. The April Plan was to set forth the concrete details for implementing the "continuum of services" defined in the January Plan. This continuum, designed to accommodate a range of student needs, from a least restrictive environment to self-contained classes, was to have been implemented by February 2, 1981. Now, given the delays involved in reaching agreement on both plans, the defendants were proposing that the implementation date be postponed. They were requesting that the continuum of service be put in operation on a pilot basis in nine or ten districts in the fall of 1981, and that full implementation citywide be postponed until September of 1982. The plaintiffs, recognizing the complexity of the issues to be settled, did not disagree with the idea of a phased-in implementation or the final dates suggested by the defendants. What they wanted, however, was a detailed implementation and monitoring plan that would set down more specific deadlines at each stage of the implementation process. They wanted a formal institutional mechanism for assuring that any differences arising during the course of these deadlines could be promptly resolved. The defendants objected to these demands, claiming that the plaintiffs were using the April Plan as a vehicle for modifying the judgment. They accused the plaintiffs of trying to extend the litigation and their monitoring role for an additional two years.

As negotiations regarding the April Plan proceeded, the relationship between the leadership of the Special Education Division and the plaintiffs became more strained. The members of the Board of Education were becoming increasingly dissatisfied with the progress made in resolving the court mandate. All this was being played out before the backdrop of a financial crisis in the city, to which the special education budget made a major contribution.

On March 10 a news story broke in the local press that another major shakeup was taking place within the Division of Special Education. The chancellor had asked for the resignations of twenty-four top-level officials, and Jerry Gross had decided to resign. Bill Rojas, the chancellor's executive assistant, who had worked as Macchiarola's liaison with the division, was "temporarily" assigned there to oversee its daily operations. Christy Cugini, deputy superintendent in Community School District 31, was made acting executive director. On the subject of Jerry Gross's tenure and departure, Carol Brownell, a press aide for the chancellor and Board of Education, was quoted in *The New York Times* as saying:

> He made a tremendous impact here because he provided the conceptual framework for handling the needs of special-education students. But unhappiness developed over his management capacity and his team's ability to put in place the programs and plans we had all agreed to. The division is a very large enterprise with a very big budget, and we need a very strong team in there to handle it.[97]

In fact, Gross had not actually been fired. Although the chancellor had asked for the resignations of a large part of the top management structure in the division, he offered to work with Gross. The problem was that by March 1981 Gross's relationship with the members of the Board of Education had hit rock bottom. They, who had always been ambivalent about his court-ordered plan, were discontented with its results. He, who had seen himself as a major advocate of special education, accused the Board of being meddlesome, petty, and overly political. As he explained,

> The Board was generally unhappy that we had a court case. They were distressed. They felt that they were losing control, that they were not making decisions.
> The first year I was the new kid on the block. They were fine. After that, when I started firing and demoting people who were dear to them, they became more involved. They continued to ask inane petty questions. This was very time-consuming. It took away from my ability to get things done.[98]

Gross also felt that he had been unfairly blamed for the overspent education budget, which had been a major source of contention between school officials and the city. He pointed out that budget decisions were really made by the deputy chancellor, but that when things blew apart, he, Gross, had to shoulder a large share of the responsibility.

> [Deputy Chancellor] Halverson blamed me because we overspent. He told me to do it. I was clearly told by him when I started, "You run the program and hire the staff. I will find the money for you." When expenditures showed up in our budget, I was put under immediate freeze for a year.[99]

While Gross was under pressure to resign from the Board, the final decision to do so was his. He left frustrated with the situation that had devloped, and disconcerted with the seven-member Board of Education, to which he was ultimately accountable.

> Macchiarola offered to go to the Board of Education to make a case for my past accomplishments and tenure. I refused. I don't like to explain on such a low level what I am doing. I can't go with hat in hand. If they can't recognize my accomplishments, the hell with them.[100]

In the end, the question remained as to whether Gross had ever managed effectively to break through the old structure of the bureaucracy with which he had to contend. Gross had a fine reputation as a special educator, and a wealth of experience, but he had never dealt with an organization as large as the one at Livingston Street. The Special Education Division was the most entrenched and difficult part of that bureaucracy, and many believed that Gross and his staff were simply not prepared for it. As one attorney in the case explained,

> Gross had a paper staff. It seemed like he had an enormous organization. Realistically, he had no control over the bureaucrats. They were tenured. They had been there for years. They had bigger offices than he did. He had a few executive assistants who were overwhelmed. They hadn't realized what they were getting into when they got here. The managerial job was enormous.[101]

NEGOTIATING COMPLIANCE: THE CONTINUING PROCESS

Two days after Gross's resignation, the superintendents' conference was held at Harrison House in Glen Cove. While the major topic of discussion at the three-day meeting was Promotional Policy, the agenda allowed considerable time for other subjects that were emerging as concerns within the community school districts. Key among these was special education. With the creation of six regional offices, the development of School-Based Support Teams, and the emergence of a new philosophy of instruction, the districts were being required to adapt to a rapidly changing model for service delivery. Most superintendents did not oppose the goals underlying the mandated reforms, but many were not pleased with the way the changes were being made. Their Committee on Special Education had prepared an analysis of the situation, and its chairman, Superintendent Marvin Aaron, presented a set of recommendations to the chancellor, his staff, and top officials of the Division of Special Education.

The superintendents' proposal was far-reaching. It called for the phasing in of a three-year plan whereby the districts would assume responsibility for special education. Under this plan, the districts would treat handicapped children as they did all others. The discussion which emerged from this proposal had enormous significance for a number of reasons. On the one hand, the plan was philosophically consistent with the legal mandate; on the other, it deviated from a ten-year history of decentralization in New York City. Historically, special education had been a central function. Special-education staff was assigned and supervised by the central division. It was not even on the district budget. Its children were not usually perceived as part of the district school population. Many district personnel, unequipped to deal with handicapped children, preferred it that way. Now, the superintendents wanted to assume a large share of the responsibility for educating these children.

Also significant was the reaction of the chancellor and school officials from the central administration. Customarily, Livingston Street guarded special education as part of its bailliwick. That was the way of the bureaucracy, for special education meant positions, and it meant dollars. But nobody objected to the superintendents' proposal; the central officials just listened. When the meeting adjourned, Macchiarola asked Alan Gartner, who had organized the conference for him, to follow up on the recommendations of the superintendents. What became known as the "Harrison House Proposal" would emerge as a significant part of the dialogue on special education in months to come.

On March 27 City Comptroller Harrison Goldin released a report on special education, drafted by his staff on the basis of the September hearings.[102] The report repeated the major themes of the testimony of various local luminaries, emphasizing once more how the special-education budget would adversely affect regular-education services in the city. To no one's surprise, the report included a demand for more federal and state aid and a request for state legislation that would establish clear lines of accountability for the currently "autonomous" Board of Education. It also suggested that parents of handicapped children be given more options for private school placements at public expense, and that the school system should contract out more special-education services. It concluded, however, with the recommendation that the efficacy of removing labels from children should be reconsidered.

On the next day the chancellor delivered a major policy address at Columbia University Law School, where he reconfirmed his commitment to the special-education mandate and defended the courts as protectors of individual rights. He singled out for criticism local officials who had directed public opinion against the special-education laws and had adopted the slogan "Get the government off our backs." He warned:

> Agencies and their officials cannot be permitted to excuse poor performance of their organizations on the basis of overregulation or "mandates without money." . . .
> . . . entitlements for the handicapped are usually singled out as oppressive. To hear some of our leaders speak, you would believe that handicapped children relish their handicapping conditions. Many in our school community have been egged on to protest what children with handicapping conditions receive.[103]

As Macchiarola was speaking before his fellow alumni on the Columbia campus, lawyers for the school system and the plaintiffs were still negotiating the details of the long-overdue April Plan. The plaintiffs were concerned that fewer than 25 percent of the ninety-one occupational and ninety-one physical therapists needed in the current year had been hired. They wanted the court to set a deadline. The defendants resisted. There was also disagreement concerning the criteria for mainstreaming handicapped students during lunch, assemblies, and other special events. The plaintiffs wanted exceptions to the mainstreaming rule provided on a short-term basis in a child's individualized education program. The defendants wanted to set down a more general policy. The negotiations continued throughout April.

In the meantime, the public debate over the reasonableness of the mandate continued. On April 28, a local radio editorial urged the chancellor to "take immediate steps" to reduce the growing backlog of children awaiting services in special education. It argued, "Lack of money cannot be blamed for this deplorable situation."[104] Two days later a local newspaper editorial appeared, entitled, "Special Education Costs Race Out of Control." It asserted, "Tragically, New York City's public schools are being brought to their knees by the ballooning costs of educating the handicapped."[105]

With negotiations between the plaintiffs and the defendants continuing, the points of difference were beginning to appear more extreme. Now at issue was the applicability of the administrative order handed down by former State Commissioner Ewald Nyquist in the *Riley Reid* proceedings of 1977, which provided that children whose names appeared on a waiting list without satisfactory public placement for more than sixty days were entitled to seek private placement at public expense. This order had been in effect since September 1977. On December 29, 1981, the executive director of the Division of Special Education issued a memorandum stating that the defendants had recently determined that the provisions of the *Riley Reid* decision were applicable only to those children awaiting evaluation or placement prior to September 2, 1977. The memorandum stated that no further applications for private school funding would be accepted solely on the basis of untimeliness, and that it would be necessary to review all students funded for private school placement subsequent to September 2, 1977. At that point the defendants also refused to distribute a parents' rights handbook that had been in use, because they claimed that it incorrectly stated the grounds for private placement.

The plaintiffs assailed the sudden freeze on a policy that had been in practice for more than three years. They demanded that the distribution of the parents' rights handbook, which had been required by the judgment, be resumed. In early May the plaintiffs initiated new proceedings seeking further relief, in the form of special summer programs for students who had been illegally denied service (for more than sixty days) during the 1981 school year. That same month the special master issued two reports to the court concerning a determination of facts and his recommended resolutions of the issues at hand. He found that the December 29 memorandum of the defendants was "conceived in faulty reasoning" and altered the generally applicable requirements of the judgment. Therefore he recommended that the defendants be ordered to distribute a new memorandum, rescinding the December 29 document, and to resume distribution of the parents' rights handbook. With regard to the summer program relief sought, the master was less sympathetic with the plaintiffs. He found that such action was not required by the judgment, that the defendants had done their best with the available resources, and that there was not sufficient time to install such a program. He recommended to the court that the plaintiffs' request be denied.

In June the recommendations of the special master on the preceding issues were approved by Judge Nickerson and were incorporated within subsequent orders. That same month the special master submitted recommendations for the resolution of outstanding issues in the April Plan, then more than a year overdue. These recommendations were also accepted by the court. However, furious battles then began over compliance, and the school system was criticized for its failure to implement the mandate adequately. In July a report was released by the Educational Priorities Panel (EPP). While put forward as a budget analysis, the document was in fact a penetrating evaluation of the organization and practices of the Division of Special Education. The report attacked the "patchwork structure" of the division, where, it claimed, "levels of authority are unclear and funding responsibilities are confusing."[106] It placed particular emphasis on the lack of integration among the central administration, the regional offices, the districts, and the school level. The report recommended paring down the administrative structure and the establishment of clear lines of supervision and authority. It also called for more timely recruitment efforts and the licensing of personnel needed to deal with the backlog in student placements.

On July 27 the plaintiffs and *amici* submitted new papers to the court, detailing outstanding issues of compliance with the judgment and seeking relief.[107] They cited an April 1981 report by the Division of Special Education,[107] which showed that 2,970 children had been illegally waiting more than 30 days to be evaluated, and 4,152 additional students had been waiting more than 60 days to be placed. By July these lists had grown even longer. With regard to mainstreaming opportunities, it was shown that only 715 of the 970 schools in the city had resource rooms in operation. Lack of compliance in this area was particularly problematic in the high schools, where only 54 out of 110 had such facilities in place. In fact, the resource-room situation had worsened over recent months, with the number of children awaiting placement over 60 days increasing from 2,062 in January to 2,319 in February, to 2,341 in March, and finally falling back to 2,319 in April. In terms of related services, the paper submitted to the court held that, as of May, 3,954 children were not receiving psychological services, and 3,165 more were not getting social work services, although both were called for under the students' individual education plans. The plaintiffs and *amici* also argued that the defendants had failed to make "maximum reasonable efforts" to ensure that children of limited English proficiency were evaluated in their native language. They noted the indefinite postponement of the "continuum of services." They criticized the inadequate reporting systems within the division and its failure to develop an integrated information system for evaluations and placements.

It was clear that the plaintiffs and *amici* had become frustrated with the rate of progress achieved by the administration at Livingston Street. They had been fighting these battles for ten years. It was no longer a question of negotiation. They were now demanding further relief by the court. Of course, the question remained how quickly the school administration could be expected to move. In July the chancellor appointed the fourth executive director to assume responsibility for the Division of Special Education in three years. The choice was Alan Gartner. Bill Rojas, who had been serving in an acting capacity since Gross's departure in March, was appointed deputy executive director.

AFTERTHOUGHTS: ASSESSING THE OUTCOMES AND THE OPTIONS

Alan Gartner assumed office on August 1, 1981. He was no newcomer to the division. Gartner had been a member of the search committee that hired Jerry Gross. He had administered the special-education training program mandated by the court under the *Lora* decree. In 1978 he had conducted the original evaluation of the Bronx Regional Office. Upon his appointment Gartner, at the request of the chancellor, was in the process of examining the feasibility of the Harrison House Proposal presented by the superintendents at Glen Cove. The new executive director was in basic agreement with the ideas that had emerged from the districts. He had a history, prior to and during his academic career, as a community advocate, and was a strong proponent of decentralization. His own report on the Bronx region had emphasized the importance of a significant district role in special education, if handicapped children were to be truly integrated into the mainstream.

Gartner began his tenure with a realistic understanding of the task before him, admitting, "The problem I face is whether I can manage this enterprise."[108] By August 1981 the waiting list for evaluations and placements had reached 12,684.[109] Thus many of the goals Gartner publicly identified for himself were dictated by the needs of the situation. They included the hiring of more teachers, the development of speedy and unbiased evaluation techniques, and the removal of architectural barriers in fifty-one more school buildings. To these goals Gartner added another, which was very distinctly his and very much part of an emerging philosophy in the division: the goodwill, cooperation, and integration of the school districts.[110]

As school was about to open in September, the chancellor delivered another major policy speech on special education. This time the occasion was a national conference on Social Policy and the Special

Education Task of the 1980s, held at the Wingspread Conference Center in Racine, Wisconsin. As he had in the past, Macchiarola told his audience that the real issue of the 1980s would remain "the right of the public to be served."[111] He once again endorsed the need for litigation and the importance of court mandates. However, he also reminded his colleagues, "The expectations of a few years ago have simply been hit by the reality of program formulation, implementation, and evaluation." Emphasizing the difference between policy formation and implementation, he explained, "The passage of legislation is really a mere statement of goals. The process of implementation is a more significant and challenging one, where unexpected problems emerge." Macchiarola then went on to articulate an argument on the limits of court intervention, which was indicative of his own past frustrations in New York and representative of a developing outlook for the future:

> Looking at our own court decree in the *José P.* case in New York, I believe strongly that the role of the courts becomes negative at the implementation stage. Having complicated decision making, and creating alternative channels of influence and accountability, it is highly likely that the courts, at the implementation stage, will actually work against what their intervention accomplished in the initial formulation of a commitment to the special student.[112]

That fall a number of significant proceedings took place before the special master and the court. A September monitoring report from the Special Education Division revealed growing backlogs in evaluation, placement, and related services, totaling 15,345.[113] At the same time school officials were continuing to resist any remedies involving private placements at public expense. These circumstances drove the plaintiffs and *amici* to seek another court order sanctioning and requiring the continuation of the *Riley Reid* administrative provisions. Thereafter, the plaintiffs renewed a request that summer school programs be made available for those students who were denied placement during the regular school year. In the meantime, a dispute broke out between the state defendants and the city defendants. It occurred when the chancellor, concerned with the teacher shortage, requested permission to use alternative criteria for the licensing of special-education personnel. The State Education Department refused. The plaintiffs and *amici* endorsed the chancellor's request. The disagreement then went before the special master.

While the legal battles were being fought at various places, Alan Gartner was implementing some significant changes in the service-delivery system housed at Livingston Street. By November, Gartner had worked out a far-reaching agreement with Nathan Quinones, the executive director of the High Schools Division. Under its terms, special-education personnel at the secondary school level were incorporated into the supervisory structure of the High Schools Division. This meant that special-education teachers and supervisors in high schools were no longer a separate entity. They would report to the high school superintendents, as did all other high school staff. More significant, under this new arrangement the special-education personnel affected would be transferred into the High Schools Division budget. These changes came about rather quietly, but their accomplishment was quite extraordinary, for they violated the cardinal rule of the bureaucracy—the protection of one's turf. Gartner was giving away personnel and dollars to another division, without a fight, of his own free will.

The high schools agreement was also significant in terms of the legal mandate. Now, handicapped students would be treated as high school students. They were no longer the clientele of another division that happened to be using the high school facilities. At that point a next step appeared obvious. Why not do the same for the elementary and middle grades? Why not incorporate special-education students and budget into the districts? That step would truly facilitate the goal of mainstreaming. However, it would not be taken easily. The central Board of Education had gone along with the first plan because it involved only shifting personnel from one central division to another. In the end, nothing was lost. Transferring resources to the districts would be another matter. Such maneuvers constituted decentralization. They violated the precious boundaries of Livingston Street. They would be heartily opposed. All indications showed that both the chancellor and Gartner supported taking that important second step. But everyone knew that things had to proceed slowly and be handled gingerly. The chancellor's plan was to approach the question managerially, not as a major policy issue. As Gartner explained, "Frank did not want the Board of Education to vote on the issue. He wanted to keep it as an administrative matter."[14]

On November 18 Gartner distributed to the district superintendents a document called the "Harrison House RFP" (request for proposals). In it, he invited the superintendents to submit proposals for participation in an experimental design for service delivery that would foster "close collaboration between the Division of Special Education and the community school districts."[115] From the proposals submitted, it was hoped, nine experimental districts would be chosen. The project was to follow the directions indicated in "Special Education in Transition" and "the initiatives begun at the Harrison House Conference." At the beginning of the document, Gartner formally recognized the continuing overall responsibility of the chancellor and his division for special-education services. However, he then went on to outline a "design for improved administration of special education" unlike anything that had ever before emerged from Livingston Street.

The Harrison House RFP outlined distinct roles for the experimental districts and the central division. Each district would have a supervisor of special education. While these supervisors would remain on the central division budget, they would be appointed by and report to the district superintendents. Together the superintendent and supervisor would be responsible for overseeing all special-education personnel serving in regional programs. They would be expected to insure that handicapped children and their teachers were integrated into the full range of activities. While the OTPS (Other Than Personnel Services) budget for special education would be distributed among the districts by the central division, local expenditure plans for each allotment would be determined by the districts. The division would retain responsibility for citywide low incidence programs, and would supervise the work of the Committees on the Handicapped. It would monitor and provide support in the areas of curriculum development, technical assistance, and training. Central officials would also continue to work directly with outside agencies such as the State Education Department, the Office of Management and Budget, and the state and federal courts.

There was a curious twist to the way the administration's position was developing with regard to special education. Some observers had seen the chancellor's initiatives on behalf of Promotional Policy as an assault on the power of the community school districts. They felt that Macchiarola, a former school board president, had become less sympathetic toward decentralization after his appointment to Livingston Street. Now, the administration appeared to be supporting an idea that called for further decentralization. Were these positions inconsistent? Alan Gartner, another advocate of decentralization, said no. He portrayed the administration's posture in terms of a widening view of the centralization-decentralization debate:

> People have always assumed that you can either have strong districts or a strong Chancellor. They saw it as a zero-sum game, where strength on one end would have to mean weakness in the other. Frank doesn't believe this. Frank wants both strong districts and a strong Chancellor. He will set standards. But he demands that they do serious things in terms of service.[116]

The Harrison House RFP was sent to the districts with neither the prior approval nor knowledge of the central Board of Education. Needless to say, when the news reached the eleventh floor at Livingston Street, the members of the Board were not very pleased with what had happened and how the move had been made. They demanded an explanation, in writing. Gartner, who was the author of the RFP, was elected to draft the explanatory response. In doing so, he criticized the current structure of special-education services for its anachronistic nature, lack of clarity or cohesion, and the limited involvement of community school districts.[117] He described his own proposal in great depth, but it was his explanation of what the plan did not represent that addressed the major concerns of the Board members:

> Responsibility for education of children with handicapping conditions remains a central one—the Board's, its Chancellor and D.S.E. This is not decentralization. No funds are to be transferred to district budgets. No staff will be on district payrolls.[118]

After several tense meetings with the Board, Gartner finally received permission to go ahead with the experimental structure. However, the scope of the project was reduced from nine districts to five districts.

On December 21, the Special Master issued another report to the court. He recommended that the plaintiffs' most recent request for a summer school program not be granted, but that they be "encouraged to exploit the *Riley Reid* procedure, both as a means of placing unserved children, and as an encouragement for the defendants to extend themselves some more."[119] On January 5, 1982, Judge Nickerson issued a Memorandum and Order supporting the Master's recommendations, and also ordered the defendants to submit within ten days a "detailed and effective plan" for the elimination of the waiting lists. The latter part of the order evoked an angry response from Board President Joseph Barkan, who threatened to "appeal the whole thing."[120] On the following day, the Board contracted with a private Wall Street law firm to act as consultants on the case. The Board members had never been enthusiastic about the original *José P.* judgment. Now, as things started to approach the breaking point, they were prepared to explore all their options. And they enlisted the best legal advice they could find to do so.

It is not difficult to understand the Board members' frustration. Over the past three years, they had been supportive of many changes within special education. They had unanimously approved "Special Education in Transition," and with it the regional plan and the dissolution of the bureaus. They had endorsed the establishment of School-Based Support Teams in order to establish the least restrictive environment possible for students and to broaden the participation of parents. Between 1978 and 1981 they had witnessed a geometric

Table 4-5
NUMBER OF CHILDREN SERVED IN SPECIAL EDUCATION

	School years						
Type of class	1978–1979		1979–1980		1980–1981		1981–1982
	9/30	6/30	9/30	6/30	9/30	6/30	9/30
Resource rooms	204	491	1,641	8,201	10,101*	15,799	18,919
All others	49,496	55,831	56,306	60,202	56,870	65,360	66,767
Total	49,700	56,322	57,947	68,403	66,971	81,159	85,686
Private	3,129	3,129	4,048	4,048	4,483	4,483	4,500
Total	52,829	59,451	61,995	72,451	71,454	85,642	90,186

Source: New York City Public Schools, Division of Special Education, "Report on Growth in the Division of Special Education: 1978–1981."
*Underestimates the actual number.

growth of the division and its service personnel. During this time the number of children in special education increased from 52,829 to 90,186.[121] (See Table 4-5.) Children in resource rooms alone had increased from 204 to 18,919. These trends were reflected in an enormous expansion in the teaching staff. Between 1978 and 1981 the number of special-education teachers increased from 5,224 to 9,447.[122] (See Table 4-6.) All this occurred while the Board was under severe political pressure to reduce its spending. Indeed, it can be said that the controversy over the special-education budget was the primary cause of attacks on the Board's political and managerial autonomy. Now, in order to comply with the legal mandate and its philosophy, the Board's own chancellor was instituting an experiment that could eventually compromise its jurisdiction over its central resources. These events notwithstanding, the Board of Education was still being dragged into court for noncompliance. The waiting list was still there to be dealt with.

On January 21 representatives of the school system appeared

Table 4-6
NUMBER OF TEACHERS IN SPECIAL EDUCATION

	School Years				
Type of teacher	1978–1979		1979–1980	1980–1981	1981–1982
	9/30	6/30	6/30	6/30	9/30
Classroom-field	5,161	5,844	7,224	7,642	8,373
Resource rooms	63	147	213	857	1,074
Total	5,224	5,991	7,437	8,499	9,447

Source: "Report on Growth in the Division of Special Education: 1978–1981."

before Judge Nickerson to submit their Plan to Eliminate the Waiting List. Their "plan" included a short history of the division's progress since the initial judgment and a listing of "constraints" on timely evaluation and placement. It outlined some "proposed measures" to be taken in order to improve the situation, but it included no specific goals or timetables. The most significant part of the paper submitted was a remarkable admission of doubt:

> The measures we propose here are sound, and we believe they will have the effect of reducing delays in evaluation and placement. We cannot, however, provide assurance that these steps will immediately eliminate evaluation and placement waiting lists, nor can we state with certainty precisely how much the waiting lists will be reduced as a result of this plan within a specific period of time. In light of future experiences, it may well be that the steps we outline here will require modification or even future abandonment.[123]

As school officials were presenting their "plan" to Judge Nickerson, Mayor Edward Koch was demanding that the Board reduce its special-education budget by $38 million.[124] On the same day, the United States Court of Appeals was handing down another decision concerning the *José P.* case. At issue was an appeal by the state defendants to be released from sharing with the city defendants liability for any court fees that resulted from the latter's failure to eliminate the waiting lists. The court unanimously rejected the State Education Department appeal. The appeal itself, however, was indicative of the worsening relationship that had developed between City and state school officials, who began the case as codefendants.

On March 3 the chancellor appeared before Judge Nickerson to present his own sworn testimony. Taking the previous points made by school officials a step further, he argued that the litigation was defeating the original goals of the judgment. He criticized the preoccupation with the number and speed of placements as opposed to a concern for "appropriate education."[125] Macchiarola also explained that the field of special education was still developing and in need of experiment, but that the constraints imposed by the judgment and the plaintiffs did not allow for experimentation. He frankly noted:

> . . . the state of the art of special-education instruction is such that we cannot state with a high degree of confidence the educational benefit that even a properly diagnosed handicapped student will derive from special-education services.
>
> There is little professional consensus, much less empirical

proof, on most issues of special-education policy, procedure, and implementation. Defendants can only offer professional judgment, not hard data.[126]

While the chancellor was not proposing a retreat from his previous commitment to handicapped children or the mainstreaming strategy that had been adopted, he was underscoring the fact that there was more certainty in the requirements of the law than there was professional consensus regarding the underlying philosophy and practices of current policies. This rigidity in the law, according to Macchiarola, stifled experimentation. He also went on to cite inadequate financial support by the federal government and lack of cooperation on the part of the State Education Department. While the chancellor did not seek relief from the court regarding the judgment, his testimony made it clear that he was dismayed at the scope of intervention that had grown out of the original mandate.

SUMMARY COMMENTS

This case study on special education has ended in very much the same place where it began, with some serious doubts about the efficacy of alternative approaches to service delivery for the handicapped. Such uncertainty has been partly responsible for the debates that have emerged within the education profession and spilled over into the political arena. The larger political battles, however, result from a general ambivalence of national policy makers concerning public priorities. In one sense, we have come a long way, for we have recognized the educational rights of a minority that has historically been denied access to appropriate schooling. However, this rising national consciousness has not been matched by resources to insure the very rights that have been recognized. Thus the major part of the financial burden for educating the handicapped has fallen on the local school districts.

This fact contributed heavily to the set of cross-pressures assailing the school administration at Livingston Street. While the legal mandate called for more and better services to handicapped children, municipal officials, troubled by shrinking financial resources, were demanding cutbacks in the school budget. In addition to financial constraints, the administration, in its attempts to comply with the mandate, had to deal with an entrenched and obstructive bureaucracy, an ambivalent school board, and a mildly supportive codefendant at the state level. Even as the administration began to make progress toward the integration of special-education programs with regular programs at the district level, the Board of Education, protective of its centralized programs and resources, emerged as a major defender of the status quo.

The case is a classic study of the role of the courts in the policy-making process. That role appears to be a significant one, since it was successful litigation that first established the educational rights of the handicapped. Several years of such litigation finally provided the needed momentum for federal legislation, which in turn propelled state legislative action and made litigation easier. But at what point does judicial intervention become counterproductive? In this case there was not only a judicial declaration of rights, but also court, or, more specifically, plaintiff intervention in school management. Thus the issues become more complex. What began as a reform of educational policy grew into a major attempt at organizational and managerial change. The aggressive stance taken by the plaintiffs is understandable. The truth of the matter was that the school administration had failed to comply with the legal mandates on time. Whether or not the deadlines in the judgment were reasonable to begin with is another question.

As one observes the situation in retrospect, a basic lack of symmetry appears between the legal and educational systems. There is more certainty about the legal entitlements in the education of the handicapped than there is about the educational principles behind those entitlements. There is more assurance about the kinds of programs school systems must provide for handicapped children than there is about the techniques for implementing them. The science of the law has perhaps moved more rapidly than the science of instruction. And this discrepancy may explain some of the distance that remains between the two sides.

NOTES

1. On the history of federal action on behalf of the handicapped, see Erwin L. Levine and Elizabeth M. Wexler, *P.L. 94-142, An Act of Congress* (New York: Macmillan, 1981); Jay B. Chambers and William T. Hartman, eds., *Special Education Policies* (Philadelphia: Temple University Press, 1982); Martin L. LaVor, "Federal Legislation for Exceptional Persons: A History," in Fredrick J. Weintraub *et al.*, eds., *Public Policy and the Education of Exceptional Children* (Reston, Va.: The Council for Exceptional Children, 1976); Alan Abeson and Jeffrey Zettel, "The End of Quiet Revolution: The Education of All Handicapped Children Act of 1975," *Exceptional Children* 45 (October 1977); Scottie Higgins and Josephine Barrese, "The Changing Focus of Public Policy," *Exceptional Children* 46 (January 1979).

2. Lloyd M. Dunn, "Special Education for the Mildly Retarded—Is Much of It Justifiable?" *Exceptional Children* 35 (September 1968).

3. Charles S. Bullock and Joseph Stewart, "Second Generation Discrimination in American Schools," *Policy Studies Journal* 7 (Winter 1978).

4. Nicholas Hobbes, *The Futures of Children* (San Francisco: Jossey–Bass, 1975); James Gallagher, "The Special Education Contract for Mildly Handicapped Children," *Exceptional Children* 38 (March 1972); G. Orville Johnson, "Special Education for the Mentally Handicapped—Paradox," *Exceptional Children* 29 (October 1962); Maynard C. Reynolds, "Framework for Considering Some Issues in Special Education," *Exceptional Children* 28 (March 1962); Alan Abeson *et al., A Primer on Due Process: Education Decisions For Handicapped Children* (Reston, Va.: The Council for Exceptional Children, 1975).

5. For an overview of the legal issues, see Jack B. Weinstein, "Education of Exceptional Children," *Creighton Law Review* 12 (1979); David Kirp, "Schools as Sorters: The Constitutional and Policy Implications of Student Classification," *University of Pennsylvania Law Review* 75 (1973); Joan N. Alschuler, "Education for the Handicapped," *Journal of Law and Education* 7 (October, 1978).

6. *Hobson* v. *Hansen*, 269 F. Supp. 401, 1967.

7. *Diana* v. *State Board of Education*, January 7, 1970.

8. *Larry P.* v. *Riles*, 343 F. Suppl. 1360, (N.D. Ca. 1972).

9. *Pennsylvania Association for Retarded Children* v. *Commonwealth of Pennsylvania*, 348 F. Supp. 279 (E.D. Pa. 1972).

10. Ibid.

11. Ibid.

12. Ibid.

13. *Mills* v. *Board of Education*, 348 F. Supp. 866 (D.D.C. 1972).

14. Among the groups active in the lobbying for passage were the Council for Exceptional Children, United Cerebral Palsy, the American Speech and Hearing Association, the National Association for Retarded Children, the National Society for Autistic Children, the Council on Education of the Deaf, the National Easter Seal Society, the National Association of Mental Health, the Institute for Research on Exceptional Children, and the National Center for Law and the Handicapped.

15. Public Law 94–142, 94th Congress, S.6, November 29, 1975.

16. See note, "Enforcing the Right to an Appropriate Education: The Education for All Handicapped Children Act of 1975," *Harvard Law Review* 92 (1979); Donald N. Bersoff and Elizabeth Veltman, "Public Law 94-142: Legal Implications for the Education of Handicapped Children," *Journal of Research and Development in Education* 12 (Summer 1979).

17. The actual authorizations defined included 5 percent in 1978, 10 percent in 1979, 20 percent in 1980, 30 percent in 1981, and 40 percent in 1982.

18. Erwin Hargrove, *The Missing Link* (Washington: Urban Institute, 1975); Aaron Wildavsky and Jeffrey Pressman, *Implementation* (Berkeley: University of California Press, 1975); Eugene Bardach, *The Implementation Game* (Cambridge, Mass.: MIT Press, 1977); Paul Sabatier and David Mazma-

nian, "The Implementation of Public Policy," *Policy Studies Journal* (Special Issue, 1980); Donald S. Van Meter and Carl E. Von Horn, "The Policy Implementation Process: A Conceptual Framework," *Administration and Society* 4 (February 1975).

19. Erwin Hargrove *et al., Regulations and Schools: The Implementation of Equal Education for Handicapped Children* (Nashville, Tenn.: Vanderbilt University, Institute for Policy Studies, 1981); Richard Weatherley, *Reforming Special Education: Policy Implementation from State Level to Street Level* (Cambridge, Mass.: MIT Press, 1979); Richard Weatherley and Michael Lipsky, "Street-Level Bureaucrats and Institutional Innovation: Implementing Special Education Reform," *Harvard Educational Review* 47 (May 1977); Chambers and Hartman, *Special Education Policies.*

20. Charles D. Bernstein *et al., Financing Educational Services for the Handicapped* (Palo Alto, Calif.: Management Analysis Center, 1976:) James Kakalik, "Issues in the Cost and Finance of Special Education," in David Berliner, ed., *Review of Research in Education* (Washington: American Educational Research Association, 1979).

21. David Kirp *et al.,* "Legal Mandates and Organizational Change," in Nicholas Hobbs, ed., *Issues in the Classification of Children,* Vol. III (San Francisco: Jossey–Bass, 1975).

22. "Progress toward a Free Appropriate Public Education," A Report to Congress on the Implementation of Public Law 94-142: The Education for All Handicapped Children Act (Washington: Office of Education, U.S. Department of Health, Education and Welfare, 1979), pp. 87–91.

23. See note 4.

24. Ravic P. Ringlaben and Jay R. Price, "Regular Classroom Teachers' Perceptions of Mainstreaming Effects," *Exceptional Children* 47 (January 1981); Barbara Larrivee and Linda Cook, "Mainstreaming: A Study of the Variables Affecting Teacher Attitudes," *Journal of Special Education* 13 (Fall 1979); B. Keough and M. Levitt, "Special Education in the Mainstream: A Confrontation of Limitations," *Focus on Exceptional Children* 8 (1978); R. Jones, "Special Education and the Future: Some Questions to Be Answered and Some Answers to Be Questioned," in Maynard Reynolds, ed., *Futures of Education for Exceptional Children* (Reston, Va.: Council for Exceptional Children, 1978); Cara Alexander and Phillip Strain, "A Review of Educators' Attitudes towards Handicapped Children and the Concept of Mainstreaming," *Psychology in the Schools* 15 (July 1978); S. Sarason and J. Doris, "Mainstreaming: Dilemmas, Opposition, and Opportunities," in Maynard Reynolds, ed., *Future of Education.*

25. See also Jere E. Brophy and Thomas L. Good, *Teacher-Student Relationship: Causes and Consequences* (New York: Holt, Rinehart and Winston, 1974); Jere E. Brophy and Carolyn M. Evertson, *Student Characteristics and Teaching* (New York: Longman, 1981).

26. Virginia L. Bruininks, "Peer Status and Personality Characteristics of Learning Disabled and Nondisabled Children," *Journal of Learning Dis-*

abilities 11 (October 1978); Tanis H. Bryan, "Peer Popularity of Learning Disabled Children," *Journal of Learning Disabilities* 7 (December 1974); Jay Gottlieb *et al.,* "Correlates of Social Status Among Mainstreamed Mentally Retarded Children," *Journal of Educational Psychology* 70 (June 1978); Gary N. Siperstein *et al.,* "Social Status of Learning Disabled Children," *Journal of Learning Disabilities* 11 (February 1978).

27. "Handicapped and Underprivileged Children—Special Schools and Special Care—Instruction in Homes and Hospitals," *Annual Report* of Associate Superintendent Margaret J. McCoovey to Harold G. Campbell, Superintendent of Schools, School Year 1933–1934, p. 6. Cited in "Legal Issues in the Classification of Handicapped Children in New York City," Office of the Deputy Chancellor, Educational Policy Analysis Unit, Board of Education of the City of New York, January 1977, p. 8.

28. Ibid.

29. Jane Stern, private interview, February 4, 1982.

30. These included classes for the neurologically impaired and emotionally handicapped, preplacement classes, readiness classes, and centers for the multiply handicapped.

31. Carol Ziegler, private interview, April 29, 1981.

32. *Reid* v. *Board of Education,* 433 F. 2d 238 (E.D. N.Y. 1971).

33. *Reid* v. *Board of Education,* 453 F. 2d 238 (2d Cir. 1971).

34. For a detailed analysis of the issues of New York State law governing the rights of the handicapped, see Barbara Gott, "Educating New York's Handicapped Children," *Albany Law Review* 43 (Fall 1978).

35. *In the Matter of Riley Reid,* 13 Ed. Dept. Rep. 117 (1973).

36. Office of the Chancellor, "Legal Issues in the Classification of Handicapped Children in New York City," p. 32.

37. *Lora* v. *Board of Education of the City of New York,* Civ. No. 75 C 917 (E.D. N.Y. 1975).

38. *In the Matter of Kelly,* 15 Ed. Dept. Rep. 427 (1976).

39. *In the Matter of Michael A.,* Ed. Dept. Rep. Decision No. 9282 (1976).

40. *In the Matter of Reid,* Ed. Dept. Rep. 127 (1977).

41. *José P.* v. *Ambach,* affidavit submitted by John Gray, attorney for Brooklyn Legal Services, February 15, 1979.

42. Ibid.

43. Ibid.

44. Alan Gartner, Marvin Taylor, Lee Ann Truesdell, *Educational Services to Students with Special Needs: A Study of their Delivery and Recommendations* (New York: Center for Advanced Study in Education, Graduate School and University Center, City University of New York, February 1979).

45. Ibid., p. 123.

46. Ibid., p. 157.

47. *José P.* v. *Ambach,* 79 Civ. 27 (E.D. N.Y. 1979).

48. John Gray, private interview, May 8, 1981.

49. *United Cerebral Palsy of New York* v, *Board of Education,* 79 C 560 (E.D. N.Y. 1979).

50. See, Michael A. Rebell, "Implementation of Court Mandates Concerning Special Education: The Problems and the Potential," *Journal of Law and Education* 10 (July 1981).

51. Michael Rebell, private interview, February 4, 1982.

52. *Aspira* v. *Board of Education,* 72 Civ. 4002 (S.D. N.Y. 1974).

53. United States District Court, Eastern District 79C 270, "Memorandum and Order," May 16, 1979.

54. *Dyrcia S.* v. *Ambach,* 79 C 2562 (E.D. N.Y. 1979).

55. *Lora* v. *Board of Education,* 456 F. Supp. 1211 (E.D. N.Y. 1979).

56. Carol Ziegler, private interview, April 29, 1981.

57. *Lora* v. *Board of Education,* Docket No. 79-752, 1980.

58. "The *Lora* Decree Staff Development Program: A Final Report," Center for Advanced Study in Education, Graduate School and University Center, City University of New York, June 1980.

59. *Lora* v. *Board of Education,* Docket No. 79-752, 1980.

60. Jerry Gross, "Special Education in Transition," Division of Special Education, New York City Board of Education, September 10, 1979.

61. Ibid.

62. Michael Rebell, private interview, February 4, 1982.

63. John Gray, private interview, May 8, 1981.

64. Frank J. Macchiarola, "Memorandum to the Members of the Board of Education, Regarding *José P.* v. *Ambach,* " November 27, 1979.

65. Letter of James G. Greilsheimar to Marvin Frankel, regarding *José P.* v. *Ambach,* November 30, 1979.

66. Amelia Ashe, "Memorandum to Members of the Board of Education and Frank J. Macchiarola, Regarding *José P.* v. *Ambach,*" December 12, 1979.

67. *José P.* v. *Ambach,* 79 C. 270 (E.D. N.Y. 1979).

68. Ibid.

69. *The New York Times,* December 22, 1979.

70. *The New York Times,* January 25, 1980. See also Edward I. Koch, "The Mandate Millstone," *Public Interest* 61 (Fall 1980).

71. "Federal Mandates," editorial, WCBS-TV, New York, June 30, 1980; July 1, 1980.

72. *Riley* v. *Ambach,* 79 C 2783, (E.D. N.Y. 1980).

73. Ibid.

74. *New York Daily News,* July 8, 1980.

75. Ibid.

76. "Costs of Compliance: A Report to the Chancellor on the Projected Costs of Providing Services to the Special-Education Population in New York City in Compliance with P.L. 94-142," Chancellor's Office of Policy Analysis, Research and Planning, New York City Public Schools, July 1980.

77. "A Survey of Special-Education Costs in Local School Districts," National School Boards Association, Washington, D.C., June 1979.

78. Cited in, "Costs of Compliance."

79. Correspondence from Comer S. Coppie to Frank J. Macchiarola, August 19, 1980.

80. "Impact of Special-Education Mandates on New York City's Financial Plan: Future Risks and the Potential for Cost Containment," Draft Staff Report, New York State Financial Control Board, August 1980.

81. Ibid.

82. Remarks of Mayor Edward I. Koch at the Hearings on Special Education, Board of Estimate Chamber, City Hall," September 5, 1980.

83. "Testimony by New York City Council President Carol Bellamy before the Comptroller's Hearings on Special Education, Board of Estimate Hearing Room, City Hall," September 4, 1980.

84. "Statement by Albert Shanker, President, United Federation of Teachers, Local 2, AFT, AFL–CIO, before a Special Hearing of the Comptroller of the City of New York on Special Education," September 5, 1980.

85. Remarks of Dr. Frank J. Macchiarola, Chancellor of the New York City Public Schools, at Public Hearings Regarding Special Education Conducted by Comptroller Harrison J. Goldin, Board of Estimate Chambers, City Hall," September 4, 1980.

86. "Chancellor's Response to the Financial Control Board's Report: Impact of Special Education Mandates on New York City's Financial Plan, Future Risks and the Potential for Cost Containment," Office of the Chancellor, New York City Public Schools, September 1980.

87. "Special-Education Funding: A Story of Broken Promises," Educational Priorities Panel, February 1981.

88. Ibid.

89. Ibid.

90. Robert Bergen, private interview, May 18, 1981.

91. Ibid.

92. "Site Visit Report: Monitoring of Progress in Phasing-In to School-Based Operations, February 3 to March 15," Office for Education of Children with Handicapping Conditions, New York State Department of Education, April 14, 1980.

93. Ibid.

94. *José P.* v. *Ambach,* 79 C 270 (EHN), "Special Master's Report," No. 3, November 8, 1980.

95. *The New York Times,* December 7, 1980.

96. *José P.* v. *Ambach,* 79 C 270, "Memorandum and Order," January 8, 1981.

97. *The New York Times,* March 11, 1981.

98. Jerry Gross, private interview, April 29, 1981.

99. Ibid.

100. Ibid.

101. Gary Tarnoff, private interview, May 21, 1981.

102. "Report on Comptroller Goldin's Public Hearings on Special Education in the City of New York," Office of Policy Management and Bureau of Performance Analysis, Office of the Comptroller, City of New York, March 27, 1981.

103. Frank J. Macchiarola, "The Allocation of Mandates and Cash to Pay for Them: The Role of Federal, State and Local Government," speech delivered at the Twenty-second Annual Columbia Law School Symposium, Columbia Law School Alumni Association, New York City, March 28, 1981. See also, Frank J. Macchiarola, "Reagan vs. the Children," *Social Policy* 12 (September-October 1981).

104. "Mainstreaming Handicapped Students," Editorial, WINS Radio 1010, April 28, 1981.

105. *New York Post,* April 30, 1981.

106. "Charting New Directions: A Budget Analysis of the Division of Special Education," Educational Priorities Panel, July 1981.

107. *José P.* v. *Ambach,* 79 C 270, "Statement of Plaintiffs and Amici on Issues of Compliance," July 27, 1981.

108. *The New York Times,* August 31, 1981.

109. Ibid.

110. Ibid.

111. Frank J. Macchiarola, "Special Education: The Costs of Experiment," paper prepared for the Conference on Social Policy and the Special Education Task of the 1980s, Wingspread Conference Center, Racine, Wisconsin, September 10–12, 1981.

112. Ibid.

113. These included 2,661 for evaluation, 3,491 for self-contained placements, 2,162 for resource-room placements, 4,728 for related services, 303 for placements in day or nonresidential public schools. *José P.* v. *Ambach,* 79 C 270 (EHN), Special Master's Report, No. 8.

114. Alan Gartner, private interview, January 21, 1982.

115. Alan Gartner, "Memorandum to Superintendents of Community School Districts, Regarding the Harrison House RFP," November 18, 1981.

116. Alan Gartner, private interview, January 21, 1982.

117. Alan Gartner, "Memorandum to Richard Halverson," December 9, 1981.

118. Ibid.

119. *José P.* v. *Ambach,* 79 C 270 (EHN), Special Master's Report, No. 9, December 21, 1981.

120. *Newsday,* January 7, 1982.

121. "Report on Growth in the Division of Special Education: 1978–1981," Division of Special Education, New York City Public Schools, November 1981.

122. Ibid.

123. New York City Board of Education's Plan to Eliminate Evaluation and Placement Waiting Lists, Board of Education of the City of New York, January 21, 1982.

124. *New York Post,* January 22, 1982.

125. *José P.* v. *Ambach,* affidavit submitted by Frank J. Macchiarola, March 3, 1982.

126. Ibid.

5
DESEGREGATION IN QUEENS

Most historians would trace the turning point of the civil rights movement to the momentous *Brown* decision of 1954, when the Supreme Court ruled that "separate but equal" educational facilities are in violation of the Fourteenth Amendment to the Constitution.[1] After hearing expert testimony by social scientists such as Kenneth Clark, the Warren Court declared that the separation of the races was psychologically damaging to black children who were denied access to certain public schools. In 1955 the Court, in *Brown II,* put teeth into its original decision when it ordered the Board of Education of Topeka, Kansas, to desegregate its educational facilities with "all deliberate speed."[2] Thus was established a standard of implementation that would set the stage for more than two decades of legal and political debate in both the South and the North, concerning the controversial issue of school desegregation.

This chapter concerns an attempt by the central school administration in New York to implement a federal desegregation order in Rosedale, Queens, against the will of the local community school board. It exemplifies the kind of conflict that continues to surround the subject of school desegregation. Moreover, from a local perspective, it indicates the level of resistance a locally elected community school board can mobilize against the chancellor, even in the face of a legal mandate imposed by the federal government. This chapter is similar to those that precede it in the sense that it again portrays a situation where the central school administration is subject to conflicting cross-pressures by outside institutions or groups. However, it goes beyond the common theme of the previous pages by dealing with a situation involving multiple jurisdictions—that is, an area of policy in which several levels or institutions of government have authority. The phenomenon of multiple jurisdictions is made highly apparent in this case by the kinds of political strategies used by each of the major actors—the chancellor and the local school board. Political scientists would call this strategy "widening the scope of conflict."[3] It occurs when a participant in a political conflict who does not derive satisfaction from a decision in one arena, takes the conflict to another arena, where a more sympathetic hearing is expected. A strategy of this sort is particularly useful in a controversy over desegregation, where the legal mandate and the guidelines for its implementation are not as clear as the original *Brown* decisions would have led one to believe.

The *Brown* decisions were followed by a decade of intense litigation at the district court level, whereby the lower federal judiciary attempted to define what the Supreme Court meant by its long-standing order. Was the Court merely outlawing de jure segregation, which was the result of purposeful state and local policy, or was it also prohibiting de facto segregation, which was not intentional? Were local school districts merely required to desegregate separate educational facilities, or were they also expected to develop far-reaching plans for integration and racial mixing?[4] These debates notwithstanding, by 1964 only 2 percent of all black children in the deep South were attending desegregated schools.[5] It was in that decennial year that Congress, under the prodding of President Lyndon Johnson, entered the picture and passed Title VI of the Civil Rights Act. This act prohibited discrimination on the basis of race or national origin in any state or local program receiving federal financial assistance. While the provisions of Title VI were not limited to education, its enactment led to the creation of the Office for Civil Rights within the Department of Health, Education and Welfare, which was authorized to initiate proceedings to cut off federal funds in cases where discrimination was found to exist. The potential impact of these legislative and executive actions became particularly significant over the next year with the passage of the Elementary and Secondary Education Act, the largest infusion of federal education dollars in American history.

It was not until 1968 that the Supreme Court began to hand down a series of decisions designed to define further its expectations with regard to school desegregation. In *Green* v. *School Board of Kent County*,[6] the Court struck down a "freedom-of-choice" plan in rural Virginia, which did not actually result in the desegregation of the races. While the Court did not declare freedom-of-choice plans unconstitutional per se, it pronounced suspect any scheme that did not achieve the goal of desegregation in situations where there was a prior history of intentional segregation. A year later, in *Alexander* v. *Holmes County*,[7] the Court raised the "all deliberate speed" formula to a more rigorous standard, declaring it the obligation of "every school district" to "terminate dual school systems at once," and to operate "now and hereafter unitary schools." It defined a unitary school system as one in which "no person is to be effectively excluded from any school because of race or color."

The inauguration of Richard Nixon in 1969 represented a rising tide of conservatism throughout the nation, and this changing mood extended to the Supreme Court with the appointment of Chief Justice Warren Burger. The dissension and violence that accompanied desegregation efforts in the South had already given birth to a deep skepticism about the merits of forced racial mixing and its practical progeny, court-ordered busing. The experience also eroded a broad political base that once supported liberal causes on behalf of human rights. In 1971 the Burger Court handed down its first major decision concerning desegregation. In *Swann* v. *Charlotte-Mechlenberg*,[8] the Court reaffirmed that school districts must take positive steps in order to undo the effects of past discrimination, and it recognized busing as an acceptable means to that end. However, reflecting an emerging conservatism within its ranks, the Court also found that one-race schools were not absolutely forbidden; it left the burden of proof of intent with the plaintiff. Writing the majority opinion, Chief Justice Burger also went to great lengths to define a limit on the scope of busing. He declared:

> An objection to the transportation of students may have validity when the time and distance of travel is so great as to either risk the health of children or significantly impinge on the educational process.[9]

By setting such limits, the Court was in effect prescribing a standard of judicial intervention which, in broad terms, required that the remedy imposed by the courts must fit the violation. In concluding his opinion, the Chief Justice also voiced strong approval for the use of freedom-of-choice plans and the gerrymandering of school district lines as appropriate remedies for desegregation. The emerging philosophy of the Burger Court was very much in accord with the political climate of the times. In 1972 Congress passed the Emergency School Aid Act, which provided funds to assist school districts in the process of desegregation. The provisions of the act, however, restricted how federal funds might be used. Money would be made available to encourage voluntary desegregation in the form of magnet schools, after-school programs, and educational enrichment programs, but could not be applied to support busing. The Equal Educational Opportunities Act, passed two years later, also contained a limitation on busing.

In 1974 the Court became involved in its first major desegregation case in the North. In *Keyes* v. *School District No. 1*[10] in Denver, Colorado, the Court entertained a presumption that if a plaintiff could prove segregation caused by "intentional state action" in a "meaningful portion" of a district, such proof raised the inference of intentional segregation in the entire school district. Here again, the Court, in an opinion written by Justice Brennan, distinguished between de jure and de facto segregation, but, under the conditions described, placed the burden of evidence upon the district defendant.

That same year the Court, in *Milliken* v. *Bradley*,[11] overturned a metropolitan desegregation plan in Detroit that involved a neighboring suburban district. In this case, the district judge had ruled that segregation in Detroit was not a local de facto situation, but rather the result of state and local de jure policies that resulted in the concentration of blacks in the inner cities and whites in the suburbs. Arguing that a Detroit-only plan would be inadequate, the judge then ordered a metropolitan remedy. The plan was upheld by the federal Court of Appeals. However, the Supreme Court ruled that it would not order an interdistrict remedy unless plaintiffs could prove intentional discrimination on the part of the suburban districts involved.

In 1977 the Supreme Court in *Milliken II*[12] sustained orders by the lower courts in Detroit that the state make resources available for the in-service training of teachers and for compensatory programs in reading and mathematics. This decision indicated a new emphasis on quality education, as opposed to the more traditional remedy of racial mixing. That same year Congress passed the Eagleton–Biden amendment as a rider to an appropriation bill, which held that the Department of Health, Education and Welfare could not order busing to achieve compliance with Title VI of the Civil Rights Act. This bill still allows the Department of Justice and private plaintiffs to sue for busing. However, since its passage the Senate has voted twice to enact laws that would strip the federal courts of the power to order busing, and both the House and Senate have voted on separate occasions for laws that would prohibit the Justice Department from pursuing court cases that could lead to busing. Moreover, under the Reagan administration, the Justice Department itself has taken a nonaggressive posture on the issue of school desegregation, leaving a major part of the responsibility for litigation with private plaintiffs.

Notwithstanding attempts by the Court to add some reason and order to the abolition of school segregation, the experience with desegregation throughout the nation has been mixed and uneven. Ironically, some of the most vehement opposition to desegregation and forced busing has occurred in the North. One of the early cases of violent reaction occurred in Pontiac, Michigan, in 1971. Perhaps the most publicized episode in racial upheaval occurred in Boston in 1974, when Judge Garrity's order to desegregate South Boston High School brought the school system to a virtual standstill.[13] Other major cities where busing plans have raised problems include Detroit, Chicago, San

Francisco, Cleveland, and Houston. However, there are also places such as St. Louis, Tampa, and Columbus, where busing efforts have proceeded more relatively smoothly. Metropolitan plans are in operation in Louisville, St. Louis, and Wilmington (Delaware).[14] In Indianapolis more than five thousand inner-city children are bused daily to school districts in neighboring suburbs. Mandatory court-ordered plans remain in place in Austin, Seattle, Dayton, and Pittsburgh, among other places. However, as the Justice Department now takes a moderate stance with regard to desegregation, many cities are being allowed to move away from forced racial mixing and instead are adopting voluntary strategies. Chicago, Buffalo, and Dallas are particular cases in point. In Los Angeles voters have passed a popular referendum that would terminate a state policy of busing to eliminate de facto segregation. That proposition has been upheld by the Supreme Court, since the program in question went beyond the federal requirements for mandatory desegregation. The fact is, however, that, despite occasional examples to the contrary, busing and forced racial mixing are still unpopular in many communities, and policy makers at all levels of government are becoming more willing to recognize and respond to that sentiment and the demands of their constituents.

The fundamental question still remains. What is to be done when minority children are denied equal access to educational facilities because of their race? Surely such a practice cannot be tolerated within the bounds of morality and the law. But some would argue that the remedy has become more troublesome than the problem. Is the cost of social equity ever too exacting in a free society? What has been the outcome of desegregation in the United States? What have been the unanticipated consequences? Have we succeeded in racial mixing at the school level? After more than a quarter-century of history with desegregation in the United States, we would hope to have learned something. Certainly there were instructional and affective objectives behind the arguments proposed to the Court by social scientists such as Kenneth Clark. Have desegregation efforts helped to overcome the psychological damage caused by racial isolation? Do black children learn more in an integrated setting? What has been the impact of desegregation on white children? Have liberal social planners placed an unfair burden on children to compensate for the inadequacies of adults?

According to the Coleman Report published in 1966, most children in the United States were still attending segregated schools a decade after the *Brown* decisions.[15] The report did show, however, that in cases where desegregation occurred, mixing poor minority children with children from middle-class backgrounds had a positive effect on the achievement scores of the poorer children. In 1973 Coleman published another major study, of trends in school segregation between 1968 and 1973.[16] It showed that school desegregation was a significant cause of declining white enrollments in public schools, thus giving birth to the well-known "white flight" thesis. Coleman's second study drew strong criticism on both its methodology and conclusions from other social scientists.[17] However, within a short period of time some of these same critics would uncover their own research findings, in basic accord with the claims of Coleman.[18] For example, in separate studies, Farley and Rossell agree that white flight does occur as a result of desegregation when certain conditions are in existence:

- when a substantial proportion (perhaps 25 percent or 30 percent) of the school population is black or minority;
- in central-city districts surrounded by accessible and predominantly white suburbs; and
- when there is a significant shift in the racial balance of schools, and primarily white reassignment is involved in the shift.

Farley and Rossell have also found that white flight is most pronounced during the first year of implementation, except when a plan is implemented in several phases. Rossell adds that white flight occurs especially when student assignments are mandatory, and when white students are assigned to minority schools. Her research also suggests that voluntary plans are not so likely to result in white flight. In an attempt to explain further the reasons behind white flight, the research of David Armour proposes that whites are motivated by a commitment to the neighborhood school concept and by the belief that neither blacks nor whites benefit from desegregation.[19] Armour concurs with Farley and Rossell that white flight is strongest during the first year of implementation, but his data also show white losses continuing over a period of four to five years.

Notwithstanding the existence of white flight, the fact remains that many schools have been desegregated. And the outcomes have been most interesting and moderately encouraging, if not conclusive. McConahay has found that, although students in desegregated schools have not reached the point where race is insignificant in choosing associates or friends, it is not as powerful a factor as gender.[20] He also observes that interracial friendships are being formed at an increasing rate, which could not happen in segregated schools. Edgar Epps has conducted a comprehensive analysis of the research literature on the psychological impact of desegregation on black children.[21] The data he uncovered revealed mixed patterns. In some cases black children have exhibited a higher self-concept in desegregated schools; in others they show more positive results in segregated settings. However, one point seems to come through quite clearly in this literature. It shows that what goes on in the classroom between teacher and student is a more critical factor in personality development than either segregation or desegregation. This conclusion agrees with the research of Felice and Richardson, which shows that desegregation produces benefits in individual development in classes including bused minority students, when the teachers are positive and supportive.[22] These findings are also consistent with the research data on effective schools.

In her analysis of sixty-four studies on the relationship between desegregation and pupil achievement, Nancy St. John has found that there is no strong evidence that desegregation will close the white-black achievement gap.[23] However, she modifies this conclusion by noting that desegregation has rarely lowered and sometimes raised the achievement scores of black children. In a more extensive review of a similar body of research literature, Weinberg provides us with a more encouraging assessment of the effects of desegregation on learning. He writes, "Overall, desegregation does indeed have a positive effect on minority achievement levels."[24] In another comprehensive review, Crain and Mahard have attempted to identify conditions under which desegregation is most successful in improving minority achievement.[25] The results of their work seem to show the same elements of effective schooling that other areas of research have uncovered. These include high expectations, appropriately trained staff, adequate facilities, and effective teaching. Crain and Mahard's findings are also consistent with the conclusions of Coleman, which suggest that mixing with middle-class students who are college-bound has a positive effect on poorer minority children. It is noteworthy however, that an implication in both works suggests that mixing by social class is more significant in terms of achievement than racial mixing.

To date, the most comprehensive assessment of desegregation in the United States is a seven-year project initiated under the auspices of the Office for Civil Rights and the National Institute of Education. Its scope includes an analysis of approximately twelve hundred previous studies, ten court cases, and desegregation activities in seventeen cities. The project team, headed by Willis Hawley, is composed of seventeen scholars from ten universities, several of whom have been mentioned in the foregoing paragraphs. The results of the team's work have been disseminated in a variety of forums since 1978. In a recent attempt to bring together some of the major conclusions of the group's research, Willis Hawley has presented a rather favorable portrait of the experience with desegregation.[26] He tells us that between 1968 and 1976 segregation has declined by 50 percent. While recognizing the causal relationship between forced busing and white flight, Hawley interestingly notes that parents of children who are involuntarily bused consistently exhibit more positive attitudes toward desegregation than parents of children who are not.

In terms of academic achievement, Hawley cites the following general findings of his study group:

- White students rarely experience declinees in performance.
- Minorities benefit academically more often than they experience negative effects.
- The earlier minority children experience desegregation, the more likely they are to react positively.
- The more carefully a school district prepares for desegregation, the more likely it will be to influence student achievement positively.

In terms of self-esteem and racial identity, Hawley presents the following conclusions:

- Desegregation causes a short-term increase in anxiety and self-doubt among minority children, but this reaction usually disappears over time.
- The key determinant of how desegregation will effect self-esteem is teacher behavior.
- Rigid tracking and highly competitive environments are detrimental to the self-image of low achievers.
- The racial identity of neither blacks nor whites is damaged by desegregation, although blacks may become more race-conscious.

If one accepts the evidence produced by Hawley and his colleagues, then one must believe that desegregation has been a relatively successful attempt at social intervention. As the work of this group has proceeded to its more advanced stages, it has given less attention to debating the merits of desegregation and has devoted more energy to defining strategies for making it most effective.[27] One cannot help drawing an analogy with the research on effective schools. That literature reached a turning point when debates focusing on the efficacy of school organizations gave way to inquiries on the characteristics of effective schools. Perhaps we are about to turn a similar corner in scholarship on desegregation. Assembling the major facets of the work in his own study group, Hawley provides us with the following strategic guidelines for effective school desegregation:[28]

- Desegregate students as early as possible.
- Encourage racial interaction in both academic and extracurricular settings.
- Avoid forms of tracking and ability grouping that highlight individual and group achievement differences.
- Organize schools and classrooms so that each has a "critical mass" of each racial group served.
- Minimize scale so as to decrease the number of students with whom a teacher must work.
- Develop rules of school governance that are fair, consistent, and equitable.
- Maintain a relatively stable student body.
- Recruit a racially diverse staff that is unprejudiced, supportive, and insistent on high standards.
- Maintain ongoing staff development efforts.
- Involve parents in instructional activities.
- Provide incentives for voluntary segregation as a supplement to mandatory programs in districts with high proportions of minority students.
- Involve the community, particularly parents, in the desegregation process.

THE NEW YORK SCENE

Racial conflict has been a significant ingredient in the educational politics of New York City ever since the beginning of the civil rights movement in the early 1950s. However, the history of desegregation in New York has been short and episodic. There was an initial decade of intense activity, dramatic demonstrations, and a series of successful school boycotts.[29] Then, by the mid-1960s, efforts to achieve desegregation gave way to a new form of racial politics—that concerning community control.

To a large extent the battle for community control grew out of the frustrations of the desegregation campaigns. It was in part a reaction to the insurmountable resistance minority and civil rights leaders encountered from white parent organizations and school officials. It was further spurred on by the rising racial consciousness of blacks and Hispanics—not to mention their dissatisfaction with the inaccessibility of Livingston Street. Thus, by the end of the 1960s neighborhood government was more relevant to the campaign for educational equality in New York than was desegregation; and its corollary, the neighborhood school, was somewhat anathema to the idea of integration.

This is not to say that segregation became an absolutely dead issue in New York. Decentralization fostered its own brand of racial politics. Occasionally it was manifested through the purposeful isolation of children on the basis of color. At times such blatant discrimination has brought litigation and has required corrective action.

In 1974 a federal court judge found intentional racial segregation at predominantly black Mark Twain Junior High School in Community School District 21 in Brooklyn.[30] He ordered the community school board to take action that would desegregate the school according to the standards established by the Supreme Court. Soon thereafter, the school board submitted to the court a plan that would convert Mark Twain Junior High School into a magnet school for gifted and talented children. After the court approved the plan, the district applied for and received $1.5 million in federal ESAA funds to help implement its new program. The federal money was used for hiring human relations coordinators, guidance counselors, and family assistants to provide multicultural educational activities. The resolution of the Mark Twain issue represented the moderate approach to desegregation that was becoming typical in New York.

In 1975 a more heated debate over desegregation began to stir in Queens, concerning Andrew Jackson High School. Jackson High School is located in the predominantly black neighborhood of Cambria Heights, approximately one mile from the Nassau County border. When the school opened in 1937, the student population in Queens was virtually all white, as was that of Jackson. By 1975 the school population in Queens was 55.4 percent white, but Jackson was nearly an all-black school. That year the parents' association from the high school petitioned the state commissioner of education to take action that would prevent Jackson from becoming a racially segregated school. Commissioner Ewald Nyquist responded by ordering that Jackson be integrated to reflect the racial composition of the entire student population of Queens.[31] Six months later the Board of Education petitioned the commissioner for a new hearing. It argued that compliance with the order would upset the racial balance in the remainder of Queens and further accelerate white flight. In 1976 Nyquist rescinded his order. He ruled that the compulsory assignment of whites to Jackson would "impair . . . racial integration of the high schools of the borough as a whole."[32] In place of his original order, the commissioner approved a voluntary plan that would give Jackson students an opportunity to choose an integrated school elsewhere. However, no white students were assigned to Jackson. At that point the parents' association of Jackson, with the help of the NAACP, took the case into federal court.

The parent plaintiffs presented their case against the state commissioner and the City Board of Education before federal district court Judge John F. Dooling, Jr. They argued that the action and inaction of the defendants represented a case of de jure segregation. They sought to enjoin the defendants from "continuing to maintain and perpetuate Andrew Jackson High School as a racially segregated facility." In the summer of 1977, after the original trial, the NAACP proposed to add nine Nassau County defendants to the case in order to press for a cross-county integration remedy.

Judge Dooling did not hand down his decision until May 1978. He then found that de jure segregation had not in fact existed because there was "no evidence that the Board has sought to segregate minorities."[33] However, he ruled that the voluntary plan approved by the commissioner in 1976 was an unconstitutional denial of equal protection because it limited the admission choices of minority students. While he denied the plaintiffs' request for a cross-county remedy, he ordered the Board of Education to present a plan to the commissioner that was in accord with Nyquist's original 1975 order. The plan was due for submission on July 1, the same day that the new school administration would take office.

Judge Dooling's ruling received considerable attention in the local media, and it was highly unpopular. A public opinion poll taken by the *Daily News* in early June showed that 54 percent of the respondents in New York City and its four neighboring suburban counties (Nassau, Suffolk, Westchester, Rockland) disapproved of the decision. Only 29 percent voiced approval, and another 17 percent responded "don't know."[34] At about the same time, the Board of Education decided to appeal the case. Several other parties filed *amicus* briefs to the court. The Queens County Democratic coalition submitted papers arguing for a reconsideration of whether Nassau County should be included in the integration plan. Two Nassau County legislators filed opposing briefs.

When the new chancellor was sworn in on July 1, only one of the 2,500 students registered at Andrew Jackson High School was white. On June 15 Judge Dooling had extended the due date for an integration plan until July 10. In the meantime, the appeal was still pending. This was all Macchiarola's problem now. But as far as desegregation was concerned, it would turn out to be the least of his worries. Another battle had been quietly brewing in Rosedale, Queens, which would develop into the most volatile public controversy ever to be faced by the new chancellor.

ROSEDALE: A STUDY IN IRONY

In most metropolitan centers, "white flight" refers to a post-1950 phenomenon in which the white middle class has fled the inner city to take up residence in the outlying suburbs. In New York's demographic

Figure 5-1
COMMUNITY SCHOOL DISTRICT 29

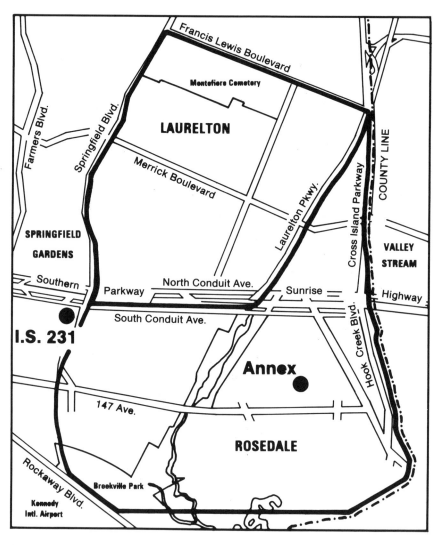

Source: *Newsday*, September 30, 1978

history there has been an intermediate step in that usual pattern. The first wave of out-migration from the inner city in New York was deposited in its own outer boroughs. Foremost among these is the borough of Queens, which, in terms of housing stock, population density, and ethnicity, bears a closer resemblance to suburban Nassau County than it does to Manhattan or central Brooklyn. The farther east one goes in Queens, the stronger that resemblance becomes. Community School District 29 is located on the eastern border of Queens, adjacent to Nassau, not far from Andrew Jackson High School. It is primarily composed of two middle-class communities: Rosedale, which is predominantly white; and Laurelton, which is predominantly black. Along the western border of the district is the community of Springfield Gardens, which is primarily black. Located in Springfield Gardens is Intermediate School 231, the original site of a major conflict on desegregation.

The Rosedale community is more than three hundred years old. Its major growth took place as part of a post-World War II building boom, when its population grew to the approximately 22,000 residents that it boasts today. Many of Rosedale's postwar settlers were city policemen, firemen, and other municipal workers, attracted to the community by the suburban-style living and the moderately priced housing. About 75 percent of the families are white, largely Jewish, Irish, and Italian homeowners. Many of the people who live in Rosedale today are there to escape the problems of the inner city, their flight propelled by the in-migration of blacks, whom they associate with crime, poverty, and dilapidated living conditions. Despite these fears, many community leaders have attempted to maintain the stability of the neighborhood and stem the next stage of flight to the suburbs that usually occurs when black migration starts to push toward the outskirts of the city. Joseph Albergo, president of Community School Board 29, who has lived in Rosedale more than twenty years and owns an automobile repair shop in neighboring Valley Stream, tells us the following about his neighbors,

> These are people who have moved three or four times already; who feel that when blacks move into the neighborhood, crime follows. I have to make them understand that when this black guy moves in, he's as happy to live here as the next guy, and he's not looking to create any problems. I tell them that these are people trying to make it the same way we are trying to make it.[35]

Laurelton is a much newer community than Rosedale. Twenty years ago it was predominantly Jewish. Today its population of 24,000 is 85 percent black. In 1963 a biracial group of residents in the community organized to form the Laurelton Block Associations. It was the first group of its kind in New York to work with state authorities to curb the blockbusting and panic selling that usually accompany demographic changes. Many of the blacks who have moved to Laurelton from the inner city were driven there by motivations similar to those of the whites. Claudette Webb, a black member of the community school board, explains, "My husband is a fireman. We moved out of Brooklyn because the neighborhood was changing. We wanted a neighborhood where everyone was working. We wanted a good school for our children."[36]

For many years, the neighborhoods that make up Community School District 29 have been praised as a model of successful integration. A local newspaper once described the community as "a racial mosaic."[37] Blacks and whites had lived together side by side in peaceful harmony and had sat together on the same community councils and school board. However, that history has not been untarnished. In 1973 an anti-integrationist group called Rights of All Rosedale (ROAR) was formed. On New Year's Eve in 1974, the home of Gloria and Ornestan Spencer, a black couple, was firebombed. Six months later a vacant house about to be occupied by another black family was set afire. These incidents brought Rosedale considerable negative attention, including a nationally televised show by Bill Moyers. Residents of Rosedale resent the negative publicity they received because of the ugly incidents. They feel that it has painted an unfair picture of the community. They claim that the leaders of ROAR have moved out. But the scars remain.

Intermediate School 231 was opened in Springfield Gardens in 1965 for students in grades 6–8. It was created to serve the students from five elementary "feeder" schools. These include PS 138 and PS 195, which are predominantly white; PS 156 and PS 181, which are predominantly black; and PS 38, which has a white/black ratio of 60/40. By 1970, IS 231 was overcrowded, in large part because of the unexpected and large population growth in southeastern Queens during the first five years of the school's existence. In 1973 the Board of Education added a new wing to the school, to provide space for 500 additional students in the 1,100-capacity facility. However, no funding was made available to provide companion additions to the lunchroom, gym, or auditorium. Therefore the school board chose to use the new wing as an early childhood center, leaving the school overcrowded. It then requested that another intermediate school be built within the district. In 1975 the Board of Education began construction on IS 240. According to the zoning plan developed by the school board, the feeder pattern of the new intermediate school was to be primarily white, serving PS 38, PS 138, PS 195, and PS 196. After one year, construction was halted because of the city fiscal crisis.

In addition to its overcrowding, IS 231 was also known to have some discipline problems. Whether these difficulties were any more severe than is usual in the case of an urban middle school is debatable. However, the Springfield Gardens school did go through six principals in a period of thirteen years. When it was discovered that construction would end on IS 240, the school board of District 29 developed a plan to create an annex for IS 231. The annex was to open in February 1977. It was to be housed on the top floor of PS 138, which is located in Rosedale, two miles from the main school facility in Springfield Gardens. The annex would draw its students from primarily white feeder schools. The proposal caused dissension among the black members of the school board and community leaders from Laurelton.

On January 24, 1977, Chancellor Irving Anker advised the community school board of District 29 that it would not be timely to open a new annex in the middle of the school year. Despite that advice, the school board went ahead with plans to implement its proposal. On January 31 the local school board received instructions from Livingston Street that no plans should proceed without approval from the central Board of Education. On February 4 a handbill was distrubuted to parents by the local school board, announcing that it had voted to establish an annex for IS 231 at PS 138. Children from PS 38, PS 138, and PS 195, all of which were predominantly white, would be given the first choice to attend. On the same day that the handbill was distributed, Chancellor Anker superseded the local school board, and the plan for the annex was dropped.

In the spring of 1977, the chancellor's office and the community school board worked together to develop a plan for opening the annex. The central school administration was interested in an arrangement that would open the annex to all the IS 231 feeder schools. In a meeting that May, it was agreed that the enrollment of students at the annex would be essentially by random choice, but that student assignments would be made, if necessary, in order to keep minority representation in the annex to a minimum of 30 percent. The annex opened in September 1977. In February 1978 the local school board advised the chancellor that it intended to zone the annex so that it would primarily serve the predominantly white feeder schools from the district. This was contrary to the agreement that had been made, but throughout April and May local school board members insisted that they would proceed with their new plan for September. In the meantime, they did not respond to requests by the chancellor for data on the racial composition of the school district.

There were many issues tied to the annex debate. In addition to complaints about overcrowding and safety in the main school, Rosedale residents claimed that the annex gave their children a neighborhood school within walking distance of their homes. Yet underlying all discussion about the annex was the more significant issue of race. Claudette Webb, a black member of the local school board, alludes to the influence of the "tipping factor"—the point at which minority children become the numerical majority in a school. She asserts, "The whites wanted out of 231 because it tipped. Integration was fine until the balance changed to 60–40 for blacks, People did not complain about overcrowding until it tipped."[38]

Linda Ovadias, a white parent leader and supporter of the annex, claims, "A large part of the issue had to do with safety. Girls were molested. Boys were beat up. So white children were moved out. When blacks are in the majority, the whites won't survive."[39]

Rosedale fits very well into the general historical pattern of the country. As the research literature on the subject shows, whites become less tolerant of an integrated situation when they are in the minority. They are less adaptable to such circumstances than are blacks. When a school tips out of their favor, whites tend to flee. Thus the annex in Rosedale soon became linked to the question of neighborhood stability. As Linda Ovadias explains, "The annex was formed because of overcrowding. But there was also the problem of white flight. The annex stabilized the neighborhood."[40]

The enrollment data on the IS 231 annex were revealing. Before its opening, the racial composition of the main school building in Springfield Gardens was 77 percent minority and 23 percent white. When the annex went into operation, its registration was 73 percent white and 27 percent minority. This left the composition of the main school at approximately 98 percent minority. When the annex opened its doors in September 1977, the Federation of Laurelton Block Associations filed a complaint with the Office for Civil Rights (OCR). The group claimed that the white majority of the nine-person community school board had intentionally created a racially segregated facility in Rosedale. The federal government initiated an investigation. This began a long, difficult scenario characterized by litigation, political maneuvering, and the constant exchange of racial epithets.

There is a real irony about Rosedale. Many of those who became embroiled in the controversy were among the original group who had labored to make integration work in their community. They hung on while others fled to suburbia. Now they were on the other side of the table. As school board president Joseph Albergo put it, "The white people who stayed and tried to integrate are the ones who are called bigots."[41]

Consider also the position of the black parents in the community. They had moved to Queens to seek a better way of life, to take their children out of the troubled neighborhoods of the inner city. Now they were the ones being excluded. The whole situation was both confusing and demoralizing. Claudette Webb, a black parent, says:

> I don't know what the whites are afraid of. The stories of violence are so exaggerated. What do they think we are going to do to them? How do you think it makes one feel to know that her children are unwanted?[42]

When the new chancellor took office in 1978, the annex was still open, in violation of the agreement that had been made with Irving Anker. The OCR investigation was still pending. On the first day of school that September, a group of parents, mostly black, held a sit-in at the principal's office in IS 231. They were demanding that the annex be closed. Two days later, Chancellor Macchiarola and the members of Community School Board 29 received a ten-page letter from the Office for Civil Rights. In it were the findings of the investigation regarding IS 231. It stated as follows:

> The City of New York is engaged in discriminatory conduct in violation of Title VI of the Civil Rights Act of 1964. . . . The violation involves the location of a school annex which resulted in a racially identifiable school.[43]

The OCR report gave rise to much speculation. Just how would the new chancellor react? Would he begin his tenure by taking on a popularly elected community board? That could be catastrophic in terms of his important and developing relationship with thirty-one other school boards and their superintendents. Could he ignore the complaints of black parents whose children were found to be the objects of illegal discrimination? Such action would send out a souring message to the minority community of the city, which makes up 70 percent of the school population. As the events concerning IS 231 slowly unfolded, it became apparent that some time would pass before the chancellor became a major actor in the controversy. Other matters demanded his attention, other debates over the difficult issue of desegregation. By the time the chancellor became immersed in Community School District 29, he would already have a record on the issue, which, under normal circumstances, would have made his behavior predictable.

THE CHANCELLOR'S RECORD: MODERATION UNDER LAW

Desegregation had not been at the center of educational politics in New York for some time. But it would arise early as an issue to be dealt with by the new administration. That was not by choice. Macchiarola's team had made it clear from the outset that desegregation would not be a significant part of its policy agenda. So long as racial isolation was not the result of intentional and illegal segregation, it was viewed as an acceptable fact of inner-city life. This administration would focus its energies on effective instruction, and racial mixing was not considered a prerequisite to that goal. Indeed, the basic premise underlying the philosophy "All children can learn" was the proposition that poor and minority schools could be made to work. Desegregation, under most circumstances, was tangential to these established priorities. As Ron Edmonds, the highest-ranking black person in the administration, explained:

> The New York City schools are predominantly minority—we accept that. It is not our intention to do anything (beyond what is already being done) to alter the racial composition of buildings or boroughs. Our energies are fixed on raising achievement.[44]

That was the plan. However, it would not quite turn out that way. As the events recounted in the previous chapters have shown, policy agendas are a result of both inheritance and design. Desegregation was to become relevant.

First there was the Jackson case. The appeal of Judge Dooling's decision was still before the court. It had to be pursued. According to public opinion polls, the ruling itself had proved to be unpopular. More important, there was a significant flaw in the legal reasoning. Judge Dooling had found that racial isolation in the Cambria Heights high school was not the result of intentional public policy. At the same time, he ruled that the constitutional rights of black children were being violated and ordered that a desegregation plan be put into action. Historically, the Supreme Court had supported such remedies only in cases where intentional or de jure segregation was found to exist.

Within the first week of his tenure, the chancellor had persuaded Judge Dooling to await the outcome of the appeal before requiring that a desegregation plan be submitted to the court. Testimony before the three-person Circuit Court of Appeals would not be presented until mid-January of 1979. The composition of that panel was relatively conservative. Hearing the case were Judge Murray Gurfein, a Nixon appointee; Judge Sterry Waterman, an Eisenhower appointee; and Judge Ellsworth Van Groafeiland, who had been placed on the court by President Ford. Arguing the case on behalf of the plaintiffs was James Meyerson of the NAACP. The Board of Education was represented by an attorney from the City Office of the Corporation Counsel. Also appearing before the court was an attorney for the state commissioner of education, who was a codefendant in the case.

Meyerson proposed to the court that Jackson High School could be integrated by busing a thousand of the thirty thousand white students from the twenty other high schools in Queens. He also offered that additional white students could be obtained "from across the Nassau line,"[45] thereby suggesting a metropolitan solution to the Jackson problem. However well-meaning these proposals may have been, they were still in disagreement with the legal precedents set by the Supreme Court.

On April 15, the United States Circuit Court of Appeals voted unanimously to overrule the lower court decision of Judge Dooling, pronouncing, "The power of the federal courts to compel desegregation in state school systems is circumscribed."[46] Citing both the *Swann* and the *Keyes* rulings, the three-member panel drew a distinction between de facto and de jure segregation. It then proceeded to explain that judicial intervention is appropriate only in the latter situation. Thus ended the Jackson case.

From both a legal and political perspective, it can be said that the new administration disposed of the Jackson case with little difficulty. One might reasonably argue that the plaintiffs never had a strong claim from the outset. Certainly, once the appeals process was in motion, the case was resolved with little fanfare. Nevertheless, the desegregation issue was still very much alive in Queens during the early part of 1979. While the Jackson appeal was still being deliberated, the NAACP had initiated another lawsuit in that borough. This time it alleged that Community School Board 24 in Middle Village had deliberately acted to create a racially isolated setting for minority children. The case in District 24 bore a remarkable resemblance to the situation that had already unfolded in Rosedale. It began when the school board decided to open two annexes in order to relieve overcrowding in Intermediate School 61. The seven hundred children assigned to the annexes were disproportionately black and Hispanic students. Moreover, the two

annexes were located outside the school district boundaries in a neighboring district (25), reflecting an arrangement that had been worked out
by the two school boards.

In a political sense, District 24 was the most complex desegregation case with which the administration had yet had to deal. Since it
concerned community schools, it went beyond the issues of Jackson,
and, like Rosedale, touched on sensitive questions concerning the
chancellor's authority vis-à-vis the districts, under decentralization. It
was even more complicated than Rosedale, because its resolution
might affect several school districts instead of one. The creation of the
two annexes had already brought two school boards into the legal
debate. When the case was finally brought to trial, NAACP attorney
James Meyerson argued for a remedy that would rezone Districts 24,
25, and 30 in order to promote desegregation.

Macchiarola was brought into court on March 5. His response to
questioning revealed that he had serious doubts about the merits of the
suit, and also a concern for its implications regarding decentralization.
Warning against policies that would further encourage white flight and
aggravate race relations, he told United States District Court Judge
Charles Sifton,

> If integration is a goal, we are going in the wrong direction as far as
> the City and the suburbs are concerned. We are short-circuited in
> obtaining integration by the limitations we have in the City school
> district. . . .
>   At this point, litigation will get blacks and whites at each
> other's throats and bring no progress.[47]

It was while he was under cross examination by NAACP attorney
Meyerson that Macchiarola came out most strongly for the protection
of district prerogatives as they were defined by the Decentralization
Law. Meyerson had asked the chancellor what effect community
school district lines had on his ability to promote integration. Macchiarola responded,

> Of course it affects our ability to do it. We had picket lines around
> the Board of Education in the 1960s because the Board of Educa-
> tion was told it didn't listen to the community. . . . Decentraliza-
> tion moved the decision-making process to the districts in lots of
> ways. . . . There were some benefits and some costs.[48]

When asked by Meyerson about the possibility of rezoning Districts 24, 25, and 30 to promote integration, the chancellor told him, "If
you get 24, 25, and 30 to agree, I'll do it."

"What if they don't agree?" asked Meyerson.

"I have to respect the policy of decentralization," Macchiarola responded.[49]

On November 14 Judge Sifton ruled that community school officials were responsible for "some, but not all" of the segregated school conditions in District 24.[50] He ordered them to submit an appropriate remedial plan by the end of the year. The judge found that the plaintiffs had "failed to establish that the segregated conditions in middle-level schools in District 24 in general are the result of intentional segregation." He noted that demographic patterns had been partially responsible for the conditions that had evolved. However, he also found the establishment of "additional segregated educational facilities" in the annexes to be "constitutional violations." In ordering a remedy, Judge Sifton suggested that the required plan could include the mandatory busing of some white students, but he also expressed hope that such action could be avoided.

By the time the Sifton order was handed down, Community School Board 25 had already closed one of the IS 61 annexes. In addition to this, the chancellor's office had developed a plan with Queens College to open a demonstration school (IS 227) in District 24 to help alleviate the problem of racial isolation. Under the plan, IS 227 would recruit students on a boroughwide basis, with a certain percentage of its 350 seats reserved for District 24 applicants. IS 227 had originally been scheduled to open as a regular intermediate school in September 1977, in response to the overcrowding in District 24. It was delayed because of construction problems. When the NAACP brought its suit over the annexes in early 1979, Macchiarola's staff began discussions with the college about establishing a demonstration school. The chancellor had mentioned this developing plan during his March court appearance, hoping that it would eventually contribute to a solution. The Louis Armstrong Demonstration School (IS 227) was opened in September 1979. Negotiations between the chancellor's office and Community School Board 24 were somewhat delayed because of disagreements over the racial breakdown of the applicant list submitted by the district. Finally, with the momentum provided by Judge Sifton's November decision, an agreement was reached that assigned approximately one-third of the 350 seats in IS 227 to students from District 24. At that point the desegregation dispute in District 24 was quietly settled.

Race remained painfully relevant in Queens. The next scene of conflict was District 26, in the Bayside–Douglaston sections. According to a memorandum of understanding signed in 1977 by the chancellor's office and the United States Office for Civil Rights, the city school system is to conduct an annual ethnic census of students and staff. These data are to be submitted to OCR as part of an annual review for monitoring compliance with federal civil rights acts. The agreement was made in response to a federal investigation of staff integration. Failure to abide by its terms can jeopardize eligibility for federal funding. In 1977 Community School Board 26 refused to conduct the required census. As a result, Chancellor Irving Anker, after much futile negotiation, suspended the school board for nearly a month and deployed his own personal staff to collect the data.

In November 1978 the school board informed the new chancellor that once again it would not cooperate in the administration of the annual census. It was joined in that threat by the school board in its neighboring district (25), which is also in Queens. Community School Boards 25 and 26 were among a group of eight that had initiated a federal suit challenging the chancellor's authority to conduct ethnic surveys in accord with the OCR agreement.[51] Macchiarola made several attempts to persuade the two school boards to comply with the standing agreement while their appeal was pending. Finally, under the threat of suspension, the school board in District 25 voted to collect the data "under protest." However, District 26 would not.

What emerged from this situation was a long, arduous legal debate between th chancellor and the school board of District 26. In January 1979 the school board obtained a show cause order from the State Supreme Court, prohibiting the chancellor from suspending or removing the elected school board without a judicial trial or hearing. In the following month Macchiarola took the case into federal court. There, Federal District Judge Jack Weinstein refused to lift the state court order forbidding the chancellor to suspend the board. However, the judge did rule that the chancellor could supersede the school board's actions and send his staff into the district to collect the data. That decision was supported by another ruling of the State Supreme Court. On June 25 Macchiarola superseded Community School Board 26, appointed Louise Latty, a member of his staff, as trustee of the district, and assigned his special assistant, Joseph Saccente, to conduct the census of pupils and staff. Those events would be repeated in the following year (1980), when the chancellor once again superseded the school board and Saccente was sent to collect the data. The long battle of wills between Macchiarola and District 26 would not end until May of 1981, when the United States Supreme Court refused to review the school board's case protesting the legality of the ethnic census. One week later, the school board voted 5–1 to collect it own data.

The chancellor exhibited a consistent pattern of behavior about desegregation. He was not a militant advocate. His administration's approach to racial equality focused on effective instruction for the poor. He was aware of the connection between forced racial mixing and white flight. A former community school board president, he was reluctant to intervene at the district level. He preferred to have the districts resolve their problems locally. However, experience had also shown that once a ruling of law was made with regard to desegregation, Macchiarola would do whatever was necessary in order to comply with the law. And what was necessary would usually be determined by the behavior of the defendants in the case.

In the recent history of New York, most problems with segregation have been resolved peacefully through voluntary plans. However, it is the cases that are exceptions to that rule that usually attract the most attention. They absorb the most energy, inflict the most pain, and bring out the worst in people. Rosedale was that kind of case. It was New York's premier exception. It would demand the strongest action.

THE COMMUNITY ARENA

Rosedale worked its way into the spotlight early in the life of the new administration. As may be recalled, the first day of school in September 1978 was marked by a sit-in at IS 231, launched by thirty black parents demanding the closing of the predominantly white annex. The demonstration lasted four days. By its end, the Office for Civil Rights had coincidentally issued its letter of findings, stating that the annex in Rosedale was in violation of the Civil Rights Act of 1964. The school board in District 29 was given ninety days to develop a plan to correct the situation. When the case first broke, Macchiarola decided to remain in the background, hoping that the school board and OCR could work out a reasonable solution to the problem. However, the mood in the district was far from conciliatory. The school board itself was polarized, with the six white and the three black members meeting separately to develop their own plans. In the meantime, black community leaders from Laurelton were persuading minority parents to remove their children from the predominantly white annex, in order to make the existence of the facility less legally defensible.

Between September and December of 1978, several negotiation meetings took place between Community School Board 29 and representatives of OCR, in an attempt to work out a compromise. On December 11 the white majority on the school board submitted two plans to OCR. One plan would have closed the annex and created seventh and eighth grades in the predominantly white elementary feeder schools for the white children attending the annex. Under this plan, black children attending the annex would be returned to the predominantly black main facility of IS 231. The other plan submitted by the school board would have kept the annex open and maintained the status quo. Both plans were rejected by OCR because, according to its director, David Tatel, "they ignored the issue of the segregated school at IS 231."[52]

Shortly thereafter, the three black members of the school board submitted their own plan to OCR. However, OCR would not accept the plan because it did not represent a proposal agreed upon by a majority of the school board. On December 28 the white majority submitted its third proposal to OCR. It called for the complete closing of IS 231 and the creation of seventh and eighth grades in all seven of the elementary feeder schools. OCR rejected that plan in early January, stating that it "further segregated the affected students."[53] In the meantime, the OCR deadline for an acceptable proposal had expired.

On April 5 approximately seventy parents, mostly white, attended a school board meeting in District 29. During that meeting, the school board, with parental support, voted 6–1 to maintain the IS 231 annex, in defiance of the orders from OCR. Desiree Greenidge, the only black board member attending the meeting, cast the one dissenting vote. David Bluford and Claudette Webb, the other two black members, were holding their own meeting with parents at PS 181 in Laurelton.

In mid-July and early August, representatives from OCR again spoke with attorneys from District 29, with the hope of reaching an acceptable agreement. There was no progress. On August 20 school board attorneys informed OCR that "under no circumstances could the district adopt and implement a desegregation plan this September."[54] Four days later, OCR announced that it was initiating administrative enforcement proceedings against both Community School Board 29 and the central Board of Education, designed to withdraw federal funds from the district. The school board was given thirty days to either integrate the school or challenge the charges. At that point the chancellor began to exert verbal pressure on the school board to take some necessary remedial action, but he still refrained from direct involvement in the case. On August 30 the chancellor's office issued a statement through an intermediary, declaring, "The Chancellor feels it is incumbent upon the local board to change the situation. . . . But since the Office for Civil Rights has put pressure on the board, he is going to stand back and see what happens now."[55]

In September 1979 the annex opened once more, for the third consecutive year. In the meantime, black and white school board members began to work together to develop a response to OCR. Any plan for rezoning the district needed approval by the chancellor. Macchiarola informed the board that he would not approve any proposal that did not have biracial support on the school board. After many abortive attempts at a compromise, it appeared that an agreement had finally been reached in February. A majority of the school board tentatively agreed on a plan that had been designed by David Bluford, a black member. Under its terms, the annex would be closed, and PS 38 in Rosedale would be converted into an intermediate school with a racially mixed feeder pattern. A science magnet program would be developed at IS 231.

The school board proposal was not well received by OCR, which claimed that its provisions did not address the problem of racial isolation in the IS 231 main building. However, Macchiarola stated that he would support the plan, regardless of the position taken by OCR, as long as it had both white and black support on the school board. When the board met in March to approve the proposal officially, a debate developed over its details. Bluford, its chief architect, reversed his position, withdrew his support, and walked out of the meeting. At the end of a rather heated discussion, the board then voted 6–2, along racial lines, to approve the plan in Bluford's absence.

In May 1980 the triennial community school board elections in New York occurred, providing, in District 29, the forum for a racially charged political contest pitting Rosedale against Laurelton. There were fourteen candidates running for the nine seats available on the board. Seven black candidates formed a Unity Slate in opposition to seven white candidates, who ran on a Community Slate. When the balloting was completed on May 6, the blacks had added one more seat to the three they had held since the previous election. However, the whites maintained a 5–4 majority on the school board.

The community school board election in District 29 was more than a symbol of the racial polarization that plagued western Queens. It was a clear illustration of a situation where a white constituent electorate chooses the governing board of a school district that serves a primarily black and minority clientele. While the racial composition of the school board of District 29 was representative of the general population of its resident community, it was not representative of the student body of the schools. That division between constituent and client was a major force behind school politics and education policy at the community level.

THE CITY AND STATE ARENAS

On May 30 the chancellor informed the school board in District 29 that he would not approve the desegregation plan it had adopted, since the proposal no longer had minority support, which was the condition he had originally set for approval. On June 11 he ordered the school board to close the annex and return its pupils to the main building of IS 231 in September. With the clock ticking away and administrative proceedings by OCR already in motion, Macchiarola wanted to resolve the annex issue before the schools were closed at the end of June. When the school board refused to carry out his order, he superseded the board. On June 17 he deployed a member of his staff to carry out the necessary administrative procedures to reassign the annex students to the main school building for the fall semester beginning in September.

School board President Joseph Albergo accused the Chancellor of "buckling under the pressure of the minority."[56] He pledged to appeal Macchiarola's action both to the central Board of Education and in the state courts. On the evening of June 23 approximately seven hundred parents, mostly white, met at PS 138 in Rosedale and raised over $3,000 in order to launch a legal battle against the chancellor. A few days later Macchiarola received a letter from Queens Borough President Donald Manes, urging him to reverse his position on the school board plan. Manes warned, "The white residents of Rosedale are adamant. They will not send their children to IS 231."[57] Manes sent a copy of his letter to Board of Education President Joseph Barkan, and asked to speak to the members of the Board before it acted on the District 29 appeal against the chancellor. Board President Barkan happened to be the Queens member of the central Board of Education. This meant that he was an appointee of the Queens borough president. Manes also came to the dispute with a reputation as a strong advocate of public education, and he was an important ally on the Board of Estimate each year when the Board of Education sought approval for its budget.

The Board of Education handed down its decision concerning the District 29 appeal on July 23. Attorneys for the local board had argued that the chancellor's withdrawal of support for the desegregation plan, based upon the reversal of the minority position, was "inappropriate and arbitrary." They contended that since OCR proceedings were still continuing, the burden of proof concerning segregation remained with OCR until an administrative court judge made a decision. The Board of Education disagreed. It ruled that in light of the OCR findings, which were the "level of initial jurisdiction," the action of the community school board was "contrary to law."[58] The Board therefore upheld the chancellor's actions as being neither arbitrary, capricious, nor contrary to law, and dismissed the district appeal.

On August 13 a group of approximately three hundred parents

met in Rosedale and voted to defy the Board of Education order to send their children to IS 231. Instead, they vowed to set up a community-run school in the annex. Within the next week, school board attorneys took their appeal into the state supreme court. Contending that the chancellor had exceeded his statutory authority in superseding the local board, they petitioned Justice Yorka Linakis to enjoin Macchiarola from closing the annex. They also warned that the transfer would create irreparable harm to the children involved and would provoke parents to withdraw children from the Queens public schools. The chancellor was represented by City attorney Mary Tucker. She attempted to persuade the judge that the issues in question were educational in nature, not legal, and that the proper forum for an appeal was the state commissioner of education, not the courts.

There was as much political reasoning behind the chancellor's position in court as there was legal thinking. School officials wanted to get the case out of the Queens courts. Most state judges sitting on the bench in that borough were products of the Queens Democratic political organization. Many of them personally owed their political and judicial careers to Borough President Donald Manes. The white electorate of Queens had often made its position known on the question of school desegregation. There was a good chance that the state judiciary in Queens, intentionally or not, was predisposed to the position of the Rosedale school board. On August 21 Justice Linakis found that the issues before the court were within the proper jurisdiction of the state judiciary. She ordered a trial, and the case was assigned to State Supreme Court Justice Martin Rodell.

Between the time of the trial and the time that Justice Rodell handed down his decision, a meeting was arranged in Macchiarola's office by Queens Congressman James Scheuer. It was attended by school board President Joseph Albergo, Vice President Doloris Grant, and Charlotte Webb and Rupert Clark, two black members of the school board. Also invited to the meeting were officials from the Office for Civil Rights. Macchiarola proposed a compromise plan. Assuming the reassignment of the predominantly white student body from the annex to the main school at IS 231, the chancellor recommended that many of the graduates from three black elementary schools who usually attend IS 231 be reassigned to another school. This would allow the percentage of nonminority students at IS 231 to increase from 12 percent to 25 percent. The plan was well received. Everyone left the meeting acknowledging that progress had been made. They would all report back to their respective constituents and give the proposal careful consideration. However, the spirit of hope was not long-lived.

Four days after the meeting in the chancellor's office, Justice

Rodell released his decision. He ruled that Macchiarola's order to close the annex was "not predicated upon any sound or accepted educational principle" but "solely upon the wishes of the Office for Civil Rights."[59] The judge also pointed out that "no determination has been made by the federal government with reference to the withholding of funds."[60] While the court recognized the authority of the chancellor to refuse a plan submitted by the local school board, it vacated and annulled his order to close the annex. In a subsequent judgment, Justice Rodell instructed Macchiarola to propose a plan of his own, "consistent with sound educational principles, City Board policy, and law."[61] This plan was to be prepared no later than October 15. Community School Board 29 was to be afforded "an opportunity of responding thereto and to submit alternative suggestions . . ." within a period of one month from the time of the initial submission.

Justice Rodell's actions certainly worked to put the local school board in a stronger position vis-à-vis the chancellor. Now it was Macchiarola's responsibility to come up with a workable plan, which the school board would respond to and comment on. Moreover, the continued operation of the annex was assured at least until February. Thus in September 1980 the controversial annex of IS 231 would be opened in Rosedale for the fourth consecutive year. The enrollment at the annex remained about 60 percent white, while that at the main school in Springfield Gardens was about 98 percent black.

Macchiarola produced his plan, as expected, on October 15. Under its terms, the annex would be allowed to remain open beyond February. However, it required that the racial composition of the annex and the main school be the same. The zone of IS 231 and the feeder schools would not be changed. Enrollment in the main building would be limited to 1,140 students. On October 23, after a raucous meeting marked by accusations and denunciations, the white majority of the community school board voted to reject the chancellor's plan. In another 5–4 vote along racial lines, the school board decided to send a letter to the chancellor, which included the following statement:

> We believe that the plan is inconsistent with the terms of Justice Martin Rodell's order of September 5, 1980, and that our students, both black and white, will suffer serious educational consequences should they be compelled to move midyear.[62]

Macchiarola responded with a letter to board President Joseph Albergo, instructing him to direct the principal of IS 231 to close the annex and return the students to the main building by February 2, the first day of the spring semester. The chancellor also advised Albergo that if the pupil capacity of IS 231 proved to be too limited, he was prepared to order the transfer of special-education classes then housed in IS 231. According to the chancellor's figures, the combined enrollment of the IS 231 main facility and annex was 1,392, including 50 special-education students. While this total was in excess of the 1,244 student capacity of the school, the amount of crowding was not unusual as far as Queens intermediate schools go.

THE CONFLICT ESCALATES

On Thursday, November 21, the District 29 school board voted (again 5–4) to direct principal Reginald Landeau to take no action on the chancellor's most recent order to close the annex. At the same meeting the white majority voted once again to appeal Macchiarola's action to the central Board of Education. On the following Sunday about three hundred residents from Rosedale organized a demonstration to protest the chancellor's position on IS 231. The demonstrators blocked traffic for forty-five minutes on the Sunrise Highway, a major artery conencting Queens and Nassau counties, as angry motorists blew their horns, shook their fists, and yelled at the Rosedale protestors. This dramatic action was the first of several that, within the next two months, would convert the desegregation controversy into a major media event on the New York political scene.

In early December a federal Administrative Court judge finally delivered a long-awaited decision concerning the original OCR findings and proceedings initiated to stop federal funding to District 29. Judge Walter Alprin's findings in the case were quite unambiguous. He ruled:

> While cloaked in such guises as relieving overcrowding in other schools, or avoiding racial physical incidents alleged but never proven . . . the various plans [of CSB 29] were in each place put forth with the obvious intent of retaining a white majority in the 7th, 8th, and 9th grades of the school district's white community.[63]

Judge Alprin ordered that federal funds administered by the United States Department of Education be terminated in pursuance of the Civil Rights Act of 1964. Another administrative decision would be needed in the Department of Education to determine how and which funds were to be withheld. The school board retained the right to appeal the decision to either the secretary of the department or the federal courts. However, the Administrative Court decision added much force to the chancellor's position, both politically and legally, and was even to strengthen his hand with regard to pending litigation before the state courts.

On December 11, the same day that they presented their appeal to the Board of Education, members of Community School Board 29 requested a "conciliation meeting" with the chancellor. Macchiarola would not attend the meeting, but he instructed members of his staff to go in his place. Community school board President Albergo was seeking permission to leave the annex open through the spring term, in order to prevent any disruption in the educational process. Under directions from the chancellor, Macchiarola's staff replied with a flat "No." That was the end of compromise. At the beginning of the next week, Rosedale parents launched a three-day boycott of the annex and of the two white elementary schools (PS 138 and PS 195) from which the annex students were recruited. As parents picketed around the school buildings, total attendance in the schools dropped from 1,576 students to 51. On the last day of the boycott, the Board of Education handed down its ruling dismissing the appeal of the chancellor's decision.

Macchiarola had no intention of letting up on the pressure anymore. According to his instructions of December 16, the school board was to direct the IS 231 principal to submit a plan for closing the annex within three days. Those orders were never carried out. On December 22 Macchiarola wrote Albergo another letter. This time he informed Albergo that he was superseding the school board. He appointed his special assistant, Joseph Saccente, as trustee of the district, and granted him "all the powers and duties attending implementation of my order of December 16, 1980."[64] Saccente was one of Macchiarola's top troubleshooters. A twenty-year veteran of the school system, he had served on the staffs of two previous chancellors. In 1969 he had played a major role in helping to convert the administrative machinery of New York's centralized school system so that it could adapt to decentralization and community control. He had been personally involved in every district suspension or supersession since the implementation of decentralization, including those that had been ordered by Macchiarola. Now his charge was to enter IS 231 and carry out the pupil programming and exchange of records required to transfer 325 students from the annex to the main building.

Macchiarola's second supersession of the Queens school board within six months brought an immediate and angry response. Queens Borough President Donald Manes fired off a public letter to the chancellor, urging him to reverse his decision and allow the annex to remain open until June. He called Macchiarola's position "educationally disruptive," and argued, "The fact that outside of a handful, all the black parents, as well as the white parents, kept their children from attending school during the three-day boycott last week, must stand for something."[65] Manes suggested that the chancellor should meet with black and white parents whose children attend the annex, in order to "try to arrive at an amicable solution." The Manes letter arrived about a week after Macchiarola had submitted his 1982 Executive Budget to the Board of Education. The chancellor would need Manes's support on the Board of Estimate to obtain the dollars needed to carry out his new program initiatives, including the recently proposed and controversial Promotional Policy.

Macchiarola, however, would not give any ground. He replied in a letter to Manes, advising the borough president that a federal judge had found that the creation of the annex resulted in intentional segregation. He rejected Manes's suggestions outright and further chided the Queens official:

> Your letter offers no constructive plan to remedy past discrimination . . . your proposal that I meet with parents from the annex overlooks the fact that these parents do not represent the district as a whole.[66]

With respect to the boycott that Manes had referred to, Macchiarola wrote, "The boycott stands for the abdication by the community school board of its responsibility to maintain education for all children in the district."[67]

On January 8 attorneys for the school board brought the case back into state court, seeking a preliminary injunction that would keep the annex open while a trial could be held on the matter. This time, the parties to the legal debate came before a different judge. Hearing the case was State Supreme Court Justice Sidney Leviss. Prior to his appointment to the state court, Leviss had served as borough president of Queens. Before that, he had been deputy borough president. He was the predecessor of Donald Manes, another product of Queens County political organizations. However, the chancellor still had a strong legal case. He came into court with the backing of both the OCR findings and the federal administrative judge's decision. The Board of Education had twice ruled in his favor with regard to the educational merits of the case.

Leviss refused to grant the preliminary injunction sought by the school board, claiming that a trial was not necessary since one had already been held by Justice Rodell in August. He said that the only thing for his court to determine was whether the Board of Education and the chancellor had complied with Rodell's order. He promised a decision before February 2.

After two weeks of deliberation, Justice Leviss handed down a ruling. His findings were a direct response to the arguments made by school board attorneys, who challenged the educational merits of the chancellor's order to close the annex at midyear. The judge found that "the only issues left involve questions of administrative discretion and adoption."[68] These, he ruled, are "issues of fact and educational policy, not of law." Under state law, such questions require the exhaustion of administrative appeals. Leviss, therefore, granted the school board a two-week stay, ordering the annex to remain open for fifteen days while an appeal could be made to the Commissioner of Education.

Neither side to the dispute was very pleased with the court's decision. There appeared to be a lack of consistency between Leviss's original pronouncements during the hearings and his final declaration two weeks later. It left the whole matter dangling in the air. Members of the Rosedale school board realized that the case would now be taken out of the jurisdiction of the state courts in Queens and turned over to the state commissioner, where the chancellor had wanted to see it from the beginning. Education officials at Livingston Street were aware that leaving the annex open beyond the first day of the new term would strengthen arguments concerning the disruptive nature of the school closing. Hence the Leviss decision drew criticism from both camps.

Black school board member Claudette Webb observed:

It's a political decision. How could he rule in favor of us and then do something like that? He is playing both sides of the street as far as I am concerned. What he should have done, if he felt that way, is to have ruled in their [the white majority's] favor so the kids would know where they were going to be.[69]

White school board member Dolores Grant lamented:

I thought the judge was going to make a decision. What he's really doing is passing it into another court. What he did was just pass the buck to someone else, and it took this time for him to pass the buck. Unfortunately, there are kids involved here, and these kids don't know if they are coming or going.[70]

James Meyerson of the NAACP, which by now was an *amicus* in the Rosedale case, declared:

The bottom line is that it's the ultimate cop-out. It took him two weeks to make this decision, and then he gave them two weeks to go to the commissioner—at the same time limiting any action [to close the annex]. He did this with the full knowledge that he would be taking it past the February 2nd date.[71]

State Commissioner Gordon Ambach lost no time in issuing a ruling. On January 29, the day before the annex was scheduled to close according to Macchiarola's order, Ambach upheld the chancellor, proclaiming:

I will not substitute my judgment for that of a board of education in the absence of a showing that the challenged decision is arbitrary, capricious, or in some manner contrary to State law or to sound educational policy.[72]

On the next day, school board attorneys were again in state court, this time appealing the Leviss decision to the State Appellate Division, making one last-ditch effort to have the annex kept open. However, by the time the District 29 lawyers argued their case before Judge Frank Gulotta, Saccente had already closed the annex and carried out the student transfers. This made the annex closing, for all practical purposes, a moot issue. Judge Gulotta ruled that since "all the necessary preparations attending the scheduled closing have already been completed," the stay requested by the school board "would not substantially serve to preserve the status quo ante."[73] However, finding that the matter before the court was "one of great concern to the affected students," the judge did rule that the case warrented a hearing before the full five-member Appellate Division of the State Supreme Court.

While the Gulotta ruling served to prolong the litigation surrounding the District 29 controversy, the chancellor's office was now confident that it had laid the groundwork for a final victory in court. It had already been successful with regard to several administrative and judicial decisions. In addition to OCR and the federal administrative court judge, Macchiarola had now received the backing of the state commissioner, the lower courts, and the Board of Education. The matter had been taken out of the Queens-dominated jurisdiction. The decision before the higher court no longer concerned the chanceilor's authority or judgment in closing the annex, but whether, in fact, he should be forced to reopen it. According to George Shebitz, the senior attorney handling the Rosedale case for the chancellor, "Our office was quite encouraged by the time the case had reached the Appellate Division. It appeared that a satisfactory resolution was imminent."[74]

However, the final rounds of the Rosedale battle would be fought not only in the courts but also in the political arena and in the streets.

In a sense, the Rosedale controversy was a classic study of community activism. As the parties involved began to recognize that the pursuit of their goals through normal and accepted institutional channels of the government would not result in the desired outcome, they sought other means. This situation contributed to increased militancy on the part of white residents from Rosedale. Such extremism further provoked drastic measures from the other side.

TAKING TO THE STREETS

On the evening of Friday, January 31, a few hours after the appellate judge refused to overturn the chancellor's order, about two hundred Rosedale parents showed up at the closed annex in the PS 138 school building and began a sit-in. On the next day the group barricaded itself in the school cafeteria in order to prevent workers from removing furniture that was to be taken to the main IS 231 building in Springfield Gardens. On Sunday a protest rally involving more than four hundred parents was held at the site, as Mayor Koch, appearing on the WCBS-TV show *Newsmakers,* commented on the situation. Koch urged the protestors to leave the occupied building and obey the chancellor's order and the law. However, when questioned further, Koch admitted, "I don't happen to believe busing is helpful to the school system. . . . In fact, it segregates."[75] The statement led Rosedale residents to believe that perhaps they could find a sympathetic ear at City Hall.

On Monday morning Koch's office was barraged with requests from organizers of the Rosedale group that he become involved in the situation and render them assistance. The mayor noted that he understood their concerns and promised that he would ask his own counsel to "look and see if the facts would warrant taking an appeal, and if an appeal is possible, we will help."[76] That same afternoon the full membership of the five-person Appellate Court delivered its ruling. In a unanimous decision, it declared that "such matters of educational policy" are "inappropriate for resolution by the courts."[77] By dismissing the appeal of the Queens school district unanimously, the court rendered it legally impractical for the Rosedale group to pursue its case further through state judicial channels.

Koch's statements on the Rosedale dispute and his expression of willingness to involve himself stirred quite a commotion. Macchiarola was furious. He immediately got on the phone with top mayoral aids to register his displeasure. He did not want to see the mayor involved, especially on the side of the school board. A group of black ministers and political leaders, who had already begun to pressure Queens

Borough President Donald Manes, also reacted. They told Koch he had the facts of the case wrong, and warned him to stay out of it. When Koch was finally informed of the Appellate Court decision, he softened his position. On Tuesday he issued a statement declaring:

> I know the frustrations of the parents, but there has been a finding by a judge that there has been intentional discrimination, and whenever there has been intentional discrimination, the city has no recourse but to support the court order ending that act.[78]

While public officials from around the city were debating the issues surrounding the Rosedale controversy, education in District 29 was being severely disrupted. With the sit-in continuing at PS 138, the home of the closed annex, only 22 out of 715 pupils at the elementary school were in attendance. Only 66 out of the 326 transferred annex students showed up at the main IS 231 building, where they were supposed to begin classes on Monday. In a show of sympathy to the demonstration, parents from PS 195, the other predominantly white Rosedale elementary school, also kept their children home, bringing attendance down to 5 pupils from a total enrollment of 550.

On Thursday evening a group of about eight hundred Rosedale residents held another rally, this time to raise money to take their legal battle into the federal courts. The group cheered as Democratic party District Leader Charles Cippola informed them that Borough President Donald Manes had just met with several high-level officials in the Koch administration to make his position known. However, that afternoon the mayor had directed his corporation counsel, Allan Schwartz, to obtain a court order to oust the demonstrators from the occupied elementary school and annex. The mayor pledged, "I'm encouraging them [parents]: Take the kids back to school. We are going to do our damnedest to make it [I.S. 231] a safe school. We are going to do our best to make it one of the best schools."[79]

In the meantime, the chancellor had sent a telephone relay to Community School Board 29, admonishing it for failing "to take any action to remove the persons illegally congregating."[80] He demanded that the members of the board come to Livingston Street for a "conciliatory meeting." That meeting took place on Friday, February 6, at which point the sit-in had been going on for a full week. The meeting was attended by one black and three white members of the board. The chancellor was represented by Joseph Saccente, who had been serving as the trustee in IS 231. Saccente noted that the demonstrators had made their point. He asked the Rosedale representatives to urge the approximately forty remaining parents to leave the school without incident. He told them that the chancellor was prepared to cite the demonstrators for trespass. The school board members promised that they would make such an appeal, but expressed doubts that the parents would listen. Their doubts were well founded. On Friday evening the school building was still occupied.

At dawn on Saturday, two police vans pulled up in front of the doors of PS 138. Approximately seventy uniformed officers filed out. Police Chief Patrick Murphy, four gold stars beaming from his collar, politely asked the protestors to leave the school. Four refused and were arrested. The rest picked up their belongings and left quietly. A few hours later, Macchiarola held a press conference and announced that he had asked Mayor Koch "to put your police at my disposal." He further explained, "There's no room for compromise when someone is in charge of a school building and they ought not to be. We had to maintain a very important principle. We expect the children to return to school. . . ."[81] In the afternoon about two hundred demonstrators returned to the PS 138 school site and peacefully picketed outside the building. The group included the four who had been arrested earlier that morning.

The next week was marked by numerous rallies and demonstrations. At one Queens meeting, six hundred white Rosedale residents chanted, "Manes for mayor," as the borough president appeared to announce his support of the continuing school boycott. By that time Manes and Koch had already engaged in an angry verbal battle over the police action at the annex. In the midst of all the anger, Koch agreed to meet briefly with four of the boycott leaders, as 150 parents and children from Rosedale marched around City Hall. Koch again tried to persuade the group to send the children back to school, and promised to ask the chancellor to meet with the leaders. Macchiarola, however, stood firm. He refused to talk with the boycott leaders as long as there were duly elected representatives of the community sitting on the school board. It was becoming increasingly apparent that the school board itself was now losing control of the situation to a more militant element in the community. Community school board President Joseph Albergo had already begun to urge parents to send their children back to school, but boycott leaders, led by Linda Ovadias of the Rosedale Block Association, were developing a momentum of their own.

As the boycott went into the second week of the new semester, word of a "mystery caravan" began to circulate among its leaders. Saccente, fearful of another incident at a school site, issued orders barring anyone but students and staff from IS 231 and its three feeder schools (PS 38, PS 138, and PS 195). On the eve of Lincoln's Birthday, a procession of one hundred cars left Rosedale and headed toward Brooklyn for what was identified as a "secret destination." When the motorcade passed through the Midwood section of Brooklyn, it became clear that the secret destination was the private home of Schools Chancellor Frank Macchiarola. By the time it arrived, the chancellor's house was surrounded by police. That did not stop the demonstrators. As Macchiarola gathered inside with his wife and three small children, a group more than three hundred strong formed a circle around the house, shone flashlights through the windows, and chanted, "No annex, no school." The protest went on for two hours in the pouring rain. On the same evening, about eighty black residents from Laurelton held a two-hour vigil outside the home of Queens Borough President Donald Manes. They carried signs bearing the inscription "All Children Should Concern Manes, Not Just White Children."

Over the next several days there were more demonstrations at the Queens Borough Hall and at City Hall. State legislators from District 29 held meetings with State Education Commissioner Gordon Ambach. By February 15, only 105 of the 326 annex students had registered at the main school of IS 231. Much to the credit of principal Reginald Landeau, business at the school proceeded in an orderly fashion. Attendance was at 91 percent, several points above the city-wide average. Nevertheless, the boycott continued.

At the beginning of the third week of the semester, the boycott organizers met at the George A. McCrackan Democratic Association to crystallize plans for privately run "freedom schools" for children who had been kept home. On Tuesday, Macchiarola met with the full membership of Community School Board 29. All promised to cooperate to end the boycott. Saccente was instructed to hold a series of open nights at IS 231 so that parents could visit the school. The chancellor conceded that he would meet with the boycott leaders if the school board deemed it necessary. In Queens, Borough President Donald Manes began meeting with a contingent of black political leaders, who by midweek had persuaded him to take a more conciliatory stance on the Rosedale situation. On Wednesday evening, Manes addressed a group of 1,800 people at the Queens Democratic Committee, and urged parents to send their children back to school. Despite Manes's efforts, boycott leaders opened "freedom schools" at five Queens locations on the next day.

As the week ended, Rosedale residents petitioned State Education Commissioner Gordon Ambach to reconsider his decision supporting the chancellor's order to close the annex. Finding that "no new evidence" or "significant new arguments"[82] had been submitted by the petitioners, Ambach dismissed their application. Since the State Appellate Division Court had unanimously denied their prior appeal, the commissioner's decision left only two other legal avenues open to the Rosedale parents. On the one hand, they might challenge the factual findings of the Office for Civil Rights and the federal Administrative Court judge through an appeal to the Secretary of Education. On the other hand, they might challenge the order, on constitutional grounds, in the federal courts.

THE JUDGE DECIDES

On February 24, the Rosedale parents filed a suit in federal district court on behalf of eight annex students—five white, two black, and one Hispanic—requesting that the annex, which had now been closed for three weeks, be reopened. The parents, who initiated their action independently of the local school board, contended that they feared losing the high quality education that had been offered at the annex, and objected to their children being "bused" two miles to the "overcrowded" and "segregated" intermediate school in Springfield Gardens. Judge Edward Neaher granted a show cause order and set a hearing for the next week on the question of a preliminary injunction for reopening the annex, pending a full trial on the overall merits of the case.

On the next day, four buses carrying nearly two hundred supporters of the Rosedale school boycott appeared in Washington, D.C. As the delegation formed a picket line around the federal building on Independence Avenue which houses the Department of Education, Linda Ovadias and Sandra Petker met with several aides of Secretary Terrence Bell. Considering the critical position that the Reagan administration had already taken on the subjects of school desegregation and forced busing, it was reasonable for the group from Queens to expect a sympathetic hearing in the secretary's office. However, Bell's chief of staff, Elam Hertzler, explained to its leaders that the matter was now in federal court and that the secretary therefore had no jurisdiction over it.

The Washington meeting highlighted a basic flaw in the legal and political strategies of the Rosedale parents. If they had appealed the factual findings of the Office for Civil Rights and the administrative court judge, the Secretary of Education would have been able to overturn the case. However, by accepting these factual findings, the parents admitted that intentional or de jure segregation existed. Given the past precedent set by the federal judiciary on this issue, it was highly unlikely that the court would overrule the previous decision.

While all parties to the case awaited the day of Judge Neaher's trial, Joseph Saccente of the chancellor's office began to hold meetings with the boycott leaders. Saccente urged the parents to send their children back to school and offered to set up an advisory committee to help the local district apply for $1.5 million in federal funds under the provisions of the Emergency School Aid Act. Saccente also instructed IS 231 principal Reginald Landeau to arrange an open-house conference for the parents of students from the annex. In the meantime, a number of editorials critical of the behavior of the Rosedale residents began to appear in the local media demanding a return to normalcy in the Queens schools.

In response to claims by Rosedale parents that IS 231 was a racially segregated (primarily black) school, a *New York Times* editorial advised the boycotters, "The way to start desegregating IS 231 is for Rosedale's white children to attend it."[83]

An editorial aired for two evenings on WABC–TV demanded that the original federal order, "should be carried out in the fullest" and that "there shouldn't be any concessions that will keep the students in the annex."[84]

Another editorial, appearing in *Newsday,* a leading daily paper in Queens, aptly observed, "The struggle over Intermediate School 231's annex in Rosedale has reached a stage where a lot of people seem to have forgotten what schools are for."[85]

By the time formal testimony at the trial began on March 4, both the NAACP and the New York Civil Liberties Union had received permission from Judge Neaher to participate as codefendants. Attorneys for the community school board argued that busing students from the Rosedale annex to the Springfield Gardens school would exacerbate the problem of white flight in the district. George Shebitz, the major architect of the chancellor's legal defense, pointed out that busing was not an issue at IS 231, since there was no cross-district registration and most children had access to the school by means of public transportation. At the end of the day's long trial, Judge Neaher reserved his decision on issuing a preliminary injunction against the annex closing. However, from the nature of both the testimony and the questioning that day, the fundamental weakness of the case presented by the Rosedale plaintiff's had become clear.

With negotiations between the chancellor's office and the Rosedale parents continuing, some signs of hope for an end to the school boycott began to emerge as the ordeal advanced into its fifth week. On March 2 a meeting took place at Livingston Street. It was attended by Joseph Saccente, representing the chancellor; Joseph Albergo, president of Community School Board 29; Claudette Webb, a black member of the local board; and Linda Ovadias, the organizer of the boycott. In return for her promise to encourage parents to send their children back to school, Saccente gave Ovadias a seven-item list of assurances designed to enhance the educational environment at IS 231 and make the Springfield Gardens school more attractive to former annex children. His list included the following points:

1. The principal of IS 231, after consulting with the PA (Parents' Association) would have the authority to employ the number and kinds of personnel necessary to insure a proper school environment. Such personnel would include school aides, school security guards, and a school safety task force.
2. The trustee (Saccente), principal, and PA officers would meet with a representative group of former annex parents to develop ways to involve these parents in various school activities.
3. There would be no cases of ethnic isolation in any classes.
4. The principal and trustee would report to parents on a monthly basis concerning the status of the school.
5. The trustee would request that the Police Department assign a patrolman to IS 231 for one hour at dismissal time every day.
6. Two-year SP (Special Progress) students who return to school by March 9 would be accelerated if they met the requirements for acceleration.
7. There would be an after-school remedial reading program two days per week for former annex students and an equal number of main-building students.[86]

Speaking on behalf of the chancellor, Saccente also agreed that Macchiarola would review for approval any rezoning and/or open enrollment plans submitted by the local school board. He stressed, however, that any such plan would need both black and white support in order to contribute to a final solution of the situation in the district.

On Sunday, March 8, Ovadias met with approximately five hundred parents at the Rosedale Jewish Center and encouraged them to return their children to school. Shortly thereafter, Saccente met with another group of approximately fifty parents at the Sons of Italy Hall and assured them that IS 231 would receive increased security as long as the situation there remained tense. On Monday students began to return to the three schools affected by the boycott. It was reported that 608 of the 716 students at PS 138, and 435 of the 523 students at PS 195 showed up for class. Only 96 of the 306 former annex students appeared at IS 231 on that day. However, by the middle of the next week approximately two-thirds of this total had enrolled at Springfield Gardens.

Judge Neaher issued his Memorandum and Order on March 17. As expected, he denied the application for a preliminary injunction against the annex closing, stating that OCR's and the administrative law judge's findings "bar any conclusion that plaintiffs have shown probable success on the merits."[87] Citing the *Swann* case, Judge Neaher advised the plaintiffs from Rosedale:

> In the face of this constitutional obligation to desegregate, the phenomenon sometimes termed "white flight" is not a countervailing consideration; nor can the concept of "neighborhood school assignment" be accepted where it in fact masks a pattern of discrimination.[88]

MOVING TOWARD A RESOLUTION

The United States District Court decision marked the end of a long legal battle over desegregation in Rosedale. However, it did not put to rest the political and racial infighting that had come to characterize the community. As the local school board went about the task of preparing a new zoning plan for review by the Chancellor, it continued to exhibit the kind of polarization that had given birth to the original conflict four years earlier. Within a few days after the Neaher decision, the school board voted 5–4 along racial lines to distribute a new zoning proposal among parents in the district. The plan, drafted principally by board member Dolores Grant, would convert PS 195 in Rosedale into a predominantly white intermediate school. It was designed to assure that no students from Rosedale would go to IS 231, and only a limited number of minority children would be admitted to the new school. Needless to say, the black community reacted to the plan with outrage. At the March 19 meeting of the school board, Barbara Weisenfeld, a black member of the IS 231 parents' association, rose to her feet and scolded the white majority in a manner expressing the feelings of the minority community, declaring, "I think you ought to be ashamed of yourselves to stand up here and salute the flag and say . . . and liberty and justice for all."[89] Weisenfeld's statement was followed by a mutual exchange of accusations of racism.

A week later, the school board conducted formal hearings concerning the zoning proposal. Approximately 1,200 spectators packed into a school auditorium built to hold 720 people as 40 speakers, mostly black, filed up to the podium to attack the plan. The school board had previously agreed to submit a formal proposal for the chancellor's approval by April 16. From the reaction of the black community, it was evident that the plan proposed by the five-person white majority was not a feasible one. When the school board met on April 9 to take a formal vote, the white majority split, as Fran Pomerance and Leo Rosen chose to abstain, and the four black members voted down the motion. Dolores Grant, surprised by the action of her white colleagues, stormed out of the meeting, yelling at Pomerance. Linda Ovadias, who was one of more than seven hundred community residents observing the proceedings, followed Grant. When questioned on her vote, Pomerance said that she wanted to see the motion tabled. Rosen more explicitly admitted that he abstained "because I thought it was time to get the chancellor involved."[90] Albergo adjourned the meeting immediately after the vote was taken.

Within twelve hours, all nine members of the community school board were in the chancellor's office for another attempt at compromise. Macchiarola complimented the group for not passing a zoning plan that would have aroused further hostility in the community. He promised to work with the board to design a plan that would be acceptable to all segments of the district. Over the next two weeks, Dolores Grant and Claudette Webb joined a cooperative effort with community school board President Joseph Albergo and community Superintendent Florence Friedlander to develop a new freedom-of-choice plan for the district. When the school board met in a closed session on May 7 to take a formal vote, it rejected the proposal, three voting for it, three against it, and three abstaining.

Fearful of a new stalemate, the chancellor began to pressure the school board to support a plan that would encourage black parents in IS 231 feeder schools to send their children to IS 59, also located in Springfield Gardens. Doing so would both alleviate the overcrowding in IS 231 and decrease the proportion of black students, thereby allowing a better racial balance. When Macchiarola sensed that the response to his recommendation was less than enthusiastic, he instructed community Superintendent Florence Friedlander to meet with parents from PS 156 in Laurelton and PS 37 in Springfield Gardens, in order to drum up support. At that point, James Meyerson of the NAACP accused the chancellor of having made a deal with the boycott leaders that would reduce minority enrollments at IS 231. Members of the Federation of Laurelton Block Associations wrote the chancellor a letter, accusing him of circumventing the decision of the courts and harassing black parents. Macchiarola denied having made any deal with the white community leaders. He explained that the federal court order required action to increase the proportion of white students enrolled at IS 231. He intended to move ahead with his idea.

On May 20 Community School Board 29 voted across racial lines to approve a new zoning plan that had been supported by the chancellor. The six-person majority included Albergo, Rosen, Pomerance, and three black members. Dolores Grant and Ann Spatola voted against the resolution. Shirley Rose abstained. According to the adopted scheme, the feeder patterns from elementary to intermediate schools in the district would be retained. However, parents would also be offered an option to send their children to IS 59. In order to make IS 59 more attractive, Macchiarola promised that he would free up money for special programs to enhance the educational offerings of the school.

By the time school opened in September, Community School Board 29, with the help of the central Office of Funded Programs at Livingston Street, had managed to obtain $300,000 in federal ESAA funds for educational enrichment programs at IS 231. The central Board of Education allocated an additional $200,000 for similar programs at IS 59. White enrollment at IS 231 climbed to 11 percent of the 1,163-member student body, a significant improvement from the 1 percent figure that had been recorded a year earlier. The enrollment data also showed that approximately 50 of the 326 annex students had chosen to leave the public school system and attend private institutions. On October 6, 1981, Chancellor Macchiarola sent a letter to Community School Board 29, informing its members that the supersession that had begun in February was finally lifted, and that it was once again responsible for administering IS 231.

With the termination of the supersession, business proceeded rather smoothly and uneventfully at IS 231. The school that had been the center of a major controversy for four years virtually disappeared from the local media. Then, on March 29, 1982, a story appeared in the *New York Daily News*. It included an account of a week-long open house being held at IS 231 for parents of prospective graduates from PS 138 and PS 195, the two elementary feeder schools in Rosedale. The story described how several supporters of the Rosedale boycott appeared before the parents and encouraged them to send their children to IS 231 because "the school has made an educational turnabout."[91] The story highlighted the "no-nonsense administration" of principal Reginald Landeau and the successful use of federal ESAA funds for the development of programs designed to reduce racial anxieties among students and parents.

Among those addressing the visiting parents was community school board President Joseph Albergo, who was quoted as saying,

> Everything about the school has changed. . . . When the school had problems, we told you about them. . . . Now we have to tell you that things are running smoothly. . . . It would be foolish for this community to abandon this school now that it's in good shape.[92]

Albergo was joined by board member Fran Pomerance, who told her neighbors, "I've made my decision about September. I'm sending my child to 231. But don't take my word for it. Go and see for yourself."[93]

SUMMARY COMMENTS

Desegregation remains one of the most volatile issues in American education. Our more than twenty-five-year history with it has shown it to be a mixed experience, and public policy, as interpreted by the courts, has not been consistent. However, notwithstanding all the debate and the occasional confusion, we know more about the subject than we sometimes pretend. What is often perceived as ambiguity of facts about the effects of desegregation is likely to be an ambivalence of values. Whatever we think about the merits or disadvantages of the governmental mandate, the law is also fairly straightforward on the question.

While the Supreme Court has modified the "all deliberate speed" formula of the *Brown II* decision, and has been more sympathetic to voluntary remedies as opposed to forced busing, the letter of the law today is quite clear with regard to the constitutional prohibition of intentional or de jure segregation by local school districts. While the question of intent has not been addressed by the Supreme Court with regard to Title VI of the Civil Rights Act of 1964, there appears to be a trend in the lower federal courts to uphold the intent standard.[94] Our experience with desegregation provides us with certain undeniable facts concerning the outcome of various approaches. We know that forced racial mixing is more likely to motivate white flight than voluntary or freedom-of-choice programs. We know that carefully planned desegregation efforts will be less disruptive to the educational process than poorly managed interventions. We know that children attending school in an integrated setting are more likely to develop positive and healthy attitudes toward peers of another race than children in segregated institutions.

We also know that there is no conclusive evidence that minority children at integrated schools are more likely to develop positive attitudes about themselves than minority children who are racially isolated. Likewise there is no conclusive evidence that racial mixing has a favorable impact on the achievement levels of minority children. It might be said that what we sometimes claim to know about the impact of racial mixing on self-perception and achievement is actually what we know about the characteristics of effective schools. To put it plainly, positive affective and learning outcomes are more directly related to quality instruction and competent school organization than they are to the racial composition of a student body.

In recent years desegregation has not been a major item on either the educational or political agenda in New York City, at least partially because racial politics within the schools has been more closely associated with decentralization, community power, and the neighborhood-school concepts, which are not usually linked to the ideas of integration or racial mixing. Of course, as this chapter shows, there have been exceptions to this rather tranquil and uneventful history with regard to desegregation. The NAACP in New York has served as an articulate advocate of desegregation and has been in the forefront of judicial battles on its behalf.

In cases where desegregation has become a relevant issue in New York, the major community and governmental actors have exhibited behavior similar to the norm established in other urban centers. Busing and forced racial mixing have been seen as major contributing factors to white flight. School officials and parents have been more receptive to voluntary approaches to desegregation, as demonstrated at Mark Twain Junior High School in Brooklyn and the Louis Armstrong School (IS 227) in Queens. The situation in Andrew Jackson High School serves as a striking example of the problems inherent in attempting to integrate an urban school system that is becoming increasingly homogeneous in its student population. While the condition at Jackson is admittedly an extreme case of de facto segregation, it points to an emerging pattern that will become more typical of inner-city school systems like New York, where white enrollment is on the decline.

Philosophically, the administration of Chancellor Frank Macchiarola was committed to maintaining a moderate approach to desegregation. Macchiarola had been a strong supporter of decentralization. His administration placed a greater emphasis on raising the achievement levels of minority children. However, the chancellor also showed that in the face of a judicial mandate couched within the law, he would do whatever was necessary to remedy a violation. He first demonstrated this with regard to the collection of ethnic data in District 26, and it was most visibly dramatized in the Rosedale situation.

The chronicle of the chancellor's attempt to implement a federal desegregation order in Rosedale develops several of the fundamental themes presented in earlier chapters. It even goes beyond the kinds of cross-pressures imposed on the chancellor's office that were documented in the previous cases. The Rosedale case involves multiple jurisdictions. While the federal Office for Civil Rights ordered that IS 231 be desegregated, other governmental institutions, most notably the state courts, had the authority to limit the chancellor's power to enforce the mandate. Before the OCR desegregation order could be carried out, legal and political victories had to be won in the federal Administrative Court, the State Supreme Court, the State Appellate Court, the State Education Department, the Board of Education, and the United States District Court.

Of course, the major political battles of the Rosedale situation were fought at the community level, within the school board. District 29 in Queens represented a far too common phenomenon at the local level, in which a school board is controlled by and accountable to the white constituent electorate of a community at the expense of a predominantly minority service clientele. In this case, the school board also showed the ability to enlist the support of the borough president, a host of local political figures, and almost that of the mayor.

Political scientists of the pluralist school have often suggested that the involvement of such a wide variety of public officials in school politics gives a superintendent (in this case the chancellor) the advantage of picking and choosing among these actors to form coalitions on an issue-by-issue basis. This case begins to highlight the precarious nature of such coalition building on an ad hoc basis, for the adversaries one encounters during a given policy debate may carry over their animosity to the next issue. For example, by taking on Borough President Donald Manes in the Rosedale issue, the chancellor was risking the loss of significant support on the Executive Budget. Community School Boards 26 and 29, which became involved in heated battles with the chancellor on racial issues, emerged as two of the most outspoken opponents of his Promotional Policy.

There are two ways to view the prospects of constituency building for the urban superintendent. The optimist might say that the involvement of many actors in educational policy making gives a superintendent many potential allies from whom to choose. The pessimist might claim that the arrangement provides the superintendent with numerous potential adversaries, all of whom are capable of obstructing his or her objectives. The negative aspects of such an arrangement might also be exacerbated in a situation where the superintendent is determined to implement a significant amount of change. The more change-oriented a superintendent is, the more likely his or her actions are to arouse resistance.

This chapter illustrates the number and variety of actors that can get involved in determining the outcome of an educational policy debate in New York. It provides us with one scenario showing the number of places where something can go wrong when a chancellor attempts to alter a practice entrenched in the politics and tradition of the existing system. However, notwithstanding the multiplicity of actors in this case, the most formidable adversary any chancellor in New York could face was absent. That adversary is Albert Shanker, president of the United Federation of Teachers.

NOTES

1. *Brown* v. *Board of Education,* 347 U.S. 483 (1954). See Richard Kluger, *Simple Justice* (New York: Knopf, 1976); J. Harvie Wilkinson, *From Brown to Bakke* (New York: Oxford University Press, 1979).

2. *Brown* v. *Board of Education,* 349 U.S. 294 (1955).

3. E. E. Schattschneider, *The Semi-Sovereign People* (New York: Holt, Rinehart and Winston, 1960), pp. 39–40.

4. See John Bolner and Robert Shanley, *Busing: The Political and Judicial Process* (New York: Praeger, 1974); Gary Orfield, *Must We Bus?* (Washington: The Brookings Institution, 1978).

5. David Kirp, "School Desegregation and the Limits of Legalism," *Public Interest* 47 (Spring 1972), 102.

6. *Green* v. *School Board of Kent County,* 391 U.S. 430 (1968).

7. *Alexander* v. *Holmes County Board of Education,* 396 U.S. 19 (1969).

8. *Swann* v. *Charlotte–Mechlenburg Board of Education,* 402 U.S. 189 (1973).

9. Ibid.

10. *Keyes* v. *School District No. 1,* 413 U.S. 189 (1973).

11. *Milliken* v. *Bradley I,* 418 U.S. 717 (1974). See Eleanor P. Wolf, *Trial and Error: The Detroit School Desegregation Case* (Detroit, Mich.: Wayne State University Press, 1981).

12. *Milliken* v. *Bradley II,* 433 U.S. 267 (1977).

13. See Robert A. Dentler and Marvin B. Scott, *Schools on Trial* (Cambridge, Mass.: Abt Books, 1981); Emmett H. Buell, *School Desegregation and Defended Neighborhoods* (Lexington, Mass.: Lexington Books, 1981).

14. On the Delaware case, see Jeffrey A. Raffel, *The Politics of School Desegregation* (Philadelphia: Temple University Press, 1980).

15. James Coleman *et al., Equality of Educational Opportunity* (Washington: Office of Education, National Center for Educational Statistics, 1966).

16. James Coleman *et al.,* "Trends in School Segregation, 1968–1973," An Urban Institute Paper, U.I. 722-03-01, August 1975.

17. Reynolds Farley, "School Integration and White Flight" (Ann Arbor: Population Studies Center, University of Michigan, 1975); Christine H. Rossell, "School Desegregation and White Flight," *Political Science Quarterly* 90 (1975–1976); Thomas F. Pettigrew and Robert L. Green, "School Desegregation in Large Cities," *Harvard Educational Review* 46 (February 1976).

18. Reynolds Farley and Clarence Wurdock, "Can Government Policies

Integrate Public Schools?" (Ann Arbor: Population Studies Center, University of Michigan, 1977); Christine H. Rossell, "Assessing the Unintended Impacts of Public Policy: School Desegregation and Resegregation" (Boston: Boston University, Report Prepared for NIE, 1978).

19. David J. Armor, "White Flight and the Future of Desegregation," in Walter G. Stephan and Joe R. Feagin, eds., *School Desegregation: Past, Present, Future* (New York: Plenum, 1980).

20. John B. McConahay, "The Effects of School Desegregation upon Students' Racial Attitudes and Behavior," *Law and Contemporary Problems* 42 (Summer 1978).

21. Edgar Epps, "The Impact of School Desegregation on the Self-Evaluation and Achievement Orientation of Minority Children," *Law and Contemporary Problems* 42 (Summer 1978).

22. Lawrence C. Felice and Ronald I. Richardson, "The Effect of Busing and School Desegregation on Minority Student Dropout Rates," *Journal of Educational Research* 70 (May–June 1977).

23. Nancy H. St. John, *School Desegregation: Outcomes for Children* (New York: Wiley Interscience, 1975). See also Nancy St. John, "The Effects of School Desegregation on Children," in Adam Yarmolinsky *et al.*, eds., *Race and Schooling in the City* (Cambridge: Harvard University Press, 1981).

24. Meyer Weinberg, "The Relationship Between School Desegregation and Academic Achievement," *Law and Contemporary Problems* 39 (1975); Minority Students: A Research Appraisal (Washington: National Institute of Education, Summer 1978).

25. Robert L. Crain and Rita E. Mahard, "Desegregation and Black Achievement: A Review of the Research," *Law and Contemporary Problems* 42 (Summer 1978).

26. Willis D. Hawley, "Increasing the Effectiveness of School Desegregation: Lessons from the Research," in Yarmolinsky *et al.*, *Race and Schooling.*

27. See Willis D. Hawley, ed., *Effective School Desegregation: Equity, Quality and Feasibility* (Beverly Hills, Calif.: Sage Publications, 1981).

28. Willis D. Hawley, "Equity and Quality in Education: Characteristics of Effective Desegregated Schools," in Hawley, ed., *Effective School Desegregation,* pp. 299–302.

29. For an analysis of these events, see David Rogers, *110 Livingston Street* (New York: Random House, 1968), Chapters 1, 4, 5, 6; Diane Ravitch, *The Great School Wars* (New York: Basic Books, 1974), Chapters 23–27.

30. *Hart* v. *Community School Board No. 21,* 383 F. Supp. 769 (E.D.N.Y. 1974).

31. *In the Matter of Parent Association of Andrew Jackson High School,* 15 Educ. Dept. Rep. 235, 239 (1975).

32. *In the Matter of Parent Association of Andrew Jackson High School,* 15 Educ. Dept. Rep. 483, 485 (1976).

33. *Parent Association of Andrew Jackson High School* v. *Ambach,* 451 F. Supp. 1077 (E.D.N.Y. 1978).

34. *New York Daily News,* July 10, 1978.

35. *Newsday,* September 29, 1978.

36. Claudette Webb, private interview, July 23, 1981.

37. *Newsday,* September 29, 1978.

38. Claudette Webb, private interview, July 23, 1981.

39. Linda Ovadias, private interview, July 19, 1981.

40. Ibid.

41. Joseph Albergo, private interview, July 19, 1981.

42. Claudette Webb, private interview, July 23, 1981.

43. William R. Valentine, correspondence to Frank J. Macchiarola and Members of Community School Board 29, September 13, 1968.

44. *The New York Times,* May 17, 1979.

45. *Newsday,* January 15, 1979.

46. *Parents Association of Andrew Jackson High School* v. *Ambach,* U.S. Court of Appeals for the Second Circuit, Docket Nos. 78-7274, 78-7307, 78-7308, April 17, 1979.

47. *Newsday,* March 6, 1979.

48. Ibid.

49. Ibid.

50. *Marcus Brody-James* v. *Macchiarola,* 77 C 876 (E.D.N.Y. 1979).

51. The other school boards included District 11 in the Bronx; Districts 18, 20 and 21 in Brooklyn; and Districts 24 and 25 in Queens.

52. David Tatel, letter to Frank J. Macchiarola, "Summary of Efforts by the Office for Civil Rights to Obtain Voluntary Compliance with Title VI of the Civil Rights Act of 1964 by Community School Board 29 and the New York City Board of Education," August 24, 1979.

53. Ibid.

54. Ibid.

55. *New York Daily News,* August 31, 1979.

56. *Newsday,* June 18, 1980.

57. Donald Manes, correspondence to Frank J. Macchiarola, June 27, 1980.

58. *In the Matter of the Appeals of Community School Board No. 29 from Orders of the Chancellor, Dated May 30, 1980 and June 16, 1980,* July 23, 1980.

59. *In the Matter of Board of Education of Community School District No. 29* v. *Board of Education of the City of New York,* Index No. 1167/80, September 9, 1980.

60. Ibid.

61. *In the Matter of the Application of the Board of Education Community School Board No. 29* v. *Board of Education of the City of New York,* Judgment, Index No. 1167/80, September 9, 1980.

62. Joseph Albergo, correspondence to Frank J. Macchiarola, October 24, 1980.

63. *In the Matter of Community School Board No. 29, and the Board of*

Education of the City of New York, and the Department of Education of the State of New York, Docket No. 79-VI-7, December 8, 1980.

64. Frank J. Macchiarola, correspondence to Joseph Albergo, December 22, 1980.

65. Donald R. Manes, correspondence to Frank J. Macchiarola, December 24, 1980.

66. Frank J. Macchiarola, correspondence to Donald R. Manes, December 30, 1980.

67. Ibid.

68. *In the Matter of the Board of Education of Community School District No. 29, Queens County v. The Board of Education of the City School District of the City of New York,* Index No. 18212/80, January 22, 1981.

69. *Newsday,* January 24, 1981.

70. Ibid.

71. Ibid.

72. *In the Matter of the Board of Education of Community School District No. 29, No. 10467, January 30, 1981.*

73. *In the Matter of Board of Education of Community School District No. 29 Against The Board of Education of the City School District of New York,* Supreme Court, Appellate Division, Second Judicial Department, January 30, 1981.

74. George Shebitz, private interview, April 30, 1981.

75. *Newsday,* February 2, 1981.

76. *New York Daily News,* February 4, 1981.

77. *In the Matter of Board of Education of Community School District No. 29, Queens County v. Board of Education of City School District of the City of New York,* 976 E, No. 38, February 2, 1981.

78. *New York Daily News,* February 4, 1981.

79. *New York Daily News,* February 6, 1981.

80. *Newsday,* February 6, 1981.

81. *The New York Times,* February 8, 1981.

82. *In the Matter of the Application of Community School District No. 29, Queens County,* No. 10475, February 20, 1981.

83. *The New York Times,* February 28, 1981.

84. Cliff Love, WABC-TV Editorial, No. 17-1981, February 25, 26, 1981.

85. *Newsday,* March 4, 1981.

86. Joseph Saccente, letter of agreement, March 2, 1981.

87. *Cheryl Rivera et al. v. Board of Education of the City School District of the City of New York,* Memorandum and Order, 81 C 558 U.S. District Court, (E.D.N.Y., 1981).

88. Ibid.

89. *Newsday,* March 20, 1981.

90. *Newsday,* April 10, 1981.

91. *New York Daily News,* March 29, 1982.

92. Ibid.

93. Ibid.

94. See Rosemary C. Salomone, "Title VI and the Intent-Impact Debate," *Hastings Constitutional Law Quarterly* 10 (1982).

6

TAKING ON THE UNION

This chapter is a study of a nondecision. For nearly a decade during the mid-1950s and early 1960s, political scientists and sociologists devoted a good deal of time, energy, and thought to the study of community power through the analysis of important policy decisions. As the conventional wisdom held, individuals who participated in important policy decisions, dominated the decision process, and benefited from the results were the true holders of power in a community.[1]

In 1962 Peter Bachrach and Morton Baratz wrote a seminal essay for the *American Political Science Review* that challenged many of the methods and conclusions put forth by their contemporary colleagues.[2] The two argued that those who truly hold power in a community are the ones who have the ability to prevent issues that are contrary to their interests from becoming part of the political or policy agenda. These "nondecisions" are the questions that are never asked, the issues that are never raised, the policies that are never seriously challenged. The groups and individuals who are the gatekeepers of the decision process can shelter themselves from adverse policy determinations and exert a substantial amount of control over local politics. With regard to educational politics in New York City, the United Federation of Teachers (UFT) is such a group. Its leader, Albert Shanker, is such an individual. The nondecision of concern here is an amendment to section 3020-a of the State Education Law, which governs the procedures for disciplining and removing incompetent or undesirable teaching personnel.

The United Federation of Teachers did not become the official collective bargaining agent for schoolteachers in New York until 1961, after years of organizing within the ranks of the work force. At that time the UFT was also granted the dues checkoff—a procedure of dues payment through an automatic paycheck deduction. Thereby New York City became one of the first school systems to recognize the legitimate right of teachers to be represented in collective bargaining. Before that time, the salary scale for teachers ranged from $4,800 to $9,100 in a fourteen-step pay schedule. Class sizes often exceeded fifty students to one teacher. If a teacher wanted health or hospital benefits, the city would pay for only one-half of an insurance plan. In fact, there was a dark period in the history of the profession when a woman could be dismissed from duty for becoming married or pregnant. Employee grievance procedures simply did not exist, and abuses of personnel were intolerably common.

As of 1980, the beginning salary for a classroom teacher in New York was $11,821—not a particularly high rate of pay for a professional, but considerably better than that which existed before unionization. A senior teacher with thirty credits beyond the M.A. degree could earn up to $25,822.[3] Maximum class sizes are contractually set at between thirty-two and thirty-four students, depending upon the level of instruction.[4] New York City schoolteachers now enjoy one of the most generous health and welfare plans in the nation. The UFT has also been an aggressive and effective force in protecting the rights and working conditions of its members.

Organizing efforts among school personnel in the city date back as far as 1916, when the Teachers Union of New York became Local 5 of the American Federation of Teachers. In 1924 the Joint Committee on Teachers Organizations was formed. This group represented sixty-five separate teacher associations. With the cooperation of other teacher groups and labor unions throughout the state, it began to concentrate a large measure of its professional and political energies on the state capitol in Albany. The focus of its activity reflected the decision-making structure in education at the time, since most of the laws and regulations governing the profession emerged from either the state legislature or the Board of Regents. The Republican-dominated legislature in Albany had always been willing to assume a large portion of responsibility in educational policy making, rather than leave discretion at the local level, where it would be controlled by city Democrats. The legacy of that legislatively dominated decision structure is still felt today. New York is the only state where the Board of Regents is appointed by the legislature. Many statutes defining the working conditions and tenure of teachers are still written in the state capitol.

In 1935 the Teachers Guild was organized in New York City by an insurgent group within the local union, in protest against the alleged left-wing ties of the union's leadership. In 1941 the Teachers Union of New York City was expelled from the American Federation of Teachers, and the Teachers Guild became the new AFT affiliate. From 1935 to 1959 the Teachers Guild unsuccessfully led a series of efforts to unite the various teacher associations in the city into a single union. By 1960 its successor organization, the UFT, could claim a membership of only 2,000 individuals from a total citywide teaching staff of 38,000. Today the UFT in New York City boasts a membership of more than 77,000. Its ranks include teachers, guidance counselors, paraprofessionals, and school secretaries. The union negotiates eight separate contracts with the Board of Education for its diverse membership. Since 1974 its president, Albert Shanker, has also served as president of the American Federation of Teachers, which enjoys a membership of more than 570,000. It is rivaled on a national scale only by the National Education Association, which claims a membership of nearly 1.75 million. The two national teachers' associations have been known to disagree frequently on professional, policy, and political issues.

Albert Shanker has also served as vice president of the New York State United Teachers (NYSUT), an AFT statewide affiliate, which exercises a significant amount of political clout in Albany. Shanker describes its potential quite bluntly in these terms:

> We are the most powerful political force in the state. NYSUT has over 200,000 members. A recent poll shows that 85 per cent of our members vote for the candidate endorsed by the union leadership. We put [Senator] Moynihan over the hump. We were decisive in Ted Kennedy's winning of the state presidential primary.[5]

Since the granting of collective bargaining rights to the UFT more than twenty years ago, Albert Shanker and his union have also emerged as a major political force at the local level in New York City. Through its VOTE/COPE fund, the UFT maintains a large political war chest, financed by an annual contribution from each of its members, which enables it to openly and actively support candidates in local and state elections. Borough presidents, elected in the city on a county-wide basis, are often beholden to the UFT for their success at the polls. The accumulation of such political debts is not inconsequential, since it is the borough presidents who appoint five of the seven members of the central Board of Education. Some observers of the municipal labor scene would also argue that by professionalizing the collective bargaining process with high-powered negotiators, the UFT has gained a significant advantage over the career educators who negotiate on behalf of the city.[6]

Combining the expertise of a professional association and the forcefulness of a large labor organization, the UFT has carved out a central role for itself in making educational policy in the city. The union instituted its first major curriculum proposal in the city school system in 1964, with the development of the More Effective Schools Program. Based upon a deficit model theory of compensatory education, the program was designed to produce teaching and learning conditions that would allow for high quality education in depressed areas.[7]

The concept displayed many similarities to the School Improvement Project implemented by Ron Edmonds more than ten years later.

In 1967 the UFT became involved in its first major wage dispute with the city, which led to a three-week strike that virtually closed all the city schools. The job action was only one of the several serious strikes the then mayor of New York, John Lindsay, faced with an increasingly militant work force. However, it was the first of its kind carried out by the teachers. In the end, the UFT was granted a generous wage increase, with a $10 million contractual commitment for the development of new instructional programs. From that point on, the union has been intimately involved with every major curriculum innovation that has emerged from Livingston Street.

The year after its first major strike, the UFT became involved in perhaps the most memorable and explosive political controversy in its history. In 1968 the union decided to side with the professional bureaucracy at Livingston Street, opposing Mayor Lindsay's plan for decentralization and community control. The battle grew particularly ugly when a group of predominantly white teachers from the UFT engaged in a near-violent debate with a black school board in the Ocean Hill–Brownsville experimental school district. What began as an argument over job security and neighborhood government ended with charges of racism and anti-Semitism. The school decentralization debate made a major contribution to the racial polarization that plagued the city in 1968. It drove a wedge of disagreement and mistrust between the UFT and the black and Puerto Rican community. Shanker's behavior during the episode was seen as uncharacteristic by many who knew him as a charter member of the Congress of Racial Equality and as a man who had marched alongside Martin Luther King to protest racial segregation in the South.

After a state law to implement decentralization citywide was enacted in 1969, the UFT became an active participant in neighborhood school board elections, using its large membership and bountiful war chest to support its own candidates and tickets. By 1973, 54 percent of those who were elected to local school boards in the city were UFT candidates.[9] The union spent an estimated $127,000 on election-related activity during that year.[10] Ten years later, the union continues to elect a majority of the local school board members in New York, thus demonstrating a basic fact of political life: that institutional restructuring does not significantly alter the power structure in a community; it merely reshapes the arenas in which the truly powerful exercise their influence.

Albert Shanker began to rebuild bridges to the black and Puerto Rican community in 1969, when he extended union membership and protection to 9,000 paraprofessionals (paras) who had come to work for the school system in 1966 and 1967. Most of these paras were black or Puerto Rican women. Many were former welfare recipients. A good number were high school dropouts. They were hired with the support of federal Title I funds to assist classroom teachers in providing small-group remedial instruction to educationally disadvantaged students. All paras are required to complete high school in order to retain their jobs. When they voted in 1969 to accept Shanker's invitation to join the UFT, the union negotiated a contract that carried a sizable package of new benefits. Among these was part-time education at the City University. The purpose was to erect a career ladder so that many of these workers would eventually join the teaching force. The union has billed the program as "an affirmative action program that works." The program has been well received in the minority community. In 1970 Shanker won favor with the minority community once again when he vigorously supported the paras' pleas for wage increases. After Shanker threatened to initiate a citywide teachers' strike if the demands of the paras were not met, the union persuaded the Board of Education to agree to wage increases of more than 100 percent.[11]

Shanker's aggressive support of the paras has certainly worked to change the relationship between him and the minority community. Throughout the next several years, the association between the UFT and the city's black and Puerto Rican population moved with slow but steady progress. However, there were occasional setbacks. Shanker, for example, has gone on record quite unambiguously as a staunch opponent of hiring quotas. This position has not sat very well with many leaders of the minority community in the city, not to mention white civil rights advocates. The quota issue became particularly sensitive with the onset of the city financial crisis in 1975 and the attendant layoff of thousands of teachers. Since blacks and Puerto Ricans are often the last hired among city employees, they have been disproportionately the first fired, undercutting efforts designed to increase minority representation and employment. However, Shanker has stuck to his position on the quota issue and remains an adamant defender of the seniority rule.

The fiscal crisis that struck New York in 1975 significantly changed the stakes of local politics. The union, once preoccupied with influencing how the education budget is spent, has become increasingly concerned with the amount of money made available for education. Thus, the UFT became a major force behind the Stavisky–Goodman bill, a state law passed in 1976, designed to protect the school system's share of the budget provided by local taxes., As the clientele of the school system has grown increasingly poor and the dollars available for education have diminished, the UFT has emerged as one of the major advocates of public education in the city, and, in an indirect way, of the minority community, which is the major user of public education. Given the demography of the city and the independent stake that the union has in the stability of the school system, this common interest was perhaps predictable. Less predictable, however, was the way the budget situation and the political affairs of the city shaped the relationship between union President Albert Shanker and new Schools Chancellor Frank Macchiarola.

SHANKER AND MACCHIAROLA: AN EMERGING RELATIONSHIP

The relationship between Albert Shanker and Frank Macchiarola took some time to forge. Shanker had been the most outspoken opponent of Macchiarola's appointment. In fact, he nearly stopped it. However, in some way, the two men would have to learn to live with each other. Macchiarola the chancellor was not Macchiarola the nominee. The union would need his support on some issues. Likewise, Macchiarola would sometimes need Shanker. There were not many strong supporters of public education left in New York, and both men understood that.

Nevertheless, there was much room for debate. Macchiarola represented management. Shanker represented labor. Macchiarola stood for change. Shanker had a certain investment in the status quo. Macchiarola had been the nominee of Edward Koch. Shanker was a militant foe of the mayor. Macchiarola was bent on achieving more staff accountability. That pledge did not sit well with labor leaders. Shanker often accused the chancellor of grandstanding. He saw the administration's attack on correspondence courses for salary credits and the chancellor's occasional denials of tenure as meaningless gestures in public relations. The UFT president was angered by the chancellor's six-month report, which he believed was unreasonably harsh on teachers. Yet Macchiarola had a message to communicate. Things would not be the same under his administration.

There were significant signs of hope. A week before his formal swearing in, Macchiarola had proved that he was capable of being an effective advocate of the school system budget. His revision of the original Anker proposal resulted in smaller class sizes in the early grades and a transitional class program for holdovers. Shanker liked those policies. The administration's School Improvement Program was very much in line with the UFT's More Effective Schools effort. So there appeared to be encouraging agreement on certain instructional and philosophical issues.

The shaping of a relationship between Albert Shanker and Frank Macchiarola was handled with political mastery from both sides. It advanced on a case-by-case basis, according to the issues. There was little room for ego. Both men were too politically astute for that. They fought tooth and nail on some matters, but they recognized the need to work together on others. It was a relationship built on mutual respect, even though it was occasionally burdened by unkind words.

Early evidence of a reconciliation appeared in the form of a relatively quick agreement on the UFT contract, which Shanker and Macchiarola had negotiated by mid-July, just weeks after the new chancellor took office. It was the first labor settlement to be reached in the city that year. A tentative agreement had actually been worked out by June 24. The rank and file of the union ratified the contract by a margin of 10–1. However, as soon as the package was put together by school officials and union representatives, Mayor Koch's budget advisers began to register their disapproval. There was no problem with the 4 percent wage increase. The major bone of contention was the UFT's paraprofessionals, who had now become a cause célèbre of Albert Shanker.

When paraprofessionals began working for the school system in 1966, most did so on a part-time basis. They accordingly received no pension rights or paid vacation time. When the school year ended in June, they would be laid off. They would collect unemployment benefits for two months and then be rehired in September. By 1978, most of the 10,000 paras employed by the Board of Education were working on a full-time basis. However, they were still treated as part-timers, without the benefits granted to other city employees. Shanker argued that these individuals should be given both pension rights and paid vacations. Macchiarola agreed. A provision to that effect was therefore placed in the original 1978 contract settlement. When Koch's budget advisers voiced disagreement with that idea, the mayor ordered Macchiarola and Shanker to renegotiate the contract. Both the chancellor and the UFT president refused to return to the bargaining table.

The original UFT settlement sat on the mayor's desk for six months while school officials and union negotiators argued with city budget analysts over the costs and affordability of the labor package. Finally, in early January 1979, Koch announced that he would not approve the "annualization" of the paras. His budget figures showed that costs of annualization would exceed the limits of the Coalition Economic Agreement arrived at by city officials and municipal labor leaders during the previous summer. He also expressed concern that the annualization of the paras in the school system would set a precedent for similar workers in other City agencies.

Since Macchiarola refused to renegotiate the union agreement, Koch decided to sit down with Shanker himself. The UFT president pledged that he would disprove the budget figures prepared for Koch by the deputy mayor and the Office of Management and Budget. When Macchiarola was informed that a meeting had been set for January 8, he remarked that he was rooting for Shanker.[12] When the meeting finally took place, the mayor rejected the para settlement for a second time. At that point, the matter was put up for arbitration.

The dispute over the paras received considerable attention in the local media. Beyond the significance of its economic implications, it was treated by some as much more than a collective bargaining issue. A notable editorial appeared in *The Amsterdam News,* which began:

> We agree with the United Federation of Teachers just about as often as we agree with Mayor Koch, which is to say rarely. But in the current dispute between the UFT and the Mayor, the union is right—and the Mayor is in the wrong.[13]

The editorial concluded with the argument:

> Paras represent a group of minority people, many formerly on welfare, pulling themselves up by hard work into the working and middle classes. They should be encouraged. It's good for them, good for our schools and our kids . . . and most of all, good for the future health of our city.[14]

The final outcome of the arbitration on the annualization of paras was a compromise. The arbitrators found that there was more money available for the paras than city budget officials had claimed, but less than the union had negotiated for. Thus it was decided that the paras would be granted some of the vacation pay requested for them; however, they were not admitted to the city pension system. While the final gains they achieved were modest in comparison to what they had hoped for, the unfolding of the issue was an important step forward in their efforts to receive full recognition as a genuine segment of the city work force. Shanker had been fighting for annualization for eight years. He had never gotten a more sympathetic hearing from an administration at Livingston Street. The events surrounding the para dispute also demonstrated that UFT President Albert Shanker and Schools Chancellor Frank Macchiarola could work together as allies, despite the "bad blood" between them previously.

Of course the labor contract told only part of the story. A comprehensive analysis of the chancellor's first year in office would show that alliances between Livingston Street and the UFT were at best tenuous. They could not survive exposure to the full assortment of policy issues. At the same time that Shanker and Macchiarola joined forces on behalf of school system employees, they were functioning as adversaries on another policy question. The second issue also involved school employees. It again included the mayor. But this time Macchiarola and Koch were in full agreement.

Mayoral candidate Edward Koch had promised that, if elected, he would institute a residency requirement for municipal workers in New York City. He reasoned that such a law would stabilize city neighborhoods, assure more positive attitudes among city employees, and allow individuals on the municipal payroll to contribute to the economic vitality of the city. Board of Education nominee Frank Macchiarola supported the Koch proposal wholeheartedly. In fact, as president of Community School Board 22 in Brooklyn, Macchiarola had established a city residency requirement for all employees of the local school district. As chancellor, Macchiarola stipulated city residency as a prerequisite for all individuals on his personal staff and for all executive personnel at Livingston Street who served at his pleasure.

In 1978 approximately 16 percent of all municipal workers in New York lived outside the city. The proportion was larger among higher-paid workers. Approximately 40 percent of the city policemen and 50 percent of the city firemen did not reside within the five boroughs. Among teachers, out-of-city residence was approximately 20 percent. There was nothing unique or unusual about the Koch proposal to pass a residency law for New York. Neighboring Nassau County had imposed such a requirement for all of its municipal employees except police personnel and community college faculty. Similar requirements exist in Chicago, Newark, Washington, Houston, Detroit, Los Angeles, and Philadelphia.

New York City had passed its own residency law for municipal workers in 1937. The purpose of the so-called Lyons law, named after its sponsor, was to alleviate the scarcity of jobs available for city residents during the depression. Enforcement of the law eventually began to waver over the years, and in 1962 Mayor Robert Wagner repealed it in order to broaden the pool of qualified applicants for city service. Nothwithstanding the historical and legal precedents, Koch's proposal for a new law was unanimously opposed by the city's labor unions. Union members worried that employees living in suburban areas near the city would be forced to relocate. They objected to the idea that workers residing in the city could not move if they so desired. Some argued that the requirement would limit the city's ability to recruit the most qualified personnel.

Despite the protestations of labor leaders, Koch's proposal was passed by the City Council on July 11, 1978, by a vote of 32–3. According to the new law, all individuals placed on the city payroll after November 1, 1978, would be required to live in the city. Employees living within the city before that date would be forbidden to move out. In reality, the final bill submitted to the Council by the mayor was a compromise. The initial bill would have been retroactive, forcing all individuals living outside the city before its passage to move back.

The enactment of the new law immediately gave rise to several significant legal issues. Attorneys for the United Federation of Teachers and the Professional Staff Congress, which represents faculty at the City University, questioned whether the law passed by the City Council could govern personnel at the Boards of Education and Higher Education, since both were independent agencies under state law. In September the two groups initiated a lawsuit in the state courts, which contested the jurisdiction of the law. Shortly thereafter, the Patrolmen's Benevolent Association (PBA) and the Uniformed Firefighters' Association (UFA) launched their own legal challenge to the law, questioning the authority of the City Council to institute a residency requirement for municipal workers without prior enabling legislation by the state legislature.

While the merits of the mayor's law were being debated in the state courts, Chancellor Macchiarola was taking his own action to assure that the intent of the statute would be preserved within the school system. He proposed that the Board of Education establish a separate residency requirement. The idea was vehemently opposed by Albert Shanker, who personally appeared at the Board of Education hearings held on the subject in mid-October to announce his disapproval. The ensuing public debate represented the first major confrontation between the union president and the chancellor since the latter's appointment. Shanker was joined in his battle by Ted Elsberg of the Council of Supervisors and Administrators (CSA). After much discussion at Livingston Street, Macchiarola's proposed regulation was approved by the Board of Education by a vote of 4–3.

The Board of Education resolution, adopted on October 18, included three major provisions:

1. As of November 1, all teachers and school personnel living within the city would be prohibited from moving out.

2. As of November 1, no person living outside the city could be hired, unless he or she assumed city residency within five months after hiring.
3. Any nonresident promoted to the position of elementary school principal or above after November 1, or who received a salary of $29,500 or more under the Board of Education executive pay plan, must establish city residency.

The inclusion of the third provision of the Board resolution, setting strict standards of eligibility for promotion or appointment to executive-level positions, amounted to making the residency standard for school personnel more rigorous than the one set by the City Council for municipal employees. On the day after the Board voted on the chancellor's proposal, Supreme Court Judge Sidney Asch handed down a ruling concerning the legality of the City Council statute as it was challenged by the police and fire unions. While Judge Asch did not question the authority of the City Council to make such a law, he found fault with the manner in which the law was written and enacted. Thus, in a twenty-three page decision, he declared, ". . . it may be legally possible to require plaintiffs to live in New York City, but not without the authorization of the New York State legislature and better legislative draftsmanship."[15]

Mayor Koch responded to the Asch decision with a pledge to appeal the ruling to a higher court. However, shortly thereafter, the Civil Service Committee of the City Council passed a resolution to delay implementation of the residency law until its validity was upheld in court. In the meantime, the Board of Education resolution was still standing. Therefore, if matters proceeded according to plan, school system employees would be the only workers in the city bound by a residency requirement on November 1. Albert Shanker and CSA President Ted Elsberg became more adamant about taking preventive action against the Board's measure. Given the similarity between the Council statute and the Board of Education regulation, the Asch decision certainly strengthened their legal hand.

On November 2 attorneys from the CSA obtained a one-week stay from State Supreme Court Judge Burton Roberts, which delayed the implementation of the Board's residency requirement. This stay was later extended by Justice Edward Greenfield until November 17, at which time school attorneys were to respond to a joint suit initiated by the CSA and the UFT. As it became apparent that a long legal battle was in the offing, the Board of Education voted on its own to postpone enforcement of the residency requirement until the legal issues were finally settled.

In July 1979 the Appellate Division of the State Supreme court upheld the decision handed down by Justice Asch nine months earlier.[16] In April 1980 a unanimous state Court of Appeals once again affirmed the lower court rulings, declaring the local statute enacted in July 1978 illegal.[17] At that point Mayor Koch promised that he would begin a new effort to have a law passed by the state legislature. Given the power that the municipal unions wield in Albany, most astute observers agreed that the prospects for such action were not very good. The handwriting was on the wall. The residency issue was dead in New York. At Livingston Street, the Board of Education, which had approved the chancellor's original resolution by only one vote when the controversy began, never took action for its implementation.

Frank Macchiarola thus lost his first major battle with Al Shanker. Nevertheless, the differences between the two leaders never became personal. There was still much room for cooperation. As the events described in a previous chapter demonstrate, the UFT was a major supporter of the chancellor's Promotional Policy. Indeed it can be said that the union played a key role in the policy design. As we have also seen, Macchiarola and Shanker would usually join forces at least once each year to defend their common ground on the education budget. In 1978 the UFT and the new school administration became involved in a large cooperative venture to operate the New York City Teachers' Center. Begun in 1977 with support from a federal grant, the Teachers' Center represents one of the most ambitious voluntary efforts at in-service training ever to have been launched in public education. It is one to which the union has pointed with special pride. When the Reagan administration eliminated funding for the project in 1981, the chancellor took measures to continue its existence through the use of public funds. The move signified a far-reaching exchange of goodwill between the UFT and Livingston Street.

But problems would continue to exist. The relationship between the union and the administration was enormously complex. There had to be differences inherent in the varying roles each played within the structure of the school system. There was the basic labor-management dichotomy, which occasionally appeared. So there were more battles. Among the most intense were those related to section 3020-a of the State Education Law.

3020-a: AN ACT OF THE LEGISLATURE

Section 3020-a of the State Education Law was enacted in 1971. Its purpose was to establish hearing procedures for tenured teachers charged with unsatisfactory performance or behavior. Under 3020-a, a tenured teacher found guilty of charges could be either disciplined or permanently removed. However, no such action could be taken until certain specified due process guarantees were observed. According to 3020-a, a teacher brought up on charges by a local school board was entitled to a hearing by a three-person panel. The membership of the panel would be chosen from a list of individuals kept by the state Commissioner of Education. One member would be selected by the school board making the charges, another member would be selected by the accused, and the third would be selected by an agreement of both sides. A fourth person, who would serve as a hearing officer, was to be appointed by the Commissioner of Education, and would be an employee of the State Education Department.

The findings and decisions of a 3020-a panel would not be binding. The local school board making the charges would maintain the right to either reverse the findings or alter any penalties recommended by the panel. This reserved power of the school board was consistent with standard practices in municipal law, which grants final discretion on employee discipline to the employing agency. Section 3020-a does guarantee that an individual brought up on charges is entitled to receive pay until a final disposition of the case is made. This holds true even if the accused person has been suspended from duty pending a hearing. This guarantee is not usually provided in municipal law, which allows employer agencies to suspend a charged individual without pay.

In 1976 the New York State United Teachers (NYSUT) launched a legislative campaign to alter the provisions of section 3020-a. A particular target of NYSUT's efforts was the legal stipulation that an accusing school board shall exercise final discretion regarding the outcome of disciplinary hearings. Understandably, union officials believed that the local school board had a built-in bias against a teacher brought up on charges. Data released by NYSUT showed that school boards ignored nearly 70 percent of the advisory rulings arrived at by hearing panels.[18] While the current law would allow a teacher to appeal a school board decision to the state commissioner or the courts, this action was not included in the hearing process. Taking an appeal through the courts involved high legal fees, and union officials thought the state commissioner had a tendency to side with local school boards in such appeals. On the latter point, the union also took exception to the requirement that panel members must be chosen from a list provided by the Commissioner of Education. NYSUT also objected to the procedure whereby the commissioner would appoint a state employee to serve as a hearing officer.

The major opponent of NYSUT's attempt to amend the State Education Law was the New York State School Boards Association.

The association, which represents school boards from around the entire state, saw the union's legislative campaign as an assault upon the sovereignty of the local school district. The school boards launched a valiant lobbying campaign in Albany, but they proved to be no match for the power of the statewide union or Albert Shanker, who had become directly involved in the legislative maneuvering. The Senate passed the union-backed bill by a margin of 47 to 7. While matters moved a bit more slowly in the Assembly, the bill, under the sponsorship of Education Committee Chairman Leonard Stavisky, was eventually approved in the lower house. Governor Hugh Carey signed the bill into law in 1977, claiming, "I'm about to sign the NYSUT bill, because I'm for fair play."[19]

Chapter 82 of section 3020-a amended the State Education Law in several significant ways. To begin with, under the new provisions a local school board no longer had authority to overrule a finding or recommendation of a hearing panel. Therefore the school board lost its ability to exercise unilateral discretion. Union leaders hailed this amendment as the most far-reaching innovation of the law. As Dan Sanders, vice president of NYSUT, put it,

> The important aspect of the bill is that it makes binding the decisions of the hearing panels. . . . The hearing panel decisions are at present advisory under the Education Law. As the years have passed since the law's adoption, these panel decisions have been more and more ignored by school boards.[20]

A second change in the new law concerned the selection of hearing panel members. As before, the hearing panel would be composed of three members—one selected by each of the parties, a third by mutual consent. However, rather than being selected from a list of eligibles prepared by the state commissioner, the third member would be chosen from a list of professional arbitrators provided by the American Arbitration Association. This third member would chair the panel and also serve as the hearing officer. The hearing officer previously appointed by the state commissioner would be eliminated. Thus, while appeals could still be taken to the state commissioner (or the courts), the role of the commissioner in the hearing process was greatly reduced.

The American Arbitration Association (AAA) is a private, nonprofit organization that maintains panels of arbitrators in various fields of expertise. Its dues-paying membership includes unions, private companies, trade associations, and arbitration panel members. Labor panels put together by the AAA consist of private individuals who are found acceptable by both employers and unions. An arbitrator's acceptability must be demonstrated by letters of endorsement solicited from each side of a dispute. Once an arbitrator is deemed acceptable, his or her qualifications are further reviewed by the AAA. For a fee, the AAA will send parties to a labor dispute or grievance a list of names of qualified arbitrators. In cases involving 3020-a procedures, the costs of AAA-endorsed arbitrators are paid by the state Department of Education at a fixed per diem rate.

The mandated use of AAA-referred arbitrators under state law has been a source of much criticism by school board attorneys. They contend that because of the regular business association between the union and AAA arbitrators, it is difficult for the latter to be objective. Some critics would go so far as to suggest a conflict of interest. One attorney from the New York City school system explains:

> The problem is that the UFT does business with the AAA on a regular basis. It has the power to blacklist AAA people if it wants.
>
> The union has a computerized record of each arbitrator. It will not use those who have been tough. The arbitrators are sensitive to that. It is their livelihood.[21]

There also appeared to be administrative problems in 3020-a, which made the hearing process both cumbersome and costly. A study prepared by the State School Boards Association for the 1977–1978 school year showed that the average length of time between a formal statement of charges and a panel decision was 36.5 weeks.[22] The same study showed that the average cost per hearing—including legal fees, staff salaries, and the salary paid to suspended teachers—was approximately $27,000.

Once the 1977 amendment to section 3020-a was written into law, the School Boards Association, its major opponent, turned its strategic efforts toward litigation. In the latter part of 1977 attorneys from the association, acting on behalf of the Belmont school district in Allegheny County, brought a suit into state court challenging the constitutionality of the law. They argued that 3020-a unconstitutionally delegates state legislative powers to a private party and violates procedural due process. The matter was transferred from the state supreme court in Allegheny County to the Appellate Division Court on March 28, 1978. On November 10, 1978, the Appellate Division unanimously upheld the constitutionality of 3020-a.

On March 24, 1980, Harvey Mandelkern, deputy counsel for the State School Boards Association, brought the case to the state Court of Appeals, New York's highest court. In addition to the constitutional issues that had been raised previously, the association attorney raised a question as to whether 3020-a represented a "private law." Specifically, he argued that the existing statute granted an exclusive privilege and franchise to the AAA. One month later the court handed down a unanimous decision, again upholding the constitutionality of 3020-a. It found:

> . . . we perceive no constitutional bar to the legislative designation of the association as a nominating body, who can reasonably be expected to present the commissioner, on an objective basis, the names of individuals exceptionally qualified by prior service.[23]

There would be other litigation surrounding the provisions of 3020-a, initiated from both sides of the dispute. The union, for example, challenged the authority of the state commissioner to raise the penalties a review panel had imposed on a teacher. The state Appellate Division upheld the commissioner's authority on that point.[24] On another occasion the Court of Appeals upheld the right of a suspended teacher to collect his salary pending the determination of a 3020-a hearing. The court ruled that while suspension without pay would not necessarily be an infringement of constitutional rights, section 3020-a, "as now worded," does not authorize it.[25]

From a litigator's point of view, it was growing increasingly apparent that section 3020-a, in the form it had evolved during 1977, was invulnerable. There was only one way to challenge the provisions of the present State Education Law. That was to take the issue back to the legislature and rewrite the law. However, given the prior experience in that arena and the power of the union, the likelihood of a legislative victory was not very high. Other than the State School Boards Association, there did not seem to be any broad constituency to support legislative reform. Nobody else wanted to touch the issue.

A statement by CSA President Ted Elsberg, who represents school principals, who are often most victimized and frustrated by the cumbersome 3020-a procedures, is very telling. He remarks:

> There are problems in dealing with certain incompetent teachers. However, there is a labor issue involved as well concerning the rights of employees. I know that the law is sometimes frustrating to supervisors, but we are not advocating any change in it. The union has won it, and we have learned to deal with it.[26]

Philip Kaplan, president of the New York City Community School Boards Association, articulates a similarly revealing attitude of resignation about 3020-a. He states:

3020-a regulations won't be changed because the union wants it the way it is. Shanker has flexed his muscle. He is too strong. We have to learn to live with it. Principals and supervisors must be taught to deal with it.[27]

After the 1977 victory by the union, 3020-a fell into the category of nondecisions that would not be seriously considered for some time. Its revision was never again formally discussed in a legislative committee. Even the state commissioner of education, whose original authority was compromised by the 1977 amendment, shied away from the issue. The New York City Board of Education, understandably reluctant to take on Albert Shanker and his union, also refused to give it purposeful attention. The issue appeared to be dead.

TEACHING AS A PROFESSION: A RELEVANT QUESTION

In November 1979 state Commissioner of Education Gordon Ambach submitted to the Board of Regents a detailed set of recommendations on "Teaching as a Profession and Teacher Competence." These recommendations were designed to provide a "comprehensive system for recognition of teaching as a profession, the licensing of teachers and supervisors, and the enhancement of teacher competence."[28] Before that time, teachers in New York received state certification essentially by completing a prescribed course of study at the college and university level.[29] Central to the proposals in the new Ambach plan was the creation of a statewide competency test for the licensing of teachers. The proposal included a prescribed one-year internship for new personnel, and called for an allocation of state funds to support in-service training for teachers, supervisors, and administrators. If adopted, the commissioner's plan would also require each local school district to develop a comprehensive system for the periodic review of all teachers, supervisors, and administrators.

The proposal presented to the Board of Regents was conceived as an appropriate complement to the developing statewide standards of competency testing for students. A major goal behind the comprehensive plan was to provide statutory recognition for teaching as a profession and to move it closer to the self-regulation that currently exists within other professions—e.g., medicine or law. The Ambach plan proposed the establishment of two state boards, a board of teachers and a board of administrators. These boards, under the aegis of the Regents and the State Education Department, would operate to some extent like other professional boards in the state. State responsibility for the disciplining of teachers, currently provided through the Regents' rules and commissioner's regulations, would be established by statute and transferred to the two state boards.

By the end of 1979, the Regents of New York had been considering and discussing ideas for raising teacher competency for more than five years. In 1977 a state task force recommended the creation of a seventeen-member board, to be composed of seven teachers, three school administrators, two university faculty members, two university administrators, one guidance counselor or psychologist, and two representatives of the public. Initially, this recommendation received the support of both the United Federation of Teachers and the New York State United Teachers. However, over the next two years effective lobbying from other members of the educational community resulted in the plan to create two boards, which was opposed by the teachers' unions. Part of their disapproval arose from the fact that the two boards would have no formal decision-making power but would serve only in an advisory role to the Regents. Labor leaders also objected to a provision that would enable the state to revoke a teacher's license for participation in a strike violating the state Taylor Law.

The Regents were to discuss the commissioner's proposal in early December. After that, public hearings on the matter were scheduled for the next several months at various locations around the state. While the Regents' approval was expected, the passage of enabling legislation through the state legislature seemed much more problematic because of the criticism the proposal had attracted from various influential parts of the education community.

When the commissioner's plan arrived at Livingston Street in early January 1980, it was not received with particular favor by the chancellor. Macchiarola was not receptive to the idea of self-regulation in the teaching profession. To him, control of a state board by the teachers meant control by the union. There needed to be, in his opinion, a stronger consumer role. The analogy between teaching and the other professions did not sit well with the chancellor, since education is a compulsory service. Moreover, nobody was impressed with either the quality or results of self-regulation in the other professions.

While the chancellor was reviewing the commissioner's proposal, a letter was placed on his desk that had been written by the principal of PS 238 in Brooklyn. The woman expressed a basic sympathy with the chancellor's efforts to improve the quality of public education in the city. But she expressed deep concern about the quality of some of the teaching staff and the problems inherent in trying to remove individuals found to be incompetent: She explained:

Everyone in the field knows that no teacher, however poor a teacher, or destructive of children he is, or unwilling to maintain professional and educational standards, is ever discharged for incompetence. . . . The process of discharge is stacked against the school system, and has no relation to the "due process" it claims to protect.[30]

The principal then conveyed a sense of frustration that grew out of the administrative procedures required by section 3020-a. It was a feeling quite common among her colleagues in schools around the city. She wrote: "Principals have to neglect many of their other supervisory duties in order to 'build a case,' only to lose the case because of a legal or administrative technicality."[31]

There was a logical connection between the issues. A comprehensive assessment of the teaching profession, its development, and its monitoring could not be advanced without a reconsideration of the questions generated by the 3020-a debate. Perhaps political realities forbade a head-on confrontation with the 1977 revisions of the State Education Law, but teacher discipline could be discussed in the context of the commissioner's proposal. Section 3020-a could be brought back into the policy arena, even if it entered through a side door. The law had been problematic for Macchiarola. It was anathema to the accountability theme that was central to the philosophy of his administration. Now was the time for a new discussion.

On Sunday, February 3, Macchiarola appeared as a guest on the CBS–TV program *Newsmakers.* As expected, he was asked to comment on the pending proposal for "Teaching as a Profession." The chancellor proclaimed that while he thought the issue of having qualified teachers in the classroom important, he was not sure that a testing program was the best way to address it. He argued instead for an effective system of tenure review. Calling the existing procedures "hidebound," he complained, "The present system does not have adequate means for us to eliminate a teacher."[32]

Macchiarola began to incorporate the theme of accountability into the speeches he was making to various audiences around the city. The chancellor made public data showing that the school system was paying $2 million per year to maintain teachers on the payroll while they were being processed on charges through state-mandated 3020-a hearings. He noted a situation where a city teacher who had been convicted of drug smuggling was kept on the school payroll for thirteen months, awaiting the outcome of a 3020-a hearing. On another occasion Macchiarola publicly applauded State Commissioner Gordon Ambach for raising the penalties imposed by a 3020-a panel on a teacher who had been found guilty of showing a pornographic film to his high school class.

Macchiarola was effectively getting out his message. On February 5 the *New York Daily News* ran an editorial entitled "Paying Rotten Teachers," blaming Albert Shanker for ramming through Albany a law that made it difficult to fire incompetent teachers.[33] On March 17 and 18, WCBS–Radio aired a similar editorial on "Disciplining Teachers," condemning the bureaucratic obstacles created by the 1977 provisions of the State Education Law.[34] On April 4, as the Regents were about to hold hearings on the state commissioner's pending proposal, *The New York Times* ran an editorial tying the plan to the question of teacher discipline. Entitled, "What Makes a Teacher a Pro?" the editorial noted that the current state laws "virtually prevent" the removal of undesirable teachers.[35] After bringing attention to the strong hold that the teachers' lobby has on the state legislature, the editorial pointed out that the plan would "hold teachers to no stricter account than before."

Macchiarola appeared before the Regents' hearings on April 9, fully intent on forcing the state board to consider the commissioner's proposal within the context of the 3020-a issue. The chancellor opened his statement by praising the new plan for "focusing our critical judgment on where we are and where we should go." But in the same breath he noted, "I must quickly add that the draft is lacking in some significant respects."[36] In customary fashion, he sounded the call for "greater accountability among our professionals" and offered regrets that "the proposals will make accountability more difficult than ever." The chancellor admitted particular disappointment that "the proposals do not address the problems created by section 3020-a of the State Education Law." He then presented to the Regents data prepared by the Office of Legal Services at Livingston Street, to illustrate the problems he hoped to highlight.

From July 1, 1978, until March 31, 1980, the administration had initiated disciplinary charges against fifty-seven tenured teachers or administrators. As of March 31, 1980, only twenty-two of these cases had reached disposition. Of these twenty-two cases, four resulted in retirements or resignations, one person died, two cases were dropped by the Board of Education, two cases resulted in dismissals following an inquest, two were settled, and eleven cases resulted in a decision by the three-member panel. Only two of the latter eleven resulted in the termination of the employee. Macchiarola followed his statistical presentation with some specific examples of the abuses possible under the existing law.[37]

The chancellor closed his statement by insisting that school systems must "have the ability to fairly and expeditiously separate incompetent staff." He urged the Regents to "focus on the real issues." He then announced that he would present to his own Board of Education "proposed amendments to improve 3020-a."[38]

Within three weeks of his testimony, Macchiarola submitted a report to the Board of Education. The report explained in great detail the provisions of section 3020-a of the Education Law and the impact that the 1977 amendments had on the disciplinary process. It explained the philosophical connection between student accountability (which the Board had so vigorously supported in the form of competency testing) and staff accountability (which was relevant to the proposals tentatively approved by the Regents). The report cited the cost data from the 1979 State School Boards Association study and the New York City data that had been presented in testimony to the Regents. Additional data showed that the average salary paid out for each of the twenty-two employees involved in the completed 3020-a hearings between July 1978 and March 1980 was $20,000.[39] This figure did not include the cost of replacement personnel, which amounted to an average of $14,000 per case. As of March 31, charges were pending against thirty-six teachers and administrators, twenty-nine of whom were suspended with pay. According to the chancellor's report, these suspensions were costing the school system over $500,000, or an average of $5,000 per day.[40] Recent data had shown that approximately six months elapsed between a finding of probable cause against a teacher and the time of the first 3020-a hearing. Therefore the school system generally incurred salary costs of $12,500 per employee charged, before the hearing actually began.[41]

Attached to the report was a copy of the letter the chancellor had received from the principal of PS 238. Also attached was a set of legislative proposals the chancellor was urging the Board of Education to endorse and submit at the next legislative session in Albany. These included the following major revisions of the State Education Law:

- Require that hearing panels in 3020-a proceedings related to New York City personnel be composed of New York City residents, or permit the use of a single arbitrator rather than a three-person panel.
- Reserve the Board of Education's right to suspend pedagogues without pay for thirty days or longer, if procedural delays initiated in bad faith are the fault of the employee.
- Provide a time frame within which a disciplinary proceeding must occur.

- Permit the filing of charges against a tenured teacher during the entire calendar year and not just the school year, as the current law stipulates.

The chancellor's recommendations to the Board also outlined a list of regulatory procedures that the state commissioner should be urged to adopt in order to expedite the 3020-a hearing process. Since these involved only administrative reforms under the jurisdiction of the Commissioner of Education, they would not require legislative action.

As might be expected, Macchiarola's legislative agenda was not received with great enthusiasm by the Board members. To begin with, there were real differences of opinion on the issues. Some civil libertarians in the city had argued that time and cost were not suitable criteria by which to judge a due process procedure. In fact, one might argue that expeditiousness is inconsistent with the principle of due process. There were also political considerations on the minds of the Board members. All knew that getting a legislative package of this sort through Albany meant doing battle with the union. Several members frankly did not want to participate in such a political encounter. The chances for success were not very high. While the chancellor had managed to bring some attention to the issue in recent months, the kind of public mandate needed to overcome the power of the union lobby did not exist.

A PUBLIC DEBATE: PORNOGRAPHY AND PENSIONS

On December 13, 1979, Ronald Drew, a New York City public school teacher, was arrested in his home and charged with promoting the obscene sexual performance of children. Confiscated as criminal evidence were more than nine hundred slides and twenty black-and-white photographs depicting young boys in various explicit sexual poses. In all, approximately fifteen to twenty different children and three adults had been used as models. At the time of his arrest Drew was assigned to Junior High School 218 in Flushing, Queens, which is located in Community School District 25. The forty-five-year-old teacher had been in the public school system for nineteen years.

Immediately after an account of the arrest appeared in the local press, Community Superintendent Joan Kenny removed the teacher from his assignment. She then called the chancellor to request his help in arranging for a nonteaching assignment outside the district. Under ordinary circumstances, a teacher who had been arrested would have been transferred to a nonteaching assignment in the district office until the case was fully adjudicated. However, since the district office in

Community School District 25 is located in a school building, Kenny wanted the accused teacher out of the district. Macchiarola responded by having Drew placed in a central administrative office in Long Island City.

Drew was indicted by a grand jury on April 7, 1980. Immediately thereafter, while awaiting trial, he began processing papers requesting retirement from the school system at the end of the school year. When Macchiarola first learned of Drew's arrest, his attorneys advised the local school board not to take any administrative action against the accused teacher until the criminal case was resolved. This was normal procedure. The chancellor, however, had never been pleased with the idea of paying someone a salary while he sat idly in a central office. When Macchiarola was informed that Drew was seeking retirement, he instructed the local school board to begin disciplinary proceedings. Under established administrative procedures, a teacher is required to give thirty days' notice before action can be taken on an application for retirement. The chancellor, annoyed with the prospect of Drew's collecting a Board of Education pension, wanted to see the teacher fired within thirty days, hoping to deny his eligibility for retirement.

Community School Board 25 agreed to consider the evidence against Drew, but it did not appoint a 3020-a panel, nor did it move with the kind of speed that Macchiarola had wanted. On Friday, April 18, the chancellor had a letter hand-delivered to the school board, which carried the following message:

> As you know, during the last week, we have been in regular communication over the question of whether your board and superintendent will meet your responsibilities to take action concerning a teacher employed by your district, who has recently been indicted for grave offenses involving children.
> . . . it has come to my attention that your board and community superintendent have been, and are, unwilling to take the immediate action necessary to pursue this matter.[42]

The chancellor's letter ended with an ultimatum to the board to take "all necessary actions to discharge your responsibilities in this matter" by noon on Saturday, April 19. Community School Board President Arlene Fleishman responded that it would be impossible to meet the twenty-four-hour deadline because Friday evening, in the Jewish religion, "is the Sabbath and we have board members who observe the Sabbath."[43]

On Saturday afternoon, with no action taken on the matter, Macchiarola informed Fleishman that he was suspending the school board.

He appointed three of his own staff members to serve as trustees in the district, thereby replacing the school board. He appointed Joseph Saccente, his special assistant, to serve as district administrator. On Sunday, Saccente presented charges to the trustees, and the trustees voted to suspend Drew pending the outcome of a disciplinary hearing. Under the provisions of 3020-a, Drew would be suspended with pay until a final determination on disciplining him was made by a three-person panel chaired by an AAA arbitrator.

On Monday morning Macchiarola obtained a stay from State Supreme Court Justice William Thompson, delaying the Teachers' Retirement Board from processing Drew's application. The Teachers' Retirement Board, a seven-person body, must review all applications for retirement and pension benefits in order to determine an individual's eligibility. The board is composed of the president of the Board of Education, two appointees of the mayor, one appointee of the city comptroller, and three teachers. Fearful that the proceedings of the 3020-a panel would exceed thirty days, the chancellor hoped to delay action by the board, pending an outcome of the disciplinary charges. In the meantime, Macchiarola had prevailed on Queens District Attorney John Santucci to turn over criminal evidence to the disciplinary panel so that it might be used in the case against Drew. The chancellor also asked State Education Commissioner Gordon Ambach to facilitate and expedite the convening of the panel.

On Monday afternoon Macchiarola modified his suspension of Community School Board 25, restoring all jurisdiction to the local board except that concerning disciplinary hearings. The latter powers were to remain with the trustees. This modification of the suspension order did not appease the members of the local school board. Within a few days the board announced that it was employing an attorney to investigate the possibility that the chancellor had violated the State Decentralization Law. Behind the announcement was an angry threat of a lawsuit against the chancellor.

The issues were becoming very clouded. What had begun as an attempt by the school administration to call into question procedures governing the disciplining of teachers was now being expanded into a dialogue over the chancellor's powers under decentralization. Added to this would be a new debate over pension rights—which was very different from the due process issue that surrounded the 3020-a procedures. Under federal law, pensions in the private sector have always been considered as deferred earnings to which the employee is entitled. Albert Shanker argued, on firm legal ground, that the same holds true with regard to public sector pensions. He also promised to challenge Macchiarola's actions in court.

The public discourse among the chancellor, the local school board, and the union gave rise to considerable editorial comment in the local press. But there was little agreement about the merits of the various issues, their relationship, or the order of their significance.

On April 22 a *New York Daily News* editorial entitled "Loophole in the Law" commented:

> Board [25] members feel that they have been treated high-handedly. But that hardly seems the issue. The major question is how a teacher accused of such a crime . . . could be allowed to stay on the payroll and file for a pension. If officials are so slow to act in such flagrant cases, maybe we need a law mandating suspension on indictment.[44]

A *Newsday* editorial, published on the next day, disagreed.

> Members of Community School Board 25 are right to raise legal questions about their brief suspension last weekend instead of just letting the matter drop. . . . Suspension, even for such a short time, is an extreme measure. . . . There are certainly more than enough questions about the suspension to warrant a thorough legal review.[45]

A *New York Post* editorial, appearing on a third day, offered more militant support to the chancellor. After citing Board of Education data on the costs and time involved in the 3020-a hearing process, it argued:

> Chancellor Macchiarola is actively seeking ways to change legislation by which a three-man panel of lawyers insures that offending teachers are retained for several years—long after their conviction in criminal courts—until a disciplinary hearing can make a further judgment. Macchiarola should be given the fullest support in his effort. . . . Our legislators should be asked in the coming election whether they are on the side of the teachers' lobby or our children.[46]

As the editorial boards of the city newspapers were airing their positions in public, the Board of Regents was holding its final round of hearings on the state commissioner's proposals regarding "Teaching as a Profession." Since the Regents had tentatively endorsed the commissioner's recommendations, it was only a matter of time before they would finally approve a redrafted version of the Ambach plan. This plan, however, would not include any measures to amend Section 3020-a of the State Education Law.

On April 23 Supreme Court Justice Gerald Held extended for two additional weeks a stay preventing the Teachers' Retirement Board from processing the application of Ronald Drew. This two-week stay, returnable on May 7, gave the chancellor the time needed to begin disciplinary proceedings against the indicted teacher. A three-member 3020-a panel began its hearings on May 1. At this point Shanker brought the whole series of proceedings into question. He called the chancellor's actions a "railroading." He complained, "There are all kinds of things which are supposed to protect due process—you are getting the equivalent of a posse."[47]

On another occasion Shanker accused Macchiarola of using the Drew case for his own political purposes. He charged:

> Macchiarola must feel he can't lose this one. If he wins the case, he's a hero in public. And if he doesn't, he will use it as another argument in the campaign he and his counsel have waged for months to get the procedure for dismissing tenured teachers changed.[48]

Shanker continued to treat the controversy over Ronald Drew as a civil rights issue—apart from the severity of the charges made against the indicted teacher. However, his sense of the political implications growing out of the case was very much on target. He had argued his position on Drew at great personal and political cost. Shanker himself had been on the receiving end of severe criticism in the press for defending a teacher accused of promoting child pornography.[49] There was not much public sympathy on his side. In the meantime, the Drew episode had allowed Macchiarola to lay the issue of teacher discipline before the popular conscience. Ronald Drew more than anyone else helped to develop a political mandate for the reform of section 3020-a, for his case provided Macchiarola with the kind of support the chancellor needed to get the ear of the legislature.

On May 13 Mayor Edward Koch and City Comptroller Harrison Goldin held a joint press conference to announce that they were instructing their appointees on the Teachers' Retirement Board to take whatever action was necessary to hold the application of Ronald Drew. Together, the mayor and the comptroller can influence the votes of three members of the seven-member body. With the Board of Education president casting the fourth vote, they could dominate a majority of the board. While the press conference was going on at City Hall, Supreme Court Justice Arthur Hirsch was hearing arguments from the chancellor's and the union's attorneys concerning the stay that had been in effect on the processing of Drew's application. While the judge reserved his decision on whether to allow the Teachers' Retirement

Board to process the application, he agreed to let the three-member disciplinary panel continue hearing charges against Drew. Under ordinary circumstances, such a hearing would not take place until the accused teacher had been convicted.

After nine days of hearings and nearly nine hundred pages of transcript, the three-person panel hearing charges against Drew finally reached a decision. On May 15 it announced a unanimous finding that Drew had engaged in "conduct unbecoming" to a teacher and was therefore unfit to serve in the public schools. The decision read:

> A person who accepts a teaching position, willingly places himself and his conduct in the arena of public attention. What may be acceptable in other walks of life, takes on an entirely different aspect when engaged in by a teacher. A teacher stands *in loco parentis*. A teacher is a role model for students to emulate. A teacher is a purveyor of community values.[50]

The decision represented a major victory for the chancellor, who announced, "I am gratified that he [Drew] will never again set foot in one of our classrooms as a teacher."[51]

The controversy was far from ended. Drew's dismissal served only to spur on further criticism from the union, which saw the rapid disposition of the case in only nine days as a violation of Drew's due process guarantees under state law. The union also maintained that holding an administrative hearing while a criminal trial was pending infringed on the defendant's due process rights under the Constitution. And there was still the debate over Drew's pension, which, many civil liberties advocates argued, was an employee's right, regardless of the circumstances surrounding his dismissal.[52] Appearing on the CBS–TV *Newsmakers* program on Sunday, May 18, Albert Shanker confidently told an interviewer that administrative proceedings against Drew would not stand up in court. He predicted that the decisions on the dismissal and the pension would be overturned.

Shanker's prediction proved to be only partially correct. On July 10, 1980, Supreme Court Justice Arthur Hirsch handed down a ruling which held that "the teacher's application for retirement will be honored and deemed filed and accepted with the New York City Teachers' Retirement Board as of May 7, 1980."[53] Board of Education attorneys had argued that a thirty-day period must elapse after application before a teacher could be considered for a pension. The court disagreed. Justice Hirsch found that applications submitted to the Teachers' Retirement Board were generally regarded by the board as "self-executing." He therefore deferred to this established administrative interpretation given by "the agency charted with the responsibility of setting the retirement laws into motion."

Justice Hirsch never addressed the broader question of whether a teacher's pension must be treated legally as deferred earnings. A ruling on that was not really necessary. The decision had the effect of assuring that Drew would receive his benefits. Macchiarola pledged to take the case to a higher court, but a suit never actually materialized. Given the legal precedent set in the private sector, which did treat pensions as deferred earnings, the chancellor's position did not seem to be based on any firm legal ground. In the meantime, however, Drew's dismissal from the school system as of May would stand and never be subjected to a serious legal challenge by the union.

It is difficult to assess who, if anyone, was the victor in the Drew controversy. All parties agreed that, if found guilty of a crime, Drew should be removed from his job. Shanker protested the manner in which the disciplinary proceedings were handled and the attempt to deny Drew his pension. He won on the latter issue, but at considerable loss to the public credibility of the union, since he was ridiculed by many for defending a child pornographer. Macchiarola managed to have Drew dismissed more quickly than would have been possible if normal administrative proceedings had been followed. However, he lost on the pension issue, incurred the wrath of a local school board, and became the target of criticism for his positions on the due process and retirement issues.

In the final analysis, the most significant outcome of the Drew case was political. By making teacher discipline a topic of popular discussion, Macchiarola began to develop a momentum behind his broader effort to revise section 3020-a of the State Education Law. He hoped to ride that momentum all the way to Albany.

THE FINAL PUSH

Following a relatively tranquil summer, there was much ado in Albany during the fall of 1980. When the New York State School Boards Association held its annual convention in October, its leadership petitioned the state Commissioner of Education, whose counsel was in attendance, to adopt regulatory reforms that would facilitate the hearing procedures under section 3020-a. Strategically, the association understood, changes in the regulations directly under the jurisdiction of the commissioner would more easily be effected than an amendment to the law. It assumed that the commissioner would be inclined to respond favorably to such an idea. At the same meeting, however, the School Boards Association adopted a resolution to "vigorously support legislation to amend 3020-a" on its own.[54] In particular, the membership hoped to reinstate the authority of local school boards to fix the penalties for employees convicted of a felony.

The School Boards Association strategists proved to be correct in anticipating a sympathetic response from the commissioner on regulatory reform. What they had not expected was an equally enthusiastic response concerning the legislative agenda they had formulated. Gordon Ambach had become deeply concerned with the rising costs of disciplinary hearings resulting from the 1977 statute—costs that would be assumed by the State Education Department.[55] He had heard numerous complaints from school administrators around the state about the cumbersome and time-consuming procedures. He had witnessed the episode of Ronald Drew in New York City. Finally, at the urging of his budget adviser and counsel, Commissioner Ambach began to draft his own proposal for amending the law, to accompany a new plan for regulatory reform.

In the meantime, on November 20, the Board of Regents adopted a set of draft regulations along the lines of the commissioner's recommendations on "Teaching as a Profession." This approval meant that both the commissioner and the Regents intended to keep the issue separate from the 3020-a debate. However, tentative approval only called for further action—first in the form of more public hearings to discuss implementation, then in the form of legislation for the appropriation of state funds. The latter issue would cause more skepticism on the fate of the proposal. The former would provide another forum for those who opposed it.

A hearing was held in late February 1981. Representing the New York City public schools was the recently appointed Deputy Chancellor for Instruction, Thomas Minter. This was Minter's first public appearance before the Board of Regents. He used the occasion to reiterate the chancellor's position that the draft regulations "fail to provide a system of true accountability," and "do not address the inadequacies of the existing system for disciplinary procedures."[56] Minter ended his statement by expressing disappointment that the Regents' tentative draft had not included recommendations for amending 3020-a—thereby revealing that city school officials did not know a move in that direction was being prepared.

After much deliberation, Ambach's grand scheme for reducing the dilatory and monetary effects of 3020-a was presented to the Board of Regents on April 22, 1981. To some extent it was more radical than the legislation the State School Boards Association had intended to advocate on its own. It was certainly more far-reaching than anything that had ever emerged on the subject from the State Education Department, and more substantial than anyone would have expected. The stated purpose of the commissioner's proposal was to "make the employee discipline process more expeditious and cost-effective," without "diminishing in any way the protections to which the employee is entitled."[57] It included four legislative amendments.

- The first statutory provision would replace the three-person 3020-a hearing panel with a single hearing officer, who would be a full-time employee of the State Education Department. This, it was hoped, would eliminate some of the scheduling problems the three-person board encountered, and therefore reduce both the time and the cost of the total process. This provision would also eradicate the role played by the AAA arbitrator, which was strongly supported by the union.
- A second statutory provision would require local school boards, when voting charges, to specify beforehand the maximum penalty to be imposed if there was a finding of guilt. This, it was hoped, would encourage some employees to waive the hearing process, if they learned beforehand that the maximum penalties to be imposed were not severe.
- A third statutory provision would empower the hearing officer to entertain and dispose of prehearing motions. These would include motions to dismiss the charges and applications for discovery proceedings outside the hearing process. It was hoped that such procedures would expedite the hearings by advance determination of certain kinds of preliminary matters.
- A fourth statutory provision would provide that where a teaching certificate has been revoked by the commissioner of education, dismissal proceedings need not be conducted in accord with 3020-a. Such revocations occur when it is found that a teacher does not possess the stipulated qualifications for a certificate.

In addition to the above amendments to the State Education Law, the commissioner's recommendation also called for several key reforms in his own administrative regulations. These changes would need only the approval of the Board of Regents, and would precede the statutory amendments. These regulatory reforms were also very much in accord with those advocated by the State School Boards Association. They included the following provisions:

- Any motion by an employee regarding sufficiency of charges should be made to the chairman either within twenty days, or five days after the selection of the chairman, whichever comes last.
- Employer and employee would be authorized, by agreement, to

waive all time provisions of section 3020-a and the regulations
of the commissioner.
- No panel member would be selected who did not provide a
  commitment in writing to commence the hearing on the date
  specified by the commissioner, and to devote not less than
  three consecutive days to the hearing.
- Adjournments of a hearing, granted by the chairman or hearing
  officer, would be made only in the interest of justice, or upon
  the showing of good cause.

The Ambach proposals evoked varied reactions from a wide
range of interested parties, some of which were anticipated, some not.
As may have been expected, the commissioner received immediate
pledges of support from both the New York State School Boards Association and the New York State School District Administrators. Also
somewhat predictable was a letter that Ambach received from the
president of NYSUT, condemning the proposed statutory charges as
"a clear diminution of the protection afforded teachers under tenure,"
and avowing, "We are unalterably opposed."[58]

City Schools Chancellor Macchiarola's response to the commissioner's recommendations was slow and somewhat surprising. It arrived in the form of a three-page letter dated May 20, which began with
an announcement of "full support for your efforts to streamline the
3020-a proceeding."[59] However, the body of the letter showed somewhat less than full accord with the details of Ambach's legislative
agenda. Macchiarola agreed with the idea of a single hearing officer
who was an employee of the state. He supported the fourth statutory
provision, concerning the revocation of teaching certificates. However, the chancellor had problems with the recommendation requiring
school boards to fix maximum penalties before the outcome of a hearing. This, he believed, robbed a school board of "much of its bargaining
position in settlement negotiations."[60] The chancellor also disapproved
of the statutory provision empowering a hearing officer to entertain and
dispose of prehearing motions. This, he argued, would not allow for
full, open, and unlimited discovery within the hearing process. The
chancellor noted support for the commissioner's regulatory proposals.
However, he cautioned that "legislative action remains necessary,"
and suggested strengthening the new time lines established for hearings
with specific sanctions.

On the same day that Macchiarola sent his letter to the state
commissioner, he submitted a more detailed memorandum to the City
Board of Education. The purpose of this document was to outline his
own legislative agenda for the repeal of 3020-a. The chancellor's legislative package was designed to complement and strengthen the Am-

bach proposals. It was not meant to be contradictory or debilitative. It was bolder than the set of recommendations he had submitted to the Board of Education during the previous year. There was a better chance now that the Board would act on the legislative proposal than there had been a year ago. The new plan to "restore to the Board of Education its management prerogatives" included several key provisions.[61]

- Section 2590-j (7) of the State Education Law would be repealed in order to establish uniform disciplinary procedures for all pedagogical personnel in the City school system. Under the existing law, different procedures existed for district and central personnel.
- There would be a rebuttable presumption that conviction for a crime constitutes conduct unbecoming to a teacher.
- Time schedules would be imposed on the hearing process, with sanctions attached to any party causing unreasonable delay.
- The tripartite panel would be replaced by a single trial examiner who was an employee of the state.

Two days after the chancellor launched his legislative campaign against 3020-a, the Board of Regents voted to support the commissioner's statutory proposals. Within the next month the Regents adopted the regulatory provisions of the Ambach plan, which represented a profound step in the direction of reform. They were put into effect immediately, by administrative fiat. However, the most significant changes concerning teacher discipline still had to be made in the legislature. In that arena, matters were much more complex.

A third bill was about to appear in Albany. It emerged from the office of Assembly Speaker Stanley Fink, whose power in the legislature was second to none. The Speaker's bill immediately became a source of great suspicion. All evidence seemed to suggest that it had been drafted by the union. Critics saw it as an alternative to change, another manifestation of union power. Fink denied these claims, but the provisions of his bill were very telling. The Fink bill proposed that the three-person 3020-a panel would be replaced by a single hearing officer chosen from a list provided by the American Arbitration Association. Thus the hearing officer would not be an employee of the State Education Department, as the commissioner and the chancellor had advocated. The Fink bill would also remove the Commissioner of Education from the appellate process, making it impossible to increase the penalties assigned by a panel or hearing officer. All appeals regarding determination of guilt would be taken through the courts.

The Fink bill was strongly attacked by the commissioner, the chancellor, and the State School Boards Association. A spokesperson for the chancellor publicly charged Fink with selling out to the teachers' union.[62] Fink denied it. He claimed that his bill was drafted in response to a proposal submitted to him by the Erie County School Board. He was annoyed with the public allegations. Finally Fink issued an ultimatum. Either his bill would be proposed to the legislature, or there would be none at all. The opposition continued. The result was a stalemate. Legislation to amend Section 3020-a of the State Education Law was never even introduced in committee. All discussion was ended. Section 3020-a survived in the form in which it had been written by the union in 1977.

SUMMARY COMMENTS

Upon close examination, there is a discernible pattern to the outcome of educational policy debates in New York City. While union support for an issue does not always assure passage, union opposition usually brings defeat. There are, of course, notable exceptions to this pattern. One was the implementation of the Decentralization Law in 1969; another was the appointment of Frank Macchiarola as chancellor in 1978. In both cases, the results had the aggressive backing of the New York City mayor. These exceptions lead to another, more general postulate that can be made about school politics in New York: Outside the school bureaucracy itself, there are two significant poles of power that influence educational policy: the mayor and the UFT.

A discussion of the mayor appears in the concluding chapter. His role is important in the present context only insofar as it modifies that of the union. The major focus here is union power and its relevance to the more general themes and hypotheses of the overall study. Two questions are immediately pertinent. First, from the perspective of the chancellor, what impact does the union have on the process of change? Second, to what extent does the union represent the interests of the school system clientele? The answer to both these questions is the same. Sometimes the union is helpful, sometimes it is not. More will be said about each below.

Let us return now to the original assertion that while union backing may not always mean success, union opposition usually means defeat, and review some of the evidence that supports it. In addition to its regular participation in collective bargaining, issues on which the union has acted affirmatively include the local school budget, annualization of paraprofessionals, Promotional Policy, curriculum reform, teacher training centers, the School Improvement Project, the seniority system, and the enactment of 3020-a. In only two of these cases has the union position been defeated—once regarding paraprofessionals, and several times on the school budget. In each of these cases the UFT was able to win some form of compromise in its defeat. In both cases its losses were again suffered at the hands of an intensely involved mayor.

Apart from the two exceptional cases already cited (decentralization and the chancellor's appointment), measures the union opposed include the residency law, hiring quotas, the "Teaching as a Profession" proposal, the denial of pension rights, and the repeal or revision of 3020-a. In all these cases, the union achieved victory.

The evidence listed above does not, of course, cover all issues, or even all the issues that are important from the union standpoint. However, one can assert with some confidence that, on the basis of those issues dealt with in this chapter, the evidence is persuasive regarding the power of the UFT.

The power of the UFT is not difficult to comprehend. Here is a large professional association with statewide and national affiliations, whose membership consistently shows a high turnout at elections. It has a competent campaign organization and resources available for contributions. It has been a major force in state, city, and neighborhood politics—not to mention the central and district school boards of New York. The influence enjoyed by the UFT in the state legislature is particularly important. There, in a major arena of educational policy making, the UFT is at a significant advantage when bills are introduced relating solely to matters in New York City. Since a majority of the legislators are elected outside the city, they are more inclined to be sympathetic to the union, which enjoys a statewide power base, than to other interested parties in the city—whether the chancellor, the mayor, or any of the many activist groups concerned with education. Evidence of this is the plethora of "New York City bills" that emerge from the legislature. A case in point is the statute of limitations, which sets a stricter time limit for bringing certain city school personnel (district) up on disciplinary charges than the standard that exists elsewhere in the state.

There are other occasions when the statewide affiliation of the union works against the objectives of local school officials in the city. This occurs when the union sees such objectives as contrary to the interests of teachers in other parts of the state. A notable example was the campaign launched by city school officials to redesign the state school finance formula for the benefit of municipal and property-poor districts. The UFT supported the campaign in principle, but the solutions it sought were not in total agreement with the goals set by city officials. City school officials sought an entire redistribution of state school funds. Teachers around the state in school districts that would lose money and jobs from such a redistribution opposed this strategy. Thus, the UFT and NYSUT would support only a "leveling up" approach, which would increase funding to underfinanced districts without decreasing it to others. The union alternative was neither a politically nor financially feasible option during a period of budgetary constraints. Its practical effect was to limit the extent of reforms made on behalf of redistribution.

In the final analysis, the union supports changes it believes to be in the interest of its members. Its approach is both reasonable and expected. However, from the perspectives of school system leadership and clientele, the outcome is mixed. The UFT, for example, has historically taken a conservative stand on the personnel issues of seniority and quotas, to the chagrin of many of the system's client groups. However, the union has also functioned as a progressive force on such questions as student competency standards, teacher training, compensatory education, school improvement, and curriculum reform. It remains the most important ally of the school administration in the yearly battles over the local school budget.

This chapter has highlighted the major and natural tension that exists between school officials and the union on the subject of teacher discipline. The union continues to deal with the question as a civil rights issue. The school administration approaches it from the perspective of staff accountability—an integral complement to an agenda that emphasizes higher standards for students. An analysis of the politics surrounding the 3020-a debate shows that it bears a marked resemblance to the cases discussed in previous chapters in that this single area of policy making involved so many individuals and institutions. The enactment, enforcement, interpretation, and repeal of 3020-a involved the following actors: a local school board, the Board of Education, the Commissioner of Education, the Board of Regents, the state courts, and the state legislature.

One factor, however, that distinguishes the 3020-a issue from the others discussed in this book is the existence of a singularly dominant interest group throughout the entire episode—the union. Even the central Board of Education was reluctant to follow the recommendations of its chancellor for the reform of 3020-a. In this sense, the UFT is unique. In the language of political science, the UFT more often resembles a "core group" of decision makers in the policy process than it does a "satellite group" that attempts to affect policy by influencing individuals with authority to make decisions. The outcomes in this case are not ambiguous. Schoolteachers are the only employees in New York who continue to receive their pay when they are suspended for disciplinary reasons. School districts are the only public agencies that do not have final discretion (outside the courts) with regard to disciplinary charges and penalties against their employees.

Certainly the power of the union in educational policy making in New York cannot be described as unilateral. There is always the power of the mayor to act as a counterforce when and if he chooses. The mayor is most likely to do so on issues that involve money—specifically, money from the city treasury. Other than occasional verbal endorsements of the chancellor's cause, there was a conspicuous absence of major activity on the part of the mayor as the entire 3020-a matter unfolded. In assessing the power of the UFT, one should also add that the union does not choose to become involved in every educational policy debate that occurs in New York. In preceding chapters we have seen the union keep a relatively low profile on special education and school desegregation. Hence it is not always part of what we might call the attentive public.

The 3020-a issue provides an opportunity to observe the dynamics of a head-on confrontation between the schools chancellor and the UFT. It demonstrates quite clearly that the union, when it chooses, can be a significant obstacle to the chancellor's campaign for change. This chapter also shows that, even in an administration where the school system and union leadership are in fundamental agreement on philosophy and strategy, the tensions inherent in the labor-management relationship are unavoidable.

NOTES

1. See, for example, Robert Dahl, *Who Governs* (New Haven: Yale University Press, 1961); Nelson W. Polsby, *Community Power and Political Theory* (New Haven: Yale University Press, 1963).

2. Peter Bachrach and Morton Baratz, "Two Faces of Power," *American Political Science Review* 56 (December 1962). See also Peter Bachrach and Morton Baratz, "Decisions and Non-decisions," *American Political Science Review* 57 (September 1963).

3. "Agreement between the Board of Education of the City School District of the City of New York and the United Federation of Teachers, Local 2, American Federation of Teachers, AFL–CIO, Covering Teachers, September 9, 1980–September 9, 1982," p. 96.

4. Ibid., p. 24.

5. Albert Shanker, private interview, June 21, 1982.

6. A. M. Cresswell, *Teachers Unions and Collective Bargaining in Public Education* (Berkeley Calif.: McCutchan, 1980).

7. See Roy R. Pellicano, "The United Federation of Teachers and the Deficit Model of Urban Education," Ph.D. Dissertation, Teachers College, Columbia University, 1977.

8. See Diane Ravitch, *The Great School Wars* (New York: Basic Books, 1974), chapters 23–36; Marilyn Gittell, "Education: The Decentralization–Community Control Controversy," in Jewel Bellush and Stephen David, eds., *Race and Politics in New York City* (New York: Praeger, 1971).

9. "The Impact of School Decentralization in New York City on Municipal Decentralization," Study Prepared by the Charter Revision Commission for New York City, June 1974, p. 66.

10. Ibid., p. 77.

11. Sterling Spero and John Capozzola, *The Urban Community and Its Unionized Bureaucracy* (New York: Dunellen, 1973).

12. *New York Post,* January 5, 1979.

13. *The Amsterdam News,* April 7, 1979.

14. Ibid.

15. *De Milia* v. *City of New York,* Supreme Court, 1 ST, July 3, 1979.

16. *Uniform Firefighters Association, et. al.* v. *City of New York,* 71 A.D. 2d 843 (1979).

17. *Uniform Firefighters Association, et. al.* v. *City of New York,* 50 N.Y. 2d 85 (1980).

18. *New York Teacher* XVIII (April 24, 1977).

19. Ibid.

20. *New York Teacher* XVIII (January 23, 1977).

21. Roy Moskowitz, private interview, April 29, 1981.

22. State School Board Association, "Legislative Sub-Committee Report on 3020-a Hearings," September 11, 1979.

23. *Board of Education of Belmont* v. *Gootnick,* 49 NY 2d 683.

24. *Adele Mockler* v. *Gordon Ambach, et al.,* 18 EDR 387.

25. *Matter of Jerry* v. *Board of Education,* 35 NY 2d 534.

26. Ted Elsberg, private interview, May 6, 1981.

27. Philip Kaplan, private interview, May 6, 1981.

28. Gordon Ambach, "Memorandum to Members of the Board of Regents, Regarding Teaching as a Profession and Teacher Competence," December 6, 1979.

29. New York City and Buffalo require teachers to take specific tests in order to qualify for an appointment to these districts.

30. Correspondence from Anna Kaplan to Frank J. Macchiarola, October 30, 1979.

31. Ibid.

32. Transcript, CBS–TV, Channel 2, *Newsmakers,* February 3, 1980.

33. *New York Daily News,* February 4, 1980.

34. Robert Hyland, WCBS News 88 Editorial, "Disciplining Teachers," 80-36, March 17, 1980; March 18, 1980.

35. *The New York Times,* April 4, 1980.

36. Statement by Frank J. Macchiarola, Chancellor, New York City Public Schools, before the Public Hearing of the Board of Regents Concerning the Draft Proposals on "Teaching as a Profession and Teacher Competency," April 9, 1980, New York, New York.

37. Ibid.

38. Ibid.

39. David Wirtz, "Memorandum to Frank J. Macchiarola, Regarding Disciplinaries and Removal of Tenured Pedagogues Pursuant to Education Law, Section 3020-a," April 7, 1980.

40. Ibid.

41. Ibid.

42. Frank J. Macchiarola, letter to Community School Board 25, April 18, 1980.

43. *Newsday,* April 19, 1980.

44. *New York Daily News,* April 22, 1980.

45. *Newsday,* April 23, 1980.

46. *New York Post,* April 24, 1980.

47. *New York Daily News,* May 11, 1980.

48. Albert Shanker, "Chancellor Railroading Accused Teacher," "Where We Stand," *The New York Times,* May 11, 1980.

49. For example, one editorial in the *New York Post,* on May 12, 1980, under the title "A Dubious Crusade," questioned the appropriateness of Shanker's attempt to protect Drew's pension. Another editorial in the *New York Daily News,* on May 13, 1980, under the title "Shame, Shame," branded Shanker's actions "scandalous."

50. Board of Education of the City of New York, News Bureau, press release, N-161, 1979–1980, May 15, 1980.

51. Ibid.

52. A CBS–TV editorial aired on May 21 and 22 agreed with Macchiarola's position that teachers should be held to high standards, but was critical of his attempts to deny Drew a pension. The editorial argued that public sector pensions, like private sector pensions, should be considered deferred earnings and should not be denied an employee because of improper behavior. A *New York Times* editorial published on July 25, 1980, similarly contended that pensions should be treated as deferred income, not as reward for good behavior.

53. *Ronald Drew* v. *Frank J. Macchiarola, et. al.* 104 Misc. 2d 1131 (1980).

54. *New York State School Board Journal,* December 1980.

55. Total state costs for the administration of Section 3020-a during the 1980–1981 fiscal year were approximately $562,000 for 160 cases, according to a memorandum prepared by the counsel to the commissioner. Robert D. Stone, "Memorandum in Support of 'An Act to Amend the Education Law, in Relation to Discipline Procedures for Tenured School District Personnel,'" June 5, 1981.

56. Statement by Thomas K. Minter, Deputy Chancellor for Instruction, New York City Public Schools, before the Public Hearings of the Board of Regents Concerning the Draft Regulations to Implement Several Provisions of the Regents Plan on Teaching as a Profession, February 25, 1981.

57. Gordon Ambach, "Memorandum to The Honorable Members of the Board of Regents, Regarding Education Law Section 3020-a—Teacher Disciplinary Proceedings," April 22, 1981.

58. Thomas Y. Hobart, Jr., correspondence to Gordon Ambach, May 19, 1981.

59. Frank J. Macchiarola, correspondence to Gordon Ambach, May 20, 1981.

60. Ibid.

61. Frank J. Macchiarola, "Memorandum to Members of the Board of Education, Regarding 'Proposed Legislation Concerning Pedagogical Disciplinary Procedures,'" May 20, 1981.

62. *New York Post,* June 11, 1981.

CONCLUSION: POLITICS AND EDUCATION IN THE CITY

Many of the patterns that emerged during the first three years of the Macchiarola administration continued into the fourth and the fifth. Governor Hugh Carey set the political stage for 1982 during the early days of the new year when he announced that he would not seek reelection for a third term. Carey wanted to leave behind a significant legacy for which he would be remembered. Among the items in the legislative agenda during his final year in office was school finance reform. At the time of the governor's announcement, the existing finance formula had been found by both the lower and appellate-level courts to be in violation of the state constitution. A final decision was still being awaited from the Court of Appeals, New York's highest tribunal.

Carey's position on the school finance issue had been consistent. He had unsuccessfully tried to bring about reform for five consecutive years. He had become a particularly strong advocate since Justice J. Kingsley Smith handed down the original *Levittown* decision in 1978. The governor wanted to achieve a radical redistribution of state education funds by decreasing the allotment made to property-rich districts and increasing the amounts to those that were property-poor or financially overburdened by the costs of municipal services. In mid-February 1982 Carey made public a new proposal, which would increase state education spending by $8.6 billion over a period of five years. Approximately $740 million of this would be realized during the 1983 fiscal year. While New York City and many property-poor school districts stood to enjoy considerable gains in their share of education dollars, many of the wealthier districts would actually experience reductions in their allocations. The full package would be paid for by a 1-percent increase in the state sales tax.

As the governor's position in school finance reform was consistent, so was that of the legislature. Lawmakers in Albany had many times before demonstrated their reluctance to redistribute state education funds by reducing spending in economically affluent and politically

307

powerful school districts. They were particularly averse to doing so in an election year. Nor were they inclined to raise the state sales tax. What emerged from the capitol in the spring of 1982 was a $310 million increase in the state education budget. Although New York City and many property-poor districts enjoyed a disproportionate share of this supplement, each school district in the state, regardless of its local tax base, would derive some benefit from the new budget. There would be no significant reform in the state finance formula. There would be no substantial redistribution of funds.

The most severe blow to school finance reform in New York State was yet to come. On June 23, 1982, the Court of Appeals handed down a long-awaited ruling that upheld the existing state finance formula and overturned the decisions of the two lower courts. In a 6–1 decision, the court found that although "significant inequalities" existed in the availability of educational funds among school districts, the situation was not in violation of either the state or the federal constitution.[1] Writing on behalf of the majority, Judge Hugh Jones declared that disparities in spending were a function of local discretion, upon which it would be "inappropriate" for the courts to intrude. While recognizing a state constitutional provision for a system of "free common schools," the court found no legal requirement that education be made available on an "equal or substantially equivalent" basis. Instead, the majority interpreted the provision as requiring only "minimal accepted facilities and services."

Thus ended any reasonable hope for a judicial remedy to the existing inequities in statewide educational spending. The final *Levittown* decision was followed by pledges from several of the plaintiffs to take the appeal into the federal courts. However, in accord with the precedent set down in the *Rodrieguez* decision, the Supreme Court of the United States denied *certiorari* to the case in January 1983. Henceforth, for both political and legal reasons, significant school finance reform in New York State remains an open and shut case.

The politics of the state gubernatorial election made its way prominently into the affairs of New York City. In 1981 Mayor Edward Koch had run virtually unopposed for reelection. Consequently, in November, he was given approval by more than 75 percent of the voters in one of the most one-sided mayoral contests in the history of the city. In the winter of 1982, a very confident Edward Koch announced his candidacy for the governorship. This meant that for the second consecutive time New York City would have an election year budget. However, the terms of election year politics in 1982 were different from those that prevailed in the previous year. In 1981 mayoral candidate Koch had run on a service budget—one that would raise popular expectations, expand agency programs, and maximize spending. In 1982 gubernatorial candidate Koch had to demonstrate fiscal responsibility. This called for moderation and some substantial cuts in the budget for fiscal year 1983. Politically, the premier candidate for retrenchment was the public schools.

Koch's Executive Budget was submitted to the City Council and the Board of Estimate in early May. It provided for generous increases in police, corrections, sanitation, and social services, and for moderate increases in fire and transportation.[2] The school budget was slated for an $87.5 million cut. After much negotiation, the Council and the Board of Estimate managed to restore $30 million for the schools. However, the remaining $57 million reduction in local funds was still severe, particularly in light of an anticipated loss of $69 million in federal aid for 1983, as promised by Ronald Reagan.

Despite the difficult budget situation, the school system continued to show signs of progress. Data from the California Achievement Test (CAT), released in June 1982, showed that for the second consecutive year New York City schoolchildren were reading above the national norm. In fact, there was a slight increase over the performance level of 1981, with 51.0 percent (as opposed to 50.8 percent) of the students in grades 2 through 9 reading at or above grade level.[3] It was the third consecutive year in which the citywide reading scores improved. A closer analysis of the data also revealed that over the past four years the percentage of students reading two or more years below grade level had been reduced from 15.1 percent to 8.8 percent.[4]

The 1981–1982 school year was the first in which a standardized mathematics test was used to determine eligibility for grade advancement under the chancellor's Promotional Policy. According to the new standard, any child in a "gate" grade (4 or 7) performing two or more years below grade level on the Stanford Diagnostic Mathematics Test (SDMT) would be denied promotion and become a candidate for remediation. Notwithstanding the anxiety produced by the new standard, the release of the SDMT scores in June proved to be another occasion for encouragement. Approximately 56.5 percent of the students who took the exam scored at or above grade level. This amounted to a nearly 7 percent improvement citywide over the 1981 scores (49.6 percent), with progress in all thirty-two of the city's local school districts.[5] Most significant of all, this was the first time in over a decade that New York City schoolchildren exceeded the national norm in both reading and mathematics.

Not all the news concerning student achievement was so uplifting. In keeping with the chancellor's Promotional Policy, 17,566 students in the fourth and seventh grades did not qualify for promotion on the basis of the spring reading scores.[6] Of this group, 8,179 also had unsatisfactory scores in mathematics.[7] The combined number of unsatisfactory scores for reading and mathematics recorded in the spring of 1982 (22,983) did, however, compare favorably with the 23,509 who had failed to qualify for promotion solely on the basis of their spring reading scores in 1981. This total number of 1982 holdovers was further reduced to 19,203 on the basis of an August retest administered after the summer remedial program.[8]

The most discouraging development emerging from the 1982 test results involved students who would fall into the category that became known as "double holdovers." Of the 23,509 students who became candidates for retention in the spring of 1981, 5,999 were promoted on the basis of the August retest, and another 1,757 met the requirements for promotion during a January 1982 exam.[9] Of the remaining students who participated in the gates remedial program through the end of the 1981–1982 school year, 3,941 still failed to meet the requirements for promotion by August 1982.[10] While this group was considerably less in number than the original class of potential holdovers identified a year earlier, and a small part of the 120,000 fourth- and seventh-grade students who originally sat for the 1981 exam, it was still a matter of legitimate and serious concern.

The prospect that nearly four thousand children would be required to pass through the same elementary or intermediate grade for the third time was disturbing. This possibility had been a major fear of the critics of Promotional Policy. Its actual occurrence rekindled many of the deep-seated doubts articulated by the opponents two years earlier. Was the school system really prepared to deal with these children? Did educators know what to do in order to improve their achievement levels? Should these children ever have been held over in the first place?

In the spring of 1982 the United Parents' Associations (UPA), a chief opponent of Promotional Policy, completed its own evaluation of the gates remedial effort. Surprisingly, the results of the study were generally positive, showing that school officials were "highly responsible" in providing the level and kinds of services they had promised.[11] However, the UPA report raised a number of important questions about the long-range plans for the program. It expressed particular concern about the double holdovers. It referred to uncertainties over the long-range future of the program. The fact of the matter is that the City had never made a long-term commitment to the program. Funding had always been uncertain, and, when received, it was usually the result of last-minute negotiations and political manipulations. Yet money remained a prerequisite for an effective remedial effort.

As it had in the past, the UPA also challenged the validity of using the CAT exam as an instrument for determining eligibility for student promotion. The CAT is a norm-referenced examination. Standard educational practice calls for the use of a criterion-referenced test for individualized student assessments. The administration had originally planned to replace the CAT exam with a criterion-referenced test after the first year of the program. However, because of doubts about the adequacy of the available tests, and a desire to remain capable of longitudinal analysis, the chancellor decided to continue with the CAT and work with a technique that had been developed to convert the scoring.

The chancellor took several measures in response to the concerns of his critics. The statewide Degree of Reading Power test (DRP), administered on an experimental basis in several districts for two years, was administered to all fourth- and seventh-grade students city-wide. The teachers of students who did not attain satisfactory scores on the CAT but did well on the criterion-referenced DRP were granted the right to appeal decisions concerning promotion. This policy introduced both a new test and a wider range of teacher judgment as criteria for promotion.

The administration also announced several new efforts on behalf of the double holdovers. Class sizes for this group would be reduced to fifteen or fewer students so as to allow for the maximum degree of individual instruction. (Class size for the regular gate remedial classes was twenty or less.) Seventh-grade students would be given specialized training in vocational education so they could develop a wider range of skills. In addition to these changes, all potential double holdovers were put through a complete medical screening to determine whether their learning problems were health-related. The decision to do this was made after it was discovered that 25 percent of the gates program children in a Brooklyn school district needed eyeglasses.

As the administration went about the task of designing alternative strategies for accommodating the needs of its first class of double holdovers, a larger effort was being planned in another part of the school bureaucracy to address the growing and no less perplexing problem of special education. By the end of the 1981–1982 school year, the number of special-education students had grown to nearly 100,000.[12] This was almost double the enrollment that had existed when Macchiarola took office in 1978. The Division of Special Education had accomplished a major reorganization. Responsibility for the delivery of school-based services at the secondary level had been effectively transferred to the High Schools Division. An experiment along the lines of the Harrison House proposal had been put into place in five local school districts.

However, litigation continued. The plaintiffs in the *José P.* case were not yet satisfied with either the quantity or the quality of services provided to the handicapped. In June 1982 the number of children backlogged on the evaluation waiting list was 4,157. The number of children waiting for placements was 3,599.[13] Both the plaintiffs and the state codefendents were raising questions about the appropriateness of placements, class sizes, the adequacy of individualized education programs, and the level of mainstreaming and support services. In the meantime the budgetary situation was becoming more strained.

In the spring of 1982 the court-appointed Special Master, Marvin Frankel, submitted his resignation to Judge Eugene Nickerson. Frankel complained that the case was beginning to absorb too much of his time. It would not allow him to follow through on his other professional commitments. As the new school year began, the plaintiffs were appealing to Judge Nickerson for the appointment of a new master with expanded administrative powers. The defendants submitted papers to the court requesting an amendment to the original judgment that was more consistent with the financial and pedagogic capabilities of the school system. In the early part of 1983, Judge Eugene Nickerson ruled that New York City school officials had failed to comply with his three-year-old order.

No one knew quite what to do with the situation in special education. The demand for services was continuing to grow in geometric proportions. The resources available to meet the costs were shrinking. There was no movement in the federal government to abide by its original financial commitment to handicapped children, as defined in Public Law 94-142 in 1975. There was still no overriding professional consensus on the merits of mainstreaming, and many educators within the school system were beginning to question the wisdom of classifying so many children as handicapped. Nevertheless, there were also students with handicapping conditions who had a legitimate need for more and better service.

On June 28, 1982, the Supreme Court of the United States handed down its first decision related to the Education for All Handicapped Children Act. The case was brought on behalf of Amy Rowley, a deaf student in Peekskill, New York. Amy had been receiving a number of special services from the Furnace Woods school which she attended. However, her parents claimed that, for Amy to fulfill her maximum potential, she should be provided with a sign language interpreter. They argued that it was her right under Public Law 94-142. The Court disagreed. It found that the "free appropriate education" guaranteed under the law "consists of educational instruction specifically designed to meet the unique needs of the handicapped child, supported by such services as are necessary to permit the child 'to benefit' from the instruction."[14] In interpreting the intent of the law, the Court found "no requirement" that states must maximize the potential of handicapped children to provide the opportunity afforded other children. While the 6–3 decision affirmed the basic objectives of Public Law 94-142, its net effect was to place a limit on the legitimate claims of the handicapped under federal law.

Shortly after the Rowley decision was handed down, the Reagan administration announced that it was proposing a revision of the federal regulations enacted to enforce Public Law 94-142. The purpose of the recommended changes was to relax the requirements for special education imposed on the states in the areas of direct instruction, support services, and due process. These proposals met considerable opposition in Congress and for the most part were eventually withdrawn. However, their announcement sent a message that had already been implicit in the Reagan administration budget: The White House would prefer to reduce the level of educational services to handicapped children rather than provide the funds needed to meet the obligations defined in the legislation of 1975. Thus the major burden for providing instruction to the handicapped would remain with the states and localities.

On June 30, 1982, the Supreme Court handed down two additional important decisions on public education. Both involved the power and responsibilities of the states regarding desegregation. In an 8–1 decision, the Court upheld an amendment to the California constitution that limited the power of the states to order busing beyond the requirements of federal law.[15] The amendment had been passed in opposition to a state court order requiring busing as a remedy for de facto segregation. Concurrently, the Supreme Court affirmed lower-court rulings overturning a Washington state law that prohibited local school districts from implementing mandatory busing.[16] While neither case represented a major breakthrough in the Court's position on school desegregation, together the two decisions served to reaffirm several basic principles that were part of the judicial precedent. Both rulings indicated that the Court continued to take seriously the distinction between de facto and de jure segregation, thereby applying intent as a significant criterion for federal judicial intervention. While the Court would not put federal sanction behind a state attempt to assume an aggressive policy in remedying de facto segregation, it would not allow a state to exercise authority that arbitrarily defined the appropriate response to a segregated situation, nor would it interfere with the use of busing as a means to end intentional segregation.

In the meantime, there was less devotion to legal precedent and past federal practice on the part of the executive branch of the government. In July 1982 the Reagan administration publicly endorsed a Senate bill that would limit the ability of the federal courts to order busing and prohibit the Department of Justice from spending any funds on desegregation suits where busing was a remedy. During the following month, the Justice Department petitioned a United States Court of Appeals in New Orleans to delay consideration of a busing plan in East Baton Rouge, Louisiana, until an attempt could be made to develop a voluntary solution to a segregated situation. The request was a first in the history of the Justice Department, which had always served as a powerful force behind school desegregation.

Many arguments can be offered on the advantages of voluntary desegregation plans over forced busing—not the least of which is the association between busing and the phenomenon of white flight. However, there is a basic irony to the Reagan administration's approach to public education. Programs that can be used to attract white children to predominantly minority schools often cost money. The White House has been steadfast in its desire to reduce the federal investment in education. As long as the federal government ignores its obligation to improve the quality of education in schools with a predominantly minority population, the only children who will attend these schools are those who have no real choice. From the perspective of an urban school system, the implications of such a policy are significant in both a demographic and political sense. We will discuss these broad policy issues at greater length. But first let us return to the affairs of New York City.

THE CHANCELLOR'S DILEMMA: CONSTITUENTS AND CLIENTS

On January 17, 1983, Frank Macchiarola announced that he was leaving his position as chancellor to become president of the New York City Partnership, a distinguished and influential coalition of business and civic groups assembled by David Rockefeller in 1979 to address some of the major economic and social issues facing the city. The announcement came a little more than a month after a bitter dispute between the chancellor and several members of the Board of Education over an educational option plan that Macchiarola sought to implement in the junior high schools. The plan would have given students a choice between spending their ninth year in junior high school, as was traditional, or moving on to high school, where they would spend four years rather than the usual three.

The idea was vehemently opposed by local community school boards, who saw it as a scheme to snatch away district enrollments and budgets. It was strongly objected to by junior high school teachers and administrators, who perceived the option plan as a threat to their job security. Several neighborhood and professional groups attacked the proposal on the ground that it was educationally unsound. In response to well-organized community pressure, several of the borough presidents instructed their appointees on the central Board of Education to reject the chancellor's recommendation. In early December 1982, a heated debate took place at a public meeting of the Board. When it ended, the Board voted to table the ninth-grade option, and Macchiarola accused several Board members of "holding up the white flag" before the districts and the unions.

The disagreement over the option plan was the bitterest public confrontation that had ever occurred between Macchiarola and the members of the Board of Education. There was much more at stake then the opportunity of students to choose the school where they would spend their ninth year of instruction. The final vote on the option plan symbolized a show of strength by Board members at the prodding of the borough presidents. It represented a new assertion of authority, which many believed had been compromised under the aggressive leadership of Macchiarola. It was a way of saying that the Board and not the chancellor would run the educational affairs of the city during the coming year. Macchiarola's resignation in mid-January made the probability even more likely.

The preceding chapters support the fundamental notion that educational policy making in New York City is a political process. The outcomes are a product of conflict and compromise factored by a multiplicity of actors. These include a host of governmental authorities and an assortment of attentive private parties. The basic causes of conflict are twofold; they include interest and ignorance. The concept of interest is by no means a novel one in the literature on politics. It derives from a political actor's perception that he or she will benefit from a particular policy. That perception may or may not be valid in any given situation. Nevertheless, conflict results when two or more actors consider their interests to be contradictory. There are several examples of such activity in the preceding pages: the battles over school finance reform, the demand for upgraded services for the handicapped, the several controversies over school desegregation, the disagreements concerning disciplinary procedures for schoolteachers. Political scientists refer to such encounters as interest group politics.

The previous chapters demonstrate that conflict also results when policy makers and interested parties have no clear or proven notion of what direction to take on a given problem or issue. Thus we have observed serious and well-intentioned debate on the merits and uses of competency testing. We have witnessed deep divisions in the professional community about the efficacy of alternative approaches to educating the handicapped. While social science research has informed these debates and helped us to distinguish between what we know and what we don't know, the evidence on such questions lacks the authority or reliability that is needed for resolution. Such an information vacuum, what we have referred to here as ignorance, causes conflict over policy options.

As a result of political conflict, whatever the source, the urban school system is the object of numerous cross-pressures. In New York City this situation creates an unenviable predicament for the chancellor. It also defines a major component of his job. In a highly charged political environment, there are few significant policy options that will not incur the wrath of some public official, governmental institution, or private group. Should the chancellor ignore the demands of retrenchment, or should he reduce services to the poor and the handicapped? Should he force a local school board to desegregate a school facility, or should he allow minority children to be denied equal access to a building? Should he tolerate a system of disciplinary procedures that invites abuse, or should he risk being seen as an adversary by the large majority of teachers who do their jobs well? Political decision making usually involves selection from among a panoply of undesirable choices, all of which generate some level of resistance.

A central role of the chancellor in New York City, like that of any other urban superintendent, is to respond to and, when possible, resolve conflict that originates outside the bounds of the school system. Ironically, however, in an administration dedicated to a significant measure of change, the chancellor himself becomes a source of conflict. Therefore the chancellor who would cast himself as an agent for change must by necessity devote a large share of his time, energy, and effort to the external environment. Let us consider for a moment the external demands made upon Chancellor Macchiarola during the first month of his tenure. These included:

- renegotiating the budget for fiscal year 1978 proposed by outgoing Chancellor Irving Anker;
- developing a strategy for the *Levittown* case;
- appealing to legislative leaders for reform of the state school finance formula;
- promoting support among community superintendents for plans involving smaller class sizes in the first grade, transitional classes for holdovers, and the extended use of school buildings;

- developing a budget proposal for fiscal year 1979;
- negotiating the UFT contract and a plan for the annualization of paraprofessionals;
- drafting a proposal for a residency requirement for submission to the Board of Education;
- responding to special-education litigation in the *Lora* case;
- responding to special-education litigation in the *José P.* case;
- responding to the state commissioner's regulations and orders regarding the education of the handicapped;
- responding to the state commissioner's initial proposal for new competency standards for high school graduation;
- responding to litigation involving the segregation of Andrew Jackson High School;
- responding to an investigation by the United States Office for Civil Rights concerning the segregated setting in the IS 231 annex.

These demands represent only a small part of the external pressures directed at the chancellor's office during the early days of his administration. More specifically, the list includes only events related to the subjects covered in this book. A complete chronicle of the administration's activities during this time would expand the size of the list several times. The important point is that a significant part of the chancellor's working agenda must focus on the external environment. At times, this kind of responsibility becomes a distraction from the internal management of the school system. Notwithstanding the peculiar influence bureaucratic organization and behavior have on internal operations, external politics remains a major obstacle to both the managerial and change processes.

One might classify the external actors with whom the chancellor deals in three categories. There are those to whom he is directly accountable on a regular basis; there are those to whom he is accountable on a less constant, issue-by-issue basis; and there are public and private groups that exercise an ongoing influence on policy, but to whom the chancellor is not formally accountable. The first category consists of the seven-member central Board of Education, which appoints the chancellor, and the mayor, who exercises discretion over the financial resources for the school system. The second includes such governmental actors as the City Council, the Board of Estimate, the state commissioner of education, the state Regents, the state legislature, the state courts, the federal courts, and the executive branch of the federal government. Although those in the latter category do not play an intimate role in local education as the first group, their impact is considerable in cases where they exercise authority.

The third category of public and private parties includes such participants as community school boards and their superintendents, the United Federation of Teachers, the Council of Supervisors and Administrators, the Educational Priorities Panel, the United Parents' Associations, Advocates for Children, the Public Education Association, and a host of professional, civic, and neighborhood organizations that have a direct or indirect stake in public education. As already noted, the chancellor is not accountable to the actors in this category in any formal or legal way. However, his dependence upon them for the support of his policies or programs is such that he is accountable to them in a political sense.

A case in point is the local community school boards and their superintendents. One might say that, formally, it is they who are accountable to the chancellor, since he has the legal responsibility to establish and enforce minimum citywide educational standards. Macchiarola used this authority to institute his Promotional Policy. Nevertheless, as that example demonstrated, practically speaking, the support of local school officials is essential for implementing policies. Because the chancellor must earn the support of these actors to be effective, he is, in fact, politically accountable to them. This same type of political relationship exists between the chancellor and the private interest groups in the third category, although perhaps more in the adoption than in the implementation stage of the policy process. Yet the point is clear: political accountability goes beyond the legal arrangements set down in the city charter or state constitution. The constituency to which the chancellor is accountable is wide and varied.

A key question still remains: Whom do these constituents represent? More specifically, is it in the interest of the clientele of the school system that they apply their influence in the policy process? Demographic data suggest that public education in New York, as in other urban centers, is increasingly becoming a poor people's service used largely by racial minorities. The institutional and political structure of the decision making does not readily lend itself to the representation of those client groups. A case-by-case consideration of the various constituents is very telling.

On the local government level, the electorate that chooses the mayor, the City Council, and the Board of Estimate is composed primarily of a white middle-class population. For practical political reasons, it is reasonable to expect that the priorities of this population will be reflected in the policies of those elected officials. That is particularly true with regard to the local tax levy budget. Longitudinal analysis of retrenchment and the cases presented on the budget bears that expectation out. Among the most severe casualties of cutbacks in New York has been the school budget.

A little more than a decade ago, the central Board of Education and the school bureuacracy at Livingston Street were among the major targets of local activists who advocated decentralization and community control. Rightfully, these reformers argued that the central administration at Livingston Street was closed to them. Their leaders pointed out that institutions inherited from the past were not responsive to the needs of a new clientele. Several observations can be made with regard to these concerns as a result of the preceding case studies. During the years of the Macchiarola administration, the chancellor's office was the beneficiary of a major shift in policy-making initiatives away from the central Board of Education. Since the administration arrived ten years after the birth of decentralization, it is safe to conclude that the shift was due less to institutional reform than to Macchiarola's aggressive leadership. While the central bureaucracy was to live on, there is good indication that its once unmitigated power had abated. These two observations are related. Since the central Board of Education has traditionally functioned as a protector of this enormous bureaucracy, a decrease in the power of the latter at least partially results from the decline in the role of the former.

There is now some evidence that under certain conditions school decentralization in New York has proved successful in improving accountability, participation, innovation, and performance.[17] However, the evidence presented in the preceding chapters is less encouraging. Particularly with regard to school desegregation, the most highly charged racial issue discussed in these pages, some community school boards have shown themselves to be insensitive and unresponsive to the demands of the minority community. Community school districts have been among the most blatant perpetrators of intentional or de jure segregation in New York. In no place is the fracture between constituent and client so apparent as in the districts, where in many cases a popularly elected, predominantly white school board governs the affairs of a local school system attended mostly by blacks and Hispanics. Perhaps decentralization represents progress over the bureaucratic mechanism that prevailed more than a decade ago, but there is still much work to be done to achieve the democratic goals articulated by its original proponents.

When one turns to the state policy arena, events during the Macchiarola administration reveal a rather mixed pattern of outcomes. The attempt by the Regents and the state commissioner to raise competency standards for high school graduation seemed to reflect a commitment on the part of these actors to improve the quality of instruction for city school children. However, their determination to implement such changes without additional financial support or the existence of a uniform curriculum raised serious questions about technique, not only within the chancellor's office but in the minority community as well. The commissioner did prove to be an important proponent for revising section 3020-a of the State Education Law. He was also supportive of efforts on behalf of school desegregation in Queens.

The most serious problem at the state level continues to exist in the school finance formula, which has historically reflected an antiurban bias that dominates the legislature. Evidently this policy is not about to change. Would-be reformers have customarily looked toward the courts for an ally in the modification of past practices. Now, however, the highest court in the state has found that inequities in educational services are legally tolerable, thereby granting judicial sanction to the unfair practices of the legislature.

The performance of the state courts on the desegregation controversy in Rosedale was no less disappointing. Any attempt by the chancellor's office to end illegal racial isolation in IS 231 was carried out despite the action of the state courts rather than because of it. Indeed the events in that case suggest that the lower level of the state judiciary functions as an extension of the county political structure— an establishment that was found downright inimical to desegregation efforts.

The most troubling development in the external environment of the city school system is in the federal government. Ever since the Supreme Court handed down the *Brown* decision in 1954, advocates of equal rights have worked through the federal judiciary to protect the educational entitlements of such disadvantaged groups as the poor, racial minorities, language minorities, and the handicapped. Ever since the enactment of the Elementary and Secondary Education Act (ESEA) of 1965, the federal government has served as a crucial source of financial support for programs designed to upgrade the quality of educational services for the poor. Now the Reagan administration has pledged to turn back the clock. The retreat is manifest not only by a financial disinvestment in public education, but also by a reluctance on the part of federal attorneys to enforce civil rights through litigation. Consequently the Justice Department has adopted a softer position with regard to de jure segregation. In the meantime, the Secretary of Education attempted to implement new regulations that would weaken the protections afforded to the handicapped under Public Law 94-142. And while financially strapped state and local school officials are held responsible for the mandates imposed by the law, federal authorities refuse to carry their share of the burden.

Without doubt, the philosophy enunciated by the Reagan administration is a response to national public sentiment. It reflects a rising conservative tide that began with the election of Richard Nixon, and has been growing in both the executive and legislative branches of the government. It remains to be seen whether this conservative ideology will also come to dominate the Supreme Court, which, since the appointment of Chief Justice Warren Burger, has more closely reflected the increasingly conservative public philosophy of the nation.

The overall evidence on the subject is rather persuasive. For the most part, those major institutions that compose the external political environment of the city school system are unsympathetic to the interests of the population that consumes its service. In the hope of establishing new policies and programs more appropriate to the needs of the school population, the chancellor must negotiate his agenda through a local government that is elected primarily by the white middle class, a state government that has displayed a traditional antiurbanism, and a federal establishment that is bent on reducing its commitment to public education. These are the public authorities to whom the leadership of the school system is accountable. And herein lies the great dilemma of the chancellorship and the urban superintendency in general. Those authorities and groups to whom the chancellor is accountable are not particularly representative of the clientele that the school system is supposed to serve.

Of course, there are private interest groups to whom the chancellor is politically accountable, which have a basic commitment to public education. However, the impact these groups exert on the policy process is inadequate to overcome the environmental constraints that exist on an institutional level. In terms of influence, we have seen that first and foremost among these groups is the UFT. While the union has emerged as a major political force on behalf of public education in the city, the fact remains that its constituency comes from those who work in the public schools rather than those who attend them. For the most part, it can be said that the interests of these two groups have coincided. However, when they do not, it is logical to expect that the union will support the position of its members.

What remains in the immediate environment of the school system is the assortment of public interest groups in the city that have historically participated in the local policy process.[18] Few would deny that these groups harbor a genuine commitment to public education and the children who attend city schools. However, most local political observers would agree that the power of these groups has subsided, along with a formerly vocal and influential middle-class population that at one time had a more direct stake in the public schools. One might also add a caveat to this generally astute political observation: the power of these groups is most formidable when it is used against the leadership of the school system itself. Most conflicts of this sort concern questions of technique and are a natural outgrowth of the state of the art in the educational profession. We have previously referred to this phenomenon as ignorance. We have witnessed its presence in discussions on how best to upgrade the competency levels of students and how best to serve the needs of the handicapped. Those individuals most likely to engage seriously in such debate are those who care most about education. The net political effect of these conflicts, however, is to strengthen the arm of those who do not.

From the point of view of the chancellor's office, the participation of these educational interest groups in the policy process often represents a rather unprofitable political trade-off. Their influence is insufficient to alter substantially the institutional and political balance of power than penalizes the school system. However, given the fact that these groups often bring their own level of expertise to debates of a pedagogical nature, their opposition is potentially devastating.

In the final analysis, the case studies in this book give us much reason to question the conventional wisdom that once prevailed concerning the bureaucracy at Livingston Street. Prior to decentralization, critics of the central administration consistently described it as a closed system that was not responsive to the wants and needs of its clientele because it was not receptive to demands from the external environment. Now that diagnosis is at best only partially true. The bureaucracy at Livingston Street is indeed an open system, susceptible to the demands of a wide variety of outside institutions and groups. The problem is that the outside actors who are most successful at manipulating the system are not by and large representative of the service clientele who rely on the schools. Implementing change under these conditions is a rather precarious and paradoxical process. It must defy political reality. It involves attempting to make what is basically a highly political institution responsive to the needs of a population that does not possess the fundamental ingredients for political power.

BUILDING BRIDGES: RECOMMENDATIONS

An analysis of the events that occurred between 1978 and 1983 has led to several conclusions about the politics of education in New York, as seen from the perspective of the chancellor's office. We have observed that the chancellor is the object of numerous cross-pressures from the external environment which, if accommodated, would hinder the development of a consistent policy agenda for the school system. The volume and intensity of these demands from the outside have been found to be both a distraction from internal management and an obstacle to change. In light of the more normative ideals of democratic government, the most serious flaw in the present institutional arrangement arises from a notable gap between those constituents to whom the chancellor is legally or politically accountable and those clients whom the schools are supposed to serve.

The individuals identified as those to whom the chancellor is most directly accountable on a regular basis include the central Board of Education and the mayor. It should be further explained that the reporting relationship between the chancellor and the central Board reflects seven lines of accountability rather than one. While it is not particularly evident in the events described in this book, the truth of the matter is that the individuals who sit on the Board are often not in agreement. The five members appointed by the borough presidents all represent different geographical localities, each with its own parochial interests. The two members appointed by the mayor are usually drawn from different racial, ethnic, or religious groups. Therefore, although the leadership role of the chancellor's office was enhanced under Macchiarola, most insiders would agree that a good deal of staff time was spent appeasing and responding to the pet concerns of the seven individuals who inhabit the eleventh floor at Livingston Street.

Largely because of its concentrated power over the local budget, the mayor's office may be considered one of the two significant poles of external influence on educational policy in the city. (The other is the United Federation of Teachers.) In the implementation stage of policy, a third significant influence includes the local community school boards and their superintendents. Assuming that institutional reform will alter neither the power of the union nor its disposition on policy issues, the recommendations in this book focus on the remaining three institutions. Based on the political realities of the situation, the plan offered here is premised on the need to instill in the local governing institutions a closer identification with the problems of the school system and the interests of its clients.

The cornerstone of this "bridge-building" plan involves recasting the authority and responsibility of the mayor in the realm of education. Specifically, it calls for the elimination of the seven-member Board of Education, and the replacement of the chancellor with a commissioner of education. As is the case with most other municipal agencies in the city, the Commissioner of Education would serve at the pleasure of the mayor and become a member of the mayor's cabinet. This change would increase the accountability of the school system and center responsibility for the quality and effectiveness of educational services on a popularly elected official.

Since the turn of the century there has been a widely held notion in American education that the more detached schools are from the political process, the better. Educational policy making, it was believed, should be left in the hands of professionals, who come to the task with training and expertise. A popular spirit could be injected into the process by the selection of a lay board of education, but politicians were to be kept out at any cost. Although we have now moved well into the last quarter of the century, large remnants of the old philosophy and tradition still exist. It is manifest through the existence of autonomous and semi-autonomous school boards, which hide behind an artificial shield that bears the inscription "Keep politics out of education." In most cases, this shield is deeply penetrated by the realities of political life. To the extent that it does provide shelter, it functions merely to protect a more narrow arena of school politics—but politics it is, just the same. The New York City Board of Education is a case in point.

Historically, the New York City Board of Education has served as protector of one of the most entrenched public bureaucracies in the history of the nation. The ranks of that institution had temporarily been infiltrated by outsiders. However, few contemporary observers would argue that the survival of the central Board has worked to remove politics from the policy process. Certainly the preceding chapters offer ample testimony to the contrary. In fact, the events described show quite clearly that, rather than serving the interests of the school system and its children, the intended separation has often worked to their disadvantage.

Admittedly, a good part of the budgetary tension between City Hall and Livingston Street is constituency-based, for those people who elect the mayor are not by and large the ones that use the public schools. However, that explanation does not tell the entire story. The present institutional setup cultivates a natural animosity, and when hostilities are played out, the schools are the losers. Because the mayor appoints only two members of the seven-person Board, he enjoys the luxury of deflecting any real responsibility for what happens in education. Given this option, a popularly elected chief executive can be expected to direct budgetary priorities toward the services for which he bears direct responsibility. As the events surrounding local budget negotiations have illustrated, the school budget has been a major source of frustration to municipal officials. Their only direct and unambiguous connection to it is on the paying end. Financial accountability has been at best difficult and generally quarrelsome. It is not surprising, therefore, that the mayor at times has been a reluctant giver. A more direct reporting line between City Hall and Livingston Street could only help to alleviate the tensions that have been so evident. It would give the mayor a more personal stake in the future of public education.

The creation of a city commissioner of education appointed by and responsible to the mayor would also carry several managerial benefits. First, there would be the obvious savings resulting from the elimination of the seven-member Board of Education, whose budget exceeded $1.5 million in the 1982 fiscal year.[19] More important, an education commissioner in the mayor's cabinet would provide a more appropriate institutional setting for the better coordination of youth-related services. There are now a number of municipal agencies in New York that provide important direct services to young people, including such general areas as health, mental health, parks, recreation, library, employment, and counseling. However, coordination among these services has been meager, particularly since schools, the agents that provide the most important service to the young, are part of a semiautonomous agency that has historically placed a high value on separation.

Mayor Edward Koch recognized this coordination problem in early 1982, when he created a Mayor's Task Force on Youth, the purpose of which was to bring about better cooperation among the various service agencies. By appointing the chancellor of schools as chairman of the task force, Koch hoped to lessen the gap that has traditionally existed between the schools and municipal agencies. While this move was a step in the right direction, it did not go far enough. The Chancellor of Schools had no real line authority over the heads of the municipal agencies that belonged to the task force, nor did the mayor have any over the chancellor. What is really needed to facilitate the coordination task is the appointment of a deputy mayor for youth services, as there once existed a deputy mayor for criminal justice. The new deputy mayor would enjoy direct line authority over all municipal agencies that provide essential basic services to youth. However, for this institutional arrangement to be effective, the group of agency heads would have to include a commissioner of education appointed by, and accountable to, the mayor.

A more moderate plan for institutional reform would maintain a semiautonomous school Board but authorize the mayor to appoint a majority or all of its members. This plan would increase the mayor's role in educational affairs but keep the official policy-making body separate from City Hall. Unlike the present Board, the members of such a body might be nonsalaried, and spend a minimal amount of time at Livingston Street. They would represent a cross section of distinguished educational, civic, business, and labor leaders from the city.

Some would argue that such a moderate plan is more likely to receive support from education groups and therefore is more politically feasible than the commissioner plan outlined above.

This moderate plan does have several drawbacks, however. For those who place a high value on political responsibility, keeping policy making in the hands of nonelected officials is somewhat problematic. While the prescription for distinguished membership is commendable, it also leaves room for subjective judgments, political bargaining, abuse, and inappropriate selections. Maintaining a semi-autonomous school board would also perpetuate the problems of service integration that now exist between the school system and municipal agencies. Increasing the membership of the Board would exacerbate the managerial problems inherent in multiple reporting lines. Nevertheless, this moderate proposal to give the mayor a more direct institutional stake in education is preferable to the present arrangement.

Conceivably, there are those who could offer a rather strong political argument against enhancing the power of the mayor in education. After all, it has already been emphasized that the political constituency that elects the mayor is not the same as the clientele of the schools. What would prevent the mayor from further decimating the school budget, along the lines of Koch's original and more drastic proposals for retrenchment? Was it not the Board of Education's political independence (or, more accurately, its semi-autonomy) that allowed it to contest the mayor's financial plan each year?

There is some validity to the above argument, but it is only partial. The seven-member Board of Education in itself did not represent a significant force on behalf of the school budget. Quite frankly, the Board does not enjoy a substantial amount of credibility on the local political scene. Perhaps the semiautonomous institutional arrangement did allow the chancellor to be a more aggressive advocate for his agency than a mayorally appointed commissioner could be. However, what made Macchiarola effective was his own personal accomplishments as chancellor. What gave him access to City Hall was the fact that he had been the mayor's own personal choice for the position that he held. What gave him credibility was his own personal relationship with the mayor, which, despite disagreements, was a good one. In the end, however, if one considers the institutional question apart from any set of personalities, the real political support for the schools must come from the communities, not the chancellor's office. This brings us to our final recommendation regarding New York City.

School decentralization has provided educators with an institutional advantage that is not available to any other local service agency in New York. That advantage is the potential for developing a broad political base. There are thirty-two neighborhood boards, popularly elected by people who live or work in the city's communities. The problem, however, as suggested earlier, is that local school boards are not always representative of the children who attend the schools. The turnout for school board elections, somewhere around 10 percent city-wide, is appallingly low. Because these contests are held at a different time from the November general elections, most people are unfamiliar with the candidates or the issues. School board elections are nonevents that take place in the city once every three years, with little recognition or interest.

The balloting for community school board members should be held at the same time as the regular November election, to maximize popular participation and provide an incentive to candidates to make themselves and their positions known. While changing the time of elections will not necessarily engage the poorest and most alienated sector of the population in political activity, the wider participation that can be expected should result in a more representative electorate, or at least, an electorate that has more in common with the clientele of the school system. For political activists who have devoted time and energy to public education, a more meaningful election for school board members can offer a significant forum for broadening the political base behind their cause.

These proposals are not meant to further politicize the educational profession in New York City. What these proposals are meant to do is recognize the political realities of educational policy making in order to erect an institutional structure more responsive to the needs of public schoolchildren. The years of the Macchiarola administration have demonstrated that it is possible to have strong educational leadership simultaneously within the central headquarters of the system and in the community districts. We must now take the next step. The schools need sympathetic and strong managerial leadership from City Hall, supported and instructed by a broad political base in the communities.

TOWARD AN AGENDA FOR URBAN EDUCATION

One question remains. What can be learned from the experiences and circumstances in New York City that is relevant elsewhere? Many people consider New York unique among urban school systems. In actuality, its most distinguishing feature is its size—a factor that more peculiarly defines the internal managerial tasks of the system than it does those critical variables which shape its external dynamics. As far as the multiple forces in its political and social environment are concerned, New York shares a lot with most urban school systems, not to mention a growing number of suburban districts that are undergoing significant changes in size and population.

Most inner-city school districts now serve children recruited predominantly from poor and minority populations. Since the enactment of Public Law 94-142, each has been called upon to become more sensitive to the needs of handicapped children. Many urban school systems have been through a tumultuous experience with desegregation, which in many cases has aggravated racial tensions in already polarized communities. No public school system in the country has escaped the painful financial retrenchment imposed by all levels of government, nor have many remained unaffected by a declining public confidence in the educational system. These are issues not just in New York; they are problems indigenous to an increasingly urbanized nation.

Local governing structures of school systems vary widely. However, all are accountable to the same assortment of public authorities at other levels of government. Notwithstanding the rhetoric and reforms of the 1960s, school districts are probably the most open of all local service-delivery systems in terms of the number of outside officials to whom they must respond. In addition to reporting to local school boards, many superintendents in financially dependent districts are accountable to municipal officials and a local legislature. Beyond the local level, all school districts must function within the rules and regulations set by a state commissioner and board of regents. One might add to this list, as in New York, a state legislature, state courts, federal courts, and the federal administrative and regulatory structure in Washington. From a political point of view, the constraints and hostilities imposed on New York by this external environment also have a more general applicability. The anti-urban bias of many state legislatures is a well-documented fact of American political life. The federal retreat from public education during the Reagan administration will exact its toll in all school districts, urban and nonurban alike.

Despite New York's distinguishing characteristics, therefore, there are some general lessons to be drawn from the events described in these pages. First and foremost, these examples reinforce the notion, becoming more common in the professional literature, that the job of the urban school superintendent is a highly political one. In addition to being the educational leader of a school district, the superintendent must also serve as chief political actor. One must further incorporate into this delicate position the roles of policy maker, manager, advocate, image maker, change agent, disciplinarian, and diplomat. The irony of the situation is that the more skilled a superintendent is at the political role, the less constrained he or she is by political forces. The fact remains, however, that, given the urban school clientele, urban superintendents enter the political arena with the odds against them.

The "across the river" mentality that characterizes Livingston Street's attitude toward the municipal government has its counterpart in other urban school systems. We have already noted that political separatism is part and parcel of the American education tradition. However, what was once a relevant and useful principle has become a nonfunctioning, if not unachievable goal. As the clients of urban school systems have become more homogeneous and less influential, there is a real danger that institutional separatism will become transformed into political isolation at the local level, where there is a dichotomy between those officials who are responsible for public education and those whose support is needed for its success. Local school systems will continue to be affected by the actions and policies of a variety of actors at all levels of government. However, as the evidence in these pages demonstrates, it is becoming increasingly important to assure that government officials at the local level have a direct interest in the operation of the public schools.

There are other important lessons to be learned from these chapters, lessons more concerned with policy than with politics, and somewhat more positive than the preceding ones. We have already spent a good deal of time discussing professional ignorance and its causal relationship to political conflict. Something needs to be said now about what we know. Again, the New York experience fits well into a pattern of research observations that have been recorded elsewhere.

The outcomes in New York are consistent with a growing body of social research, conceived largely in the early 1970s, which tells us that, in an appropriate educational setting, inner-city children can be effectively taught, regardless of race or class. This research on effective schools also tells us that an appropriate educational setting for minority children does not necessarily include the presence of white classmates. We now know that minority children do not need to be mixed with white children in order to derive the benefits of effective instruction. They are perfectly capable of constituting an appropriate collegial setting on their own, so long as other instructional, affective, and material factors are provided within the school environment. To some of us, this conclusion may not sound very astounding. However, we must keep in mind that it runs contrary to the conventional science wisdom that once dominated the educational profession and, unfortunately, still prevails in many places today.

What we are saying here about effective schools has significant implications beyond the realm of instructional strategy. It also impinges upon the more controversial issue of school desegregation. Since the original *Brown* decision in 1954, we have learned much about desegregation. Taken together with what we know about effective schools, the research on desegregation can tell policy makers a good deal about the consequences of various actions. While there is no persuasive evidence that school desegregation has a significant impact on either the self-image or the achievement levels of minority children, we do know that forced integration and busing result in white flight. There is also some indication that integrated schooling helps cultivate racial tolerance among children, but the evidence is inconclusive. Whether forced integration breeds such tolerance remains highly questionable.

What does all this tell us about the efficacy and desirability of our policy options? It certainly does not mean that intentional racial isolation is more tolerable now than it was thirty years ago. De jure segregation remains both ethically and legally indefensible. Also, there are those among us who personally believe that a racially integrated school setting is preferable to a segregated one. However, the evidence warns against a public policy that treats racial integration as a goal in itself, no matter what the cost. It suggests that, where feasible, it is advisable to achieve desegregation through voluntary means rather than by methods that lead to resentment, conflict, and the further abandonment of public education by the middle class. Given what we now know about effective schools, perhaps there is no longer any need to mourn the flight of the middle class because of its atmospheric effect on the learning process. However, white and middle-class flight is costly, for it weakens the political base of the urban school system. And, as our chronicle of the budget wars has shown, this political base determines the level of resources available to the schools.

The most constructive way of attracting the middle class back to the public schools is to demonstrate that these schools can be instructionally effective. From the research literature that has been mentioned, we are now aware of the environmental and human variables essential to do this. First and foremost are positive attitudes among classroom teachers. If children are confronted with adult convictions of their own uneducability, then we can expect that it will have an adverse effect on student achievement. This is true of black students and of white, whether they be in an integrated or segregated setting.

The magnitude of the evidence on the effect of teachers' attitudes is so persuasive that it dictates a policy calling for a larger investment of public resources in teacher training. Such instruction should emphasize the affective realm of the classroom, but it must also go beyond this. The level of confidence that a professional brings to an inner-city school does not depend totally on racial attitudes. It also reflects a sense of preparedness in the subject matter, teaching technique, and classroom management skills. Thus there is a serious need for further public investment in the development of the teaching force.

The case study in the preceding chapter documents the kind of institutional obstacles that can prevent school administrators from the proper disciplining or removal of undesirable teaching personnel. This is not a problem that is peculiar to New York. The case points to a widespread need to develop fair and effective means for processing charges against teachers. However, the issue of discipline is only part of a much larger problem that is just beginning to reach the public consciousness. It calls for a total reassessment of the teaching profession.

One might argue that recognizing the problems pervading this troubled profession is the first step toward remedy. However, popularization of the issue also carries some inherent dangers. It paves the way for piecemeal observations and simplistic solutions. We have rediscovered in the eighties, what we already knew in the sixties and seventies, that public education is in trouble. However, blaming the teachers is no more appropriate now than was blaming the kids in previous decades. This situation calls for a comprehensive examination of the education, certification, compensation, development, rewards, assessment, and supervision of individuals within the teaching profession. It requires a shared responsibility among universities, state education boards, public officials, budget planners, and school administrators at all levels. It requires commitment and support.

We now know that if we want children to improve in their basic reading, writing, and computation skills, we must stress the importance of these subjects. Such emphasis need not be at the expense of all other subjects, but it should go beyond a mere declaration of expectations. It must also involve the proper support services and regular feedback to students on their success or progress. It must guarantee the availability of remediation for those children who fall behind. Whether or not using competency tests to determine eligibility for grade advancement is preferable to social promotion is still debated among professionals. However, the experience in New York did show that, with the appropriate support services, performance on competency tests did improve. It also suggested that if we raise our expectations and challenge, then students will respond with a higher level of achievement.[20]

We can also conclude from the outcome of the promotional gates program in New York that there is a population of inner-city schoolchildren who cannot be adequately reached through traditional modes of instruction. In New York they are called the double holdovers. These children have much in common with many of those who exhibit behavioral problems, who have been labeled "handicapped," about whom professionals also feel uncertain when it comes to selecting appropriate strategies for instruction. The existence of such a substantial and ever-growing population for whom we are ill prepared emphasizes the need for more experimentation and research in the field of alternative education. Recent literature on the subject shows that alternative education does not necessarily mean a total break with the mainstream, nor does it require the dilution of standards or traditional instructional objectives.[21] A greater public investment in alternative education would allow educators to recognize the diverse needs of our pluralistic urban populations without necessarily burdening children with labels that are detrimental to human development.

We now have at our disposal a voluminous body of social research that demonstrates quite convincingly that throwing dollars at problems does not make them go away. Alas, an entire field of evaluative research has also emerged to document the failure of social programs and the waste of public money that accompanies such failure. Many of these assessments have been in the field of education, and their results have been used, sometimes inappropriately, as part of the rationale for a federal disinvestment in services to the young. The fact remains, however, that much work still needs to be done. While more dollars alone will not provide us with the resources necessary to get the job accomplished, further cutbacks in federal, state, and local spending could assure failure. Innovative efforts along the lines of smaller class sizes in the early grades, remedial instruction, teacher training, and experimentation or research on alternative approaches all cost money. Maintaining a safe, comfortable school environment through the proper upkeep, cleaning, and heating of school buildings costs money. Because of inflation, more money is needed to maintain services at a consistent and acceptable level. Because of serious local retrenchment, urban school districts are more dependent on federal support than ever before. Thus, any serious attempt to improve the performance of urban schools necessitates a restoration of federal funding beyond the levels that have existed over the last several years.

Inner-city school administrators in general, and superintendents in particular, will have to make better use of the public resources available to them. Intergovernmental transfers can no longer be considered free money, and used to swell local coffers without any recognizable impact in the classroom. There must be a greater focus on managerial accountability. But accountability should not be translated to mean less spending. Rather, it implies accepting responsibility for the quality and effects of services delivered at the school level. It means making better use of available dollars. It requires more sophisticated management and financial control systems than are commonly found in school districts.

The major task before the urban superintendent is to regain the credibility that public education in the City once enjoyed. Of course, the first step in this direction is to produce positive results. That is a weighty assignment in itself. However, the obstacles to good public image go beyond considerations of merit. They are philosophical and psychological. They are found in a deep-seated public skepticism about urban schools and the educability of the children who attend them. The good news notwithstanding, many of those who make decisions about the future of public education are predisposed to put more stock in the stories of failure. Negativism has become part of a public tradition. Therein lies the most difficult and enduring challenge.

NOTES

1. *Levittown* v. *Nyquist,* 57 N.Y. 2d 27, 453 NYS 2d 643 (1982).

2. Koch's executive budget called for increases in the following services: police, $46,495,000; corrections, $22,148,000; social services, $113,080,000; fire, $15,955,000; sanitation, $27,164,000; transportation, $14,657,000.

3. Board of Education, City of New York, press release, June 15, 1982.

4. Ibid.

5. Ibid.

6. Ibid.

7. Ibid.

8. Frank J. Macchiarola, "Memorandum to Members of the Board of Education, Regarding Summer Promotional Gates Program," September 8, 1982.

9. Board of Education, City of New York, press release, June 15, 1982.

10. Frank J. Macchiarola, "Memorandum to Members of the Board of Education, Regarding Summer Promotional Gates Program," September 8, 1982.

11. "Monitoring Promotional Policies: A Parent Documentation" United Parents Associations, May 1982.

12. Office of the Mayor, City of New York, "The Mayor's Management Report," January 1983.

13. Ibid.

14. *Board of Education of Hendrick Hudson Central School District* v. *Rowley,* 50 U.S.L.W. 4925, June 28, 1982.

15. *Crawford* v. *Board of Education of Los Angeles,* 50 U.S.L.W. 5016, June 30, 1982.

16. *Washington* v. *Seattle School District No. 1,* 50 U.S.L.W. 4998, June 30, 1982.

17. See David Rogers, "School Decentralization: It Works," *Social Policy* 12 (Spring 1982); "Does Decentralization Work?" *The Urban Lawyer* 14 (Summer 1982).

18. Among those already mentioned are the Educational Priorities Panel, the United Parents' Associations, Advocates for Children, and the Public Education Association. However, the list of groups that actually exist is much longer.

19. This figure includes the budgets for the Board of Education, the secretary and counsel to the Board of Education, and the legislative representative of the Board of Education.

20. On the subject of the relationship between challenge and achievement, see Jeanne S. Chall *et al.,* "An Analysis of Textbooks in Relation to SAT Scores," prepared for the Advisory Panel on the Scholastic Aptitude Test Decline, jointly sponsored by the College Board and Educational Testing Service, June 1977; Jeanne S. Chall, "Some Thoughts on the Status of Literacy" (paper presented at the National Academy of Education, May 1982).

21. See Mario Fantini, "Mainstreaming Alternatives," *Social Policy* 12 (September–October 1981).

ADDENDUM FOR SOCIAL SCIENTISTS

The case studies in this book have allowed us to explore the relationship between a large public bureaucracy and its external environment. Its findings suggest that the governance of this institution is influenced by a number of external actors, and that the interaction among them is highly conflictual. The conflict was explained in terms of the different policy preferences of the actors, as they perceived situations in terms of their own welfare (interest), and the uncertainty surrounding the means by which policy goals could be best achieved (ignorance). It was pointed out that the first factor is consistent with a tradition of interest group theory prominent in political science. The entire explanation was derived from a well-known model of organizational decision making conceived by Simon, refined by Thompson and Tuden, and later espoused by Landau.[1] The model suggests that judgment, compromise, bargaining, and, one might add, conflict result when there is disagreement or uncertainty regarding either the ends or means of decision options. The existence and importance of the model suggest that uncertainty (or ignorance) in the realm of organizational decision making is not peculiar to the institution that was the subject of our case studies, nor is it limited to the field of public education.

It was concluded from our case studies that the dichotomy which exists between the constituents and clients of the institution studied has a negative impact on its internal management and its aptitude for responsiveness and change. This analytical distinction between constituent and client is relevant to other urban service institutions that serve a predominantly poor clientele, and it has theoretical implications beyond these case studies. The following discussion addresses the significance of this analytical distinction within the context of the existing social science literature on organizational environments.

ORGANIZATIONS AND ENVIRONMENTS

Students of complex organizations have long recognized the importance of investigating the relationship between bureaucratic institutions and their environments. Even Max Weber, who is usually associated with the "closed system" approach, examined the impact of social structure on bureaucracy during the course of his comparative historical studies. In his early discourse on the role of the executive, Chester Barnard brought attention to the influence of social variables on both the viability and decision structures of organizations.[2] Barnard's ideas were further developed by Herbert Simon. In a refinement of Barnard's equilibrium theory, Simon observed that in order to keep an organization operable, an executive not only must provide employees with incentives to adopt organizational goals, but also needs to maintain the support of outside clients and suppliers.[3] With James March, Simon went on to demonstrate that scarcity of resources in the organizational environmment has a causal effect on the level of internal conflict.[4]

As the "open systems" approach grew popular in the professional literature, it became more common for scholars to view organizations as being responsive to ever-changing environmental inputs, and to portray structure and behavior as being in a constant state of flux.[5] Thompson and McEwen wrote that since goal setting is essentially a process of defining desired relationships between an organization and its environment, a change in the latter requires an alteration in the former.[6] Adopting the environmental context, Etzioni and Perrow would later introduce the concepts of power and conflict into organizational models of goal formation.[7]

Gouldner described the new theoretical orientation in terms of a "natural" as opposed to the traditional "rationalist" approach.[8] Burns and Stalker distinguished between an "organic" and "mechanistic" approach.[9] Behavioral scientists were reacting to a once commonly held notion that organizations could (or should) be kept separate and apart from the larger social setting—a boundary that was presumed to maximize managerial control and efficiency.

James Thompson later sought to integrate the two traditions. While recognizing that organizations are constantly subject to the uncertain influences of a changing environment, he found that they also attempt to achieve rationality through closedness.[10] Building on the work of Talcott Parsons, he assigned the task of mediating the boundary of external interference to the managerial leader.[11] This protective phenomenon was regularly exhibited in the previous case studies, particularly when political actors sought to involve themselves in educational policy making or implementation. Thus, while developing his model in an open system context, Thompson asserted that certain organizational actors could influence and modify the level of external interference on internal operations.

A substantial literature has emerged over the last two decades that is concerned with the description, classification, and significance of various types of organizational environments. Emery and Trist focused on the causal texture of the environment, which they treated as a quasi-independent domain, and developed a four-class typology ranging from "placid randomized" to "turbulent."[12] Their purpose was to design a conceptual technique for assessing whether particular external settings had a stabilizing or a disruptive influence on organizational life.

Among the early empirical contributions to the research was the work of Paul Lawrence and Jay Lorsch, who examined corporate structures in the plastics, food-processing, and container industries. Lawrence and Lorsch challenged the idea that there is any "one best way" to design an administrative structure. Instead they found that, since differing environments place differing demands upon organizations, high performance levels are more likely to result when organizations adapt their structure to the needs of the environment.[13] This approach has become known as contingency theory. Shortly thereafter, Terreberry completed a comprehensive review of the existing research literature. It resulted in a two-point hypothesis that would serve as a precursor to a substantial and significant body of future work.[14] The first point suggested that organizational change is increasingly becoming externally induced. The second proposed that organizational adaptability and survival are a function of the ability to learn and perform according to changes in the environment.

Two important lines of thinking followed.[15] A "resource dependence" approach grew out of the understanding that no organization is capable of generating all the resources necessary for goal attainment or survival.[16] It focused on the interorganizational exchanges that take place, and gave particular attention to the strategies institutional leaders adopt to enhance their bargaining positions and prevent their organizations from becoming overly dependent upon others. A "natural selection" model, born out of a tradition of social Darwinism, treats organizations as populations rather than individual systems.[17] It utilizes a concept of environmental adaptation to explain how certain organizations survive or thrive while others become extinct.

As the analysis on the preceding pages indicates, notable progress was made in our understanding of environmental contexts during the middle and late 1970s. However, while this literature made a rich contribution to behavioral theory, the fact remains that a large portion of the empirical work on the subject focused on private sector organizations. While this work has been informative and useful to students of the public sector, its applicability has been limited. Nobody who has read the preceding case studies needs to be told that the resource dependence model is relevant to the public sector. Political economists have adopted this model and used it productively in their own research.[18] As retrenchment and termination become more common themes in government, so will the concern for organizational survival.[19] Nevertheless, the questions remain: Have public sector scholars made the best use of private sector models? Has there been adequate refinement and adaptation?

To some extent public sector analysts, in an attempt to reap the benefits of the work done by their private sector colleagues, have let the latter set their agenda. This at times has been inappropriate. While survival may be the bottom line issue in the corporate world, it is one of many important concerns in the government agency. Normative inquiries that deal with issues such as representativeness, responsiveness, and equity are at least of equal importance. As the research in the preceding chapters suggests, the student of public administration might more appropriately investigate the environmental conditions under which government bureaucracies are most responsive to the needs of the clientele they are supposed to serve.

THE PUBLIC PERSPECITVE

There is no intention here to suggest that empirical research on the relationship between public bureaucracies and their environments is either nonexistent or insignificant, for that is not the case. Peter Selznick's case study of the Tennessee Valley Authority was one of the first empirical analyses of the environmental context.[20] In education, Burton Clark demonstrated how adult clients in a service environment could have a direct impact on the organizational goals of a college.[21] In the health field, Levine and White documented the interdependence of public agencies and their need to establish exchange networks in order to be successful.[22]

Notwithstanding important contributions to the professional literature like the aforementioned, a good deal of the research on public bureaucracies and their environments has been one-dimensional. Taking its cue from the private realm, the public administration literature has displayed a preoccupation with the question of organizational survival. Political scientists, for example, have given much attention to the role that powerful client or constituent groups play in helping government agencies secure, maintain, or increase their operating budgets.[23] They have observed that government agencies, in order to cultivate the support of such outside groups, have often fallen under the control of the interest groups they are supposed to serve or regulate.[24] But the focus of this research on the budget process has served as a proxy for the more general issue of agency survival, and in this sense has been limiting.

In a recent study of finance departments across the United States, Marshall Meyer presented and verified a four-point hypothesis on the relationship between public agencies and their environment. He found:

1. The structure and behavior of public bureaus are largely shaped by external forces.
2. This pattern is not necessarily dysfunctional because it may mean that government agencies are properly more open to external pressures than popular beliefs suggest.
3. Environmental effects may be mediated by a variety of mechanisms, such as the stability and nature of organizational leadership.
4. Many ongoing organizations do not change fast enough, and hence are rendered inconsistent with their environment and are replaced.[25]

The first finding, concerning the influence of external forces, is consistent with the private sector observations previously cited. The fourth finding, dealing with adaptation, is indicative once more of the consistent concern for survival in public administration research. The third directs us to the characteristics and strategies of organizations that enable them to deal with complex environments. It is particularly relevant to the case studies in this book. Enough has been said about these issues already. We will here focus on Meyer's second point.

Meyer's second hypothesis is indicative of a more general normative concern that is central in public administration. It is connected to a fundamental and aged question, which can be articulated as follows: "Given that those officials who run the public bureaucracy are not elected, can they be responsive to the external political environment?" In other words, are these institutions closed systems that are remote from such influences? Meyer, like many before him, has found that public bureaucracies indeed are open systems. However, like others, Meyer does not take the question to its logical conclusion. "To whom," we might ask, "are these institutions open?" Like most institutions in government, our public bureaucracies are often responsive to particular constituencies. But the crucial question is not whether our bureaucratic institutions are responsive to public influence, but whether those groups that exert influence are representative of the entire public, or at least that public for whom specific services are to be provided. It is for this reason that the analytical distinction between organizational constituent and organizational client is significant. It is for this reason that the analytical distinction has normative implications concerning social equity.

BUREAUCRACY AND EQUITY

The question of the relationship between bureaucratic organization in government and the goal of social equity is an old one. Max Weber, one of the first and foremost students of the subject, found the relationship to be quite definite. Weber recognized the threat bureaucratic institutions pose to both democratic government and the human spirit. However, he also found that these institutions, which he believed were capable of making decisions according to "purely objective considerations"[26] without regard to preference or favor, were an effective ally to the principle of equality. Weber understood that, in an attempt to operate in a rational and efficient way, in accordance with established rules of procedure, administrative officials would provide each individual in society with "equality of treatment," regardless of social status.[27]

A review of the research literature on service distributions within urban public bureaucracies gives credence to the notion of equity articulated by Max Weber. A number of multi-agency studies in several American cities show that internal rules of procedure that influence bureaucratic decision making contribute to a pattern of distribution that is fair and nondiscriminatory.[28] In some cases the pattern of distribution actually was found to favor the poor, whose service needs tend to exceed those of the general population. Given the notion of bureaucracy that dominated the professional literature during the 1960s and early 1970s, these findings were rather startling. They gave rise to a new optimism concerning the role municipal bureaucracies might play on behalf of the interests of the poor. Nevertheless, one must be careful not to overstate the case.

To begin with, the role service agencies play in the local allocation process is a limited one.[29] Crucial decisions concerning the resource levels that specific agencies have available to them are generally determined legislatively—usually with the input of the local chief executive. As our case study on the budget process has demonstrated, agencies that cater to a predominantly poor clientele are at a competitve disadvantage in such highly political contests. Moreover, the evidence on bureaucratic decisions regarding agency service distributions, though encouraging, is mixed. In some cases the poor have fared better than in others. Henceforth, an appropriate line of inquiry would attempt to identify conditions under which local agencies are most likely to make distributive decisions according to criteria that are fair. That question once again brings us to the environmental context.

My own research, both primary and secondary, suggests that equitable distributive decisions are more likely to emerge from agencies where external political interference is minimized.[30] The logic here suggests that the poor are at a distinct disadvantage when distributive decisions are a function of influence. Conversely, the poor are more likely to fare well when distributive decisions are made according to objective bureaucratic criteria of service need. Thus there appears to be a correlation between closed decision structures and equitable outcomes. These findings are consistent with the Weberian model of bureaucracy, which links technical rationality and equality of outcomes. However, the findings also run contrary to another traditionally held notion in public administration which associates the "closedness" of bureacratic institutions with their inability to respond to the needs and wants of the poor. Nearly a decade of social reform was dedicated to the goal of making urban bureaucracies more open and accessible to the public, so that they might be more sensitive to the diverse needs of inner-city populations, especially the poor.[31] And it was here in particular that a lack of conceptual clarity concerning the distinction between constituent and client tended to lead us astray in terms of both our research inquiries and our prescriptions for institutional reform. True, decentralization changed the procedural rules for administrative politics at the local level, but it is questionable whether it succeeded in altering the power relationships among different groups.

The campaign for decentralization and community control that grew out of the 1960s was based upon two important but faulty assumptions. The first held that urban service organizations were closed systems, remote from the influence of the external environment. The second held that institutional reform would lead to a greater degree of control by those population groups that were the primary service recipients. To state it differently, there was an implicit understanding that an absence of client influence was tantamount to a closed system. Conversely, there was an underlying expectation that increased openness would result in greater client control. The fact of the matter is that in most instances local agencies are responsive to the demands of an external constituency, but in many cases that constituency is not representative of the agency client. This is particularly true in service agencies with a predominantly poor clientele. Thus, from a normative perspective the analytic distinction between organizational constituent and organizational client is a significant one.

CONSTITUENTS AND CLIENTS

Political and social scientists have always understood the difference between constituents and clients. However, there has been a tendency in the professional literature to use the terms interchangeably. There has been an implicit assumption, often correct, that the constituents and clients in a given organizational environment had a common identity. The result, however, has often been analytical confusion—not to mention faulty assertions and conclusions.

Part of the confusion can be traced to the origin of the terms themselves. The term "client" comes to us from the sociological literature on organizations. It refers to customers or service recipients. While it was clearly understood that organizations must accommodate the needs of their clients in order to survive, the concept of client did not originally involve any notion of accountability. The term "constituent" is derived from the political science literature on legislatures. It refers to those population groups that elect a legislator to office and to whom the official is accountable.[32] References to organizational or agency constituents grew out of a later understanding by political scientists that public bureaucracies are political institutions in need of external support, and therefore are accountable to outside groups. The two concepts (constituent and client) were finally merged with the discovery of the "iron triangle" relationship, sometimes known as subsystem politics, which exists among interest groups, legislative committees, and public agencies.[33] The merger was reasonable, in the sense that the constituency to which legislators and executives were accountable were often one and the same with the agency client. In return for access and service, these constituent groups would support the election campaigns of legislators and the budget requests of agencies.

An examination of the logic behind such triangular relationships is very telling. As Wilson explains it, client politics results in a situation where a relatively small, easily organized group will benefit from policies in which the costs are widely distributed and insignificant at a per capita rate.[34] Client politics works when the incentive for a small influential group to support a policy outweighs the incentive for a broader political population to oppose it. In such cases, the client is the only active political constituency in the policy arena. It often achieves victory by default, because of the apathy or disinterest of the larger population in the issue at hand.

Let us now consider another scenario—that concerning the local social service (or public education) agency in an urban setting. Here the clientele cannot ordinarily be expected to be politically influential.

While it is generally composed of a popular and racial minority, its membership is large and therefore the costs of the service can be relatively high. The costs are particularly conspicuous in a period of retrenchment or scarcity, when resources committed to one service can cause reductions in others. Here the incentive for opposition by those without a direct stake in the social service is real. Hence the attentive constituency in the larger decision arena is no longer synonymous with the client. In fact the interests of the client and constituent are at loggerheads. In such situations the subsystem breaks down and no longer works to the benefit of the client. Under such conditions the analytical distinction between constituent and client is quite significant.

Now let us consider the internal dynamics of a public organization where the client and constituent are not the same. The professional ethos among service providers in such a setting may dictate a primary commitment to service recipients. However, political realities may require that an inordinate amount of energy be devoted to appeasing those constituent groups which can influence the viability of the agency. Thus while professionals in a social service agency may espouse one orientation, they can conceivably be torn in another direction when political forces are not sympathetic to the interests of their clients. To use the terminology of Argyris and Schon,[35] the "espoused theory" and the "theory in use" that prevail in the organization are inconsistent. Thus, there is confusion with regard to expectations, behavior, loyalties, commitment, and the criteria by which performance should and will be evaluated.

Finally, let us consider the role of the leader in an organization where there is a dichotomy between constituent and client. As the preceding case studies indicate, that situation exacerbates the political demands on the agency head. It means that policies initiated on behalf of the client must often be carried on despite external pressure rather than because of it. Such situations require a leadership style characterized by temporary and fleeting alliances rather than the long-standing coalitions that characterize subsystem politics. To adapt Thompson's framework,[36] it becomes extremely important for the leader to maintan and protect the boundary of external interference—requiring that he or she devote an extraordinary amount of energy to constituent groups, with the hope that agency personel will thus be allowed to focus more attention on the wants and needs of clients.

In conclusion, it can be said that the analytical distinction between organizational constituents and organizational clients is highly significant in public sector research. It has serious implications regarding the normative issues of representativeness and responsiveness. It can provide us with more sophisticated tools for defining the conditions under which public agencies are capable of operating according to fair and equitable standards. This analytical distinction also allows us to understand more clearly the leadership role in service agencies that are meant to serve the poor. It serves to illustrate that organizational change does not necessarily mean making urban service systems more open to external pressure. Urban service agencies are indeed open systems. Change on behalf of the poor requires tampering with relationships that already exist between the organization and its environment and violating the political premises upon which they are founded.

NOTES

1. Herbert Simon, *Administrative Behavior* (New York: Collier-Macmillan, 1947); James D. Thompson and Arthur Tuden, "Strategies, Structures and Processes of Organizational Decision," in J. D. Thompson et al., eds., *Comparative Studies in Administration* (Pittsburgh, Pa.: University of Pittsburgh Press, 1959); Martin Landau, "Decision Theory and Comparative Public Administration," *Comparative Political Studies* 1 (July 1968).

2. Chester Barnard, *The Functions of the Executive* (Cambridge: Harvard University Press, 1938).

3. Simon, *Administrative Behavior*.

4. James G. March and Herbert A. Simon, *Organizations* (New York: John Wiley, 1958). See also Richard Cyert and James G. March, *A Behavioral Theory of the Firm* (Englewood Cliffs, N.J.: Prentice Hall, 1963).

5. Daniel Katz and Robert Kahn, *The Social Psychology of Organizations* (New York: John Wiley, 1966).

6. James D. Thompson and William J. McEwen, "Organizational Goals and Environment," *American Sociological Review* 23 (February 1958).

7. Amitai Etzioni, *Modern Organizations* (Englewood Cliffs, N.J.: Prentice-Hall, 1964); Charles Perrow, "The Analysis of Goals in Complex Organizations," *American Sociological Review*, 26 (December 1961).

8. Alvin W. Gouldner, *Patterns of Industrial Bureaucracy* (New York: The Free Press, 1954).

9. Tom Burns and G. M. Stalker, *The Management of Innovation* (London: Tavistock, 1961).

10. James D. Thompson, *Organizations in Action* (New York: McGraw-Hill, 1967).

11. Talcott Parsons, *Structure and Process in Modern Societies* (Glencoe, Ill.: The Free Press, 1960).

12. Frederick E. Emery and E. L. Trist, "The Causal Texture of Organizational Environments," *Human Relations* 18 (February 1965).

13. Paul Lawrence and Jay Lorsch, *Organization and Environment* (Cambridge: Harvard Business School, 1967); "Differentiation and Integration in

Complex Organizations," *Administrative Science Quarterly* 12 (June 1967). See also Jeffrey Pfeffer and Husein Leblebici, "The Effect of Competition on Some Dimensions of Organization Structure," *Social Forces* 52 (December 1973).

14. Shirley Terreberry, "The Evaluation of Organization Environments," *Administrative Science Quarterly* 12 (March 1968).

15. For a comparative analysis of the two approaches, see Howard E. Aldrich and Jeffrey Pfeffer, "Environments and Organizations," *Annual Review of Sociology* 12 (1976).

16. David Jacobs, "Dependency and Vulnerability," *Administrative Science Quarterly* 19 (March 1974); Jeffrey Pfeffer and Gerald R. Salancik, *The External Control of Organizations* (New York: Harper and Row, 1978).

17. Michael Hannan and John Freeman, "The Population Ecology of Organizations," *American Journal of Sociology* 82 (March 1977); Howard E. Aldrich, *Organizations and Environments* (Englewood Cliffs, N.J.: Prentice-Hall, 1979).

18. Gary L. Wamsley and Mayer N. Zald, *The Political Economy of Public Organizations* (Lexington, Mass.: D. C. Heath, 1973).

19. See, for example, Herbert Kaufman, *Are Government Organizations Immortal?* (Washington: The Brookings Institution, 1976).

20. Peter Selznick, *TVA and the Grass Roots* (Berkeley: University of California Press, 1949).

21. Burton Clark, *Adult Education in Transition* (Berkeley: University of California Press, 1956); *The Open Door College* (New York: McGraw-Hill, 1960).

22. Sol Levine and Paul E. White, "Exchange as a Conceptual Framework for the Study of Interorganizational Relationships," *Administrative Science Quarterly* 5 (March 1961).

23. Aaron Wildavsky, *The Politics of the Budgetary Process* (Boston: Little Brown, 1964); Richard Fenno, *The Power of the Purse* (Boston: Little Brown, 1966); Francis E. Rourke, *Bureaucracy, Politics and Public Policy* (Boston: Little Brown, 1969).

24. Avery Leiserson, *Administrative Regulation* (Chicago: University of Chicago Press, 1942); J. Leiper Freeman, *The Political Process* (New York: Random House, 1955); Marver H. Bernstein, *Regulating Business by Independent Commission* (Princeton, N.J.: Princeton University Press, 1955).

25. Marshall Meyer, *Change in Public Bureaucracies* (New York: Cambridge University Press, 1979).

26. Max Weber, "Bureaucracy," in H. H. Gerth and C. W. Mills, eds., *From Max Weber* (New York: Oxford University Press, 1946), p. 215.

27. Ibid., p. 224.

28. Frank Levy *et al.*, *Urban Outcomes* (Berkeley: University of California Press, 1974); Robert Lineberry, *Equality and Urban Policy* (Beverly Hills, Calif.: Sage Publications, 1977); Joseph P. Viteritti, *Bureaucracy and Social Justice* (Port Washington, N.Y.: Kennikat Press, 1979).

29. See Joseph P. Viteritti, "Bureaucratic Environments, Efficiency and Equity in Urban Service Delivery Systems," in R. Rich, ed., *The Politics of Urban Public Services* (Lexington, Mass.: Lexington Books, 1982).

30. Viteritti, *Bureaucracy and Social Justice;* and "Bureaucratic Environments, Efficiency and Equity in Urban Service Delivery Systems."

31. See Frank Marini, ed., *Toward a New Public Administration* (New York: Chandler, 1971); H. George Frederickson, ed., *Neighborhood Control in the 1970's* (New York: Chandler, 1973); H. George Frederickson, *New Public Administration* (University, Ala.: University of Alabama Press, 1980); Alan A. Altshuler, *Community Control* (New York: Pegasus, 1970).

32. See, for example, Julius Turner, *Party and Constituency* (Baltimore, Md.: Johns Hopkins University Press, 1951); Warren E. Miller and Donald E. Stokes, "Constituency Influence in Congress," *American Political Science Review* LXII (March 1963).

33. See note 23.

34. James Q. Wilson, "The Politics of Regulation," in J. Q. Wilson, ed., *The Politics of Regulation* (New York: Basic Books, 1980).

35. Chris Argyris and Donald S. Schon, *Theory in Practice* (San Francisco: Jossey-Bass, 1974).

36. Thompson, *Organizations in Action.*

INTERVIEWS

The list below includes individuals who were formally interviewed by the author at least once. Titles and affiliations represent relevant associations these individuals had with the New York City public school (NYCPS) system between 1978 and 1983, and may not represent their present status. In cases where an individual has held more than one position, the most recent is listed first.

Stephen Aiello, Special Assistant to the President of the United States; President and Member, Board of Education of the City of New York.

Joseph Albergo, President, Community School Board No. 29, NYCPS

Anthony Alvarado, District Superintendent, Community School District No. 4, NYCPS

Kathy Archelin, lead analyst, Office of Management and Budget, City of New York

Amelia Ashe, Vice President and Member, Board of Education of the City of New York

Joseph Barkan, President and Member, Board of Education of the City of New York

Robert Bergen, attorney, Office of Corporation Counsel, City of New York

Edward Burke, Deputy Director, Office of Management and Budget, City of New York

Richard Carman, Executive Assistant to the Executive Director (Jerry Gross), Division of Special Education, NYCPS

J. Robert Daggett, Executive Assistant to the Commissioner of Education, New York State

Ronald R. Edmonds, Senior Assistant to the Chancellor for Instruction, NYCPS

Ted Elsberg, President, Council of Supervisors and Administrators

Sandra Feldman, Executive Director, United Federation of Teachers

Dall Forsythe, Assistant to City Council President Carol Bellamy; Director, Office of Budget Operations and Review, NYCPS

Carlotte Frank, Executive Director, Division of Curriculum and Instruction, NYCPS

Richard Frankan, Deputy Assistant Director, Office of Management and Budget, City of New York

Alan Gartner, Executive Director, Division of Special Education, NYCPS; Director, Center of Advanced Study in Education, City University of New York Graduate School

Bernard Gifford, Deputy Chancellor under Irving Anker, NYCPS

James Gifford, Assistant to the Chancellor, NYCPS

Susan Glass, Director of Public Affairs, United Federation of Teachers

John "Chip" Gray, attorney, Brooklyn Legal Services

Jerry Gross, Executive Director, Division of Special Education, NYCPS

Jerome Harris, District Superintendent, Community School District No. 13, NYCPS

Helen Heller, Executive Director, United Parents Associations; Coordinator, Educational Priorities Panel

Philip Kaplan, President, New York City Community School Boards Association; President, Community School Board No. 15, NYCPS

Edward I. Koch, Mayor, City of New York

Nancy Lederman, attorney, Office of Legal Services, NYCPS

Stanley Litow, Executive Director, Educational Priorities Panel

Frank J. Macchiarola, Chancellor, NYCPS

Harvey Mandelkern, Deputy Counsel, New York State School Boards Association

Alfred Melov, Assistant Superintendent for Promotional Policy, NYCPS; President, New York City Superintendents' Association; District Superintendent, Community School District No. 15, NYCPS

Thomas Minter, Deputy Chancellor for Instruction, NYCPS

Roy Moskowitz, attorney, Office of Legal Services, NYCPS

Linda Ovadias, President, Rosedale Block Association

Arlene Pedone, Assistant to the Chancellor, NYCPS

Janet Price, attorney, Advocates for Children

Nathan Quinones, Executive Director, Division of High Schools, NYCPS

Stanley Raub, Executive Director, New York State School Boards Association

Michael Rebell, attorney representing United Cerebral Palsy of New York

David Rogers, author, *110 Livingston Street*

Waldemar Rojas, Deputy Director of the Division of Special Education, NYCPS; Executive Assistant to the Chancellor, NYCPS

Joseph Saccente, Assistant to the Chancellor, NYCPS

Reuven Savitz, Senior Assistant to the Chancellor for Business, NYCPS

Meryl Schwartz, President, United Parents Associations

Albert Shanker, President, United Federation of Teachers

George Shebitz, Deputy Director, Office of Legal Services, NYCPS

Jane Stern, attorney, Advocates for Children

Gary Tarnoff, attorney, Office of Corporation Counsel, City of New York

Mary Tucker, Counsel, Board of Education of the City of New York; attorney, Office of Corporation Counsel, City of New York

Robert F. Wagner, Jr., Deputy Mayor for Policy, City of New York

Claudette Webb, member, Community School Board No. 29, NYCPS

Jack Weinstein, Chief Judge, United States District Court, Eastern District, New York

David Wirtz, Counsel to the Chancellor and Director, Office of Legal Services, NYCPS

Carol Ziegler, Special Assistant to the Counsel to the Chancellor, NYCPS

BIBLIOGRAPHY

I. POLITICS, EDUCATION AND SCHOOL GOVERNANCE

Bailey, Stephen K., *et al. Schoolmen and Politics*. Syracuse, N.Y.: Syracuse University Press, 1962.

Bailey, Stephen K., and Edith Mosher. *ESEA: The Office of Education Administers a Law*. Syracuse, N.Y.: Syracuse University Press, 1968.

Boyd, William. "The Public, the Professionals and Educational Policy Making: Who Governs?" *Teachers College Record* 77 (May 1977).

Callahan, Raymond. *Education and the Cult of Efficiency*. Chicago: University of Chicago Press, 1962.

Coons, John, *et al. Private Wealth and Public Education*. Cambridge: Harvard University Press, 1970.

Cronin, Joseph. *The Control of Urban Schools*. New York: Praeger, 1973.

Cuban, Larry. *Urban School Chiefs under Fire*. Chicago: University of Chicago Press, 1976.

Fantini, Mario, and Marilyn Gittell. *Decentralization: Achieving Reform*. New York: Praeger, 1973.

Fantini, Mario, *et al. Community Control and the Urban School*. New York: Praeger, 1970.

Gifford, James P., and Frank J. Macchiarola. "Legal, Technical, Financial and Political Implications for School Finance Reform in New York State." *Tulane Law Review* 55 (1981).

Grimshaw, William J. *Union Rule in the Schools*. Lexington, Mass.: Lexington Books, 1979.

Horowtiz, Donald L. *The Courts and Social Policy*. Washington, D.C.: The Brookings Institution, 1977.

Iannaccone, Lawrence, and Frank Lutz. *Politics, Power and Policy*. Columbus, Ohio: Charles Merrill, 1970.

Kerr, Norman D. "The School Board as an Agency of Legitimization." *Sociology of Education* 38 (Autumn 1964).

Lehne, Richard. *The Quest for Justice*. New York: Longman, 1979.

Murphy, Jerome. *State Education Agencies and Discretionary Funds*. Lexington, Mass.: Lexington Books, 1974.

Peterson, Paul. *School Politics Chicago Style*. Chicago: University of Chicago Press, 1976.

Rebell, Michael, and Allen Block. *Education Policy Making and the Courts*. Chicago: University of Chicago Press, 1982.

Salisbury, Robert. "Schools and Politics in the Big City." *Harvard Educational Review* 67 (Summer 1967).

Tucker, Harvey, and L. Harmon Ziegler. *Professionals versus the Public*. New York: Longman, 1980.

Tyack, David. *The One Best System*. Cambridge: Harvard University Press, 1974.

Wirt, Frederick, and Michael W. Kirst. *Schools in Conflict*. Berkeley, Calif.: McCutchan, 1982.

Wise, Arthur. *Legislated Learning*. Berkeley: University of California Press, 1979.

Wise, Arthur. *Rich Schools, Poor Schools*. Chicago: University of Chicago Press, 1968.

Ziegler, L. Harmon, and M. Kent Jennings. *Governing American Schools*. North Scituate, Mass.: Duxbury Press, 1974.

II. NEW YORK CITY GOVERNMENT AND POLITICS

Auletta, Ken. *The Streets Were Paved with Gold*. New York: Random House, 1979.

Bailey, Robert. *The Crisis Regime*. Albany: State University of New York Press, forthcoming.

Bellush, Jewel, and Stephen M. David, eds. *Race and Politics in New York City*. New York: Praeger, 1971.

Caro, Robert A. *The Power Broker*. New York: Knopf, 1974.

Gittell, Marilyn. *Participants and Participation*. New York: Praeger, 1967.

Kaestle, Carl F. *The Evolution of an Urban School System*. Cambridge: Harvard University Press, 1973.

Lowi, Theodore. *At the Pleasure of the Mayor*. New York: The Free Press, 1964.

Morris, Charles R. *The Cost of Good Intentions*. New York: W. W. Norton, 1980.

Newfield, Jack and Paul Du Brul. *The Abuse of Power*. New York: Viking, 1977.

Ravitch, Diane. *The Great School Wars*. New York: Basic Books, 1974.

Rogers, David. "Does Decentralization Work?" *The Urban Lawyer* 14 (Summer 1982).

Rogers, David. *110 Livingston Street*. New York: Random House, 1968.

Sayre, Wallace, and Herbert Kaufman. *Governing New York City*. New York: W. W. Norton, 1960.

Shanas, Bert. "Albert Shanker: The Politics of Clout." *New York Affairs* 5 (Summer, Fall 1978).

Shefter, Martin. "New York City's Fiscal Crisis." *Public Interest* 48 (Summer, 1977).

Tabb, William K. *The Long Default*. New York: Monthly Review Press, 1982.

Temporary Commission on City Finances. *The City in Transition*. New York: Arno, 1978.

Viteritti, Joseph P. "Managing 110 Livingston Street." *Urban Education* 15 (April 1980).

Viteritti, Joseph P. *Police, Politics and Pluralism in New York City*. Beverly Hills, Calif.: Sage Publications, 1973.

Viteritti, Joseph P. "Policy Analysis in the Bureaucracy." *Public Administration Review* 42 (September–October 1982).

Viteritti, Joseph P., and Daniel G. Carponcy. "Information, Organization and Control." *Public Administration Review* 41 (March–April, 1981).

III. BUREAUCRACY AND ORGANIZATIONAL ENVIRONMENTS

Aberbach, Joel D., and Bert A. Rockman. "Bureaucrats and Clientele Groups." *American Journal of Political Science* 22 (November 1978).

Aldrich, Howard E. *Organizations and Environments*. Englewood Cliffs, N.J.: Prentice Hall, 1979.

Aldrich, Howard E., and Jeffrey Pfeffer. "Environments and Organizations." *Annual Review of Sociology* 12 (1976).

Argyris, Chris, and Donald A. Schon. *Theory in Practice*. San Francisco: Jossey–Bass, 1974.

Bacharach, Samuel B., ed. *Organizational Behavior in Schools and School Districts*. New York: Praeger, 1981.

Carlson, Richard D. "Environmental Constraints and Organizational Consequences." J. V. Baldridge and T. E. Deal, eds. *Making Change in Educational Organizations*. Berkeley, Calif.: McCutchan, 1975.

Emery, Frederick E., and E. L. Trist. "The Causal Texture of Organizational Environments." *Human Relations* 18 (February 1965).

Gouldner, Alvin W. *Patterns of Industrial Bureaucracy*. New York: The Free Press, 1954.

Katz, Daniel, and Robert Kahn. *The Social Psychology of Organizations*. New York: John Wiley, 1966.

Lawrence, Paul R., and Jay W. Lorsch. "Differentiation and Integration in Complex Organizations." *Administrative Science Quarterly* 12 (June 1967).

Lawrence, Paul R., and Jay W. Lorsch. *Organization and Environment*. Homewood, Ill.: Richard D. Irwin, 1969.

Lefton, Mark, and William Rosengren. "Organizations and Clients." *Administrative Science Quarterly* 31 (December 1966).

Levine, Sol, and Paul E. White. "Exchange as a Conceptual Framework for the Study of Interorganizational Relationships." *Administrative Science Quarterly* 5 (1961).

Levy, Frank, *et al. Urban Outcomes*. Berkeley: University of California Press, 1974.

Lineberry, Robert L. *Equality and Urban Policy*. Beverly Hills, Calif.: Sage Publications, 1977.

March, James D., and Herbert Simon. *Organizations*. New York: John Wiley, 1958.

Meyer, Marshall W. *Change in Public Bureaucracies*. New York: Cambridge University Press, 1979.

Meyer, Marshall W., *et al. Environments and Organizations*. San Francisco: Jossey–Bass, 1978.

Pfeffer, Jeffrey, and Gerald R. Salancik. *The External Control of Organizations*. New York: Harper and Row, 1978.

Rosengren, William R., and Mark Lefton, eds. *Organizations and Clients*. Columbus, Ohio: Charles Merrill, 1970.

Rourke, Francis E. *Bureaucracy, Politics and Public Policy*. Boston: Little Brown, 1969.

Sergiovani, Thomas J. and F. D. Carver. *The New School Executive*. New York: Harper and Row, 1980.

Scott, W. Richard. *Organizations*. Englewood Cliffs, N.J.: Prentice Hall, 1981.

Simon, Herbert. *Administrative Behavior*. New York: Collier–Macmillan, 1945.

Terreberry, Shirley. "The Evaluation of Organizational Environments." *Administrative Science Quarterly* 12 (March 1968).

Thompson, James D. *Organizations in Action*. New York: McGraw-Hill, 1967.

Viteritti, Joseph P. "Bureaucratic Environments, Efficiency and Equity in Urban Service Delivery Systems." R. Rich, ed. *The Politics of Urban Public Services*. Lexington, Mass.: Lexington Books, 1982.

Viteritti, Joseph P. *Bureaucracy and Social Justice*. Port Washington, New York: Kennikat Press, 1979.

Weber, Max. "Bureaucracy." H. H. Gerth and C. Wright Mills, eds. *From Max Weber*. New York: Oxford University Press, 1946.

IV. COMPETENCY TESTING, STUDENT ACHIEVEMENT, SPECIAL EDUCATION

Blatt, Burton. "Public Policy and the Education of Children with Special Needs." *Exceptional Children* 39 (March 1972).

Bloom, Benjamin. *Human Characteristics and Learning*. New York: McGraw–Hill, 1976.

Brookover, Wilber, *et al. School Social Systems and Student Achievement*. New York: Praeger, 1979.

Brophy, Jere E., and Carolyn Evertson. *Student Characteristics and Teaching*. New York: Longman, 1981.

Brophy, Jere E., and Thomas L. Good. *Teacher–Student Relationships.* New York: Holt, Rinehart, and Winston, 1974.

Chall, Jeanne S. *Leaning to Read.* New York: McGraw-Hill, 1967.

Chall, Jeanne S. *Stages in Reading Development.* New York: McGraw–Hill, 1982.

Coleman, James S., *et al. Equality of Educational Opportunity.* Washington: Office of Education, National Center for Educational Statistics, 1966.

Dunn, Lloyd M. "Special Education for the Mildly Retarded—Is Much of it Justifiable?" *Exceptional Children* 35 (September 1968).

Edmonds, Ronald. "Effective Schools for the Urban Poor." *Educational Leadership* 37 (October 1979).

Glass, Gene V. "Standards and Criteria." *Journal of Educational Measure* 15 (1978).

Glass, Gene V., *et al. School Class Size.* Beverly Hills, Calif.: Sage Publications, 1982.

Haney, Walt, and George Madaus. "Making Sense of Competency Testing." *Harvard Educational Review* 48 (November 1978).

Hargrove, Erwin, *et al. Regulations and Schools.* Nashville, Tenn.: Vanderbilt University, Institute for Policy Studies, 1981.

Hobbes, Nicholas, ed. *The Future of Children.* San Francisco: Jossey–Bass, 1975.

Jencks, Christopher, *et al. Inequality.* New York: Basic Books, 1972.

Jensen, Arthur. "How Much Can We Boost I.Q. and Scholastic Achievement." *Harvard Educational Review* 39 (Winter 1969).

Madaus, George F., *et al. School Effectiveness.* New York: McGraw–Hill, 1980.

Maeroff, Gene I. *Don't Blame the Kids.* New York: McGraw–Hill, 1982.

McClung, Merle S. "Competency Testing Programs: Legal and Educational Issues." *Fordham Law Review* 47 (1979).

Mosteller, Frederick, and Daniel P. Moyniham, eds. *On Equality of Educational Opportunity.* New York: Vintage, 1972.

Pipho, Chris. "Minimum Competency Testing." *Phi Delta Kappan* 59 (December 1977).

Reynolds, Maynard C., *et al,* eds. "Symposium on Public Policy and Educating Handicapped Persons." *Policy Studies Review* 2 (January 1983).

Rutter, Michael, *et al. Fifteen Thousand Hours.* Cambridge: Harvard University Press, 1979.

Tractenberg, Paul, and Elaine Jacoby. "Pupil Testing: A Legal View." *Phi Delta Kappan* 59 (December 1977).

Weatherley, Richard. *Reforming Special Education.* Cambridge, Mass.: MIT Press, 1979.

Weintraub, Frederick J., *et al,* eds. *Public Policy and the Education of Exceptional Children.* Reston, Va.: The Council of Exceptional Children, 1975.

V. DESEGREGATION AND RACE IN EDUCATION

Buell, Emmett. *School Desegregation and Defended Neighborhoods.* Lexington, Mass.: Lexington Books, 1981.

Coleman, James. "Trends in School Segregation, 1968–1973." An Urban Institute Paper. U.I., August 1975.

Dentler, Robert A., and Marvin B. Scott. *Schools on Trial.* Cambridge, Mass.: Abt Books, 1981.

Farley, Reynolds. "School Integration and White Flight." Ann Arbor: Population Studies Center, University of Michigan, 1975.

Fiss, Owen. "Racial Imbalance in the Schools." *Harvard Law Review* 78 (1965).

Hawley, Willis D., ed. *Effective School Desegregation.* Beverly Hills, Calif.: Sage Publications, 1981.

Kirp, David. *Just Schools.* Berkeley: University of California Press, 1982.

Kluger, Richard. *Simple Justice.* New York: Knopf, 1976.

Orfield, Gary. *Must We Bus?* Washington: The Brookings Institution, 1978.

Orfield, Gary. *The Reconstruction of Southern Education.* New York: John Wiley, 1969.

Pettigrew, Thomas F., and Robert L. Green. "School Desegregation in Large Cities." *Harvard Educational Review* 46 (February 1976).

Raffel, Jeffrey A. *The Politics of School Desegregation.* Philadelphia: Temple University Press, 1980.

Salomone, Rosemary C. "Equal Educational Opportunity and the New Federalism." *Urban Education* 17 (July 1982).

Salomone, Rosemary C. "Title VI and the Intent–Impact Debate." *Hastings Constitutional Law Quarterly* 10 (1982).

Stephan, Walter, and Joe R. Feagin, eds. *School Desegregation.* New York: Plenum, 1980.

St. John, Nancy. *School Desegregation: Outcomes for Children.* New York: Wiley Interscience, 1975.

Wilkenson, J. Harvie. *From Brown to Bakke.* New York: Oxford University Press, 1979.

Willie, Charles V., and Susan L. Greenblatt, eds. *Community Politics and Educational Change.* New York: Longman, 1981.

Wolf, Eleanor P. *Trial and Error.* Detroit, Mich.: Wayne State University Press, 1981.

Yarmolinsky, Adam, *et al.,* eds. *Race and Schooling in the City.* Cambridge: Harvard University Press, 1981.

Yudof, Mark. "Equal Educational Opportunity and the Courts." *Texas Law Review* 51 (1973).

INDEX

Italicized page numbers indicate material in tables or figures.